Organizations and Unusual Routines

Everyone working in and with organizations will, from time to time, experience frustrations and problems when trying to accomplish tasks that are a required part of their role. This is an unusual routine – a recurrent interaction pattern in which someone encounters a problem when trying to accomplish normal activities by following standard organizational procedures and then becomes enmeshed in wasteful and even harmful subroutines while trying to resolve the initial problem. They are unusual because they are not intended or beneficial, and because they are generally pervasive but individually infrequent. They are routines because they become systematic as well as embedded in ordinary functions. Using a wide range of case studies and interdisciplinary research, this book provides researchers and practitioners with a new vocabulary for identifying, understanding, and dealing with this pervasive organizational phenomenon, in order to improve worker and customer satisfaction as well as organizational performance.

RONALD E. RICE is Arthur N. Rupe Chair in the Social Effects of Mass Communication and Co-Director of the Carsey-Wolf Center for Film, Television, and New Media at the University of California, Santa Barbara. He is the author of several books, the most recent of which include *The Internet and Health Care* (with Monica Murero, 2006) and *Media Ownership* (2008).

STEPHEN D. COOPER is Professor of Communication Studies at Marshall University, where he teaches courses in business and professional communication, computer-mediated communication, group communication, organizational communication, and research foundations. He is the author of *Watching the Watchdog: Bloggers as the Fifth Estate* (2006).

Organizations and Unusual Routines

A Systems Analysis of Dysfunctional Feedback Processes

RONALD E. RICE
University of California, Santa Barbara, California

STEPHEN D. COOPER
Marshall University, Huntington, West Virginia

CAMBRIDGE
UNIVERSITY PRESS

CAMBRIDGE UNIVERSITY PRESS
Cambridge, New York, Melbourne, Madrid, Cape Town, Singapore,
São Paulo, Delhi, Dubai, Tokyo, Mexico City

Cambridge University Press
The Edinburgh Building, Cambridge CB2 8RU, UK

Published in the United States of America by Cambridge University Press,
New York

www.cambridge.org
Information on this title: www.cambridge.org/9780521768641

First published 2010

Printed in the United Kingdom at the University Press, Cambridge

A catalog record for this publication is available from the British Library

Library of Congress Cataloging in Publication data
Rice, Ronald E.
  Organizations and unusual routines : a systems analysis of dysfunctional
  feedback processes / Ronald E. Rice, Stephen D. Cooper.
    p.   cm.
  Includes bibliographical references and index.
  ISBN 978-0-521-76864-1
  1. Organizational behavior.   2. Organizational change.   3. Organizational
  learning.   I. Cooper, Stephen D, 1950–   II. Title.
  HD58.7.R525 2010
  302.3′5–dc22
  2010021890

ISBN 978-0-521-76864-1 Hardback

Contents

List of figures	*page* viii	
List of tables	ix	
List of boxes	x	
Preface	xi	
Acknowledgments	xiv	

1	Crazy systems, Kafka circuits, and unusual routines	1
	Two stories of mundane complexity and dysfunctional feedback	1
	Crazy systems	5
	Unusual routines	17
	The rest of the book	19
2	Causes, symptoms, and subroutines of unusual routines in six computer information/communication systems	21
	Causes of unusual routines in three ICTs	22
	Causes, symptoms, and subroutines of unusual routines in three ICTs	40
	Conclusion	60
3	Getting personal: unusual routines at the customer service interface	67
	Customer service, dissatisfaction, and complaining	68
	Examples and analysis of unusual service subroutines, routines, and organizational (non-)response	81
	Conclusion	106
4	A multi-theoretical foundation for understanding unusual routines	107
	Five foundational theories for a preliminary model of unusual routines	107
	Developing a preliminary model of unusual routines	139

| | Five propositions | 149 |
| | Conclusion | 152 |

5 A detailed case study of unusual routines 155
- Method 155
- Proposition One 160
- Proposition Two 167
- Proposition Three 173
- Proposition Four 177
- Proposition Five 191
- Conclusion 199

6 Summary and discussion of the case study results 200
- Proposition One 200
- Proposition Two 201
- Proposition Three 201
- Proposition Four 202
- Proposition Five 203
- Discussion 204
- Conclusion 215

7 Individual and organizational challenges to feedback 217
- Feedback challenges inherent in human communication behaviors 218
- Feedback challenges inherent in organizations 227
- Conclusion 249

8 A multi-level and cross-disciplinary summary of concepts related to unusual routines 252
- Cognitive and social processing errors 252
- Social traps and dilemmas 266
- Organizational complexity 269
- Organizational paradoxes 274
- Organizational deviance 280
- Technological complexity 287
- Conclusion 305

9 Recommendations for resolving and mitigating unusual routines and related phenomena 306
- Encourage customer service feedback from all stakeholders 306
- Apply socio-technical systems theory, involve stakeholders from design through walkarounds 310

Reduce blaming and defensive approaches to
   cognitive dissonance   312
Manage paradoxes and sensemaking   314
Foster learning through feedback   317
Heighten awareness of predictable surprises and
   avoid overreacting to worst-case scenarios   319
Understand and resolve social traps and social dilemmas   320
Discuss and resolve conflicting goals, vicious cycles, and
   workplace deviance   321
Avoid simple and individual approaches to complex
   technology and system error   322
Apply and combine linkage and routines analysis   325
Conclusion   329

10 Summary and a tentative integrated model of
    unusual routines   331
    The allure of unusual routines   331
    Our preliminary models   333
    A proposed integrative model of unusual routines   336
    Conclusion   342

References   344
Index   373

Figures

1.1 Initial model of unusual routines, derived from
Singer's crazy systems model   *page* 19
4.1 Extended model of unusual routines   153
6.1 Dynamics of single-loop and double-loop learning
in unusual routines   208
10.1 Concept-level integrated model of unusual routines   337

Tables

3.1 Model of unusual routines, expanded from Singer's model of crazy systems   *page* 101

3.2 Aspects of unusual routines in the case examples   103

4.1 Aspects of routines, workarounds, and meta-routines   140

4.2 Conceptual rationales associated with each proposition   152

5.1 Interview guide   157

5.2 Examples of subroutines in the case   197

6.1 Working taxonomy of the single-loop process from the case   209

6.2 Working taxonomy of the double-loop process from the case   210

7.1 Development of defensive routines   246

10.1 Primary components of general concepts in Figure 10.1   338

Boxes

2.1 Summary of causes and symptoms of unusual routines
    in six ICT implementation cases   *page* 60
7.1 Summary of individual and organizational challenges
    to feedback   250
8.1 Individual processing heuristics, with example application
    to unusual routines   264
8.2 Organizational and social processes, with example
    application to unusual routines   301
9.1 Recommendations for avoiding, analyzing, mitigating,
    and resolving unusual routines and related processes   307

Preface

When something goes wrong
I'm the first to admit it
I'm the first to admit it
And the last one to know.
When something goes right
It's likely to lose me
It's apt to confuse me
It's such an unusual sight.

   (Paul Simon, *Something So Right*, © 1973)

This book identifies, describes, and analyzes the pervasive and frustrating experiences people have with dysfunctional feedback in organizational and societal contexts, by showing that they are symptoms and consequences of unusual routines. An unusual routine is a recurrent interaction pattern in which someone encounters a problem in trying to accomplish normal activities by following procedures, then becomes enmeshed in wasteful and even harmful subroutines while trying to resolve the initial problem, creating and reinforcing unintended and (typically) undesirable outcomes, to some set of people, subsystems, organization, or society, either within or across system levels (or both). Often, the feedback loops about this initial unusual routine are either non-existent, dysfunctional, or deviation-reinforcing, creating a second-level, or meta-, routine. The term "unusual routines" is intentionally oxymoronic. The processes and consequences, when known, would be considered unusual, unacceptable, or negative by one or more stakeholders. Although the phenomenon is pervasive, any particular instance may be infrequent and difficult to identify. Nonetheless, the process and consequences are systematic, to the point where they become routinized and embedded in other routines. The subtitle emphasizes that the book takes a social systems analysis perspective, although technical aspects of information and communication systems also play a role throughout the book.

Chapter 1 begins the book by reviewing the inspiration for this work, Benjamin Singer's concepts of crazy systems and Kafka circuits, and introducing an initial, more general, model of unusual routines. The following chapters provide a wide range of empirical case analyses, from implementation of information and communication technology systems (Chapter 2), and unsatisfying customer service interactions (Chapter 3), to a detailed analysis of the implementation of a university networking system (Chapters 5 and 6). Each of these attempts to advance an interdisciplinary model of unusual routines. The foundations for an interdisciplinary model of unusual routines, based in systems theory, sensemaking theory, diffusion of innovation theory, socio-technical systems theory, and, especially, organizational routines theory appear in Chapter 4.

Interestingly, while many theoretical and pragmatic approaches to problems such as unusual routines recommend increased feedback, Chapter 7 shows, through a broad review of literature, that the process of feedback itself is often quite problematic, and even implicated in the generation and reinforcement of unusual routines. Feedback is treated from both a communication and an organizational perspective as a complex and often dysfunctional process, involving activities such as ignoring available information, seeking versus receiving, discourse and language, multiple layers of content and relation, reflexive loops and undesirable repetitive patterns, skilled incompetence and competence contradictions, reporting errors, feedback timing, tensions between behavior and learning, organizational memory, the unreasonableness of rational systems, vicious circles, and defensive routines.

Chapter 8 is specifically intended to show how this common and pervasive experience is related to, and a generalized example of, many other issues, such as tragedy of the commons, social traps and social dilemmas, personal heuristics, cognitive dissonance, errors in logic, predictable surprises and worst-case scenarios, organizational complexity, unanticipated consequences, organizational paradoxes, organizational deviance and employee mistreatment, technology complexity, system manipulation, normal accidents, automated systems and system error, system drift and workarounds, among others. Chapter 9 reviews a variety of recommendations, derived from the research and theories underlying the prior chapters, about ways to help avoid, mitigate, resolve, or at least identify, unusual routines. Chapter 10 integrates the main arguments and insights from each chapter, providing a tentative comprehensive model of, and initial suggestions for analyzing, unusual routines. The reference section provides an extremely broad and diverse set of sources for these chapters. Both the table of contents and the index provide multiple access points into the materials.

The first intended contribution of this book is an identification and articulation of a set of core concepts, terms, and recommendations about unusual routines, leading to an integrated model of unusual routines, that will help researchers, practitioners, designers, customers, and clients identify, analyze, and possibly mitigate this pervasive but sometimes invisible phenomenon. The second intended contribution is an implicit critique of the idealizing of functional approaches to systems and routines, and of sensemaking theory, as social, communicative processes that necessarily counter organizational dysfunctions and necessarily create social benefits for all concerned. The third intended contribution is an emphasis on the experiences, perceptions, and implications of users, consumers, clients, employees, supervisors, and administrators, rather than, as is usual in information systems or organizational behavior books, executives, strategists, and industries, or, as are often the focus of psychology or user interface books, specific individuals.

Acknowledgments

We are grateful to Ms. Paula M. Parish, Commissioning Editor in the Business & Management series of Cambridge University Press, for her support and guidance in getting this book published. She managed several iterations of seeking, providing, and framing reviewer comments. We also thank the anonymous reviewers for their focused insights and very helpful suggestions about related literature. We also thank Gail Welsh for the great copyediting job.

The cases in Chapter 2 are substantially edited, reorganized, and integrated versions of six course projects. In these projects, the graduate students, all working professionals, were asked to use the initial unusual routine model to interpret and critique behaviors and events in their own organizations. The first three systems examples are derived from papers written for Rice's 1995 course on "Social Aspects of Implementing Technology" at the Macquarie University Graduate School of Management, Sydney, Australia. The labor cost management system is based on Richard Hale's study, Martin Dare provided the analysis of the Home Sale Automation system, and Elizabeth Barclay reported on the voicemail system. The next two cases came from projects for Rice's course, "Management and Information Technology", at the University of Southern California Annenberg School of Communication. The technical issue help system case was provided by Tina Phoenix, and the online database query system case by Brian McGee. Finally, the employee time reporting systems case came from a study by Ann Bemis for Rice's course "Social Aspects of Implementing Information Systems" at Rutgers University's School of Communication, Information and Library Science. We appreciate the contributions and insights of Elizabeth Barclay, Ann Bemis, Martin Dare, Richard Hale, Brian McGee, and Tina Phoenix, and their permission to allow us to work with their case materials.

Materials in Chapters 5 and 6 are significantly adapted from Cooper, S. D. (2000). *Unusual Routines and Computer Mediated Communication Systems.* Unpublished dissertation. New Brunswick: Graduate School, Rutgers, The State University of New Jersey. A considerable portion of Chapter 8 is adapted from Rice, R. E. (2008). "Unusual routines: organizational (non)sensemaking." *Journal of Communication*, 58(1), 1–19 (with acknowledgement to the journal, the International Communication Association and Blackwell Publishing).

Ron thanks Claire Johnson for her routine support of this topic, and of her tolerance for the unusual time and effort devoted to the book.

Stephen thanks Sandy Hamon, for believing in me, and God, from whom all my blessings flow.

1 | *Crazy systems, Kafka circuits, and unusual routines*

Two stories of mundane complexity and dysfunctional feedback

In most organizations (whether corporations, academic departments, retail stores, government agencies, hospitals), most everyone at least at some time is trying to improve, suffering from, attempting to avoid, or complaining about, some aspect of the organization or particular system. Unfortunately, the improving, suffering, avoiding, and complaining are rarely linked. After a while, complaints disappear as people develop workarounds or ways of overcoming, without solving, the problems, or avoid them, or disengage from the process, or displace the costs to others. But the tension and frustration percolates throughout the organization and its environment, and different people who have to interact with the system (employees, customers, technical support, administrators) continue to pay in varying psychological, professional, pedagogical, or just practical ways. Such interactions would seem nonsensical on the face of it: why would organization members regularly behave in ways that frustrate them, weaken their performance, or create other kinds of negative outcomes? And why should it prove so difficult for well-intentioned people to change such patterns? Consider these two stories, one a seemingly trivial frustration of daily life, the other a seemingly ineluctable feature of public bureaucracy.

Sweeping it under the rug

Recently, I went to the local grocery store to rent a carpet shampooer. I went to the shampooer stand, took the one and only shampooer, and went to the Express line, as I had only one item. Of course the Express line was the slowest line, and I spent that time worrying whether renting a shampooer was acceptable in the Express line, and whether they would take a check in the Express line (though there was no sign saying "Cash Only").

Finally when I came up to the checkout clerk, the checkout person didn't see the shampooer (because only the top of the handle was in my hand, which was pulling the cleaner on the floor), and starting checking out the next person's stuff. I'm not sure why she thought I was in the line if I didn't appear to her to have anything to pay for. So I showed her the shampooer (causing some frustration for the person behind me who expected to be served), and she said she didn't know what it was. I said it was a shampooer. She said, no, she didn't know what it cost. I began to go to the stand to read the rental cost, but she said no, she had to get the price from a manager. To do this she had to close down her register and leave her stand, creating ripples of frustration in the line of customers who were there precisely to receive "express" checkout. She got the attention of the manager (who was checking out customers a few rows down), who said no, I should have taken it to the customer service window. I asked the checkout clerk if the stand had any sign telling people that's what they had to do. (I had now spent fifteen minutes worrying about doing the right thing, only to find out it was wrong.) She got upset, as though I was raising a forbidden topic. (There was no such sign.)

I left the Express line on the way to the customer service desk, and when I was next to the manager I said that if they had put the information on a sign on the stand I would have followed it, but there was nothing there. She ignored me, obviously angered that I questioned this whole thing.

It never occurred to either the checkout person or the manager that some process at the *store* might be at fault; this may be because that's an abstraction. Because there's no *person* associated with the display stand for the shampoo machines, it can't be the *stand's* fault. And it wasn't the manager's fault, or the checkout clerk's fault, because they were just doing their job. All these things are *true*. So my predicament *must* be my fault – the customer's fault. But this is *not* true! It was obvious to her that I should have known to take it to the customer service desk, because to her there was a policy in place, and they would have prior awareness through multiple instances. But I only rent a carpet shampooer once or twice in a lifetime, and never from the same place, so it is an extremely unusual event to me; how am I supposed to *know* this, when there was no sign saying so? What might possibly be a *usual* routine to them is a very *unusual* routine to me, but, worse, the interactions following from trying to deal with or recover from that disjunction also involve an unusual routine for both them and me.

Possibly the worst implication of this situation is that not only did the checkout clerk learn nothing about a transaction which created delays and frustrations for a number of customers, but the manager didn't realize a repeat of the various aspects of the incident (my distress and their secondary distress) could be avoided by simply placing a sign at the shampooer display. Perhaps this is because the manager doesn't really pay any consequences of the *store's* oversight (the first problem); she only pays the consequences of a *customer* raising the issue of the predicament (the consequent problem). So the easiest and most sensible approach was to put the costs on the customer (and, as a byproduct, the checkout clerk and other customers), and deflect learning by making a negative judgment about an unhappy customer. Everyone loses, and the process only confirms each participant's view of the process. I'm a dumb customer, they're unfriendly checkout clerks, the Express sign is misleading, and the store is a faceless bureaucracy.

Ironically enough, my trip to the store was the consequence of another system's failure. A previously reported but nonetheless unrepaired problem with my office air conditioning had caused water to leak onto the carpet. The university's maintenance crew had been unable to remove the water spot, so I had decided to take care of it myself. The chain of events illustrates potential interdependencies among presumptively independent systems, percolating through the most mundane situations (for an elaborate story of unusual routines in trying to deal with multiple new media, see Rice, 2009a).

A poetic license to steal

Umberto Eco, known primarily for semiotic analysis and his very successful novel *The Name of the Rose*, was a journalist early on in his career. In one story, he wryly describes a classic problem and contorted solution (1994). He lost his wallet in Amsterdam. He received his commercial credit and press cards in short order, but a permanent replacement of his driver's license was another story. This situation occurred in Italy, but it is by no means unique to that country.

He received his temporary license in two months, but only because of his position, education, and contacts. It still involved three cities, six institutions, numerous personal contacts, and a newspaper and magazine. Each visit unearthed new requirements, forms, sources of delays. In one instance, he was told he would have to return to the original place of issuance in order to obtain a document number to trace license documentation, not the actual license number itself, in order to issue a temporary license. But the original location was very far away, impossible to reach without a car, which he could not use because he had lost his license. Also, the main issuing office could not retrieve the license information based only on the driver's name; they needed the license number. But the license was now lost, of course. He initially tried to use the license number written on one of his past rental car receipts, but that turned out to have been written down incorrectly by the rental car office.

The temporary license was finally issued, but only in a series of six-month extensions awaiting the permanent license. The temporary document had no real value and could easily be forged, so there must have been many illegal temporary documents around. Also, he had to purchase an annual tax stamp for the temporary document, but was told by the seller not to cancel it, because he'd just have to buy a new one when the real license arrived. But not canceling it would probably be a crime itself! When he finally received his permanent license nearly two years later, it was not sealed, so it could have been printed by anyone; it seems likely there were lots of forged and illegal permanent licenses in use. That is, it would be very easy to create illegally, and terrorists did (and do) this quite well, so why was it so hard to obtain a permanent license legally? He suggests, in the best Swiftian tradition, why not just have a coin-operated machine available in public places for purchasing a license, or why not hire repentant terrorists in the license office, thus reducing prison costs and improving administrative efficiency in one move.

Just stories?

Are these just random, idiosyncratic occasional occurrences? Are these kinds of experiences primarily noise in the music of social interaction? Is there any way to talk or think about these kinds of situations based on more than frustration, irony, bemusement, complaint, resignation? We argue that there is. The primary goal of this book is to develop a detailed vocabulary and conceptual framework for identifying, understanding, analyzing, and possibly resolving such phenomena. The chapter begins by first describing an early perspective on dysfunctional organizational and societal feedback loops by the sociologist Benjamin Singer, involving *crazy systems*. The chapter then introduces the more general concept of an *unusual routine* (UR), along with a preliminary model of unusual routines, which will be developed throughout the book.

Crazy systems

An early framework for identifying and assessing these situations is what Singer (1980) called *crazy systems* and *Kafka circuits*. Briefly, Singer proposed that organizations suffer from psychotic and pathological behaviors much as people do, but are rarely diagnosed, critiqued, or treated as such. The dysfunctional organizational behaviors often take the form of "crazy systems" that generate "confusion, error, and ambiguity" and even "inscrutability and unaccountability, involving harm to the victim and often to the system itself, [breeding] a new kind of organizational trap" called Kafka circuits. These involve "blind alleys, crazy situations," and processes that "end where they began" (p. 48).

One does not have to agree with Singer that organizations or systems can be literally "crazy" in order to readily recall such interactions with systems; we use the term metaphorically. Other terms such as wasteful, silly, dangerous, or foolish, while indicative of some of the characteristics and consequences of these systems, do not quite capture the frustrating sense of dysfunctionality reinforced, of processes seemingly taking on a life of their own, diverging from even the best-intentioned designer's, employee's, or client's aims.

Causes

Singer and others have identified the following factors as contributing to the emergence of crazy systems.

Conflicting goals

Most organizations are rife with latent goal conflicts (Cyert and March, 1963). James March and Karl Weick, among others, have argued not only that a plethora of goals – even inherent paradoxes (Putnam, 1986) – represents the ordinary state of organizations, but that both the presence of conflicting goals and the awareness of them are salutary for organizational learning and performance. Eisenberg (1984), for instance, argues that ambiguity (such as in the meaning of organizational mission statements and logos) helps achieve strategic goals such as commitment, by allowing individuals to invest some of their own meaning into shared words. The folly of apparently inconsistent reward structures may mask a deeper organizational wisdom, due to the need to serve multiple contradictory goals (Boettger and Greer, 1994). Kerr (1995), however, disagrees, arguing that rewarding A while hoping for B is organizational folly.

"Organizations perform in contradictory ways because they must satisfy contradictory expectations" (Fairhurst *et al.*, 2002, p. 502). This is particularly the case in complex environments, as organizational adaptation and success requires internal variety matching environmental variety (Weick, 1979). Fairhurst *et al.* relate this to Giddens' (1984) structurational argument that every social system involves an antagonism of opposites, whereby systems have structural properties that are both shared and opposed. Typically there is one primary contradiction (about the nature of the system itself) and possibly many secondary contradictions, which emerge from, and, ironically, sometimes worsen the primary one.

"Organizations are inherently paradoxical" (Ford and Backoff, 1988, p. 82), involving, for example, control vs. independence, nonconformity vs. conformity, centralization vs. decentralization, order vs. variation, etc. Sometimes these conflicts are embedded in what might appear as a consensual goal. For instance, principles and goals of just-in-time manufacturing engage the tensions of quality and low cost, high current performance and adaptability to change, full-capacity efficiency and organizational slack to allow for errors and experimentation, push scheduling of production and pull demand triggering production, and standard production and customized product lines (Eisenhardt and Westcott, 1988). As another example, Total Quality Management seeks to achieve the unifying goal of high-quality climate, products and services, but through multiple goals which themselves include conflicts: seek diversity, but build a shared vision; encourage creativity, but be consistent in everything; focus on continuous process improvement, but make breakthrough change an important part of the job; use autonomous work groups to enhance performance, but ensure careful and uniform control of product and service quality; build a cohesive work team, but welcome conflict when critically analyzing ideas; set realistic, yet challenging, goals for maximum performance, but use stretch targets to dramatically improve performance; and reward team effort, but create a high performance climate for individuals (Thompson, 1998). These multiple conflicts may be summarized as a fundamental tension between the goals of *learning and control* (Simard and Rice, 2006). Managers attempting to achieve both goals must adopt multiple, sometimes incompatible, roles.

Typically, important goal conflicts are rarely identified, understood, or publicized. Instead, there are multiple requests/goals/commands from multiple stakeholders, with different time lines and feedback cycles, involving explicit as well as tacit pressures of varying kinds. Organizations may have explicit goals that are both vague and incompatible, which Dorner (1989/1996, p. 68) refers to as "documentary integration of incompatibles." Attempts at resolution of incompatible goals are influenced by explicit and salient rewards, incentives and norms, and are often seen as a source of professional expertise and pride. However, the actual resolutions and the actual influences are largely invisible outside the local context, so no one learns about their existence or their consequences. Related to the presence of documentary integration of incompatibles, one study analyzed short narratives from 560 MBAs at eighteen US university human relations management classes about one of their recent on-the-job communication problems resulting from their understandings of one of their organization's communication rules (Gilsdorf, 1998). The respondents reported twenty-two different types of sources (mostly non-written) for such rules. The study found instances of written guidelines that were functional but not reinforced, causing people to turn to an unwritten rule for guidance, which might have been less functional. But noticeable consequences of this decision were often evaluated against, and punished according to, the written (but unreinforced) policy. "If an organization's management does not consider which communication behaviors it wishes to foster for its success, the signals it sends to employees may be inconsistent or counterproductive ... Resulting patterns may be dysfunctional to the organization" (p. 175).

Boettger and Greer (1994) point out four conditions in which conflicting goals are likely:

(1) Operative and avowed goals can both be important yet divergent. Operative goals require practical and effective activities, involving drifting and adapting from the initial avowed goals, while supporting the official avowed goals rewards stakeholders and strengthens accountability.

(2) Periods of complex change may require short-term inconsistencies to foster long-term goals; a simple solution in the short-term may hobble a long-term solution.

(3) Some situations present individuals with two sets of contradictory but justified responsibilities (say, product and function, or efficiency and quality).

(4) Loose coupling between formal structures and ongoing work activities increases the likelihood of inconsistent reward structures.

We will return to these issues in Chapter 4.

Poor feedback

Systems can become "crazy" if feedback mechanisms are not built into their processes that allow users to communicate information with regard to error or malfunction. This lack of feedback, whether intentional or due to oversight, dissuades users from complaining to, or, in the long run, even interacting with, the organization (Singer, 1980; Chapter 7, this volume). One specific kind of organizational pathology is where the only feedback loops are through a flawed system itself, so perceptions of the system are inherently constrained or distorted.

 Singer noted the general decline in access to feedback with institutions and organizations, with specific indicators such as the increasing use of one-way addresses or phone numbers, recorded messages, warranties without addresses (1973, 1977). Not only do these decrease motivations and a sense of legitimacy in contacting the organization, they also raise the cost to the consumer to communicate with organizations; even then, many calls or contacts are ignored. Even when those who persist do make contact, they may well receive irrelevant, perhaps formulaic, communications, which serve (whether intentionally or not) to distract the customer or end the interaction. This opaqueness may also be related to organizations becoming pervasively mediated through information and communication technologies (ICTs) (Singer, 1977; Zmud, 1990; Chapter 2, this volume).

Organizational non-response takes various forms. These include *hiding out*, primarily through increased mediation (one-way addresses or phone numbers, recorded messages, warranties without addresses; increased costs to the consumer to communicate with organizations; simply not responding to calls or contacts), *irrelevant responses* (formulaic, superficially indicating response, but serving to distract or end the interaction), and *work circuits* (increased ratio of work to goal benefits, such as requiring specifically-formatted letters or other "formwork," forcing users to communicate on the organization's terms). Other techniques include blaming the victim, cooling out techniques, cover-ups, insufficient compensation, semantic manipulation (reinterpreting the error as correct), bureaucratic diffusion of responsibility, and attrition through time (Singer, 1978, p. 30, referring to Mintz and Cohen's 1976 review of case studies of the consequences of unaccountability). Making excuses is a form of non-response, as it suppresses resolving both the customer's problem and the internal system problem (Bear and Hill, 1994).

In turn, client or customer responses to this increasingly pervasive and intolerable situation include apathy, helplessness, unquestioning compliance, tolerance of insults, explosive, "irrational" behavior, and counter-bureaucratic coping (applying one's civil rights, developing some countervailing power) (Singer, 1978).

Symbolic uses and manipulation

One factor that seems to contribute to the development and maintenance of Kafka circuits (and URs) is what Feldman and March (1981) call the symbolic value of information. Briefly, traditional models of organizational decision-making assume that before decisions are made, organizational members conduct a rational analysis until they obtain relevant and sufficient information, and then use that information as criteria for a reasoned decision. However, there are many instances where irrelevant information is collected, information continues to be collected after the decision is made, the decision may be made before any information is collected, and people demand more information even when they are surrounded by relevant information which they continue to ignore. Feldman and March's theoretical insight is that information in organizations serves two conceptually different purposes. Information is used as a *denotative signal*, representing the "facts" or the results of system analysis, as well as a *connotative symbol*, representing various values and images necessary to the maintenance of organizational roles, subunit goals, and public accountability. For example, if the corporate library is managed as "overhead," other units are implicitly encouraged to engage in irrelevant information requests because the benefits from surveillance and monitoring, as well as the symbolic value of appearing "informed" (even if the information is never used), reduce future risks as well as lend legitimacy and accountability to any solutions stemming from that unit – yet without (direct) cost to the users. However, in this situation, the corporate library can never show evidence of success, and ends up being rewarded for disseminating more irrelevant information, or punished for always being behind in service delivery and above budget allocations.

However, it is not simply the symbolic nature of information that fosters manipulation, deception, or fraud. Organizations and their structures often provide the very resources and positions that allow some to distort, suppress, or misuse information (Singer, 1980; Chapters 7 and 8, this volume). There may be low levels of perceived responsibility of the individuals making the product, or the executives guiding the organization. Kafka's servants in *The Castle*, Eco's inquisitor, Bernard Gui, in *The Name of the Rose*, Gilliam's bureaucrats in the movie *Brazil*, and the head Vogon (alien) bureaucrat, Prostetnic Vogon Jeltz, in the book and movie of Adams' *The Hitchhiker's Guide to the Galaxy* all fulfill their job descriptions and use resources so effectively that there is no recourse for the innocent, efficient, altruistic, or reasonable. Bureaucracies may, by their very nature – efficiently applying, through multiple levels of authority, the same set of rules to every situation – foster dysfunctional behavior (Mieczkowski, 1991).

Zmud (1990) argued that characteristics and uses of ICTs make some organizational functions especially vulnerable to *strategic information behaviors* such as manipulation or distortion. This may happen in two primary ways (in the content of a message that a system transmits/stores/distributes, or in how a message directs operations of the system itself) and in a variety of system nodes (sensor, filter, router, carrier, interpreter, learner, and modifier). It is not the technological complexity of computer systems per se that facilitates manipulation, but the pace, abstraction, and distancing possible in communicating through such systems. Flanagin *et al.* (2009) identified five types of destructive communication activities associated with ICTs. The first is *counterproductive activities*, or uses that conflict with organizational goals, or create employer risks through illegal behavior (downloading music at work, online gambling), create data security risks (viruses, network attacks, denial of service), or involve unauthorized use of the system. Most of these, they argue, go unreported. The second is *nonproductive activities*, such as social communication, cyberloafing/online procrastination, visiting inappropriate websites, conducting personal business, or using company resources. The third is *inappropriate activities*, such as flaming, sharing inappropriate jokes or pornography, releasing confidential information (sometimes used in the name of exposing truth). The fourth is *deceptive and equivocal activities* such as dishonesty, lying, knowingly sending messages to generate an incorrect conclusion. Related activities include identity deception and misrepresentation, identity concealment, use of avatars to reduce anxiety while misrepresenting oneself, and greater opportunities for ambiguous and misinterpreted messages. The final category of ICT-related destructive communication is *intrusive activities* which interrupt work activities or cognitive focus, shift one's focus, fragment tasks, and require time for recovery and refocus.

Barriers to perception

Singer (1978, 1980) argues that crazy systems and even their subroutines often become invisible, impervious to critique, or tolerated due to what he calls barriers to perception. These include such tendencies and practices as inherent organizational incentives to maintaining components of these systems, mechanization and bureaucratization of processes, ascribing normalcy to otherwise bizarre procedures simply because they occur in familiar situations, projecting an air of rationality onto technological and rationalized processes, perceiving legitimation cues in organizational and authority activities no matter how inconsistent, and the fragmentation of both perceptions and routines so that it becomes difficult to even identify a pattern of craziness or to allocate blame. Not only does technology itself promote a sense of rationality, but forms of communication about technology may foster a sense of rationality, which may diminish the ability to question or even identify potential problems. For example, referring to

NASA briefings on Challenger, "Bulletized presentations were central in creating local rationality, and central in nudging that rationality ever further away from the actual risk brewing just below" (Dekker, 2005, p. 39).

Crazy systems create systematic malfunctions either perceived as normal, or not perceived at all. The easily articulated goal-, algorithmic- and rule-driven nature of a crazy system may contribute to the visibility problem, making it harder to recognize the problem as a problem. The elegance of the rationale for the problem obscures its real-life costs. Taleb (2007, pp. 62–9) discussed the human tendency to reduce complexity by inventing narratives, or explanations of events, what he calls *false confidence*. Crazy systems may arise because organizational policies are created explicitly to obtain intended consequences, but when the policies have unintended negative consequences, the motivation, intention, and subsequent narratives of normalcy inhibit the perception of the unintended. A highly unlikely (Black Swan) event in an organization might make an existing crazy system visible, leading to an effort to codify procedural rules to prevent and deal with future occurrences. But the new procedure may itself be a crazy system or induce one elsewhere in the organization, because the emphasis on the very low probability of the initiating event precludes considering the surrounding high-probability (White Swan) context.

In addition to legitimation cues, Singer (1978) points to the *quasi-institutionalization of error*. Increased complexity and bureaucracy generates errors in databases, documents, and procedures. Large organizations have greater difficulties in correcting, or enabling victims to perceive, organizational errors (Mintz and Cohen, 1976). When errors become embedded and routinized in large and complex organizations, they are more likely to be perceived as idiosyncratic rather than systemic, or misperceived as external to the system. Those actually responsible for the error – say, designers, producers, executives – are distant from the event and can evade responsibility. Clients or customers tend to assume that the only reasonable explanation is that it is their fault. And, of course, some errors are in fact known but tolerated for various reasons, such as cost-effectiveness, detachment through risk assessment, knowing that most customers will not return the defective product, or the difficulty in completely identifying consequences.

The inability to perceive errors increases people's tolerance of them, both members and outsiders, and thus allows organizations to commit more of them. It becomes less costly for organizations to commit them, leading to people becoming used to lower standards and expectations. Individuals seeking information are often confronted with *authoritative organizational statements* that decrease their confidence and likelihood of pursuing the error. Errors come to seem idiosyncratic and infrequent, and therefore "cannot" be the fault of organization. Errors are tolerated or ignored especially when attempts to correct errors are made difficult (sometimes intentionally); organizations, after all, have much greater resources available to them than does any single "complaining" individual (Chapter 3, this volume). Moreover, society in general seems to have a false confidence in large technology, fostered by the size and pervasiveness of such systems and their public face, such as advertisements, logos, or branding images.

Boundaries become transparent yet impenetrable, individuals can see only limited aspects of the whole system, obligations and difficulties with roles get confused with specific personalities, resources are never sufficient, and people fill uncertainty with preferred interpretations. So specific organizational procedures (or lack of them) or decisions (or lack of them) that might seem to any particular individual as crazy, bureaucratic, unreasonable, or just wasteful, yet are not caused by peculiar action on the part of the individual, become rationalized, routinized, acceptable, and eventually invisible.

"Common sense" and "sensemaking" may well be another barrier to perception of crazy systems and URs (Weick, 1979, 1995; Chapter 4, this volume). Double-loop learning (learning how to learn by both the system and its users) can be inhibited, constrained, or manipulated at points of single-loop learning (understanding or behaving according to current schema) without it even being noticed. Perhaps more subtle is that the persistence of these kinds of problems indicates that the outcomes of sensemaking – that is, the reduction of equivocality through interactions that enact the environment, make sense of the phenomenon, and then retain this sense in organizational routines – are not necessarily self-reflexive, insightful, or even healthy for an organization and its members. The very drive to "make sense" of a situation may also institutionalize crazy systems and URs.

Kafka circuits

Singer explained that people directly experience crazy systems in the form of various Kafka circuits. The name comes from Franz Kafka's stories of apparently innocent people becoming entangled in pervasive paranoia, guilt, and confusion, while others treat the situation as rational and natural, or avoid dealing with the person by hiding behind bureaucratic procedures. "In Kafka's most important novels, *The Trial* and especially *The Castle*, the victim 'K' repeatedly finds himself struggling to attain some important but ambiguous objective against guilt, but this very objective seems to disappear as he becomes trapped in endless subsystems of irrelevant tasks" (Singer, 1980, p. 47). Here, again, the word "circuit" is used metaphorically, with human beings constrained by these problematic behavioral patterns much as electrical current and its applications are constrained and directed by electrical circuits, with associated routed energies and potential for shocks and short-circuits. Kafka circuits in crazy systems include:

- work circuit – trying to solve a problem generates more work, much of which may be fundamentally unnecessary, and which may quickly generate more costs than the initial individual instance of the problem, discouraging organizational action and learning;
- delay circuits – users or clients get no response, are actively stalled, are made to go through endless "channels," and have to wait until any benefits of resolving the initial problem have long since disappeared;
- error circuits – users or clients get caught up in a series of linked errors set off by their attempt to resolve an initial error.

Work, delay, and error circuits impose their costs and obstacles not just on the individuals involved, but also on the very processes involved in trying to evaluate the problematic system. In later chapters we will elaborate on these, and identify other circuits, which, in line with the emphasis on routines, we will generalize to the term "subroutines."

While using different terminology, other literature has touched on these kinds of costs. Similar costs were identified by Marschak's economic theory development work (1968), which in turn relied heavily on Shannon and Weaver's information theory. Marschak showed how encoding and decoding are related to the decision-making components of inquiring, transmitting, and deciding. He further explained that every step in the process has associated costs. These can readily be identified, for example, in interactions with ICTs, a primary context for discussing URs in this book. The first type is an *access cost* (similar to work subroutines) – the efforts and expenses associated with using a channel. Examples of access costs in ICT use are developing critical mass, search and uncertainty in both acquiring and then knowing how to use the system, and achieving sufficient user experience with an ICT (King and Xia, 1997; Markus, 1987; Rice, 1990; Rice and Shook, 1988; Rice *et al.*, 2001). The second type of cost is an *error cost* – incongruities in meaning between senders and receivers that occur throughout communication processes. ICT-related misunderstandings can happen because of channel capabilities. For example, emotional conversations and persuasion may be better handled using a medium that is "richer" or has more social presence (Daft and Lengel, 1986; Rice, 1993). The third type of cost associated with ICTs is a *delay cost* – including delays in communication such as the time it takes to compose and send messages, and wait for the other person to check their email inbox, read, obtain the necessary related information, and respond to the message.

A more general approach to nonproductive costs associated with organizational media includes what Rice and Bair (1984) call *shadow costs* and *media transformations*. Shadow costs are expended resources (time, money, social capital) associated with getting to the point of actually communicating with someone through some medium. The classic example is the time and costs associated with meetings: scheduling, off-topic talk, waiting for people to show up, group process losses, difficulty in accurately recalling content from earlier meetings. These costs in no way contribute to the productivity of the meeting, are nowhere accounted for, are always associated with using the communication channel of the meeting, may be substantial, and may generate secondary costs (such as leaving some members out or delaying an important decision). Media transformations, more laborious in the analog age, are all the intermediate transcribing, copying, interpreting, re-transmitting and delays associated with getting the information provided by one person in one medium to the intended person in a different medium. The classic example is a secretary answering a phone call, attempting to summarize the message on a small pink memo sheet, leaving that in a box to be picked up by the party for whom the call was originally intended, and then the recipient trying to interpret what the few words mean. Such internal organizational shadow costs and media transformation are examples of more general office transaction costs (Ciborra, 1987).

One especially insidious example of broad social costs is what Feeley (1992) calls *procedural injustice*. The experience of being arrested, incarcerated, and processed through pre-trial court procedures is a form of punishment administered by the lower criminal courts; defendants pay direct and indirect costs before they are tried. Thus some may chose to plead guilty rather than contest a charge, only because that may be less costly than defending oneself even when the legal complaint is unwarranted. For the individual, avoiding the short-term costs in this way may generate long-term costs, including damage to reputation, credit ratings, and job prospects. This lack of procedural justice in the lower criminal courts may, at the system level, impair public safety by reducing voluntary compliance with law enforcement, thus achieving the opposite goal motivating the original legal procedures.

Symptoms

According to Singer, symptoms of crazy systems include:

- catatonic non-responsiveness (lack of feedback, the inability to use the system itself to solve problems involving the system, making the client responsible for verifying the problem);
- denial (ignoring initial indicators of problems or complaints);
- pathological rigidity (inflexible rules and regulations, following problematic procedures blindly or claiming the procedures are fixed so as to avoid blame, false rules generated ad hoc, rules that may be intentionally misinterpreted, etc.);
- psychopathic manipulation (rigged systems that are biased against some users or clients, systems that encourage or facilitate outright fraud even while appearing legitimate, responses that label the person with a system problem as paranoid or a troublemaker); and
- suspicion and secrecy (turf battles within organizations, hiding useful information or explanations from users and clients).

Unusual routines

Singer's crazy system perspective provides a foundation for the book's topic: unusual routines. An unusual routine (UR) is a recurrent interaction pattern in which a system allows or requires a process which creates and reinforces, through dysfunctional (non-existent, obstructive, or deviation-reinforcing) feedback, unintended and undesirable outcomes, either within or across system levels (or both).

URs do not include accidents, errors, ignorance, breakdowns, evasions, or sabotage, although they may be mistakenly labeled as, or cause, these. They may be periodic, or repeated as part of everyday organizational life. They may be the outcome of choice, or avoidance of a choice. They may be the consequence of some "acceptable" error level. (Because perfection is either impossible or infeasible, systems must operate within some cost–benefit ratio, which may or may not correspond to some appropriate level of beneficence in its operation.) They may even be intentional, devised by one stakeholder to gain or maintain an advantage over another. The term "unusual routines" is intentionally oxymoronic, and both words have at least two meanings for our purposes.

They are *unusual* because they are dysfunctional, may be unexpected, may appear idiosyncratic to any one actor yet pervade organizational and social interactions, and involve participants, processes, policies, and goals in interactions that not only reinforce the unusual but also resist mitigation. They are unusual because attempts at mitigation may generate additional or unproductive work, create new errors that then also have to be fixed, or impose further delays. Each of these may end up creating more costs than just continuing to live with the initial problem, but the costs are not known in advance, often are not even identified as costs related to attempts at resolution, and are frequently displaced from the participants. They are unusual in that they may occur rarely, only in a particular context and combination of other interactions, or they may be fairly common across many organization members and customers, but only rarely experienced by any specific person. In these conditions the UR may persist and become entrenched, as no one experiences the pattern more than very infrequently, so is easily misperceived as noise, mistake, localized error, or due to an external agent (such as a customer), and thus difficult to identify as something systemic. They are unusual because there are often no explicit organizational or system processes for learning about such routines, or for communicating solutions to implementers, system designers, users, and customers.

They are *routines* because they are systematic, persist, are reinforced, and often become routine aspects of organizational life. Indeed, they are themselves generated through and become embedded in other ongoing routines and processes. Because they become embedded and often central to accomplishing some kinds of work, they also become routinized, in the sense that specific procedures, understandings, and patterns accrete around the first occurrence. They are routine in that organization members or outsiders doing what they are supposed to be doing, or what the system encourages, may become trapped in a manifestly dysfunctional process. What should be recognized as problematic takes on both the appearance, and the procedural and consequential reality, of the routine, thus becoming invisible to organizational developers and managers, and hence difficult for users and clients to recognize, much less resolve. When they are noted at all, they are often defended as "the way things are," caused by someone's "mistake" (the client or the user), justified as normal procedures, or dismissed as an "exception." URs become internally justified, whether implicitly or explicitly, and bureaucratized. An especially troublesome characteristic of a UR is that the larger context in which it is embedded (such as the complete organization, or the social system as a whole) makes it difficult to even perceive the initial problem *as* a problem.

While feedback may indeed be necessary for systematic organizational improvement – and poor feedback may indeed be a cause or characteristic of URs – feedback alone will likely be insufficient to cure a specific UR, much less an organizational penchant for them, and may well reinforce the problem. (As we will see in Chapters 4 and 7, because of the potential second-level dysfunctional feedback, the system cannot or will not identify this as a UR and thus cannot or will not attempt to resolve it, and may even impose additional delay, error, or work subroutines on anyone trying to do so.) Thus, these routines can prove maddeningly difficult to prevent, mitigate, acknowledge, or even identify, as the system itself is resistant to feedback or other corrective efforts about both the problem and the subroutines. Over time, the unusual or aberrant becomes both routine and routinized.

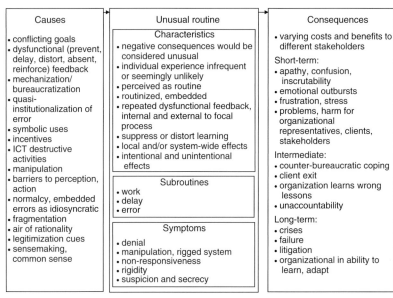

Causes	Unusual routine	Consequences
• conflicting goals • dysfunctional (prevent, delay, distort, absent, reinforce) feedback • mechanization/ bureaucratization • quasi- institutionalization of error • symbolic uses • incentives • ICT destructive activities • manipulation • barriers to perception, action • normalcy, embedded errors as idiosyncratic • fragmentation • air of rationality • legitimization cues • sensemaking, common sense	**Characteristics** • negative consequences would be considered unusual • individual experience infrequent or seemingly unlikely • perceived as routine • routinized, embedded • repeated dysfunctional feedback, internal and external to focal process • suppress or distort learning • local and/or system-wide effects • intentional and unintentional effects **Subroutines** • work • delay • error **Symptoms** • denial • manipulation, rigged system • non-responsiveness • rigidity • suspicion and secrecy	• varying costs and benefits to different stakeholders Short-term: • apathy, confusion, inscrutability • emotional outbursts • frustration, stress • problems, harm for organizational representatives, clients, stakeholders Intermediate: • counter-bureaucratic coping • client exit • organization learns wrong lessons • unaccountability Long-term: • crises • failure • litigation • organizational in ability to learn, adapt

Figure 1.1 Initial model of unusual routines, derived from Singer's crazy systems model. (This model integrates the components of Singer's model of crazy systems with the central aspects, including two levels, of unusual routines.)

These contradictory and frustrating URs paradoxically generate completely sensible and even effective outcomes for some organizations, system users, organizational representatives, customers, and clients, while generating negative consequences for others. The consequences may be intended or unintended (the more subtle and difficult case), short-term or long-term, within the same process level or at different levels, and with different temporal feedback loops. Consequences may include frustration, apathy, helplessness, unquestioning compliance, tolerance of insults, stress, "irrational" behavior, sabotage, counter-bureaucratic behavior, exit, corporate litigation, and organizational failure (Singer, 1977).

The rest of the book

Chapter 2 applies the initial model to the implementation of six information and communication technology systems, while Chapter 3 looks at unsatisfying customer service interactions. Chapter 4 reviews the foundations for an interdisciplinary model of URs, based in systems theory, sensemaking theory, diffusion of innovation theory, socio-technical systems theory, and, especially, organizational routines theory. Chapter 5 applies this model and related propositions to an in-depth analysis of the implementation of a university networking system, while Chapter 6 summarizes the results and their implications. Chapter 7 shows that the process of feedback itself is often quite problematic, and even generates and reinforces URs. Chapter 8 shows how URs are related to, and a generalized example of, many other concepts and experiences, across a broad range of disciplines. Chapter 9 presents a variety of recommendations, derived from the research and theories discussed in the prior chapters, and initial suggestions for analyzing URs. Chapter 10 integrates the main arguments and insights from each chapter, providing a tentative comprehensive model of unusual routines. The Preface and the Contents provide more details about each chapter.

2 | Causes, symptoms, and subroutines of unusual routines in six computer information/communication systems

WITH ELIZABETH BARCLAY, ANN BEMIS,
MARTIN DARE, RICHARD HALE, BRIAN
MCGEE, AND TINA PHOENIX

This chapter begins to explore the phenomenon of unusual routines in six cases of organizational information and communication technologies (ICT – including computer-mediated communication systems). Unusual routines associated with ICTs are rarely acknowledged, diagnosed, or addressed by systems personnel or management, and only minimally by information systems researchers. Further, most systems analysis approaches emphasize the development of systems according to planned uses and expectations, and do not well anticipate dysfunctional uses, negative outcomes, and components resistant to diagnosis and correction. Markus (1984) and Bostrom and Heinen (1977a) noted that a frequent assumption of system designers is that problems with systems are due to user inadequacies ranging from lack of training to resistance to incompetence, rather than inadequacies of the system (similar to the "operator error" explanation of complex system failures, in Chapter 8). (For exceptions clearly emphasizing the social aspects of systems analysis and implementation, see Hirschheim, 1985; Kendall and Kendall, 1999; and Markus, 1984.) Users and clients may know they are experiencing difficulties with the system, but rarely do they identify these as URs.

The interactions, procedures, and processes are designed into the regular operation of the system or organization, and organizational structures or policies rarely allow the identification or mitigation of associated URs. The problematic processes are due, in the broadest sense, to faulty system design, impermeable organizational boundaries, and limited understanding of the complex, ambiguous, and changing social environments in which people use such systems. As Chapter 1 explained, their implications or requirements are essentially "unusual," but they become accepted – indeed often can only be understood – as "routine."

The case analyses of six ICT systems in this chapter are our initial step toward a deeper understanding of the structure and dysfunctionality of URs. One specific addition is the identification of a *blame* subroutine (discussed in the Time Reporting case, and in Chapters 3 and 4).

Causes of unusual routines in three ICTs

This first section considers three newly implemented ICTs – a labor cost system, a housing relocation program, and a voicemail system – as examples of socio-technical systems which have developed URs. They illustrate the potential that computer systems have, in general, for nurturing URs. To that end, we first describe the systems, then analyze them with regard to those problems of conflicting goals, poor feedback, symbolic and manipulative uses of information, and barriers to perception.

Labor cost system

Managing commercial projects typically requires accurate records of the time spent on a project and its subcomponents. This information is sometimes used as the basis for charging clients. More often, though, it is used as a time control and analysis device so that resource usage can be measured against allocated budgets for a project. In most projects clients prefer to agree to an upfront fixed price for a fixed scope of work; this allows the project manager to develop an explicit budget. Labor time cost systems have been developed to handle these issues.

The simpler labor time cost systems generally limit the data recorded to employee identification, budget identities against which to record usage, and a numeric field in which to enter the amount of labor used. More sophisticated systems have fields to record the actual task performed, and other project-related information and analysis tools. Overall, labor time cost systems are databases that record information ready for aggregation and interpretation. The recording of labor time expenditure on tasks and projects has obvious advantages for managing resources, and is therefore perceived positively by management. Like all monitoring and control systems it provides a measure of performance (Markus, 1984), although here it focuses on cost. The advantages of recording labor time include the ability to:

(1) charge clients and customers for the work being performed on a project, and justify those charges;
(2) monitor the labor being used and its associated cost;
(3) measure the accuracy of labor estimations against actual labor used;
(4) identify resources available for use on projects by analyzing the time spent by each staff member on client billable tasks compared to time spent on non-billable tasks;
(5) quickly examine data about labor costs and resources in electronic format that would not be available if the data were recorded manually; and
(6) improve subsequent resource planning as more data are gathered.

Labor cost is also a measure that is well understood in all organizations.

More and more, however, such systems are also used for employee performance evaluation. The *reinvention* (adaptation of an innovation after its adoption; see Johnson and Rice, 1987; and Chapter 4, this volume) of labor time cost systems as performance evaluation devices has raised some interesting issues, such as the recording process and how the information itself is interpreted by the various stakeholders including users, management, and customers.

Conflicting goals

A labor cost system's information is generally used as a means to track the labor billable to a client and also to manage costs within budgetary limits. The latter use is most common and applies in projects where a fixed price is agreed with a client for a defined objective or deliverable.

This seems to be quite reasonable and rational behavior and fits nicely with the efficient and effective management of a business. Or does it? What happens when there are two goals in conflict, such as the objective to meet labor time cost budgets that are tight, and the other to deliver a high-quality product or service to the customer? Assuming that the system user is even aware of these two goals, (s)he is often torn between meeting time cost constraints and producing a quality product. This is amplified when the company has a strong commitment to both quality and client satisfaction, as so many explicitly state.

But a more fundamental difficulty is embedded in such systems: how are labor costs actually assessed? Most systems have to use a notional cost for labor since the actual cost of using labor is not just limited to an employee's salary. Overhead such as desks, floor space, and equipment should be included. A more subtle difficulty is that labor time cost systems use "rubbery" internal labor rates – that is, they are generally estimated, rather than actual, costs. Generic labor charge-out rates are often used for each type of functional role performed by a company. For example, "project management" rates are different from "design" labor rates because the task involves different skills that are essentially valued differently, reflecting the market value of the services offered. The various rates also cover salary costs as well as company overhead, general employment costs and, in the commercial world, a profit margin. As a rule of thumb, staff at all levels within a company are paid differently, so the cost differential between the charge-out rate and actual cost for each employee may vary widely. Labor costs within systems cannot, therefore, be "accurate," because the real cost of labor is not actually known a priori.

Another source of inaccuracy with labor time cost systems is related to the actual recording of labor hours. The time taken to perform tasks and the amount of time recorded on projects can vary significantly between individuals. If labor time costs are managed against budgets, individuals will tend to use the available budget. In other words, labor time cost systems are not, as systems, intuitive about labor task efficiency. Labor task efficiency analysis needs to be performed independent of the data contained within the system, as these systems are designed mainly to record and aggregate labor usage records, and to report usage against compartmentalized budgets. However, because most labor cost systems are used both to record (rubbery) labor "costs" as well as to analyze task efficiency based on those costs, the systems are used for internally conflicting goals.

Time cost budget overruns, particularly in an environment where quality is crucial to success, can thus become (sometimes intentional) procedural traps. The employee who overruns the allocated time cost but produces a quality product could receive a bad performance review or dismissal. In contrast, the employee who meets the time cost budgets but does not meet the client expectations might be praised for finishing the project on time and on budget. As a result, the company may lose a client (or become embroiled in litigation or contract penalty fees) because of the poor product or service. Often clients pay for work they are not happy with, but later vote with their feet rather than confront or complain about the unsatisfactory product (Chapter 3). This is a classic symptom of a UR: the ambiguity between what the company wants to achieve (customer satisfaction) and a system that provides management with what seems like reasonable information about performance (cost overruns) that prompts them to take irrational actions (employee sanctions) that cost them the desired result (customer loyalty) yet does not allow the organization to learn from this experience (as they rarely know that a customer has not "returned").

Poor feedback

The data in labor time cost systems is generally simply recorded with reference to quantity. It is a system of counting and calculation, and reasonably inflexible. Emphasis is placed on the billable time that a company can charge to a client. The data tends to be aggregated into total number of hours. Once the data has been entered into the system and aggregated in this way it is perceived as being more homogenous and robust, providing legitimation cues, and an air of normality that is difficult to question.

A budget overrun in the system may mean that the employee or the project manager has to spend additional resource time checking the overrun, a work subroutine. The lack of feedback from the system allows this event to occur within the organization-wide system and this event in itself creates more work. Adequate feedback from the system and data verification at the time of entry could prevent this extra unproductive work from occurring. For instance, budget balances could be reported by the system before and after data entry to allow information that could be used in managing the time more actively. Post-event feedback rarely helps to improve performance in the current project (and usually not much in future projects either), whereas on-the-spot feedback allows more flexibility in action and decision-making.

It is important to realize that, as designed and implemented, the basic process of recording labor time costs adds no intrinsic value to the work being performed. It typically only represents a cost, with no value added; it is essentially a transaction cost. Also, from an employee's perspective, there may be a tendency to feel as though "big brother is watching you" and that individual autonomy is being taken away. This can lead to inconsistencies in the information recorded as employees behave in ways that allow them to reclaim their autonomy (also a form of symbolic uses and manipulation). For example, an employee who has a large amount of non-billable time on their time sheet may face being loaded with more work that is billable. This in turn may reduce the amount of free time available for legitimate internal, but non-customer-billable tasks. Therefore, there is a tendency for the employee to overstate billable hours, allowing the employee a greater amount of freedom for such tasks. This is similar to bogus "typing productivity" figures (Johnson and Rice, 1987; Markus, 1984). That is, the system requires feedback, but as the user receives negative reinforcement (explicitly or implicitly) for providing this information, the user may provide suspect feedback to the system. This means the system will "learn," and later reinforce, the wrong thing (Kerr, 1995).

Employees may not see the system as advantageous since the system may be limited in the type and format of the feedback it can provide. Often labor time cost systems do not provide appropriate user interfaces to help the user understand the information being recorded in the system. This can lead to incorrect assumptions being made about the data being recorded, and in the end information that is misused or misinterpreted. Consider, for example, using billable hours data as a performance measurement to counsel or praise an employee without having adequately assessed the environmental circumstance to evaluate the legitimacy of the performance data.

Symbolic uses and manipulation

Stakeholders within the organization are prone to misrepresent information about labor usage. Senior management, from a cost perspective, would like to reduce labor overhead since this has a direct effect on the bottom line. Line managers, on the other hand, may receive salary benefits for the more staff they control and would benefit by using labor information to justify more staff. As Feldman and March noted, "Information is gathered and communicated in a context of conflict of interest and with a consciousness of potential decision consequences" (1981, p. 176). Labor time cost information can be viewed symbolically as a means to show results, the fruits of one's labor, or proper decision-making procedures. Alternatively, it could also be viewed as a symbol of control, particularly for those who have access to the information and the ability to control its presentation (Feldman and March, 1981).

The mere availability of labor time cost data facilitates its use as a measure of employee performance. Management may use this information in a way that gives the appearance of legitimacy and objectivity in conducting performance appraisals (Singer, 1980). If the data is used for performance appraising it is often used covertly rather than overtly. To extract performance information, the data is often manipulated to meet what appears to be legitimate evaluation criteria (see the discussion of performance measurement by Paton, 2003, in Chapter 8). The problem, however, is that labor time cost information is often decoupled from its context, such as the organization's environment and events associated with producing each end product. The underlying assumptions about the information and the benchmarks need to be continually reviewed for the information to be useful and coherent for making management decisions.

Lack of context is even more of a problem if the end products are unique or have not been created before, such as the process of designing a new and unique product (Johnson and Rice, 1987). In specialist task environments, like project management, time cost systems cannot reflect the variability and nuances of each task. Under such circumstances, the time taken to create the product becomes a matter of academic argument. Therefore, the measurement against any time cost goal can only really be used as a statement of fact rather than of performance measurement, since typically there have been no real performance criteria set, or adequately reflected in the system's input filters (see Sless's (1988) discussion of forms as organizational interface, Chapter 3).

Nonetheless, data within a time cost system is often used to measure performance for which there have been no criteria set. Once an employee becomes aware that the data can be, and is, used in this way, it can lead to concern and even paranoia. If the system is simple in nature, the data can be easily manipulated by employees to give the appearance of high performance. This essentially defeats the original purpose of the system which is to have an accurate record of client billable hours. The employees who manipulate the data in these ways may very well be rewarded for their apparent performance and thus their actual manipulation. This in turn encourages them to manipulate the data even more. On the other hand, the organization may seek to reprimand honest employees, who in management's judgment have not met the performance standards, but at the same time have not manipulated the data in their favor (somewhat similar to Edmondson's (2004) analysis of error reporting by nurses, Chapter 4).

Barriers to perception
In regard to the costs of collecting data for the labor cost system, the following issues are often neglected:

(1) the labor time it takes each person to record the information including data-entry time if centrally entered into a system;
(2) the systems, paper and storage cost associated with holding the data (sometime held in both paper and electronic format by multiple parties);
(3) indirect and opportunity costs associated with time and distraction of recording data that is not directly associated with a person's core role or responsibility;
(4) the cost associated with analyzing and manipulating the data into a useful format; and
(5) the indirect costs associated with using information that is not relevant, or is inadequate or unreliable.

Some of these are understood transaction costs; some are shadow and media transformation costs; and some of these may be work subroutines. These costs are often not perceived, and not easily quantifiable, but nevertheless could be substantial. Their invisibility becomes a barrier to perceiving some of the negative implications associated with using the system.

Reliability of the information is affected by the accuracy of entry, which has a lot to do with how valuable and important the information is perceived to be by the recorder. Individual belief in regard to the intention of information use (for example, if the information is to be used for reward or punishment) can also affect how reliably they record the information. Thus there is a disjuncture between responsibility for provision and responsibility for use of the information, and an asymmetry of information in the principal–agent relationship (Feldman and March, 1981; Chapter 3, this volume).

The (mostly implicit) reinvention of a labor cost reporting system into a performance evaluation system generally is reinforced by the pervasive notion that the system's information is all-encompassing and believable. For example, an accountant may use the information to examine employee efficiency and report what is believed to be accurate data about each employee. The more information that can be gathered about labor usage costs, the more rational the decisions appear. If the information is presented to management, the information tends to be accepted as being accurate because it was presented by the accountant and was obtained from the computer – both symbols of accuracy and precision, creating an air of rationality and legitimation. The reasonableness of the data is often unquestioned, unless, however, the results are sufficiently outside the range of expectations as to be noticed.

An example of this is when reports from the system indicate budget overruns. When notional labor costs are conflated with actual costs, the attempts to find the causes of the apparent inefficiency may themselves create work, delay, and error subroutines. The root cause in actuality may be the false presumptive accuracy of the system's reports. Labor time cost systems tend to become entrenched, or routinized. This is made more difficult when at least some of the use of the system does not provide or add any value to the work that it is expected to support.

Conflicts in more sophisticated construction systems

As a side note, this fundamental problem of conflicting goals infests even the most sophisticated, integrated industrial systems. Building Information Modeling (BIM) systems bring together, in a 3-D modeling system, the components from different companies of the mechanical, electrical, plumbing, and fire and life safety systems during design and construction of buildings. The construction projects are tightly coupled technologically (including design, coordinate, optimize, install, and maintain iterations), and the BIM system provides an integrated perspective into, and tracking of, all the components. However, in practice, the components, their management, and their actual use in the system are separated according to the respective professions and companies (mechanical engineer, architect, building owner, general contractor, fabricator, and mechanical subcontractor) (Dossick and Neff, 2010). So, in reality the BIM consists of a network of several loosely-coupled independent digital models. As each is revised, the implications for the other models may or may not be known or carried through. And those responsible for revising and integrating the components are removed from the decisions made by the various subcontractors. Each separate company has its own bundle of reasons to resist any particular innovation, or a shared innovation, such as BIM: legal risks, intellectual property, financial risks, necessary training, project specifics, corporate culture, trust in the other companies, etc. (Nithamyong and Skibniewski, 2006).

Thus there are inherent tensions between obligations to the work scope (with attendant expertise about regulations and standards, etc.), the project, and the company, in the form of who is in charge, the level of organization (individual, team, firm), the mission (from producing documents to producing a building), tasks (translating from blueprints to surviving a competitive market), actions and values (advocating for the task to optimizing time and money), relationship to other obligations (from project budgets to staffing), and approach to collaboration (from timely exchange to avoiding exposure). A wide range of conflicting obligations across scope, project, and company arises from this situation. Pervasive obstacles to consistent and comprehensive communication develop, so the need to move forward allows or requires individual leadership, such as a project engineer, to take the place of integrated project organization. This of course puts that individual in a generally untenable position of attempting to obtain all relevant recent information across boundaries without sufficient authority or even knowledge. More specifically, the lack of coordination and communication across the project and professions encourages local commitment to one's work scope instead of the overall project. Thus, multiple, and often unidentifiable and undiscussable, goal conflicts ensue (Dossick and Neff, 2010).

Home Sale Automation system

Companies and their employees are on the move. In the United States, the employee relocation industry is huge, requiring both personnel and system support ($24 billion in 2009, according to 1888PressRelease, 2009). The system referred to here as a Home Sale Automation (HSA) system provides services to clients who require assistance in the relocation of their employees. The HSA system tracks the employee's property through a number of phases: inspection, offer, acquisition, inventory, and resale. These phases constitute the "property life cycle."

Using this system, there are two major steps in employee relocation. The first involves counseling the transferee in the program's parameters, arranging for inspections of the house by a variety of vendors (such as appraisers, brokers, inspectors, title searchers, etc.) and then arriving at a fair market value for the house. This step is handled by a Relocation Coordinator. Once the transferee accepts the offer, the property passes into inventory and the second step begins. The Real Estate Specialist becomes involved and concentrates on packaging the house for resale. After the sale is finalized, the system generates a final invoice for the client, although there may be partial invoices rendered during the process as well. The HSA system has interfaces with back office computer systems such as accounting, management reporting, and client reporting. The client reporting system supports the activities of the Client Relations Manager, who ensures that the client's requirements are satisfactorily addressed.

This particular HSA system was embroiled in a change of corporate cultures. The relocation company was acquired by another company about halfway through the rollout of the HSA system. The original owner of the company had managed a string of realty companies and had acquired the relocation organization primarily to feed business to the realty division. However, the new acquiring company's attitude toward the relocation business, and the HSA system, was vastly different. This company's core competency was insurance, and they very much understood the value of human relationships. They immediately saw the system's value, accelerated its implementation, and involved users in future releases of the software. They saw that a system that allowed their staff to know essential details about a particular customer would allow them to provide personalized service that would exceed the industry's current standards.

The HSA system eventually was considered a success, but this mixed cultural heritage affected the course of the implementation. As is typical in many system implementations, the initial agenda, strategic design, and vision were set by upper management and were quite broad and general (Johnson and Rice, 1987). The branch offices, however, determined and established operational and tactical issues, which were quite specific and procedural. Thus, dedicated technical resources and a help desk were set up to support the ongoing integration of the HSA system into work flow. As problems were encountered and solutions proposed and implemented, the branches were able to see the organizational commitment in support of their efforts to genuinely improve the system.

Conflicting goals

Decisions made during the implementation of the HSA system reverberated throughout various uses of the system. The HSA system was designed for online, interactive application. One advantage of the new system's design was that it separated various data-entry stages, to better match the life cycle of the property, and better correspond to the manual processes of moving the property. The new HSA system was designed to assist Relocation Coordinators, who were not, and did not contemplate becoming, skilled computer operators. While the prior system had few editing requirements and only really checked that the required data was present at certain key points in the life cycle, primarily at client billing stages, the HSA system's screens were designed to accept small amounts of related information at a time, allowing for consistency and providing advisory messages; they did not allow entry of all relevant information at once. As a consequence, input errors and inconsistencies were now displayed one at a time and would not allow a user to go forward without resolving the first error. This was, after all, one of the responsibilities of Relocation Coordinators – to resolve inconsistencies and advance the process.

Due to cost constraints, however, the management of the relocation company decided that not every user could have their own terminal. Also, the secondary costs of training users in how to operate the system were high. Therefore, the system designed for use by the Relocation Coordinators was actually installed for use by data-entry operators located in each branch. The system was designed to allow only limited data entry and to stop for each error to be resolved, but the data-entry operators did not understand the transaction relationships (because that was not their job). It is not surprising that the data-entry operators intensely disliked this piecemeal discovery of errors, because they often had to abandon the whole data-entry process for a particular transferee as they were not in a position to resolve problems then and there. In some instances, the transaction was rejected as many as four times before it was finally accepted by the system. Further, the data-entry operators bore the brunt of the system's teething problems, and were forced to act as advisors to the other branch staff who had not received training in how to use the system.

The error messages displayed on the screen, designed to provide instant feedback to the Relocation Coordinators, presumed that the user had a certain industry-level knowledge, and was capable of resolving the reported error immediately. As the data-entry operators did not have this information, they had to physically write the error on a piece of paper so that the Relocation Coordinator could deal with it later. Once the correct information returned from the Relocation Coordinator, the operator would re-enter the data, only to have it rejected on the basis of another error further into the processing cycle of the transaction but not yet validated due to the previous error stopping processing at a prior point. This ironic effect is inherently dysfunctional, as it prevented some of the very benefits justifying the information system, created delayed and decontextualized error feedback, and caused work, delay, and error subroutines.

From the Relocation Coordinator's point of view, they were now confronted with a batched set of data entry forms that had to be fed to a system designed for interactive operation. However, the Relocation Coordinators had no direct experience with the system, because the data-entry operators were the only ones actually using it, yet had little ability to correctly analyze any technical reasons why the system had rejected the transaction. A side effect of this data-entry problem was that some Relocation Coordinators would save up their transactions until the entire case had been completed. While this minimized errors because basically all information was present by that time, the planned value of the HSA systems in providing, as it became available, incremental information to related systems was diminished. Users' reasonable avoidance of delay and error subroutines reduced the inherent value of the system to the organization and clients.

The system was adapted over time to better fit the relocation process to the extent of actually embedding particular clients' requirements as business rules into the processing cycles of the HSA system. When the relocation company considered altering its service delivery program to differentiate itself from the services offered by its competitors, and address particular clients' requirements, it had to change these embedded rules – which had now become procedural traps. This had two effects that were somewhat contradictory to management's initial agenda.

The first was that the salespeople involved in creating and offering these new programs had to be made aware of how the program's parameters were implemented – throughout all of its components – so that changes would be consistent throughout the life cycle processing of the properties. Previously, the old system had relied entirely on the Relocation Coordinator's understanding of the customer relocation program, and his/her resolution of any inconsistencies and discrepancies before a case was entered into the system. An interesting paradox associated with the new system, therefore, was that as the routinization of the new system was in part designed to reduce the skills involved in administering the programs and thus minimize impacts of staff turnover, a broader cross-section of staff had to become more aware of how the system operated, not just those directly involved with its operation. In actuality this generated more widespread but diffuse effects of turnover.

Once the system was fully implemented, the Relocation Coordinators used the system on a transaction-by-transaction basis, rather than waiting for a whole portion of the process to be completed. But this caused the second effect, that inconsistencies in the input were not discovered until later in the life cycle. Such problems generated a whole host of political issues with regard to which unit or person was responsible for dealing with these inconsistencies, and what should be done about it. Here, a delay subroutine also created obstacles to feedback, thus generating other kinds of problems.

Paradoxically, the (decentralized) branch operations were now finally beginning to drive the (centralized) company, in part because evidence of achievements and information about the activities of the branch were now becoming more widely disseminated and understood. Interestingly, associated with this broader availability of information, senior branch managers were beginning to migrate to positions of power within the relocation company and take up management positions at the head office.

Poor feedback

A major problem involving poor feedback occurred in the sources of the system evaluations. The relocation company had specific staff called Client Relations Managers who interacted with the client's personnel department and assisted in interpreting the output and results of the HSA system. While the branch operations personnel handled the relocation of individual transferees, the success of the relocation process was judged by the client's personnel department staff, normally in their head office. The Client Relations Manager position was seen as essential in maintaining a good working relationship between the relocation company and the customer. But it was a head office, not branch, function; the head office rarely received feedback about local processing and system problems. Further, the consolidating of evaluation processes at the head office reflected the company's attitude that the activities in the branches could be routinized, and that the personal relationships that ensured ongoing success were best managed from the head office. This indicated that upper-level management had not fully appreciated the valuable contribution that the Relocation Coordinator and other branch staff added to the whole process, and made it difficult for them to either properly reward behavior or assess the source of problems.

Symbolic uses and manipulation

The name of the system – Home Sale Automation – symbolically implied a routine, rationalized process; however, it was really quite unstructured and contextual. These mismatches created considerable complexity for the data-entry operators. They now had to understand the flow of information in the branch and become more actively involved in solving problems. Eventually, because of the expertise gained in this area, many operators were able to transfer into Assistant Relocation Coordinator positions when the large-volume data-entry requirements disappeared. This may be considered an unintended, but positive, outcome similar to the outward and upward migration of word processing operators over time in Johnson and Rice's (1987) study. But at the time, the operators disliked the system not only because of the unplanned changes in their task structure, but also because of the clearly conflicting goals in interface design and task requirements. Indeed, the mismatch considerably slowed down apparent benefits from the new system, leading senior management to seriously consider abandoning the HSA system and returning to the prior system. These are all clear examples of work, delay, and error subroutines, and some ways in which symbolic values of information and technical systems may be inconsistent, or even manipulated.

To some extent, the system had been designed to support both branch users' and management's expected outcomes, but did not require either culture to actually interact and thus adapt to achieve the outcomes. That is, each culture was able to maintain its symbolic interpretation of the expectations, nature, and value of the system. For example, an inconsistency in the symbolic expectations of the system's use occurred in the underlying motivation for, and the actual extent of, data collection, in the HSA system. Management now required that all related information be entered into the HSA system incrementally, as the information was generated (in spite of the data error-correcting work and delay subroutines noted above). The objective was to collect information for use in analyzing the relocation industry in general, in near real-time, and then to eventually rationalize and routinize the processing. As a result, a great amount of information was collected by the system about each stage of the property and transferee life cycle. Senior management could report back to the relocation company's owners and point to their efforts to understand the industry and therefore either make, or at least appear to make, the most informed and effective decisions.

Few HSA system reports that contained this information were designed for, or distributed to, the branches and users. The only online screen output was a summary report. In this instance the head office management was effectively penalizing the branch operations by making the branches collect data to provide information that would educate management about the relocation process and industry, rather than to support the branches in making particular decisions. Note, as well, that as the system was routinized to collect all this information, even once management "understood" the industry, the HSA system continued to require branches to collect and input all related information. In other terms, local users experienced work subroutines, without feedback about the benefits of that work.

Senior management also had a hidden agenda for HSA: using it to record dates associated with each stage of an entire relocation case, which could be used to compare the processing time required by each branch employee. The use of system data in performance evaluation revealed that senior management presumed the relocation process was a sequence of rational decisions that could be improved by reducing variations based on individual employees, and that all necessary information could be captured by the system.

Barriers to perception

In spite of the obvious subroutines and conflicting goals in the HSA system, the system was implemented and used, due to ascriptions of normalcy and fragmented perceptions (Singer, 1980). First, branch operations personnel had become used to filling in data-entry forms, and as the prior system had not provided more feedback than did the new HSA system, so the additional complexity was seen in an incremental light. Branch staff were also instructed to expect some teething problems associated with the implementation, but as the amount and nature of inconvenience was not specified, the branch staff ascribed any inconvenience to the implementation of the system, rather than to the system's features or inherent design. Second, the Relocation Coordinators were asked to complete only portions of the data-entry form, so the size of the task did not become so large that they would perceive it as a significant burden. Also, as they dealt with multiple transferees, all at slightly different points in their individual relocation programs, it was hard to assess the absolute level of additional burden.

Voicemail system

The voice processing system discussed here, typically referred to as "voicemail," was implemented in a university of some 20,000 students and employees. The mid-range system offered voicemail/messaging, call processing, automated attendant, and voice information (audiotex) services to all university personnel twenty-four hours a day. (For some studies on voicemail or messaging systems, see Rice and Danowski, 1993; Rice and Shook, 1990; Rice and Steinfield, 1994; Rice and Tyler, 1995.)

Two pilot implementations were involved. The Office of the Registrar's system allowed callers to press their telephone keypad buttons in response to voice menus to request course information. The Office handled over 12,000 inquiries during the pilot test. A complicating factor was that responsibility for the implementation had just been transferred from the telecommunications department to the Office of Computing Services. Thus the Office of Computing Services was the other pilot test site, so that they could better understand their role as the new manager of overall implementation for voice processing throughout the university.

Some benefits were obvious, and others more subtle. For example, while previously callers would wait until business hours to leave more detailed inquiries (approximately 20 percent of all calls were simple requests for information), the Registrar Office noticed that calls now were more evenly spread out during the twenty-four-hour period. And the Office of Computing was aware of the opportunity to be perceived as a university-wide innovator. Of course, many were concerned at the possible loss of the "personal touch" potentially available through "live" telephone operators, even though prior to the system the operators could often not handle the volume of calls, or did not have the required information (see, for example, Rice and Shook, 1990; Rice and Steinfield, 1994).

Poor feedback

Lack of feedback can take on more subtle forms than simple lack of interaction. For instance, potential users of the university voice system were offered training on how to send and receive messages, but not on how to use the system to support communication with outside callers, project groups, or chains of interactions (i.e., how to use the system features for messaging instead of just answering, in order to increase feedback across traditional communication boundaries; see Rice and Shook, 1990). Another example was when the Office of the Registrar recorded extensive messages for some system menu choices, but provided no opportunity to ask that the information be repeated. This made it difficult for the user to process or remember all the information, leading to wasted time and frustrating experiences (delay and error subroutines). However, as an example of designing the system to learn about such negative subroutines in other parts of the system, the designers had also included a menu choice for leaving comments. Review of these recorded comments highlighted this problem, which designers then solved by shorter menu responses and the ability to repeat any segment. This ability of a system to allow meta-communication about the system (and thus avoid work, delay, and error subroutines in order to provide feedback) seems a crucial factor in dealing with URs.

An extreme case of poor feedback is a catatonically non-responsive system (Singer, 1980, p. 48). In the voicemail system, without regular maintenance some hard disk storage will be wasted on non-users while other users' accounts will fill up, preventing anyone from leaving additional messages for those users. Note that external users, not the account owner, experience this error (and probably work) subroutine directly; internal system constraints and design choices generate costs for others external both to the system and to the organization!

Individual voice account owners may also be directly non-responsive to any outside messages. The initial complexity of the system actually made it fairly difficult for new users to respond to outside messages, generating a "non-responsive" system from the outside callers' perspective. Further, other users who got no response from these account holders began to perceive the entire system as non-responsive, generating negative implementation attitudes and increasing system-wide non-responsiveness (a problem that Markus, 1990, calls a failure of *communication discipline*, creating a critical mass of non-responders).

Symbolic uses and manipulation
In a decision process, participants may request additional information to attempt to clarify issues, or to provide evidence or rationality as a pre-defense against later criticism (Feldman and March, 1981). Indeed, much information was gathered during the pilot voicemail studies, including studying others' failed implementations in an attempt to counter possible worst-case scenarios (Chapter 8). However, little of this background material was actually made available, as a consequence of the ill-will generated by the transfer of control from telecommunications to the computing office. Only the system sales agreement, various product brochures, and a page of evaluation criteria were available for the computer office system evaluator to assess. This withholding of information clearly functioned as an exercise of power over information available for decision-making. However, this required work and delay subroutines in the form of duplication of efforts in obtaining information about potential uses and users, and related technical and cost information. Paradoxically, this withholding of prior information may have speeded up the implementation process, as there was no symbolic investment in or allegiance to prior

decisions about how to progress, yet there was exceptional pressure to move ahead.

An organization may choose to implement a voice processing system entirely as an automated attendant and callers have to choose an extension when prompted. However, if the callers do not know the extension, they must listen to a complete announcement before they can reach an operator, who may not always be available. Thus the caller must either return to the message loop, or hang up. Even if an operator is available, this *rigged system* design wastes time and frustrates the caller.

Causes, symptoms, and subroutines of unusual routines in three ICTs

This section describes three more case studies utilizing the initial UR model as the analytical framework. They go into more detail than the preceding cases, with regard to symptoms of URs, associated subroutines, and causal linkages within the organizational context. The intent here is to further illustrate the analytical value of the UR theoretical framework, and further connect our model to other literature. The case studies concern a technical issue help request system, an online database query system, and an employee time reporting system. The first two cases reveal specific manifestations of causes, symptoms, and subroutines. The last case shows how causes, symptoms, barriers to perception, and subroutines are highly integrated.

Technical issue help request system

A bank's Worldwide Technology Services (WTS) system, called "Falcon," was developed and implemented to improve the quality of technical support service provided to the bank's employees by imposing more rules and stricter policies on the technical services team. The Falcon system imposed deadlines and restrictions that limited the flexibility of its users, thus limiting the possibility of the system's reinvention. As a result, members of the WTS team often found themselves using workarounds (Chapter 4) and both suffering from, as well as generating, URs, in their attempts to provide technical support to employees. Not only did the system not succeed in providing better technical support to employees, but it also frustrated them and the

WTS team. The Falcon system was housed on its own server, which had limited capacity. Its users were assigned login IDs and passwords to access the system. To allocate the server's limited space, IDs and passwords were only assigned to WTS employees whose daily responsibilities involved Falcon requests. For this reason, the Falcon system was limited to a handful of WTS employees. The limited communication potential through and outside of the system generated a number of problems.

Cause: conflicting goals

Falcon users were often involved in both the individual request work generated by the system and the project work that existed outside the system. Since many WTS employees had virtually no knowledge of Falcon requests, projects and schedules, they were unaware of the amount of work some of their teammates were engaged in from day to day. This created conflicts of interest when assigning projects and designing project schedules that required the time and participation of Falcon users, as well as secrecy symptoms (see below, pp. 45–5).

Falcon, in conjunction with the policies and procedures that accompany it, exerted extreme control over its users by holding them to strict deadlines and restricting them from filtering the information passed from person to person and from group to group. The deadlines imposed on Falcon users prevented them from finding ways to reinvent the system because they were preoccupied with meeting these deadlines. Instead of reinventing the system, users actually found themselves manipulating the system to avoid being penalized by the system or those who managed its use.

Technically, the Falcon system could have been improved by expanding the server's capacity, making use of more of the system's features, and linking other departments via server access. However, it seemed that management did not wish to adapt the system until the initial WTS users could utilize the current version more efficiently. The money and resources required to increase server size and to train users in other departments on the system could not be justified until the existing processes were perceived as effective by requestors and managers. Thus there was little opportunity, or justification, for analysts, operators, and assignment coordinators to explain that many of the problems with the system could be resolved. Thus, while development and evolution of the system were feasible, they were unlikely to occur any time soon. So the initial users had to learn to fully and effectively use a flawed system before the flaws and limitations would be fixed, which would enable users and the system to be more effective, which was the initial goal of the system.

Cause: poor feedback

Requiring all technical requests to be submitted through the Falcon system itself created two sets of individuals, separating the users from the analysts who resolved their issues. This distorted the clarity of the requests made (as Zmud, 1990, proposed), added layers to the process of completing the work requested, and strained the personal relationships bank employees once had with their technical support analysts.

"Help Desk" operators translated users' requests and then entered those requests into the Falcon system. The operators passed the requests along to assignment coordinators, who then assigned the ticket to an analyst based on region and skill level. This added another layer of administration to the processing of the request. The operators rarely passed along completely accurate information – not intentionally, but largely because they were required to interpret what were, after all, inherently uncertain questions, and possibly highly contextual responses. Furthermore, since they had no knowledge of the analysts' job, they were also unaware of what information to ask requestors to provide. As a result, after receiving requests through the system, analysts typically ended up calling the users to clarify the requests, defeating some of the purpose of the operators.

This process also created confusion for the analysts since most assigners were unfamiliar with the skill level of the analysts they assigned to these requests, so analysts may not have had the appropriate type or level of expertise (either too low or too high) for the particular problem. Finally, by having two administrative points in between the user and the analyst, users could not directly contact the person handling their request. The bank employees in a specific region, before the implementation of Falcon, were familiar and quite friendly with the telecommunication analyst(s) who typically processed their requests. Analysts had previous knowledge of the existing equipment and programming for most bank employees, so were very in tune with their specific needs. (This issue of the need for ongoing communication relationships between service requestors and providers across boundaries was a central topic in Johnson and Rice's 1987 study of the design of stand-alone word-processing jobs and procedures.) Again, operators and assignees did not have this information. Now, users were forced to place requests with individuals they were not familiar with and who had no specific or ongoing knowledge of their needs. Furthermore, when an analyst was forced to work around the system by calling users to clarify the work they requested, users became frustrated, since they had to verbalize the request a second time, and sometimes try to retrieve their problem statement while in the middle of some other task. This impact of the system strained the once pleasant relationship that existed between users and analysts in addition to making users less satisfied with their process for reporting telecommunication troubles. Since the phonecalls were made outside of the Falcon system, there was now no record within the system as to this stage or content of problem resolution – exactly contradictory to one of the formal procedures and purposes of the system.

Cause: symbolic uses and manipulation

By imposing strict deadlines, the system, and those who managed it, communicated that meeting the deadlines imposed was the top priority. When a ticket read "DEADLINE ALERT" in all bold capital letters, it was intended to signal that a deadline was imminent. However, it also symbolized the importance of that deadline and the severity of not meeting the deadline assigned. While quality of service could be somewhat managed by viewing comments and updates included in the ticket, it was not viewed as important as meeting deadlines; thus there was also a conflict between goals generated by, and explicit in, the system. The text of the tickets was monotonous to read, and most people were not likely to scroll through an entire ticket of information to assess the quality of service provided to the requestor. However, the "DEADLINE ALERT" could be easily found at the very top of a Falcon record in its own field, marked Alert Status. The difference in the way deadlines and quality of service were monitored and displayed in the system clearly demonstrated their varying levels of importance. Whereas, prior to the use of Falcon, quality of service was viewed as more important than deadlines, now deadlines were viewed as more important, and the quality of service provided to users often suffered. It is unlikely that this shift in goals was intended, or even perceived.

Symptom: secrecy

Bank employees were only able to view the Falcon tickets they submitted. While they were given access to the updates on their requests, they were not allowed to view others' tickets. This created a problem in the system for several reasons. First, members of the same department often ended up submitting requests for the same work, because a procedure may be relevant for multiple members of a work group, but in different forms, stages, or manifestations. This generated duplicate (but differently described) requests in the system, and since these requests were typically not made at the same time, it also generated different due dates for the completion of the work. WTS employees who used the Falcon system then become responsible for closing out all of the requests opened, even if they were what the Falcon system classified as "duplicate requests."

Another problem resulting from bank employees not being able to see others' requests is that they were never aware of the number of requests submitted before their own. For this reason, they generally had little understanding of why their requests could not be fulfilled immediately. Finally, since only members of WTS were privy to the requests made through the Falcon system, they were often burdened with the responsibility of passing on pertinent information provided in the system to other departments, and held responsible (i.e., blamed) for both the duration and outcome of any problem resolution. For example, most one- or two-person moves from building to building or within a building required technical support in addition to furniture, electrical additions, and the permission of site managers to use the designated space. That is, although it seems as though it's "just" one or two people moving, an entire system of interdependencies was involved and affected. Users typically opened Falcon requests for technical support without knowing about (and thus considering) the rest of the necessary items. As a result, WTS employees tended to begin processing work that had not been approved by the other relevant parties, or missed their assigned system deadlines waiting for those requests to be approved. Often WTS employees had to provide the tickets they received to other departments, so that those departments' teams could begin fulfilling the other required items of the move.

The inability to *filter information* (filtering being one of Schein's (1994) and Zmud's (1990) information technology characteristics) in the Falcon system also imposed control over its users. Since anyone

who could access the system could access any of the final information (i.e., not including requests) in any Falcon record, analysts and
administrators often felt scrutinized by requestors, managers, and
each other. For this reason, almost everyone who used the system con-
formed to a standard way of resolving and reporting issues, so as not
to draw attention to their work. Because the text of all Falcon records
was viewable by anybody and everybody on the system, operators,
assignment coordinators, and analysts were not likely to try use the
system for any purpose other than the ones it served initially, for fear
of being penalized by the system, its managers, and others who use it.
Furthermore, since most of the WTS employees who used the system
were unhappy with the way it worked, they did not wish to used it
for any of their other tasks, or to submit their co-workers to its flaws.
Thus experimentation, adaptation, and reinvention were suppressed
(Johnson and Rice, 1987), and the organization could not learn.

Symptom: manipulation

Feedback and boundaries between the system and the wider organizational environment were not well designed. While the system was
expected to have an impact on certain external factors, the impact
of external factors on the system was not carefully considered. One
external factor that had a detrimental impact on the system is one
aspect of the organizational context: a constant sense of urgency
among bank employees, generated both by the nature of their work,
and by the nature of the Falcon system design. As employees were
aware that the system imposed specific deadlines for certain requests,
they often manipulated the system to ensure their requests were fulfilled right away. As a result, bank employees were more likely to
request work later than they should, relying on system manipulation
to get their requests processed and completed immediately. This over-
whelmed both the system and the WTS employees who used it with
requests, and indirectly punished those who followed procedures and
did not try to manipulate the system. This sense of urgency, in turn,
had an effect on the environment via the Falcon system. Failing to
report issues when they first appeared not only created tighter deadlines for WTS employees and a greater number of analysts using the
system at one time, but also put the technical system at greater risk
of failure, since some issues were not specific to an individual's equipment, but related to the overall health of a building's equipment. That

is, system motivations for manipulating the system created negative externalities both for other individuals, as well as for the collective system.

Symptom: rigidity

As noted above, Schein (1994) and Zmud (1990) identified an important characteristic of information technology as *routing* and *filtering* capacity, used to provide the right information to the right people, without overloading any one individual or group with erroneous information. Falcon's routing abilities were quite useful. Even though the system's communication capacity was limited, anyone who used the system could send records and the information in them to anyone else who used the system, although that was a limited subset of WTS employees. The filtering capacity of Falcon, however, was extremely poor and often negated the benefits of the system's routing abilities. While records could be sent to anyone, the records themselves could not be edited in any way. Users could only add information tickets. All information, even incorrect and insignificant information, remained in the records. There was a search function within the system that allowed users to identify specific records or groups of records, but this was only useful to those who processed general Falcon information, mainly statistics. For most users, who typically needed to find a specific item within a ticket, the search function left much to be desired. The only way to search for information within individual records was to scroll through them. Since the records could not be edited, many users were forced to scroll through several pages of notes and updates to find the information they sought, and of course they may have overlooked it, whereas specific single or multiple keyword searching would retrieve every instance of it. Furthermore, the routing abilities of the system required that updates be made to records before they were routed to another individual or group, further increasing the amount of text Falcon users had to sort through. This not only generated work and delay subroutines as users attempted to retrieve information from the system, but it also made it difficult for them to understand their role in processing the request and where the request should be routed to next (possibly generating error subroutines), since this information could be buried in the massive text of the records.

While operators and assignment coordinators could typically regulate their own work, analysts enjoyed none of the same privileges.

The deadlines that analysts had to adhere to were assigned by the system and monitored by everyone who used the system. They were also not able to assign work to themselves and to each other. The requests made through the system were assigned to the analysts by the assignment team. As a result, analysts had very little control over their Falcon activities and even less over the amount and type of work that flowed their way. While they did have the ability to reassign work that was mistakenly assigned to them, they had to do so immediately, because there was no way to change the deadlines that were assigned. This prevented analysts from being able to correct misrepresentations of their performance in the system. Once a ticket was reassigned to another analyst, the new analyst only had the remaining amount of time, from the date the ticket was opened to the deadline alert date, to fulfill the request. Sometimes, tickets took longer to trickle down from the operators to the analysts, so tickets were received by analysts already in "DEADLINE ALERT" status, a considerable delay subroutine! Even though the analyst had never seen the request, he/she was held accountable for the missed deadline (a blame subroutine, see Chapter 4, p. 144).

Online database query system

This case study observed the transition from an interactive/online, but aged, query system (called QMF, for "query the mainframe," providing interactive real-time queries) to a new batch system (called BFQuery, for "batch query," in which the system stores users' queries and later processes them according to some predetermined schedule or criterion). Though ongoing increases in storage, transmission, and processing power would suggest such transition from an interactive to a batch system was a technological regression, under certain system, job, and user conditions, collecting and submitting queries in batches may be more efficient, and free up processing power for other applications during predictable periods. Over this period, BFQuery became the only official method of running database queries at the company, providing opportunities to see how the new system was working and how normal users were responding to the successes and failures. As the company had fully implemented this new technology, it was possible to identify some problems inherent in the system and its interactions with jobs and the organization. The interaction of the

new system, and how the users' jobs are designed, generated a variety
of symptoms of URs and associated negative subroutines.

Symptom: non-responsiveness

Typically this would refer to something about the system or the organizational management which was unresponsive to users or customers.
However, non-responsiveness may occur in other ways; for instance,
the users themselves may not give any feedback to the organization
and the system may be incapable of rectifying problems through its
own means. This was particularly evident in the BFQuery system
because many people tended to complain about the problems of the
new system rather than ask the developers to solve the bugs. But there
must be something in the social or technical system that fosters this
user non-responsiveness for this to be a symptom of a UR.

One user's experience suggested a possible explanation. When trying to use multiple lines for the same variable in a query (apparently
an acceptable form of query, based on the formal documentation),
the job kept encountering an error. The user went to one of the better
batch programmers in the unit and asked him if he could tell what
was wrong with the query. After some investigation, the programmer decided there was something wrong with the programming in
the BFQuery job, so he needed to send an email to a member of the
technical team (all of whom worked at headquarters in a different
city). After the technical member got back to the programmer, the
programmer got back to the user, and said they had made a production fix to resolve the problem, and the user needed to wait until the
following day to run the query. This made it seem as though the user
was the first person, out of the thousands who used the system to
submit hundreds if not thousands of queries each day, to submit this
kind of formally acceptable query. The only available explanation is
that of catatonic non-responsiveness among the other users, where all
others experiencing this kind of problem would rather have someone
else deal with trying to resolve the problem – and in the meantime
either figure out another way to run the query (a workaround), or
simply avoid running that query – than bring it to the appropriate
programmers or technical team themselves. This can be seen as a case
of the costs of inquiring preventing collective benefit, a type of social
dilemma or a kind of inverted tragedy of the commons – in this case an
underutilization of an individual's resource generates increasing costs

to everyone (Chapter 8). Although the substance of the resource – information – is generally costless itself (though of course its development costs are not), the transaction costs associated with sharing the information are excessive for any particular individual (Lamberton, 1996; Shapiro and Varian, 1999).

Symptom: secrecy
Suspicion and secrecy occurs when useful information or explanations are hidden from the users and/or the clients. This was certainly the case with the BFQuery system because the development team never put together any easily accessible documents on how to use the system. In addition, they never announced any of the successes or failures that they encountered, which might have helped people understand the problems that they were experiencing themselves. Instead, the development team and organizational communications reported how much money the company was saving because of switching from the old QMF system to the new BFQuery system. Paradoxically, this approach did not enhance general users' confidence in how well the new system was working. If the developers and organization executives had discussed some of the problems that associates in the firm were facing in using the new system, it would have indicated the company was aware of the problems and was actively finding ways to fix them, generating an atmosphere of both realism as well as of understanding and support.

Another aspect of secrecy relates to keeping the old system running parallel to the new. Even though the new system was "fully implemented," users were still able to run queries on QMF in the "test environment." This actually undermined the stated goal of decreased operational costs of the BFQuery system, because many people ran their queries in test mode to check their results before submitting it through the batch query job, effectively doubling the systems cost for running a query. Although many people were aware that they could still do this, no one actually talked about it publicly. The company knew that people were still using QMF in test mode, but there was little communication instructing people to avoid using it. This usage undermined the goal of operational savings through the new batch query system, but the secrecy about the test mode use prevented measuring how much the intended cost savings were diminished and, in fact, any shared knowledge about the outcomes. If, for example, users had been explicitly encouraged to do this for a given period of time, with the goal of verifying the credibility and accurate results of the new system (by comparing results from the two runs), this particular symptom of secrecy (and the associated conflicting goals) would have been resolved and users would have had greater confidence in the new system.

Symptom: manipulation

Psychopathic manipulation occurs when the system is biased in some way (possibly intentionally, but not necessarily so) against particular users or customers (Singer, 1980). It is exacerbated when these users are then punished in some way (from loss of social capital through firing and litigation) when they bring the problems to light (see, for instance, the research on *organizational whistleblowing* in Vardi and Weitz, 2003). With BFQuery, the system was not necessarily biased against one type of user per se, but the fact that it was based in batch programming did add another dimension to the complexity of each query for some types of users. Anyone in a technical role would have at least a basic knowledge of Structured Query Language (SQL), which allowed one to run queries against the database. Even though everyone writing and submitting these queries had some sort of technical role (usually they were quality assurance analysts), not all of these associates were proficient with batch programming. When encountering some sort of error with BFQuery, most people needed to go to one of the batch programmers in their unit to debug the job for them (i.e., identify what was missing, incorrect, or inappropriate in the wording of the query). Often, the batch programmers could not figure out the problem because it was specific to the BFQuery job set-up (and not the database query itself), which, because it was new, they were not yet familiar with, so they had to send their question to the technical group (at the headquarters) responsible for the new system.

This interdependent resolution process could make the quality assurance analyst seem like a pest to the batch programmer and, subsequently, the batch programmer seem bothersome to the technical resource (generating multiple principal–agent relations; see Chapter 3). Conversely, however, the technical resource could seem like an additional cost and possibly non-responsive to the batch programmer, and the batch programmer could seem the same way to the quality assurance analyst. In the old system, a user was only concerned with the SQL syntax of their query, which the most basic technical person was familiar with, but having to also know the language and syntax of the batch job added a new level of complexity to a formerly mundane task, requiring users to become involved in a series of requests, with attendant work, delay and, of course, error subroutines.

Symptom: denial

In this organization, denial was often associated with users' difficulties in entering their queries. In general, system designers may intentionally cover up problems or complaints to make the system appear more successful than it is. This was particularly rampant with BFQuery because there was no centralized database to log issues with the new system, and it was often difficult to get someone to admit that there were problems. There were no publications distributed or posted that explained the programming bugs that people were experiencing, nor were there any updates on system enhancements that had been installed to correct those problems. The only thing that was being said about the system was how much money the company was saving because of the operational efficiency of the new system. But those costs did not take into account the time lost or errors made due to missing or queried results or abandoned queries (involving work, delay, and error subroutines) by associates while waiting for their BFQuery job to get fixed.

Symptom: rigidity

Pathological rigidity may emerge when the organization has strict rules governing the system, which end up making it difficult or even impossible to solve the problems created by using that same system. This was a symptom of experiences with the new system, particularly in regards to the way that users could save their queries. In the old QMF system, users could save particularly helpful queries under their system ID, to be used or shared later. (The concept of knowledge sharing and reuse is central to the study and practice of knowledge management – Heinz and Rice, 2009; Markus, 2001; Simard and Rice, 2007.) This was very efficient because users did not have to keep re-writing queries that were used on a regular basis; one could just retrieve a relevant prior query, change the variables, and re-submit the query. Since BFQuery was based in batch mode, one could no longer retrieve or use those prior saved queries through the system itself; this was a crucial aspect of this UR. This created a multitude of problems. Users now had to develop anew, and maintain a library of, their common queries in the database, and were required to keep a list of all of these queries with descriptions as to what they did and what variables were used. This discouraged many users from saving helpful queries because of the regulations, restrictions, and costs imposed on them. Rather than going through all of this, some users resorted to just saving a screenprint of their query, in case they wanted to use it again. But this printed version could not be used by others, and required re-keying of the information. Further, upgrades or fixes to the system could easily change the exact format of the screen, making the helpful screenprint an occasion for confusion and errors. This paradoxically defeated the purpose of having an electronic library to house this information but, for many people, this was the only way to get around the rigidity and costs of the routine.

Subroutine: work

Although the organization was now saving a lot of systems (processing) time, the cost in man hours to convert the saved queries in QMF to the new system was staggering. As there were a few thousand people working with this system, and each of those people had dozens of queries that they wanted to save in the new query libraries, the amount of work and time spent on just that activity was extensive – if and when they were motivated to do so – but also invisible (shadow costs).

Subroutine: delay

Most of the knowledge about BFQuery was concentrated in the technical team that developed the new system. There were several problems with this, particularly that all of these people were located at headquarters, so the only way that anyone could get in contact with them was either through email or voicemail. But this made it very difficult to solve errors because one needed to leave a detailed but unavoidably incomplete message (because of contextual, conditional, and iterative communication necessary to clarify the problem and the solution), and then wait on those individuals to return the message before one could begin to fully explain and identify the problem.

This did not include the time required to actually debug the BFQuery job, which could take even longer than the time required to get in touch with the programmers. Note that delays associated with *debugging* a job are an actual task function that is reasonably associated with technical work (there is always uncertainty, complexity, changing standards, learning costs, coding errors, etc.), and thus not a UR subroutine per se. However, to the extent that debugging BFQuery errors was work generated by other dysfunctional subsystems or subroutines, and those processes were not identified and resolved, then some proportion of the "debugging" delay was in fact a UR subroutine. More relevant here is that the nature of the centralization of knowledge about the new system, interacting with the asynchronous and less-than-effective communication channels, created delays associated with debugging.

Subroutine: error

Errors, error subroutines, and linked and interdependent errors could be particularly damaging in an environment where the output of the batch queries might be passed on to other system processes or the customer. Typically the organizational users looked at the query output as fact, not considering that the job might have had some sort of internal coding error (an example of a barrier to perception due to technical legitimacy and to fragmentation of work). This would be even worse if the results were only slightly inaccurate, so the numbers would seem reasonable upon general inspection (a legitimation cue; why would one doubt each result enough to submit it to verification, such as through using the test mode of the QMF system, which was not officially sanctioned or publicized?) and thus would not arouse suspicion (the perception barrier of normalcy). This information could be passed on to the customer, who was trying to rectify some problems in their own, independent, system and was looking for this company to verify some figures. This would cause the customer to think there was something wrong with *their* database, and the error subroutine would spread, without anyone knowing the problem was actually due to some problem in the BFQuery system or in the query.

An employee time reporting system

The operative word at R&D Company (RDC) during the period of this case study was "change." The company was working to shift from being a research and development consortium to becoming a profit-driven, commercial company (involving, among other things, reorganizing the company into Strategic Business Units and Business Units, with profit-generating responsibilities). Ownership had recently changed hands from several publicly-held regulated companies to an employee-owned defense-oriented systems integration company. The owner companies which were formerly RDC's exclusive customers were becoming a dwindling percentage of the entire domestic and international market which RDC sought to capture, and RDC was in the process of being sold to an outside company.

These large-scale changes, involving new strategic and operational goals, resulted in significant alterations in daily operations that directly affected employees. As part of these changes, RDC implemented PeopleData, a corporate employee time reporting system. PeopleData was part of a centralized financial and human resources information system which provided links to multiple databases that contained information used to manage client billing, assist in project management, and monitor resource utilization.

PeopleData generated a variety of URs, arising from defense mechanisms adopted by the organization, and enabling RDC to defer accountability and misrepresent reality. PeopleData, as a corporate-wide application, affected all members of the organization. However, depending on the practices of different business units, the magnitude of the UR symptoms varied. These symptoms became evident upon close scrutiny of the system, and were likely identifiable by those who used the system. However, constructive feedback either had not been solicited or was ignored by management. Without this feedback, PeopleData seems to have instead provided an air of rationality and stability to upper management in the time of change, strengthened by the belief that computers and technology could be trusted. However, people could be pressured into misusing such systems in order to force compliance with the institution's rules, procedures, and goals, thereby contributing to and perpetuating several URs.

Symptom: denial

There was a time at RDC when hourly time reporting had little impact on business operations. All work projects were done for the owner-companies, which annually committed major funding for RDC work done throughout the year. The money for a project rarely ran out and, if it did, there was always another over-budgeted project to charge against.

This situation changed drastically when RDC positioned itself as a market-driven, profit-earning, consulting firm. Now the company had to compete on the open market for customers. Contracts were bid against competitors that were able to undercut RDC's relatively high cost structure. To break into this market and obtain a base of new customers, RDC, as do many companies entering a new market, had to underbid contracts. Under these circumstances, where clients have committed limited funds for specific work efforts, accurate time reports that could be credited against client accounts are a critical component of business operations as well as strategic analysis. But these principles, and the close accounting of time, were initially foreign to RDC.

Out of this situation arose the need for an integrated time reporting system such as PeopleData, which provided the capability to monitor business inputs and outputs. The system was fairly sophisticated in its ability to manipulate data entered into the databases. Where it seemed to suffer weaknesses was at the input level, where RDC had to define the manner and type of data which could be entered (i.e., an issue of forms, or system interface, design; Sless, 1988).

RDC employees were required to be 100 percent billable, allocated across all their specific projects. Over time, the understanding of what this actually meant changed. (More conceptually, the feedback process changed the control criterion, a double-loop learning process. But double-loop learning is not necessarily positive for the system or for specific units. See Chapter 8 for many more examples.) Within most corporate environments, it is understood that some of the time that an employee spends in the office is what can be referred to as "administrative time:" time spent attending general meetings, completing various correspondence related to corporate activities such as reading email and inputting time reports, and attending company-sponsored work-time social gatherings.

The former Unix-based time reporting system, UTR, provided a mechanism for recording hours that were spent in these company-sanctioned non-billable activities as "ADM," or administrative hours, which were considered part of normal company overhead. Similar to ADM time, hours worked on a project that were over and beyond the hours contracted with a client, but found necessary for completing the job, were recorded as "Non-billable Overtime" (typically, entered as "NOT-time"!). Initially NOT-time was acceptable, and recording of required work on under-billed projects appeared to be desired by management. One long-term benefit of this system was that such data could be used to assist in pricing future projects more accurately.

Over time, while the UTR system was still being used, the interpretation of NOT-time drifted. Although the option of entering NOT-time remained, it no longer always meant "non-billable," and the entering of hours under this category by an employee was sometimes viewed negatively by middle management charged with managing project resources (because of the new goals of not only profitability, but also cutting costs to win initial contracts). Although never clearly articulated to most employees, there were cases when NOT-time *was* charged back (i.e., not absorbed as overhead similar to ADM, so it actually *was* time) to either internal or external sources, depending on how the project was initially negotiated. Because it was often difficult to get accurate information on the terms of each project's contract, many employees stopped recording NOT-time altogether, since doing so presented the risk of displeasing middle management, required entering what could be construed as false data, and created downstream corrections through chargeback. The result of this misrepresentation was the creation of evidence that seemed to indicate that there were *no* inaccuracies in the pricing of projects – i.e., that exactly enough hours had been allotted to complete the work. In actuality, employees were working unrecorded (and thus also unpaid) overtime to complete contracted work, which, as a negative byproduct, would subsequently provide an incorrect basis for future contract bidding, generating even more need to misrepresent time spent and hours billed!

There were similar changes in the way in which ADM time itself was recorded. All time spent in the office was required to be associated with a project (essentially ADM time was being charged to a client's project), and management also had imposed strict limits on how much time could be recorded under this category (usually 0.25 hours maximum each day). This meant that hours allotted for doing project work would likely be needed to be used for administrative time spent in the office. However, the new PeopleData system accepted no less than 7.5 hours per day from full-time employees; therefore each day 7.5 billable project hours had to be entered into the system, whether or not the employee actually spent that time (whether more or less) working on the project. Therefore, if a general corporate meeting was called, the employee was still required to enter 7.5 hours of time charged to one or more assigned projects, because it had been made clear that only minimal ADM time was acceptable. Thus whenever an employee attended general corporate functions (which supposedly have diverse benefits to the employee as well as the organization), that time would have to be replaced with overtime hours that compensated for lost billable time during the day. (Here, costs are uncoupled and distributed away from benefits, costs are increased, and individuals are essentially punished for following required, but dysfunctional and conflicting organizational goals.) The alternative was to work less time on the project, produce a lower-quality product, and salvage one's personal life.

PeopleData added to the problem, as employees needed to spend even more ADM time to learn the new system. (See Johnson and Rice, 1987, on the need to provide and encourage learning and experimentation time when implementing new systems.) That is, learning how to use the system to accurately report time allocated to corporate functions as well as project activities was not considered either a corporate function or a project activity, leading to inaccurate time reporting, both in the short run, and accumulated over projects.

Several symptoms emerged from the implementation and use of the PeopleData time reporting system at RDC. First, management seemed to be in denial that projects were frequently underpriced and that they required more hours to complete than had been contracted with the client. This placed many employees in work, error, and blame subroutines, where the responsibility for rectifying the errors of the corporation was their responsibility, with the "reward" of additional as well as unrecognized work.

Employee frustration resulting from this situation was high. Some of the RDC divisions were more affected by these problems than others, due to the nature of their work they did. This inconsistent treatment of employees across the company was also likely to add to feelings of frustration and dissatisfaction in those areas most affected. This situation may have contributed to the high attrition rate which RDC was experiencing, of course further reducing the ability to meet the new, general organizational goal of becoming both a high-quality and profitable vendor.

In order to camouflage the fact that the under-billing situation existed, management constructed a set of rules and regulations for time reporting that paradoxically negated the validity of the time reporting system. The rules were issued and reinforced by the restrictive interface to the time reporting system, which provided limited selection categories in the system's menus. Management did not address or explain to employees how they were to realistically manage these rules and effectively attend to their work. Instead, employees were led to believe that this was "normal" procedure for consulting firms (and thus an example of symbolic uses).

Employees responded to the conflicting demands by misrepresenting hours worked, borrowing billable hours from projects that had been overpriced, and avoiding both attending and reporting all ADM activities (which are usually to the organization's benefit) that took away from billable time. In some cases, this led to ignorance of corporate goals and missions (the awareness of which may have provided better understanding of RDC strategies, the clients' projects, and the rationales of the system), because meetings communicating this type of information were avoided. In turn, because participation was minimized, morale suffered.

Subroutine: error

For reasons that were not entirely explained, a deadline of December 16, 1996 was imposed for corporate-wide activation of the new PeopleData employee time reporting system. The system that was actually implemented by this deadline did not meet the needs of the organization, employees were dissatisfied with the interface, and performance and functionality were inadequate. This assessment was confirmed by a memo (dated March 28, 1997) circulated throughout the company by the Executive Director of Internal Business Systems (IBS), which explicitly mentioned response time and usability issues. These were due to the time and cost restrictions imposed by the implementation deadline, which led to decisions to minimize customization of the system and integrate it with the pre-existing database system. The memo also acknowledged that the aggressive implementation deadline prevented IBS from following some normal deployment procedures. Thus, because of the inflexible early deadline, rules, goals, and procedures were imposed upon IBS and the system users that took precedence over what would normally be the primary objective, to implement an integrated financial data system that would effectively meet the new needs of the corporation and highlight RDC's innovativeness and high performance.

Unfortunately, these efforts to meet the goals set by upper management appeared to have resulted in only short-term resolutions, leading to much higher long-term expenses than originally anticipated. The subsequent proposed solution for resolving the response and usability issues of the IBS system was to develop and redeploy Web-based versions of these applications. RDC members and the organization wasted uncounted hours in learning and using an inefficient system, and developing and implementing the alternative system. This was an ironic situation, when the company was trying to impress its new owner with its software development expertise and profit-generating capabilities.

Subroutine: blame

RDC had an internal, centralized network operations center called ITC for many years. ITC had responsibility for selecting and delivering networked applications to employees, and in general did this reasonably well. Therefore, it was somewhat surprising to find that when the company decided to implement the networked PeopleData employee time reporting system, the responsibility for developing this system was given to the Internal Business Systems (IBS) division, which was directly related to the Finance division, rather than to ITC. ITC was given its usual responsibility for providing access to the system through the network to users' desktops, but control of the PeopleData system itself was maintained by the Finance division. This led to numerous misunderstandings by employees as to who was actually responsible for providing assistance with the PeopleData application. Normal practice would lead employees to call the ITC helpline when encountering problems with networked applications. However, for PeopleData problems (and there were many), responsibilities were ambiguously split between the two departments; worse, most problems that arose regarding the application were completely beyond the control of ITC.

In a sense, this system had been rigged to give the appearance of being legitimized as an ITC system (a symbolic use), where mechanisms were already in place for dealing with client requests. Instead, the responsibility for handling these issues resided within Finance, which appeared to have much less formalized procedures for managing user issues. One instance where this was evident is illustrated in the difficulty users encountered in attempting to obtain remote (i.e., other than from their desktops) access to the system, usually failing in these attempts because there was no clearly defined procedure for requesting the appropriate software and security passwords. This ambiguous/split responsibility placed users in a situation where they usually had a higher probability of encountering continual obstacles than achieving success. The absence of a clearly defined responsible party for the application also enabled (or caused) the two divisions sharing responsibility to blame each other for delays and failures. Further, lacking formal procedures for resolving client requests increased the probability that resolutions would stall before completion, all contributing to the inability of users to achieve success without excessive work, delay, and blame subroutines.

Conclusion

Box 2.1 summarizes the variety of causes and symptoms of URs in the six case studies. The cases suggest a number of general observations about URs associated with ICTs. It is important to note that a given UR is unlikely to display all possible symptoms and unlikely to evolve all subroutines in our typology.

Box 2.1 Summary of causes and symptoms of unusual routines in six ICT implementation cases

Causes

Barriers to perception
fragmentation of tasks reduce ability to assess overall costs and
   problems

---

misattribution of source of problems

neglecting relevant information (such as costs)

overestimation of accuracy and completeness of information

salience of information to person recording the information

weak connection of actual interdependencies

Conflicting goals

accuracy vs. feasibility

avoidance of subroutines prevents achieving larger goal of real-time analysis

control/deadlines vs. learning/innovation

costs of data collection and analysis vs. efficiency of project

different bases for assessing labor costs

different deadlines and criteria from different stakeholders

efficiency of batch processing vs. control and flexibility of interactive input

fragmentation of input, management, and uses

interface halt for error-detection vs. forced abandonment of case processing

local and professional commitment vs. overall project commitment

local task demands vs. external project demands

rationalization of local entry vs. need for broader network of expertise

recording vs. analysis

saving local costs vs. externalizing costs

skills, knowledge, and goals needed to use system vs. those of users

time and labor budgets vs. quality product and service

Poor feedback

aggregation

constraints on interaction or meta-communication following feedback

inaccurate and manipulated input

limited range of feedback topics (such as more expansive uses of a system)

limited responsiveness due to system projected onto other users

local contextual information not available to higher, centralized client or user support

Box 2.1 (*cont.*)

mediation between users and support/help analysts

narrow categories (constraints) on content of feedback

negative effects of monitoring

poor user interfaces

reporting after project completed

reporting only to and by management

solving mediation obstacles by using informal channels prevents organization from identifying and solving problems

system failures prevent using system to provide feedback or questions about system

Symbolic uses and manipulation

ambiguity in interdependencies allowing units to maintain divergent interpretations

biasing actions toward rewards and measures

collecting information for justifying decision or pilot-testing, but not providing results

formatting of messages affects sense of authority, consequence, and priority of content (deadlines vs. service)

information as symbol of control, position, validity

legitimacy of computer reports

misrepresenting information

post-hoc performance criteria

system name obscuring or biasing interpretation of actual processes

Symptoms

Denial

cover-up system problems

denial of the problem of denial vitiates the purpose of the system

interface and reporting constraints deny existence of relevant activities, creating distortions throughout (such as biased reporting or inadequate work in other categories)

no process for logging problems

no recording of subroutines associated with trying to report or find solutions

Manipulation

requestors managing system to meet their deadlines, creating task
  bursts and system overloads

system usage requiring specific skills or knowledge without providing users those skills; leads to asymmetric information, dependency, social capital costs, and power relations

Non-responsiveness

users not taking personal time and resources to provide feedback;
  complaining without taking action, so everyone continues to
  suffer the same problem

Rigidity

limited, constrained features, such as limited editing/searching and
  forced reading/scrolling of complete, long entries

system-assigned fixed deadlines and timelines, even when task
  transferred to another person

inability to save and retrieve locally re-usable information

Secrecy

concern about surveillance leading to self-imposed conformity and
  silence

inability for co-workers to see others' help requests and thus being
  unable to help them or understand broader context or prioritiza-
  tion of work, generating redundant work

non-existent or inaccessible problem or solution documents

running shadow systems without acknowledging or legitimizing

Invisibility, embeddedness, and routinization of unusual routines

We can see from the cases that the ICT dysfunctionalities are both
frequently occurring, although often only under certain conditions
and experienced only by certain actors, and rarely identified, so as
to become "routine." Further, they are rarely identified as systemic
processes or problems; when they are noted at all, they are often
defended as "the way things are," caused by someone's "mistake"
(usually the client's, sometimes the user's), justified as normal procedures, or dismissed as an "exception." The unusual becomes routine,

with considerable short- and long-term subtle costs. The case studies reveal that the perceptual barriers can be formidable. This may explain, to a considerable degree, the prevalence of URs in contemporary organizations.

In many organizations, especially those that are implementing new ICTs, someone is always improving, suffering from, or complaining about, aspects of the system. Unfortunately, the improving, suffering, and the complaining are rarely linked. Curiously, once the URs have become established, they tend to be resistant to change in the form of deliberate efforts to mitigate them. This suggests there may be particular factors in organizational environments that can support and sustain URs, giving them a tenacity beyond what a rational cost–benefit calculus would support. We will elaborate on our notion of this cultural substrate in Chapters 4, 5, and 6, and feedback challenges in Chapter 7.

After a while, complaints disappear as people develop *workarounds*, ways of overcoming the problems, avoiding them, or disengaging (Gasser, 1986; Chapters 4 and 8, this volume). But the tension and frustration percolates throughout the organization and its environment, and people who have to interact with the system continue to pay in psychological, professional, pedagogical, or just practical ways. As these URs continue to generate work, error, delay, and blame subroutines, customers, users, and designers learn to live with, work-around, or simply exit, if not overtly damage, the system. Further, there are few organizational or system processes for learning about such subroutines, or for communicating solutions to implementers and system designers. One specific kind of organizational pathology is where the only feedback loops are through a flawed system itself, so of course perceptions or feedback about the system are inherently constrained whenever the system experiences problems.

Unusual and unintended consequences of unusual routines

The cases also show the familiar problem of unintended consequences, part of the unusual aspect of URs. No doubt each of the implementations was intended to improve some aspect of the organization's functioning and, arguably, each did provide at least some amounts of the intended benefits. Nonetheless, each also spawned negative subroutines as the new systems became part of the organizational environment in which organization members acted, reacted, and made sense of their experiences. Change within an organization – in these particular cases, an ICT implementation – creates the opportunity for URs to develop, even when (and perhaps most ironically when) those systems are implemented partially to resolve, remove, or prevent other URs.

One might be tempted to attribute such consequences solely to incompetent design and poor implementation of a system, perhaps to manipulative or coercive intent on the part of management, insufficient time and resources, or possibly to user resistance, lack of training, or even incompetence. But we feel the sheer prevalence of such problems indicates that other factors contribute to the pattern. Put bluntly, we are not satisfied that the human failings of incompetence, venality, or disengagement are a complete (or in some cases, even partial) explanation for the existence of URs.

To the contrary, these cases suggest that the design stage of a system implementation can be "smart" and motivated by "good intent," and many intended benefits may follow, yet it may nonetheless also create problems. As we noted above, an observer can get a sense that URs are almost beyond the control of any organizational actor, even at high levels of authority in the organization. It may help to begin by distinguishing two levels in the implications of these system implementations, an idea we will elaborate in Chapters 4, 5, and 6. The first-level effects relate to the system as a tool to be utilized by organization members to improve current, or provide new, processes. The intended consequences in each of these cases was some sort of efficiency gain, quality improvement, or new information-handling capability. The second-level effects relate to the system as a constraint upon organization members. Some of the unintended consequences of the above cases were some sort of loss in, or obstacle to, effective processes, manifest as harmful subroutines. These first-level and second-level effects are related to Sproull and Kiesler's (1991) and Rogers' (2003) analyses of the effects of new technology in particular and innovations in general, but our use emphasizes the constraint and process aspects. As several of the cases note, and as Singer's notion of symbolic uses and manipulation emphasizes, symbolic uses of ICTs are another contributing factor to the development of URs (Feldman and March, 1981; Sitkin *et al.*, 1992). We will further explore these observations concerning the symbolic value of various organizational behaviors in Chapter 8.

These examples of system manipulation and problems are in no way the most subtle or complex instances, as Chapter 8 shows. New ICTs will always create and involve mistakes, problems, and new things to learn. Further, as Chapter 7 discusses, the very efforts to seek and provide feedback about these problems may themselves be imbued with, and foster additional, URs. But identifying and learning from these URs should be encouraged rather than repressed. More importantly, social systems analysis should be an integrated part of traditional technical systems analysis and should include the identification, avoidance, and resolution of unusual routines.

3 | *Getting personal: unusual routines at the customer service interface*

Perhaps the most familiar unusual routine is the combination of a customer's experience with and then complaint about some unsatisfactory interaction with an organization, its service, or its product, and the organization's lack of, insufficient, or mismatched response. The main assumption behind this claim is that most customers are not asking for any particularly exceptional or unusual service, product, or information; they are simply following the standard, normal, or explicit procedures associated with an advertisement, offer, instruction, standard retail clerk interaction, attempt to use the product or service, or inquiry. Despite this, they experience difficulties or problems with one or more of these, suggesting that others – possibly everyone – also following the procedures will experience the problem as well. When they attempt to communicate with the organization to gain an understanding of the situation, resolve it, return the product, get a refund, possibly institute legal action, or simply to convey their feelings the effort involves a variety of work, delay, error, and blame (as well as straightforward financial cost) subroutines, along with general frustration. And it may not result in a favorable response, or, for that matter, any response at all. So there are two levels of problems here: the original UR experience, and the UR experience in trying to communicate about the original experience.

This chapter begins by reviewing some of the central concepts in analyzing customer service, dissatisfaction, and complaining, and the important roles of different kinds of customer – and service provider – feedback. It then provides several examples from the first author's (unfortunately extensive) collection of attempts at resolving a problem, providing feedback, and seeking responses to that feedback, ending with a brief analysis of each case.

Customer service, dissatisfaction, and complaining

Service behaviors range from personalized (emphasizing individuation of the customer), to courteous (generalized positive service), to manipulative (deceiving or controlling customers) (Ford and Etienne, 1994). Incomplete or inadequate service quality creates costs in service rework, compensation, customer defection, negative word of mouth, and lower employee morale (Bitner *et al.*, 1994). Customers complain about these unsatisfying service behaviors, either to the representative, the company, or their family and friends – and, increasingly, as noted below, on blogs.

There is a deep tradition and research area concerning consumer complaining, or, to use a more positive description, customer satisfaction. Certainly there are detailed studies and guidelines about all kinds of customer problems, threats, risks, and legal protections. Kaufman (1999) explains the foundations, risks, rights, and resolutions involved in buying and selling, protecting self and others (especially from credit debt and fraud), the fallacies and misleading nature of self-help products, the complex service industries surrounding automobiles and car insurance, recourse to small claims courts and arbitration, and how to find relevant information about rights and procedures. Rosa (1995) provides a classic, ironic, and satirical litany of attempts to communicate with organizations about service and product problems, largely to no avail, or generating nonsensical and strange responses. The letters and replies indicate that organizational representatives may not understand their own organization's products, services, or procedures, and, worse, may not know that they do not understand. Charell (1974, 1985) combines both perspectives, showing how his communications with organizations spotlight problems, generate responses, and provide financial and service benefits. Later in the chapter we provide a small set of such examples, noting aspects of URs in each.

Wexler *et al.* (1993) provide an excellent source for a wide variety of short customer service vignettes, both positive and negative. Most customers or clients do not take the time or effort to complain, are not allowed to, or are somehow punished for doing so. This does not mean, however, that there are no consequences to the organization from the problems. In most cases the organization never receives any explicit feedback about the problem so does not know it exists and cannot fix it; in turn, the person will not return to the business, the person complains to others, and those people then avoid the business as well. More interestingly, how the problem is handled (the *recovery process*) is in some ways more important than whether the problem is fixed. If the service representative responded to the complaint as "friendly, caring, nondefensive, enthusiastic and committed to the relationship," the customer will most likely return to the business even if the problem is not fixed. However, even when the problem is fixed, when the customer perceives the opposite attitude and behaviors, (s)he will stop doing business with the organization (Wexler *et al.*, 1993, pp. 176–7). What is worse, from a deviation-amplifying feedback loop perspective, an environment of hostile or defensive responses to complaints will filter out the more considerate complainers, leaving only the more aggressive ones, making the representatives more resentful and dissatisfied, generating more hostile and defensive responses (p. 179).

The consensus in customer relationship management (CRM), total quality management (TQM), and consumer behavior research is that seeking out, rewarding, and responding to consumer complaints and dissatisfactions is a necessary and valuable process for organizational learning and improvement. In general, insufficient or ineffective upward communication between customer contact personnel and top management suppresses an organization's understanding of consumer expectations and satisfaction (Fornell and Westbrook, 1984; Zeithaml *et al.*, 1988). Culnan (1989) notes studies showing that consumers in general are highly dissatisfied with how their complaints are handled, while only a small percent of top executives refer to customer complaints as a basis for assessing quality of products and service. Yet complaints and other inputs from all stakeholders (from vendors to customers) represent significant sources of corporate intelligence, early warning, and environmental scanning. Consumers should be encouraged to provide, and be rewarded for providing, feedback of all kinds, in the expectation that such consumers actually become more loyal through the experience (Barlow and Moller, 1996; Davidow and Malone, 1992).

Complaints and satisfaction

A 2004 national Canadian survey of 1,000 shoppers found that 40 percent experienced at least two problems every time they bought something, and the overall satisfaction level was lower than in a 2000 poll (CBC Marketplace, 2005). The most frequent complaint was having to wait; the next most frequent category was problems with frontline staff, such as not being helpful or courteous or not being knowledgeable about the company's products and services. Part of the cause of these problems is that companies tend to cut costs through reducing staff, so there are fewer, and less knowledgeable, company representatives for customers to interact with. Similarly, companies reduce the number of telephone complaint lines as a way to deal with the increased complaints. So there are fewer people to represent the company, more complaints from customers, but fewer people to complain to. Now the organization has even fewer opportunities to learn, and the customer is more likely to complain to their friends, a negative outcome for the company.

Complaint behavior (of any kind) and level of satisfaction are not necessarily directly related (Halstead, 2002). Complaint behavior is also affected by the person's tendency toward complaining, their emotional states and blame attributions, the seriousness of the problem, costs of complaining, prior complaining experience, and both self-efficacy and response-efficacy of complaining (Susskind, 2000, p. 355). Some complaining is not due to dissatisfaction, but an aspect of fraud, or motivated by organizational commitment/loyalty, or a way to reinforce prior decisions.

One form of complaint behavior is *negative word of mouth* (WOM), or telling others of one's bad service or product experience. Negative WOM is more frequent, or at least more widely diffused, than positive WOM. A survey of 400 carpet consumers found that negative WOM was greatest for those who voiced complaints directly to the vendor (Halstead, 2002). Thus, complaining supplements, rather than detracts from, later dissatisfaction. Negative WOM is especially high when consumers do not feel their complaints were satisfactorily managed, while it is reduced substantially if the customer is even minimally satisfied with the company's response (Halstead, 2002). Susskind (2001) found that efforts to correct a restaurant service error were not successful when the server made excuses, appeared indifferent to the problem, or exhibited a bad attitude while fixing the problem. Customers who said they would not return to the restaurant after complaining told about three times more people than those who planned to return, and about four times more if not satisfied with the complaint remedy. In the Canadian survey, just over 50 percent of those who heard a story about a negative shopping experience from someone else would subsequently avoid that store.

Organizational responses to customer complaints based on timeliness, facilitation, redress, apology, credibility, and attentiveness help foster positive post-complaint customer behavior (Davidow, 2003; Kasouf *et al.*, 1995). If the person is very satisfied with the organizational response to a complaint, then they are likely to engage in positive WOM. So, preventing customer dissatisfaction has longer-term effects, such as reducing negative WOM, while suppressing complaining increases negative WOM.

Service fairness

Service encounters are inherently risky because, like information goods in general, one cannot experience the service beforehand. This is especially true when services are difficult to judge because they are too technical, abstract, future, distant from the customer, or provide limited recourse (Seiders and Berry, 1998). So service customers are likely to feel vulnerable.

Thus one subtle but crucial aspect of service provision is a sense of *fairness* (Seiders and Berry, 1998). Fairness is required for trust, the most important variable (both positive and negative) in service exchanges, and thus loyalty, because of the inherent riskiness in the intangibility of service encounters. A sense of unfairness is not the same as poor service, and unexpected fairness can foster very positive perceptions. Unfair service practices may include exploitation, lack of accountability, or discrimination. *Exploitation* includes deception, misrepresentation, and invasion of privacy. *Lack of accountability* means it may be difficult or impossible to identify those responsible for neglecting service operations, wasting customers' time, denying responsibility, failing to enforce regulations, hiding behind unreasonable policies, or exploiting one's monopoly. *Discrimination* may involve targeted biases or selective manipulation, especially of vulnerable groups such as those with lower education, dependencies on the service, or cultural attitudes about confrontation and power. These are similar to some of Singer's causes of URs: poor feedback and symbolic manipulation.

Seiders and Berry (1998) develop a model of how discrepant service interactions, beliefs about justice, fairness perceptions, and subsequent responses unfold. A customer's interpretation of some service discrepancy or problem can foster a perception of unfair services, depending on the customer's expectations and norms about fairness. Perceptions of unfairness may arise due to breakdowns in distributive, procedural, or interactional justice. *Distributive justice* is an assessment of the outcome of decisions or allocations, based on principles of equity, equality, or proportional need. *Procedural justice* is an assessment of the extent to which unbiased, accurate, correctable, consistent, and representative procedures or systems are used in determining outcomes (see Feeley's 1992 example in Chapter 1). *Interactional justice* is an assessment of the nature of interpersonal treatment, including respect, honesty, and courtesy. The customer may perceive the unfairness more intensely as the outcome is more severe, frequent, or seen as controllable by the provider. Discrepancies the customer believes are under the company's control are more likely to be perceived as intentional, and thus blame-worthy. Seiders and Berry (1998) note that customers generally assume that companies (represented by the clerk at the desk or person on the other end of the phonecall or email) have access to complete and correct information, even if the personnel (or even the companies, as a whole) do not, thus increasing the sense of intentionality and therefore blame. Under these conditions, customers experience a sense of unfairness (depending on the extent of the outcome, the participants' loyalty, and the potential for correctability). Perceptions of service unfairness quickly generate either instinctive responses (such as emotional or other retaliation; Huefner and Hunt, 2000) and/or reasoned responses (such as requesting correction or compensation, complaining to the company or to others, loss of loyalty, litigation, etc.). Few of these are pleasant for the customer or beneficial for the organization.

Service feedback mediation

Often, it is only the consumer who experiences the product, service, or process in what appears to be an unusual or dysfunctional way. Unfortunately, neither feedback system developers nor organizational representatives are likely to have the same experience the consumer had, so cannot themselves identify such potential problems. So a central problem in processing customer service or product feedback is the extensive mediation of those experiences and the responses.

Media in general, and information systems in particular, can both facilitate or constrain feedback about organizational services, products, and systems. Customers may initiate contact with organizations on a wide array of topics and problems, so external feedback may be highly equivocal, both in form and meaning. Therefore, organizations need to structure potential feedback dialogues that do not constrain content but are matched to the attributes of the produce or service stimulating the feedback, to enable distribution to and response from vertical and horizontal levels in the organization (Culnan, 1989). While Culnan focuses on feedback from customers, we would generalize this point to include internal users' and implementers' feedback as well. Organizations and governments are just beginning to understand the value of not only traditional feedback channels, but also a variety of social media, from online rating systems to microblogs such as Twitter (Shirky, 2008).

Structured feedback systems, such as closed-ended comment cards, foster faster routing (especially if optical character recognition (OCR) is used to scan in the responses or online suggestion/complaints systems are provided), easier summarizing (if the response process is integrated with a database and analysis system), fewer delays (depending on where they are collected), and allow less internal modification (if the cards or online comments are directed to headquarters instead of the local service location) (Culnan, 1989). However, organizational media and information systems represent a recursive occasion for both stimulating URs as well as enabling feedback (positive, negative, accurate, or inaccurate) about them (Zmud, 1990). Different transaction processing systems may support or constrain different message processes: *routing* (selectively distributed, limiting overload); *summarizing* (reducing amount of message without loss of information); *delays* (intentional or not, beneficial or not); and *modification* (distortion, due to motivations or cognitive limitations) (Huber, 1982).

Semi-structured systems such as toll-free telephone lines or Internet homepages can be designed to include meta-level tracking of the nature and topic of calls, providing cues that user documentation for certain products or services is inadequate (Culnan, 1989). Note, however, that the frequency of letters will likely be in inverse relation to the complexity and difficulty of the problem or the complaint forms, as greater work subroutines will suppress clients' willingness to provide feedback. There may also be external and internal routing delays because the writer does not know exactly to whom to send the letter or make the phonecall, or how to identify and explain the problem, and the organizational recipient may not know how to categorize it once received.

But processing customer-initiated feedback through technology is difficult, as feedback can be highly equivocal not only in content but also in form and structure. Comments may be about unanticipated topics, allowing no standard response; these represent exceptions not only in the problem but also in the feedback communication (i.e., the organizational representative or system cannot easily process the feedback in the first place, to even identify the internal exception). Even if such feedback can be captured, natural language is hard to retain, associate, and retrieve, especially if it is voice-based. The design challenge is to develop systems to remove equivocality of format, but not equivocality of content. So, organizations seeking mediated feedback need to structure potential dialogues without constraining content, matched to product attributes, to enable distribution and response from vertical and horizontal levels in the organization (Culnan, 1989).

This is by no means straightforward. Forms in general, and customer complaint forms in particular, have an unpleasant ability to contribute to URs. Forms are a "major mode of discourse" of structured communication, and a primary interface among governments, organizations, citizens, and administrators (Sless, 1988, p. 58). Forms are manipulated by different interest groups within bureaucratic systems, and the progressive stages in a form's evolution are not necessarily indicators of coherent rational processes. More likely, the final version is a combination of competing rationalities and administrative sedimentation, and thus lacks coherence as a functional document. Implications of the possibly constrained and dysfunctional format and content of the form's questions and the resulting answers percolate throughout the organization. Ideally, these formats are designed to match the needs of a particular unit or process, but those same formats create constraints in other units or processes, and possibly for the intended unit over time. Some information is created by and for the bureaucracy, because forms require it (asking for estimates when actual figures are not available, or in providing categories created by tax law, etc.). The meaning of the questions, and thus the answers, on the form may not match the interpretations or needs of the person completing the form. Because the format and wording of the form are designed from organizational positions (such as regulators, accountants, data-entry operators, designers) far removed from the site at which the forms (texts) are actually read or processed by the user, what appears highly routine (the standard, formal, legal form) by its very nature can generate both external and internal repeated, systemic misunderstandings and mismatched processes, contributing to URs (Sless, 1988).

Technology and service literacy as feedback mediator

Even providing multiple media and systems to stimulate and distribute feedback presumes that organizational members and clients are in some way technically knowledgeable enough both about the problem and the systems used to support feedback. Unfortunately the nature of a UR itself will typically be beyond the limits of responsibility or knowledge of either the customer or the representative. In a world that depends on technical knowledge and flow of information, most consumers are, in fact, technically ignorant (not "dumb") – far more, relatively, about their world than were pre-industrial peasants about theirs (Blumberg, 1989, p. 60). There is growing concern with literacy and the general distribution of knowledge in various domains, especially health and the sciences. For example, by some criteria, 85 percent of the people in the United States in the early 1990s were functionally technologically illiterate (Lukasiewicz, 1994). Even if this weren't true, or as true, the increasing specialization and complexity of systems raises the dilemma of decreasing the possibility of any one person knowing enough about each of the parts to integrate the whole (Thayer, 1988). Thus, everybody is vulnerable to the expert knowledge of others, while none of those others actually understands the existence or interdependencies of the entire system (Chapter 8), fostering the exploitation of ignorance, through deception or manipulation, intentional or even unintentional.

This lack of technical knowledge is probably most extreme in the consumer electronics industry because there are few moving or even visible parts, and upgrades and new technologies make current understanding quickly obsolete. The very user-friendly nature of these systems exacerbates the problem, as use is nearly (and desirably) completely decoupled from technical understanding. And, back-office technical repairs (sometimes taking the form of sabotage, superficial treatment, or sheer incompetence) are invisible to the consumer, while pleasant service demeanor (sometimes knowledgeable about the back-office deception) provides the basis for customer satisfaction (Blumberg, 1989, p. 75). The paradox here is that pleasant over-the-counter service generates positive client behaviors, which rewards the individual fronting the UR of bad technical service, while also generating client attributions of service competence and thus repeat business, reinforcing the system. There are many protective laws, such as the customer's right to request in writing, before car repairs, to receive the original parts that are replaced, but few people know or take advantage of this; many people are ignorant about protections against their own ignorance. Further, often the probability of any particular deception being detected, and the resultant fines, is much less than the likely gain from it.

Perceptions and attributions of service quality

Another mediator in managing customer service feedback is that the provider and the customer will likely disagree about the causes and resolutions of service problems. Bitner *et al.* (1994) applied role, script, and attribution theories to analyze 774 encounters reported by employees in hotel, restaurant, and airline industries. Their review of prior research showed some large discrepancies between employees' perceptions of their own service quality, and customers' perceptions of those encounters. Attribution theory would predict less similarity in perceptions when there are differences about the underlying causes of the events, and about the failure or success of the service. Especially relevant here is the *self-serving attribution bias*, whereby people tend to take credit for successes, and deny responsibility for failure by blaming others or events (Fiske and Taylor, 1984; Chapter 8, this volume). Indeed, Bitner *et al.* (1994) found that employees are more likely to blame service dissatisfaction on customer or organizational systems, while customers are more likely to blame the employee or the organizational system. Employee actions in customer service encounters consisted primarily of (a) responses to service delivery system failure, (b) responses to customer needs and requests, (c) prompted and unsolicited employee actions, and (d) problem customer behavior (including, for example, verbal and physical abuse). This last result provides a check on the slogan that "the customer is always right" – which, when followed rigidly, can create conflicts in goals and behaviors (see the section below on problematic customers, pp. 80–1). Thus, most satisfactory experiences (from the employee's perspective) were associated with the employee's being able to adjust the system to accommodate customer needs.

Related to the self-serving attribution bias are face-saving and impression management. In order to continue appearing to live up to the moral standards one associates with a preferred impression – either one's own, or that of the organization providing the service or product – people have to spend considerable time and effort trying to maintain the show. In one sense, this is itself, ironically, an amoral act, while also necessary and beneficial. Two of the ways of accomplishing this are through performing *emotional labor* (Hochschild, 1983), or a *line* of acts and expressions that both evaluate one's own impression as well as others' (Dillard *et al.*, 2000, referring to Goffman, 1967, p. 405), such as routinized courtesy and denying responsibility for problems. Effective line management bolsters one's *face* (positive social value) and even the face of one's job or organization. However, because of the dual agency problem, described below, service providers are in the position of needing to maintain at least three, often contradictory, lines: toward the customer, toward their co-workers, and toward the organization.

Mediation of service feedback through roles and positions

As noted above, higher-level organizational members typically have little contact with customers. Thus front-line employees become the mediator between customers and managers, and the associated organizational goals (Grisaffe, 2000; Schneider and Bowen, 1993; Susskind *et al.*, 2003, p. 180). Agency theory provides one perspective on why this link often fails or produces contradictory or inconsistent customer service.

Principal–agent theory asserts that the goals of a principal and the goals of the agent hired by the principal are not aligned, as the parties have different preferences or interests and are differentially informed about each other, and because monitoring is difficult and/or expensive (Eisenhardt, 1989; Sandler, 2001). In this context, the principal can view the final outcome, but not the agent's actual effort or action creating that outcome. Further, an agent's actions rarely fully correspond to the final outcome. In either case, the final outcome does not completely represent the agent's actions or the principal's interests. In these conditions, the agent may take advantage of this *asymmetric information* to provide suboptimal levels of effort (called the *moral hazard*), become frustrated if the reward for the outcome does not reflect a high level of effort, or divert the principal's resources to agent interests.

Applying this perspective, Ellis *et al.* (2001) explain that the frontline service provider is the agent in not just the traditional superior–subordinate relationship, but also in the provider–customer relationship. When the customer feels that the service provider shows insufficient effort but the provider is following procedures, it's not clear how the provider can satisfy both the customer and the organization. So service provided to customers is in a *dual moral hazard*, with the provider attempting to jointly maximize both the customer and the organization relationships. These moral hazards are due to information asymmetry between the customer and the provider, and between the provider and the organization. But of course these are weighted differentially, so the customer–provider relationship may be conditional on the organization–provider relationship (and vice versa). This imposes a ceiling on provider satisfaction and customer service satisfaction, and thus the relationship between the two. The provider–customer satisfaction relationship will be lower, the greater the disparity between the provider's implicit contracts with the organization and with the customer.

One approach from the organization's perspective is to monitor service, with penalties for inadequate service. But, as principal–agent theory shows, this generates wasteful costs, and is likely to be only moderately successful. So organizations need to design the service arrangement to allow service solutions while reducing uncertainty as well as monitoring costs, which should affect the overall level of *customer satisfaction*. But note also that the provider has asymmetric information about the context and service needs of the customer. In this sense, the customer becomes an agent for the service provider. So, in turn, the service provider must expend monitoring costs to obtain the information and provide the service. But the customer may be unwilling or unable to provide those agency costs, placing an upper limit on the provider's service and the customer's own satisfaction. So, as with other relationships, the customer service provider needs to balance monitoring costs with risk-sharing and motivation, and those influence *service provider satisfaction* (separately from the more familiar customer satisfaction). The implication is that, from the perspective of the service provider, both the customer's and the organization's objectives must be aligned (Ellis *et al.*, 2001) and avoid conflicting goals, which contribute to URs. Clearly, this is an inherently difficult task.

Mediation of feedback by blocking and non-responding

Some companies, perhaps especially online companies, either provide no customer support through phone calls or hide those support numbers, reserving them for elite customers (Hafner, 2004). Withholding telephone contact information may be reasonable from the company's perspective, as when companies providing accessories to a popular device sold by another company get deluged with technical questions about that other company's device, especially if the initial customer support or warranty period has expired. While in this case the customer "should" know which company to contact, it's often difficult to distinguish the accessory from the device (especially given the technological illiteracy noted earlier). Companies may provide online customer request forms, but there is no guarantee of a swift – or any – response, even if the customers or organizational representatives can make good sense out of them. Such obstacles to obtaining customer feedback reduce satisfaction, and thus return business, of the customer (Hafner, 2004).

Frustrated customers are becoming more proactive, representing what McGregor (2008) calls *consumer vigilantes*, due both to the increased access to online information and systems, increased distrust of corporations, and increasing gaps between company promises and client experiences. They send mass emails to top layers of management, track down direct phone numbers of executive customer-service teams, post their experiences on blogs and online videos, etc. An increasing number of customer activist websites provide internal phone numbers of customer support or high-level executives, sometimes obtained through the registration information associated with the company's website's domain name, sometimes through inspecting the HTML (source code) of the website (Hafner, 2004). They suggest techniques for bypassing this feedback blocking, such as immediately pressing 0 several times at the initial phone menu or selecting the rotary phone option. Online discussion groups, blogs, and social networking features also allow these consumer vigilantes to become aware of others' experiences, and offer advice both about solving the particular problem as well as about how to complain or even litigate (see, for example, the section on consumer complaint letters at www. theconsumerist.org or websites for sharing consumer complaints such as www.measuredup.com or www.complaints.com). Insightfully, some companies have used these sites, as well as microblogging (e.g., Twitter) to identify and respond to these complaints, bypassing their own customer service processes (McGregor, 2008). Unsatisfied customers may become complaint activists, generating much more publicity, shareholder opposition, and class-action suits, blending into the area of media counter-usage called *hacktivism* (Lievrouw, 2008). Digital media-savvy consumer vigilantes can edit or animate corporate logos, create downloadable songs or videos that satirize the company, or set up counter-websites. Many organizations realize that widely shared awareness of customer service problems harms their reputation and decreases their business, so are motivated to deal at least with these more public cases. Companies can either ignore and defend against these (Bear and Hill, 1994), or use them as important sources of insights and customer sentiments (Kasouf *et al.*, 1995).

Problematic customers

Unusual routines and dysfunctional feedback loops are not solely attributable to provider or organization behaviors, of course. Blithely ignoring customer feedback is dangerous and harmful, but blithely accepting and encouraging all customer behavior, suggestions, and interpretations of services, products, and interactions may also be misleading, or harmful to the organization, its representatives, and even the consumer (Black, 2004). Customers may just as well be manipulative, deceitful, exploitative, fraudulent, insulting, discourteous, and unresponsive to feedback. Customer complaints may simply be cranky, uninformed, and frivolous, when not fraudulent or pathological. The long-running television program *Saturday Night Live* had an occasional routine involving the Letter-Writing Cowboy, who, sitting by the campfire with the other cowboys, would tell them of his most recent letter complaining about some problem with the Wild West or sagebrush. Altering well-reasoned and justifiable policies and procedures to satisfy a particular customer may create personnel and organizational conflicts, send inaccurate signals to more customers, and foster workarounds, preferential treatment, and even corrupt and illegal routines (Chapters 7 and 8).

Jones and Sasser (1998) dispute two common beliefs about improving customer satisfaction. The first myth is that it is not worth the cost to raise customer satisfaction from satisfied to completely satisfied. They argue that, except in rare cases, complete customer satisfaction is necessary to secure customer loyalty and long-term financial performance, especially in more competitive industries. Providing customers with many feedback opportunities to express their satisfaction creates both loyal and positive word-of-mouth customers. The second myth is that it is a good investment to try to raise the satisfaction level of the least satisfied customers. It may be that a company has attracted the wrong type of customer (difficult or too costly to serve, chronically unhappy), and that it is wise to realize, and publicize, the limits of service. It is obvious that companies must decide what level of support, service, and customization they can afford. That is, customers with more specialized needs and expectations become disproportionately more expensive, and, depending on the organization's desired clientele, may simply be outside that boundary (Davidow and Malone, 1992). High-end, expensive, service-oriented companies may seek out and court such customers, at a premium price; mass, low-cost, commodity-oriented companies may be very explicit that customers should expect no additional services. Neither choice is inappropriate; however, not being clear about such goals and expectations, and not providing integrated and complete support for and feedback about those, is harmful and provides fertile ground for UR growth.

Examples and analysis of unusual service subroutines, routines, and organizational (non-)response

The rest of this chapter presents a small selection of the first author's real-life adventures in attempting to solve a problem, seek a response, and then provide customer/client feedback, in a variety of contexts. (For a detailed experience of cross-system interdependencies and dysfunctions, see Rice, 2009a.) None of these organizations responded to the letters printed below. Again, our intent is to underscore what might in principle seem inexplicable: given the lip service paid to the "customer is number 1" or "the customer is always right" goal, how is it that in most cases the initial service was so flawed, and then various forms of the customer's feedback were ignored? This inability or unwillingness to process feedback from people outside of the organization (and, as we will see, from inside as well) – apart from the contorted, costly, and frustrating experiences of the original problem – is a central feature of URs. So, too, is the work subroutine, in which it took the first author considerable time to find the exact names and addresses of the possibly relevant people in the appropriate offices in different states, rather than the general "customer service" address. Unfortunately, the reader will most likely have had similar experiences.

1. *Your checks are safe with us*

Dear Mr. [County Bank Executive]:

I turn to you because of three levels of frustration I've had:

1. One of the branches seems to have lost two of my checks, and I'm quite frustrated. (Though just an hour ago, many weeks after I deposited them, they found the checks … see below.) 2. Every person I talk to has a different interpretation of policy, when it's known at all, and it's pretty peculiar. 3. In some cases I've been treated as someone who doesn't know what I'm talking about and who's guilty of the problem in some way.

Here's the story, with others' and my interpretations:

- My account at the [local name] branch is XX. The account name is [name], ITF YY. My social security number is ZZ. I used to live at TT [near the local branch].
- We recently bought a house at AA. My phone number there is BB.
- As you can imagine, there was a flurry of banking activity in June, July, and August, concerning mortgages, closing, remodeling, etc. On July 25, I obtained the last of several certified checks (my check #1369), and at that time provided the teller with a signed, official change-of-address form. Keep this in mind.

- Earlier, on July 19, I deposited three checks into the downtown ATM machine (because the [local branch] office doesn't have one, and I was going out of town the next day):
  - one for $7,000, made out to me
  - one for $85.65, made out to me and YY, from Lawyer 1 Attorney's Trust Account #9999
  - one for $1,125.19, made out to me and YY, from Lawyer 2 Attorney's Trust Account #9998
- I just returned home a week ago. When I opened my statement of 7/26/91 a few days ago, it shows the ATM deposit of $8,210.87 on 7/19, but also shows a "ATM debit adjustment" in the amount of $1,210.84. This is the total of the second and third deposited checks.
- Because I have lots of remodeling, appliance, and mortgage payments due shortly, I was concerned about this amount, and called the 800 number. They couldn't help me, and told me that my home branch would have the explanation. I called the local branch. They had no information on this, and said that where I made the deposit would have the information. I called the downtown branch. They said that all adjustment paper is sent to the local branch. I called the local branch. I talked with Cosmo [her name, really] at that time and since. Their computer was down, so she began looking through her paperwork, but there apparently was a lot, so after a while she said, no, the branch of deposit should have the information. I called the downtown branch.

Aha! The downtown branch just today discovered photocopies of the checks and provided the following explanation.

- Because the second two checks were made out to both me and YY, but my account name is in only my name (with YY as ITF), even though we both signed the checks, they couldn't be deposited into my account. This seems understandable; however, both of my lawyers expressed surprise at this, and they and others told me that they have been able to deposit such checks in similar circumstances. They may be right, or they may be wrong. Your bank may have a particularly stringent policy, or a widely accepted one. I don't know. I didn't know at the time. However, even if this is proper legal policy, it's not as though I caused all the subsequent problems, which is how some bank representatives have couched the problem.

- Here's where it gets real murky. So I ask the downtown branch what to do, and where are the checks. I know that unless I have the checks in my hand, neither lawyer will just write me another check. Ironically, we have two other accounts with your bank, both in both our names. Had we, or had the bank, known of the problem, the checks could have been deposited there. They told me that the policy is to send the checks to the local branch, which should then send the checks to me by certified mail. However, they did keep photocopies of the checks. Remember, this original (mis)handling of the checks is all around July 23 or 24. All these calls are around August 19–21.
- The local branch says, no, the downtown branch is wrong; the deposit branch should handle the checks.
- I call the downtown branch. They say, no the local branch is wrong, that they should have sent the checks. I've dealt with Ms. C. at the downtown branch, who has always been very courteous with me. She checked my account and found that my address was still listed as at the old address, TT. She, and everyone else since then, felt that this was the obvious explanation: that I didn't submit a change of address form, that somehow I've caused the problem. But I did – see # 3 above – which indicates another area where the local branch dropped the ball. I explained to her as well as to everyone else that (a) I did submit a change of address form, and (b) if the checks were mailed to TT, they would be forwarded to my new address, as all our other mail is being forwarded, or they would be returned to the local branch office. Neither of these has happened. In spite of these facts, Ms. C. first suggested that I check with the Post Office to see if something was lying around for me. I called, and they said no. Ms. C. suggested I wait awhile to see if the checks show up. It's now almost a month after the debit adjustment was made; I can't imagine they will now "show up."
- I call the local branch. Cosmo has no record of receiving, mailing, or receiving back undeliverable checks.
- The downtown branch also suggested that now was the time to ask the two lawyers to write stop payments and write me new checks. I comply, though I suspect that this is again passing the buck, so to speak. Lawyer 2 is on vacation this week, so his secretary took a message and I'll hear from him on Monday. Lawyer 1 was surprised at this request. First, because the bank caused the problem; they

feel that the bank lost the checks, and the bank should make good on the checks. Second, because they were now supposed to take their time and pay the stop payment fees. Third, because (they both said) Attorney Trust Accounts are heavily regulated in New Jersey, it's extremely difficult to make a stop payment and write another such check. They may be entirely correct. They may be exaggerating the situation to avoid the hassle. I don't know the "truth." I'm not a lawyer. However, that's what they say.

- I call Ms. C. and tell her what the lawyers say. She expresses surprise and generously offers to call the lawyer. Later, she tells me the Lawyer 1 folks were rather indignant and that they explained their regulatory constraints. She feels that they are wrong, that they could put a stop payment and write another check quite easily. She may be entirely correct. She may be exaggerating the situation to avoid the hassle. I don't know the "truth." I'm not a lawyer. Then again, neither is she. However, that's what she says.
- I call the local branch back. I relate all this to Cosmo. She also latches on to this issue of the change-of-address. She says she'll call me back. No one seems to "get" the fact that the local branch seems not to have submitted or entered my change-of-address form; rather they all think that I did something wrong. But this is irrelevant, as well as wrong – even if I did not submit such a form, the two branches should still have the same policy (which they don't), should have records of who was responsible for the checks (which they don't), should have records of sending out the checks (which they don't), and should have records of receiving them back if they were undeliverable (which they don't).
- Her message on my machine was that she talked with her supervisor, who said they'd pay the lawyers for their stop-payment order. Whether it's the lawyers' responsibility or the bank's responsibility is hotly debated by the lawyers and the bank; from my perspective, however, I'm out $1,210.84, with a mortgage payment coming up.
- I called Cosmo today to ask her for the name and phone number of the regional branch manager, because it was clear that her supervisor was not going to be very helpful.

As a side-story along with all this, your bank is closing down the local branch, and the former manager left several months ago, so the temporary supervisor neither knows about where things are (so I was

told; this may be wrong or it may be right; it's probably a bit of both),
nor probably has much commitment to the branch and its customers.
Further, Ms. C. at the downtown office said that all the local branch
accounts would be moved to some larger center, though she wasn't
sure which of two it would be.

- Cosmo instead put her supervisor on the phone, who treated me
  in a very hostile and condescending way. She tried several times to
  place the blame on me because the current records show my old TT
  address instead of my new address. She grilled me on who the name
  of the teller was that I gave the form to, and since I couldn't remember, then of course I didn't really submit the change-of-address,
  and was I sure it was on the proper form? (Though the certified
  check of that date should show which teller it was, although that
  proves nothing concerning the change of address form.) I couldn't
  get her to understand that it was (a) irrelevant, and (b) not true that
  I didn't submit a change of address. She felt I caused the problem in
  this way. Finally I got her off that, simply pleading that I've tried to
  do all the right things, but, since I'm neither the bank nor the lawyers, am stuck in the middle. She turned to the issue of the original
  checks and pointed out that since I deposited them to my account
  but they were made out to us jointly, then how could I say I didn't
  do anything wrong? Finally, she did say that she would personally
  call the lawyers to get them to put the stop payments and write
  new checks. Perhaps she will have better luck than all the rest of
  us. But nowhere in the conversation did she "get" the fact that the
  two branches have very different stories (if not policies), that one
  of them lost the checks, and that the local branch didn't enter my
  change of address form.
- The local branch supervisor just called to say that *indeed* they
  did find the checks. They were in the "lost and found," or I guess
  suspense file. Seems they *were* mailed to my old TT address, and
  returned, *but* since they hadn't actually/yet entered my change of
  address form, they didn't know where to send them. However, they
  do have my employer's address in their files, so they could have
  tracked me down. The supervisor indicated that I shouldn't have
  given the form to the teller (or, rather, the teller should have asked
  me to take it to the front desk), because she doesn't know what the

teller did with it. So, I'll pick up the checks, and deposit them into a suitable account.

Since they just found the checks, there's nothing to do about all this, really, but you should know what it's (sometimes) like as a customer dealing with your organization.

Yours truly,

2. *Risky investment: figuring out how to fill out forms (in homage to Sless, 1988)*

Dear Mutual Funds Company Correspondent:

This note is not about any financial account of mine, so this won't fit into your regular processing. However, I would like a response, just for my information.

- Some of your company's materials are contradictory and confusing. Now, these are "minor" problems in the overall scheme of managing billions of dollars, but they frustrate me and they probably do the same to others. And I'm sure these contradictions cost your company money and time, not to say customer dissatisfaction.
- On the Express application, note that it says to return the information to PO Box XXXX, with a ZIP of YYYYY. Also, the correspondence control sheet has that same address (twice). However, the enclosed return envelope has no PO Box, and a ZIP of ZZZZZ. Now, I'm sure that it all ends up in the right place. But, here I am wondering – should I send the correspondence inquiry (this note) with the correspondence control slip, in the return envelope, but send the application to the "correct" address? Should I include it all in one envelope? If the addresses *should* be different, won't that slow down, and possibly mislay, my applications? This probably is of no importance to you – you know that it all ends up in the right place. But that's because you deal with it all the time. Customers do this only a few times, and I'm not clear as to what the right thing to do is. It probably doesn't matter, but it creates a sense of confusion and incompetence.
- On the Express application, section 2, it asks for Bank Account Number after the Bank address information. Now, if I stopped

right there, I'd probably interpret that to mean you want my bank account. But, the next blanks call for checking, savings, or NOW account. Aha! *That*'s my banking account. So the company must mean the *Bank*'s banking account above. I just happen to know where to get that information – the preceding section of the MICR on the check – because I used to work in a bank. Lots of people don't know that.

- But it's worse than that. Note that in the Bank Authorization Agreement For Electronic Funds Transfer, it asks for the signature of the "Bank Account Owner." Now, if the company meant *Bank* by Bank Account above, that would mean the company also meant owner of the *Bank* here – but obviously it means the owner of the *account*. So you use the term "bank account" differently in two places or you're asking for redundant information above (Bank Account Number is same as checking, savings, or NOW account). Neither makes sense.

- Even worse still. Now, below the signature you ask for Bank Account Number. Now, for me to be consistent, I should put in the same number I put in for the Bank Account Number in section 2. I had decided that meant the account of the *Bank*. So I put that in here. But, when the bank officer sees this, they'll need to know the number of my bank account (checking, savings, NOW). So, to avoid having the bank and you send it all back to me, I put in *both* numbers. Now the bank officer will think I'm causing trouble. (It just so happens in this case, that the bank officer *will* think I'm causing trouble, because they had trouble with a bank transaction from Canada and thought I was a troublemaker because I wondered why they messed it up.)

- Yet another question. Because my mutual fund accounts have a JT WROS and NOT AS TEN COM, I had to obtain signature guarantees of that JT WROS. Okay. But, note on the Bank Authorization Agreement For Electronic Funds Transfer, it asks for the signature of the "Joint Tenant, if any." I'm assuming you are referring to the checking account (I can't say Bank Account here, to avoid confusion), not the mutual funds account, here. But note that my checking account, unlike my Vanguard account, doesn't have a joint tenant – it's my name, in trust for the other person. So the bank officer will be confused if they see the other person's signature here, and again may return the stuff, saying, nope, that's not the correct account ownership. But if the mutual funds company name means the mutual funds company name JT here, then it *does* require the other person's (JT) signature. I assumed the first, because it's the bank's concern, but wrote in a note (NO JT ON BANK), which is likely to cause a question or rejection.

Seriously, I would like someone to comment and respond to all this. As this whole set of stuff comes up only once, or a few times, for any one person, and then it's resolved, it never becomes a recurring problem for any one customer, so no one does anything about it, so every new person has to deal with it – and your company has to deal with its implications (mostly invisible) all the time. Surely the company can do a better job of reducing such confusion on a two-page sheet.

Yours truly,

3. *Running out of gas*

Dear XYZ Gas Co. Correspondent:

Here are two things I'd like to resolve. I know that the person who handles the first problem probably has little interest in or ability to do anything about the second problem, but they are somewhat related, and I'd like a response to both anyway.

The first is paying an outstanding bill and putting it in the correct name and address – mine. The second is a question about finding out how you deal with suggestions that could avoid some problems for customers and your phone service providers alike.

Here's the first problem: for some reason, when Ms. A [former resident] moved out of [my new rental address] in July, the gas service was not only not turned off, but the billing information was never changed. Now, when I moved in, I was new to the area, so did not know that even though PSEandG stands for electric and gas, it did not in fact provide our gas. Yes, you're shaking your head because how could someone NOT know that, but in fact, it makes perfect sense if you don't know that someone else provides the gas, and the name of this company includes the word "Gas." So naturally I didn't seek out any other company about the gas, and in fact I continued to get gas. So, for many months, somehow either the XYZ bill was never sent out or it never reached Ms. A, and it didn't arrive at the old address either.

But I had a gas problem (see the second problem, below), which is when I found out that PSEandG was *not* the gas provider, and told XYZ about the accounting problem – that I was perfectly prepared to actually pay the back months since Ms. A moved out – but because I didn't know the account number (how could I? I never got a bill), and because they couldn't allow someone who didn't actually hold the account to phone in a change of account, they couldn't do anything about it. So I figured a bill would show up sometime.

Well, it did, and here it is; about $88 in back payments due, with a delinquent notice and a threat of cutting off gas. Ms. A received it in the mail, finally, and was kind enough to forward it to me before they cut it off with all sorts of attendant charges.

So, what I'm doing is:

- including a check for the full amount
- requesting that the account now be put in my name and address
- without having to disconnect, reconnect, or anything.

I hope that's easy to do – after all, I'm doing the right thing and just want to continue with service and I'll even pay the bills if and when I get them.

Here's the second, much more interesting, problem: if you're the person who handles billing and accounts, you can probably stop here and pass it on to someone else, because this isn't your problem. Probably it'll be interesting to find out whose problem it is.

I read the notice the very moment I got it, this Saturday. On the notice, it says very clearly to call a specific number to avoid the cut-off and the attendant multiple charges. I thought – that's just what I'll do, because I don't want to have my gas cut off and pay all those multiple charges, so I'll straighten this out right away. So I called the number. The woman answered nicely, and allowed me to start explaining this, but then told me that billing hours were Monday–Friday. Now, on the face of it, this is fine, and most people would just hang up and wait until Monday. But consider this from the dumb customer's point of view: I did just exactly what the notice told me to do, and the phone operator essentially says that I'm wrong and I should call again in a few days. I was curious as to how the notice information could be wrong (which it is, because it doesn't say to call only Monday–Friday), but, moreover, curious as to how this situation could have continued, because certainly I couldn't be the first person to encounter this.

Think about it – every time this happens, it (a) ties up your phone service person, (b) makes the customer feel like they've done something wrong, and (c) makes them a bit more frustrated with "those utilities."

So, it seems to me that your company would actually be glad to hear from someone about this problem and would actually try to solve it, like just noting on the notice that the number is for Monday–Friday, you can't handle billing or new accounts on the weekends, *and* you won't penalize folks who thought they were told to, and wanted to solve the problem on Saturday but couldn't call until Monday. But the question is, how can someone like me actually get into your organization to suggest this, and who would care anyway?

Having nothing more responsible to do, I briefly raised this question to the phone service person. I wondered if there was any mechanism for her to report such problems. She immediately interpreted this as though I was asking her to take time out right now to solve my billing and account problem! She started explaining how it wouldn't be fair to those who actually had emergencies for her to take the time out. I said that wasn't what I was after. (It's so strange for a customer to suggest some improvement, and so unlikely that a representative has any authority or channels for passing on such suggestions, that naturally she interpreted it in the way I had suggested – the customer has done something wrong.)

I explained the situation (silly, cause why didn't I just hang up and call on Monday, after all?), and when she grasped the point, I asked her whether this has happened before, because I can't be the first, because it's a common and systemic situation. She said *yes it does happen*. So why didn't anyone try to fix it? She says that the company might respond if a lot of customers report it, but they wouldn't respond to her suggestion (which she doesn't have time for anyway) unless it was a "real serious" problem. Note that that puts the burden on the customer, which is again not what the company wants to do, and stress on the service person, which I think isn't what the company wants to do. Most customers will just forget about it, leaving the next customer and service person to suffer it. And your company will never learn about it, though even the phone service person will think this is all pretty stupid.

So there you have it:

- this oversight in the notice information causes the same problem for every customer who tries to respond to the notice on a weekend;
- your telephone service person has to waste her time explaining to customers that they've called at the wrong time;
- customers just keep on getting upset; and
- there's no way for your company to improve this situation.

So, my second question is, why does this kind of thing happen? It happens all the time, with many companies. There's no way for an ordinary customer, client, or user to get into the organization's system to point out that the organization is wasting time, money, and customer goodwill. What's worse, the organization doesn't appreciate these kinds of suggestions anyway, ends up actively discouraging such suggestions, and doesn't provide its representatives with any way to handle it or be rewarded for solving such problems!

Just curious; I really would like a sincere reply, by someone who's intrigued about these kinds of problems and might even want to improve their company's dealings with customers.

Yours truly,

4. *Please call back at your convenience*

Dear National Telecom Service District Manager:

I'd like to recount to you a long and frustrating string of interactions (only some of them actually got to the stage of interaction) with Telecom [country]. I don't write this to ask for any specific request; I'm more interested in wondering how these things can happen, and how your company might respond to such occurrences so as to prevent them from happening in the future. One of the problems was that there seemed to be absolutely no way to get the people on the phone to actually deal with this larger question: how does Telecom actually learn about customer and system problems? Mostly, they just wanted to transfer me on to someone else.

Here's the sequence of events.

On Wednesday, June 25, I wanted to make a call to the United States from my hotel phone. I had done so a day or so before, dialing direct through the hotel phone, without any problem, though I did not at that time understand how to use the international operator number (114) so as to use my telephone credit card. So the prior call worked, but it cost me more.

This time, I dialed 114. The first four times, I got interminable busy signals. The fifth time, I got someone whom I could hear but could not hear me. They finally hung up (a reasonable response). The sixth time, I got long beeps.

So, I gave up and dialed direct (knowing that this would now cost me more, as it went through the hotel processing system). The first two times, I could hear the party in the United States, but they couldn't hear me. The third time, we had a conversation for about one minute, when the line was disconnected. The fourth time, I got a wrong number.

So, I gave up on the idea, but at least wanted the charges backed out since all my calls were unsuccessful. Here's where things got really frustrating.

Not knowing whom to call, I dialed 0 several times. It was busy each time. So I called 114 again. It was busy each time. I wondered whether 10 would work. It was busy each time. I tried 198 – knowing that the "accounts" number wasn't right, but maybe someone would answer. Someone did. I explained my story. He was sympathetic, but couldn't help me. He gave me the number for customer assistance (777747).

I dialed that, was connected, and explained my story again, this time including this most recent connection. The person forwarded me to someone else. I explained my story again, this time including this most recent connection. The person forwarded me to a manager. I explained my story again, this time including this most recent connection. The manager forwarded me to another manager. I explained my story again, this time including this most recent connection.

This person said she'd back out my charges. I gave her the hotel phone number (which she knew, of course, as that's where I was dialing from) and my room number. She repeated it. So, although I never made my call that day, I finally got through and figured my charges would be corrected.

Of course, when I checked out, the hotel bill *did* include the charges for the calls. I explained the story (well, part of it – who would want to hear it all?) and said that the charges should have been reversed out of the hotel's phone bill. She said that the phone company couldn't do that, especially as it was to a room. That put me in the position of being "wrong" – as the phone company told me one thing and the hotel person told me another contradictory thing. I insisted on the story, and she finally decided just not to charge me.

So, the outcome:

I was extremely frustrated with Telecom, and was put in a bad situation with the hotel person. Telecom personnel spent a fair amount of time with me, but in the end learned nothing from the experience and did nothing to correct it. I was told contradictory information. The hotel may end up covering the phone charges.

I'm back in the United States, and I guess I should just have forgotten it all and paid the bill. But I'm really curious: how could such terrible technical and business service occur? How can the customer response process be so completely non-responsive, bureaucratic, and incorrect? And how is it that there seems to be absolutely no way (or perhaps no motivation) for personnel to provide feedback about such problems to Telecom?

Yours truly,

5. *Next time we just wreck your car*

Dear Major Auto Repair Store General Manager, and Auto Manager:

Just what you need. Another complaint letter. Usually I'm pretty adaptable and far too courteous to complain. But this experience deserves a letter, and a response.

Last evening, July 6, I came to your Auto Services and paid in advance, by check, for services to be performed today, Wednesday, July 7, because (a) I wanted all the paperwork done so that when my wife drove in her car behind me so I could drop my car off and then I could drop her off at the train station, she wouldn't have to wait long. Today, Wednesday, was the only really convenient day for me to have this done because we both have to drive several places on Thursday, Friday, and Saturday, and then we go out of town for a week. So I planned ahead to make things simple and easy.

So this morning I arrive at 7:20. There was only a nice older couple waiting before me, in front of the customer door. The door opened about ten minutes late, which wouldn't have been a problem in itself. But of course one guy walked in the employees' door instead of the customers' door and was waiting at the desk when we finally came in. The counter person saw this but the older couple and I had to wait until after the guy, of course. No big thing, but it adds to the setting.

Then finally a guy came to the front desk. It turns out his name is [Mr. A]. I presume he was in a bad mood from something else; I hope he doesn't always treat his customers this way. He asked me what I wanted. I showed him my copy of the Estimate Copy/Claim Check (#9999). He said what did I want done. I said it was listed on the sheet. I also mentioned to him that the name on the sheet was incorrect, because your company's system automatically prints the name of the person with an account at the same phone number, so it was listed under my wife's name instead of me. I also said that although it wasn't printed on the sheet, there was a handwritten note about my loose muffler. He asked me where the paperwork was. I said I only had this sheet. He looked around for a second then asked me again, sharply, where was the paperwork. I said I was only a customer, and how should I know where the paperwork was. He said where's the key. I gave him my key. He proceeded to walk to the shop door. I asked him when they were open to and could I pick it up this evening. He said 9 p.m. and disappeared. He never greeted me, and was at best gruff, and certainly discourteous. I gave him no reason for treating me this way.

So my wife calls from the train station at 7:20 p.m. for me to pick her up, and we go to get my car. I notice the car is still in the same lot (#3) I left it in, and the tires hadn't been changed! I went in, and there was no one at the desk for about five minutes. Again, during that time, a couple came up with some purchases, and went right to the desk, and were served first when a service person came to the desk. This gets kind of old.

So when the service person came to the desk, I was a bit frustrated, and asked how it could be that my car, which I paid for the prior evening, and dropped off at 7:30 a.m., was still not serviced, at 7:45 p.m. that day? He asked for the paperwork, and I showed him my claim sheet. Strangely, he asked for the car key, and I said of course I don't have it, because I gave it to the person this morning. He went away, and came back about five minutes later, with the plastic envelope, and the key (on a red tag, with my wife's name, even though I told Mr. A that my name was entered in the customer block, but the computer system printed my wife's name in the top of the costs section). In the plastic envelope was the paperwork with a red note (Waiting for Customer to Arrive) because they couldn't find the key.

It turns out the key was *not* put in the envelope. Mr. A apparently put it on a shelf somewhere, and not with the paperwork. And it wasn't clear that the paperwork was in the "in process" shelf in the shop, or elsewhere. Note, however, that the claim sheet in the envelope *did* have my proper telephone number on it, because that's how the system retrieved my wife's name. No one called me at home to ask about this problem. I have an answering machine, and I was home all day, this being my only free day.

I thought for a minute about asking for a full refund. But since my car was already there, it would cost me a lot more to schedule to go somewhere else. But this is *not* a way to treat any customer. The service person at the counter this evening was understanding, and I know and acknowledged to him it was not his fault.

So.

- Mr. A treated me at best discourteously and thoughtlessly, and at worst he sabotaged me, messing up my and my wife's schedule.
- There seems to be a systematic problem with handling certain kinds of paperwork; I didn't do anything weird that would have made this an exceptional transaction, so this situation could apparently happen again. In fact I'm a good customer – I paid in advance the night before, and dropped off the car the first thing in the morning, without requiring it be serviced until the end of the day.
- No one took the responsibility to call me at home to ask about the key.
- On Thursday, I now will have to take a train to work, walk to work, then walk to the train, and get a train back here, and walk from there at 8:30 p.m. for a meeting, and then meet my wife, who will drive us home.

Here's what I would like to know:

- Whether this matter is discussed with Mr. A, and what comes from this discussion.
- Whether you have any plans to make the waiting-in-line process both a bit quicker (I know cutbacks result in fewer sales people, increasing tensions for both salespeople and customers) and fair

(there should be some sort of line, like at airport counters, so that people get served in their fair turn).

• What policy you have for compensating people for these kind of dislocations – this will cost me two train tickets and about an extra hour out of my day tomorrow, two more days of coordinating shared rides (so I can pick my car up Friday morning), in addition to the frustration, poor treatment, and making my wife take a later train. Yours truly,

6. *Reproducing problems*

For this case, to help illustrate how the other cases were coded as shown in Table 3.2, *the text notes[in brackets] where instances of the three main components of the model (Conditions and Influences, In-process Subroutines and Symptoms, and Consequences) occur.*

Dear Copy Store Manager:

I would like to share with you some of our experiences this semester with Copy Store. You should know that at the moment several faculty here are upset at Copy Store's service this semester, and some of them may not return to you in the coming semesters. I will, however, only note my own experiences. Please consider this as intended as useful customer feedback. I have enjoyed Copy Store's service in the past, and I want you to provide good service so I and other faculty can keep using you. For example, Copy Store is very good at preparing clean pages and calling me about missing pages, etc., and this helps me provide a better reading packet for the students.

Background: I provided Copy Store two sets of materials, way back in May, before my summer travels. I always provide my materials very early to give your staff enough time to get all the permissions, so that the course packets are ready before classes begin. We dive right into the materials, and if the students can't get their packets right away – by the first class – the classes immediately fall behind and the students get aggravated by the obstacles.

The two packets were for 449 (undergrad Telecommunications Processes and Policy) and 602 (PhD Research Foundations). Both of them included a set of articles, and a set of computer manuals and related pages. All of the articles and the computer pages were different for each of the packets.

For example, here's part of my cover letter, to show you how much I try to make things easy for Copy Store:

"Here are my materials to go in to a reading packet for 602, Research Foundations. Enclosed are:

- a copy of the table of contents of the reading packet, with notes concerning permission information. Do NOT put this in the reading packet.
- the copies of the permission materials, including permanent personal permission letters.
- the table of contents for the reading packet, to go into the reading packet.
- a complete set of materials, articles, and book chapters. Each one of these is in a particular order, as listed on the table of contents. There are no two-sided pages."

Here's a summary of what happened (or didn't):

- Come beginning of the semester, even though I got a call that the reading packets were ready, some of the students had to come back several times to get their packets. I give the Copy Store phone number in the syllabus to have them call up ahead of time so the packets would be ready. In some cases, it wasn't until over a week after classes started that people had their packets. Some, but not all, of the undergraduates were told that they had to leave a deposit or pay for the packet in advance (I can't remember which) and the packet wouldn't be ready for three days. This is very inconvenient for students, and, again, this meant they couldn't keep up with the coursework. [Organization: inconsistencies; subroutines: work, delay, error; short-term: frustration, problems.]
- It turns out the PhD students (602) didn't get the computer manuals and pages in their packet. Several of them also said in class that they ended up paying different amounts for their packets. I called Copy Store and was told that, yes, they had accidentally left out the computer materials. The students could come back and pick those up. Again, this caused inconvenience, delays and confusion. [Organization: inconsistencies; subroutines: work, error; short-term: problems.]
- Some PhD students came back saying that they were going to be charged an additional $31 for the computer section (in addition to

the $34.50 for the initial part of the packet). Other students were quoted a total of $75! As none of these computer materials required permissions, I couldn't believe it would cost this much. I called up Copy Store and was told that there were 300 pages to this section, and yes it would cost $31. I figured out that Copy Store had confused the readings part of the 449 packet with the computer materials part of the 602 packet! That is, there were 300 pages of articles (not including the computer materials) in the 449 packet, which cost $31. So at least one person at Copy Store didn't even understand what was involved here (in spite of the very detailed instructions). Eventually the PhD students got their materials and for the most part ended up paying nothing extra, as the $34.50 for the packet had included the cost for the (missing) computer materials. [System: poor design; organization: inconsistencies.]

- This past Tuesday, in the middle of a computer lab with the undergrads for 449, I said, "turn to the back of your reading packet where instructions for today's computer activities are included." None of the students who had their reading packets with them had the computer section in their reading packet (not all of the students brought them, so it's possible that some of the unbought reading packets did include the materials)! I checked several of them, and sure enough, they ended at page 300, and the packet cost $31. Yet, my own professor reading packet *did* have the computer materials in it, so I had just assumed that all the student ones did too. You can imagine that this made it nearly impossible for me to conduct the computer lab, and just increased the students' confusion and anxiety about using computers. The students often think these kinds of problems are my fault, due to my incompetence, and they correspondingly rate me negatively on their course evaluations. [System: mismatched costs, benefits; short-term: confusion, inscrutability; frustration, stress; harm for stakeholders.]

- By now I was pretty frustrated because of how difficult it was to conduct my classes because of the continual mess-ups by Copy Store. I called again to try and explain what had happened. As with all my earlier calls, it was nearly impossible for me to get a chance to fully explain the situation clearly; I kept having to deflect assumptions and misunderstandings about what I was talking about, what was involved in the reading packets, even which classes were involved. And, the remaining 449 course packets at Copy Store *did* have the computer materials in them, so maybe only the early packets didn't have them? [Organization: inconsistencies; symptoms: non-responsiveness, denial.]

• Several times that I called Copy Store from late summer on, I got people who had no idea about my reading packets; many times the copiers were running and the phone is near them so it was almost impossible for the person on the phone to hear what I was saying; sometimes the radio was playing near the phone so it was difficult for me to have a clear conversation. So, in addition to all the mistakes and inadequate processing, the general nature of interaction with Copy Store is very unprofessional and frustrating. This is simply no way to run a business. If you want to run this as a toy "student" operation, fine, but then you will eventually get no business from serious customers. [System: poor feedback through, about the system; organization: culture; subroutines: work, error; symptoms: non-responsiveness; intermediate: exit, loss of user motivation.]

As you can see, from the customer's perspective – and that includes me as well as all my students – the Copy Store experience has been unsatisfactory, in many ways. It doesn't matter to the customer what the reasons are – several Copy Store people tried to explain all these things as having to do with hiring new people, copying machines breaking down, etc. Indeed, providing all these excuses, regardless of how true they are, just worsens our perception of Copy Store. [Organization: training, socialization; symptoms: denial; intermediate: loss of worker motivation; long-term: organization does not learn.]

So. I'm just summarizing my own experiences, and not those of other faculty. You can decide to ignore these warning signals if you want, but I'm offering them as an outsider's experience and perception of Copy Store. I would think a manager would want to know about these perceptions and experiences, and figure out ways to prevent them in the future. After all, it's your business. If your employees don't care about these kinds of things, then they're not being managed according to customers' needs.

The next time we use Copy Store services, we hope the students and faculty will have a smooth and satisfying experience. Based on their experience this semester, some faculty may not give Copy Store a next time. [Intermediate: client exit.]

Yours truly,

Table 3.1 *Model of unusual routines, expanded from Singer's model of crazy systems*

Causes and conditions	In-process effects	Outcomes
Individual: • symbolic use of information, meta-phors, discourse • barriers to perception • strategic manipulation of information, system • subsume role and process in individual • incentives • common sense, sensemaking • habits • psychological and cognitive processing System: • system complexity • poor design • limited conceptualization of "user" • unlinked costs and benefits • poor feedback • aura of rationality	Unusual routines: • should be conceptualized as unusual but not • perceived as routine • embedded as a routine • repeated deviation-amplifying loops, internal and external to focal process • suppress or distort learning • generate wasteful subprocesses • varying costs and benefits to different stakeholders • local and/or system-wide • intentional and unintentional Subroutines: • work • delay • error • blame	Short-term: • client frustration • stress • problems for organizational representatives, clients, stakeholders • apathy, confusion, inscrutability • emotional outbursts • exit/exclusion Intermediate: • client exit • loss of worker/user motivation • embedded workarounds • turnover • unaccountability • organization learns wrong lessons • employee sabotage • organization does not learn, adapt

Table 3.1 (*cont.*)

Causes and conditions	In-process effects	Outcomes
Organization: • conflicting goals • changing uses, contexts, conditions • organizational culture and socialization • impermeable intra-, inter-organizational boundaries • inherent paradoxes • incentives • fragmentation mechanization/ bureaucratization • normalcy • legitimization cues • job/task features Interactions among: • individual • system • organization	Symptoms: • non-responsiveness (lack of feedback, inability to use system to solve system problem, resolving problem becomes client's burden) • denial (ignore, reject symptoms) • rigidity (rules, regulations, blind following of procedures, falsely claiming problems are fixed, ad hoc false rules, intentionally misinterpreting rules) • manipulation (rigged/biased systems, encourage fraud while seeming legitimate, label problem reporter as paranoid or troublemaker; symbolic use of information, metaphors, discourse • suspicion and secrecy (turf battles, not invented here, hiding useful information or explanations)	Long-term: • organization does not learn, adapt • harm to the system/organization itself • harm to external stakeholders • litigation • crisis • failure

Table 3.2 *Aspects of unusual routines in the case examples*[a]

	1	2	3	4	5	6
Conditions and influences						
Individual:						
barriers to perception, action (tolerance, fragmentation, costs; requires specialized knowledge)	x	x	x		x	
role, process subsumed in individual	x				x	
strategic manipulation of information, system					x	
symbolic use of information, metaphors, discourse			x			
System:						
aura of rationality, normalcy, legitimization		x				
poor design		x				x
poor feedback through, about the system	x		x	x		x
system complexity		x		x		
unlinked, mismatched costs, benefits			x	x	x	x
Organization:						
bureaucratization, formalization	x		x	x	x	
changing uses, contexts, conditions	x	x	x			
conflicting goals, criteria	x					
impermeable intra-, inter-organizational boundaries	x			x		
inherent paradoxes, inconsistencies	x	x	x			x

Table 3.2 (*cont.*)

	1	2	3	4	5	6
organizational culture, training, socialization	x				x	x
Interactions among:						
individual: habits, relations	x					
system: social, technical features		x		x		x
organization: interdependencies; mismatched timing, level of feedback, context	x	x	x	x	x	x
Subroutines and symptoms						
Subroutines:						
work	x	x			x	x
delay	x			x	x	x
error	x	x	x		x	x
blame	x	x	x	x	x	x
Symptoms:						
catatonic non-responsiveness	x	x	x	x	x	x
denial	x			x	x	x
pathological rigidity	x					
psychopathic manipulation					x	
suspicion, secrecy					x	

Consequences

	1	2	3	4	5	6
Short-term:						
apathy, confusion, inscrutability	x			x	x	x
emotional outbursts	x					
frustration, stress	x		x		x	x
problems, harm for organizational representatives, clients, stakeholders	x		x	x		x
Intermediate:						
client exit					x	x
embedded workarounds				x		
employee sabotage					x	
loss of worker/user motivation			x			x
organization learns wrong lessons		x				
unaccountability	x					
Long-term:						
harm to the system/organization					x	x
legal issues, litigation		x				
organization does not learn, adapt	x		x	x		x

Notes: The six cases referred to in the table are as follows: 1 (Your checks are safe with us); 2 (Risky investment: figuring out how to fill out forms); 3 (Running out of gas); 4 (Please call back at your convenience); 5 (Next time we just wreck your car); 6 (Reproducing problems).

Conclusion

We can now begin to expand upon Singer's (1980) original model of crazy systems and Kafka circuits (subroutines), by integrating more causes, intermediary processes, and outcomes, presented in Table 3.1. Table 3.2 indicates the extent to which each case includes components of this expanded model of unusual routines.

These tables are meant to anticipate the development of our UR model in later chapters. The reader will note that not all the elements of these tables are apparent in the cases described above, for a number of reasons. First, because we are intentionally, knowingly, and explicitly applying aspects of URs to these cases, some of the cases will not have as many entries as they might were these analyses of others' experiences. For example, simply being aware of the concept of URs, and the related entries, should help to reduce the *barriers to perception*; someone aware of the phenomenon and aspects of URs would likely perceive such experiences differently from someone who is not. Second, only deep analyses within the specific organization can begin to identify a variety of aspects, such as *strategic manipulation of information, limited conceptualization of user, unlinked costs and benefits, changing uses, contexts, conditions, conflicting goals and criteria, organizational culture, training, socialization,* and *organizational context* (see Chapters 5 and 9). Third, in addition to a deep knowledge of internal organizational processes, one would have to analyze entire sets of unusual routines over time to begin to identify some of the *intermediate* and *long-term consequences*. (See Chapters 4 and 9 for discussions of analyzing routines.)

4 | A multi-theoretical foundation for understanding unusual routines

Chapters 1 through 3 have provided a good basis for identifying, describing, and, to some small extent, explaining unusual routines. So far the analysis has primarily applied extensions of Singer's crazy systems perspective. However, both the phenomenon and the explanations are much more complex and subtle, and require the application of multiple theories, primarily from organizational and communication research.

The purpose of this chapter, then, is to further elaborate the conceptualization of URs, with the ultimate goal of developing it as an analytic tool and diagnostic. The first section summarizes five central theoretical approaches that form the basis for the case analysis in the following two chapters – systems theory, sensemaking theory, diffusion of innovation theory, socio-technical systems theory, and, especially relevant to our topic, organizational routines theory. The next section outlines a working model of URs with levels of analysis. The concluding section presents five general propositions about the creation of and change in URs, which the case study in Chapter 5 explores.

Five foundational theories for a preliminary model of unusual routines

Systems theory

Systems theory is not really a single theory, but several approaches with related sets of principles. Of relevance to our discussion of URs is general systems theory, social/open systems theory, and cybernetic systems theory.

General systems theory argues that "systems" are an integral structure of nature, and occur at all levels, from biological through astronomical (Bertalanffy, 1968). Four central principles of natural systems are that they consist of irreducible principles within a whole (i.e., wholeness, emergent), they strive to self-maintain in a changing environment, they arise in response to that environment, and there are coordinating interfaces within a hierarchy of larger systems (e.g., nature) (Laszlo, 1972, p. 23). Systems are also non-summative or emergent (more than the sum of its parts). Further, interactions of systems generate supersystems, which also display the same principles.

This generality of systems theory allows concepts and empirical relations to be considered at multiple levels. As an example, in celestial mechanics there are cumulative interactions between gravitating bodies, called *resonances*, that reinforce each other and critically influence the overall motion of the bodies, leading to possibly significant changes in orbits. For instance, in the band of asteroids between Jupiter and Mars, some asteroids have elliptical orbits that have resonances with Jupiter's orbit. Simple whole-number ratios of the orbits, reflecting convergence of the two orbits in reoccurring numbers of years, lead to cumulative gravitational effects, generating instability in the asteroids' orbits, eventually flinging some of them out of the band. Indeed, there are gaps in the asteroid band around these resonances, reflecting the large differences in orbits over long periods due to small initial differences (Peterson, 1993, pp. 168, 185). For our purposes, this may mean that social and organizational interactions that cross paths at infrequent but regular intervals may in fact generate instabilities, whether minimal and largely undetectable, or large but minimally predictable. This generation of instability "gets rid of stuff" (flings them out of proximate relations), leading to quasi-stability of the system as a whole, but eccentricity and deviance for a particular local system. Conversely, a critical problem occurs when an "accident" generates a regularity – that is, that can provide influence and feedback for future interactions. Even by chance some accidents will become frozen, and over time more frozen accidents produce regularities (Gell-Mann, 1994, p. 371). Some selection processes promote complexity, so complex regularities due to accidents become difficult to identify, much less change.

Open systems theory is founded on the principle that systems exchange energy, matter, and information with their environment. "An open system is a set of objects [or events] with attributes that interrelate in an environment. The system possesses qualities of wholeness, interdependence, hierarchy, self-regulation [or autopoiesis], environmental interchange, equilibrium [or homeostasis], adaptability, and equifinality" (Littlejohn, 1983, p. 32; bracketed terms from Gunaratne, 2008, p. 179). While some critiques argue that systems theory ignores social interaction per se, this problem was redressed both by Rogers and Kincaid's (1981) systems-oriented network analysis approach and by Weick's (1995) sensemaking approach. *Social* systems engage in (or are constituted through) communication or information to reduce complexity through selecting or processing (attributing meaning to, or constructing meaning from) only a portion of the environmental information. They maintain their identity through reproducing communication meaningful to the system itself. Habermas (1984) and Weick (1995), among others, argued that consensual meaning is created through iterative and adaptive communication (rational discourse, double interacts) referring to social norms and values.

In organizational theory the *open systems perspective* (Katz and Kahn, 1966) emphasizes that individual behavior creates structures at an organizational level (Taylor *et al.*, 2000, p. 99). An organization is an open system (Morgan, 1986, pp. 44–8). It is an entity which can be distinguished from its environment by a boundary; it is meaningful to talk of things "inside" and "outside" the organization, and we should note that what is inside and outside may vary over time. The boundary is permeable, so the organization can be influenced by forces in the external environment, including technological innovations. In response to a stimulus, the organization exhibits a tendency to maintain stability; a technological innovation will trigger an effort to establish a new equilibrium state. Within the organization we can identify subunits, each with their own boundaries; subunits can be tightly coupled (i.e., be highly interdependent) or loosely coupled (i.e., have little interdependency) (Weick, 1979, pp. 111–12). Because the organization is a socio-technical system (Hirschheim, 1985, pp. 167ff.), it is important to attend to both the (first-level) changes in efficiency, and the (second-level) changes in the social system (Sproull and Kiesler, 1991) which a technological innovation may trigger (discussed below).

Cybernetic systems theory proposes that systems attempt to maintain homeostasis through functional systems of control and feedback, or, more generally, regulation (Wiener, 1948, 1950/1967). A goal or criterion is set, often with an acceptable range of variance around that goal. The system seeks feedback about whether the current level of the criterion is within the acceptable range of variance. If not, the gap or discrepancy activates a system process for either increasing or decreasing the process(es) that affect the level of the criterion, intending to bring the level back within the acceptable variance range. Cybernetic theory characterizes internal and external feedback loops as *positive* or *deviation-amplifying* if the feedback information and the resulting internal processes increase the deviation from the criterion level; alternatively, they are *negative* or *deviation-reducing* if the information and processes decrease the deviation, back toward the criterion level. The classic example of a simple cybernetic control system is the thermostat.

Feedback loops may be *overdamped*, when feedback leads linearly to smaller deviations from a criterion level or goal; *underdamped*, when feedback oscillates about the criterion, but eventually converges; and *critically damped*, with very quick return to the criterion level (Barnett, 1997). Oscillations occur when the response exceeds the appropriate level or the system takes a long time to respond to the deviation in which case much energy is expended each time to respond to the prior over- or delayed reaction. Another outcome is possible: an organization may be unable to reduce the deviation in a consistent way, either because responses always exceed the criterion, or have no effect at all. In addition to this directional nature of feedback loops, there is a level aspect – *single-loop* learning and *double-loop* learning. The simple thermostat illustrates single-loop learning, where the goal criterion is the basis for both responding to, and evaluating the feedback. However, second-loop learning may also occur, involving the adaptation or changing of either the goal itself or the processes used to maintain that goal. In this case, the new process and feedback loops may create what appears to be deviation-amplifying single-loop learning, as the system seems to be diverging, perhaps radically, from the original criterion level, while operating within the acceptable variance of a higher-order system. Feedback loops may not only operate with different periodicities, but are not necessarily linear – that is, they may work faster or slower at different stages of the cycle, may shorten or elongate over time, and may or may not always activate their intersecting processes (Anderson *et al.*, 1999, p. 234).

Sensemaking theory

A subjectively-oriented application of system theory is *organizational sensemaking theory*. Weick's theory (1979, 1995) labels the state of confusion and uncertainty that can stem from confronting, dealing with, and resolving such complex problems as *equivocality* or *ambiguity*. One of the aims of organizing (organizational processes and interaction among organizational members) is to reduce this equivocality or ambiguity. From Weick's (1979, p. 27) point of view, "organizing consists of adapting to an enacted environment, an environment which is constituted by the actions of the interdependent human actors." Thus he emphasizes the "activity of organizing rather than the structure of organizations" (Bantz and Smith, 1977, p. 171). Weick (1995, p. 17) explores seven core characteristics that set sensemaking apart from ideas such as interpretation, attribution, and others: grounded in identity construction, retrospective, enactive of sensible environments, social, ongoing, focused on and by extracted cues, and driven by plausibility rather than accuracy. Four sets of interlocking processes constitute organizational sensemaking: *ecological change*, *enactment*, *selection*, and *retention*.

Sensemaking begins with ecological change, "when there is some change or difference in the organizational environment, resulting in disturbances or variations in the flows of experience affecting the organization's participants" (Choo, 1998, pp. 5–6), detected directly or comparatively. Enactment is the process whereby individuals create their environments through attending to and interpreting certain aspects of the larger environment. Organizational sensemaking identifies enactment (called "framing" by others) as part of the process of making sense of things. One must do more than just "discover" – respond to changes detected in environment – but also "enact" – proactively interpret the environment through experiments and probes. For example, often the nature of work and organization must be reconceptualized, setting a new agenda, in order to take advantage of the potential of a new practice or technology (such as word processing – see Johnson and Rice, 1987). "The process of innovating involves actively constructing a conceptual framework, imposing it on the environment, and reflecting on their interaction" (Brown and Duguid, 1996, p. 74).

Then, the process of organizing requires organizational members to select an explanation of what this enacted environment means, from the range of possible explanations. Selection occurs through iterative communication among the members (Eisenberg and Goodall, 1997, p. 109). During the selection process, communication generates possible and plausible answers to the question: what is going on here? (Choo, 1998). Then, selections that are deemed useable or functional at that moment are retained for future use, thus generating routines. "Retention is the storage of the initial information, the action taken, and the evaluation of the action for future reference" (Bantz, 1992, p. 173). Retention is one form of organizational memory or knowledge stock, and provides a mechanism for knowledge reuse (Markus, 2001; Walsh and Ungson, 1991). This sensemaking may be retained in the form of tentative or well-developed measures, routines, and organizational memory, which are now the new basis for sensing environmental equivocality.

Overall, organizing is an ongoing, cyclical process. An individual might engage in several cycles to reduce equivocality regarding a particular problem or issue, and each of these cycles both stimulates and is embedded in the reactions and responses of other individuals. Each of these cycles typically includes an *act*, an *interact*, and a *double interact*: "The person performs some action [act], which is accepted or rejected by a second person [interact], after which the first person makes some response to what the first person did [double interact]" (Weick, 1979, p. 74). It is the actions and behaviors involved in these cycles of social interaction and interpretation that foster sensemaking. Structures of meaning and action arise through the double interacts among people and subunits, or in the negotiation of scripts among organization members. People enact the structures by the actions they take, and take actions constrained by the structures they enact (Weick, 1979, p. 5; Weick, 1995, pp. 30–1). Organizational members need to experiment with different narratives to see which one best recreates the context of the problem and provides the best understanding about how to resolve it. This also leads to a revised, convergent narrative that will be useful in future situations; that is, this socially constructed narrative contributes to organizational memory and facilitates knowledge reuse. Constructed narratives – including knowing what and when to tell – also help develop the individual worker's identity as well as the identity of the community of practice. However, the concept of narrative does not reject the concept of causation or the utility of routinized measures. Indeed, the goal of a coherent account from users, clients, other workers, specialists, revised through working with the system or problem, is just such a causal account, however tentative or subjective. The need for, and the development of, such complex causal narratives, indicate just how subtle, ambiguous, and challenging work is (Brown and Duguid, 1996; Choo, 1998).

The more that subsystems (people, units, processes) are *loosely coupled* (less tightly interconnected and interdependent), the greater the possibility for adaptation and recovery from error (if only by buffering other subsystems through delays or insufficient strength of consequences), but also a greater potential for limiting clear understanding of the sources and causes of consequences (both positive and negative) of those other subsystems (Vaughan, 1999; Weick, 1979). Enactment is thus not only necessary but also fundamentally misinforming, by retrospective definition (through sensemaking) of the process as having been rational or at least consensually meaningful. Enacting or framing episodes, by selecting aspects for attention and associating them with general notions, may be more or less appropriate or suitable as a basis for later or others' actions, generating *ordinary troubles* (Goffman, 1974). Different frames of reference help characterize how employees process information differently, allowing the identification of problems and solutions, and affecting actions, which should be connected with actions in the organization (Westenholz, 1993). "The individual stays within his or her existing frame of reference and chooses the environmental responses that confirm this frame of reference" (p. 38, referring to March and Olsen, 1976). As the frame is a self-production process, environmental responses are not independent influences on the object of an individual's frame of reference. Thus, any responses within this perspective are likely to be single-loop learning, as the limits of one's frame of reference are not easily challenged (highlighted in discussions of barriers to feedback in Chapters 7 and 8).

Sometimes, though, this behavior cannot be explained within the identified frame of reference. This may be due to experiencing a paradoxical situation, whereby two incompatible frames are possible (Chapter 8). New frames may be socially constructed, and they may allow understanding and appropriate action. These may facilitate or constrain organizational change. Westenholz (1993) argues

that deframing may be able to cause the person to see how erroneous the prior perception of environmental responses was, so a new
frame must be constructed, possibly socially. In particular, a *cognitive paradoxical process* (p. 40) is needed, whereby different frames
are applied (Quinn and Cameron, 1988), which may appear as paradoxical actions. Examples in Westenholz's case study include balancing a company's internal vs. external affairs, and worker solidarity
vs. differential market wages. To these issues, employees took either
a *self-referential logical approach* (different members believed in
different models unambiguously, based on their separate logics), a
pluralistic approach (different members supported different models but tolerated differences), or an *inconsistent/varying approach*
(accepted the ambiguity of models, the difficulty of linking interests
and actions, and changing support for different models over time).
Experiencing differences in each of these approaches would be attributed to, respectively, ideological misunderstanding (the other is wrong,
resolve through persuasion or power), interest group conflicts (resolve
through negotiation, voting, or localized/fragmented solutions), and
inherent contradictions (passivity, confusion, loss of agency, devalu-
ing of meaningfulness of differences). Each approach, applied to other
members supporting other approaches (as described by Westenholz,
1993), generates its own examples of paradoxical or ironic perspectives, without the members being aware of them.

A foundational intersection between cybernetic control theory and
sensemaking is the double bind. A *double bind* involves "contradictory injunctions in that one is damned whether there is compliance or
disobedience to the demand made; in addition, one cannot discuss
or leave the situation or the relationship which is the source of the
injunction" (Siporin and Gummer, 1988, p. 210, referring to Bateson
et al., 1963). The double bind involves four conditions (Tarnas, 1991,
p. 419):

(1) an actor (classically, a child) is dependent, so accurate communication (classically, from the mother) is crucial;
(2) but the dependent receives information that is contradictory or
incompatible at different levels;
(3) the dependent is not allowed to ask questions to clarify the communication or resolve the incompatibility; and
(4) the dependent cannot exit.

From a psychological perspective, this untenable situation distorts both inner and outer realities, with serious psychopathological consequences. Inner feelings are repressed and denied (apathy), inner feelings are inflated (narcissism, egocentrism), the dependent slavishly submits to the external world, and the external world is aggressively objectified and exploited. The dependent tries to flee through escapism, drugs, or other behaviors. But, if unable to exit, then "anxiety, paranoia, chronic hostility, a feeling of helpless victimization, a tendency to suspect all meanings, an impulse toward self-negation, a sense of purposelessness and absurdity, a feeling of irresolvable inner contradiction, a fragmenting of consciousness" may occur – in the extreme, "self-destructive violence, delusional states, massive amnesia, catatonia, automatism, mania, nihilism" (Tarnas, 1991, p. 421).

Beyond the familiar psychological double bind, Jamieson (1995) considered more sociological and political aspects. Here, a double bind is a situation that involves "a powerful and a powerless individual, or … social and institutional norms and a vulnerable class … a double bind occurs if two or more persons, one of them the victim, undergo a repeated experience in which one 'primary negative injunction' conflicts with a second, both 'enforced by punishments or signals which threaten survival,' and from which the victim has no means of escape" (p. 13). She suggests several types of double binds, and specifically their manifestations for women. Imposing an either/or, positive/negative frame on a situation creates a *no-choice choice*. One kind of a *self-fulfilling prophecy* is being condemned for not doing what you are forbidden to do. *No-win (neither/nor) situations* occur when one is judged against the opponent's standard. *Unrealizable or contradictory expectations* require excessive or mutually exclusive abilities or characteristics. And the all-too-familiar *double standard* involves being treated and evaluated on different grounds, or differently on the same grounds, than those who are doing the treatment and evaluation.

Related to the general process of sensemaking, and the particular condition of unusual routines, is the *antipattern*. If a problem is difficult to first identify or diagnose, it will surely be difficult to correct. As discussed above, over time, through sensemaking and retention, organizations and individuals develop recurring ways to respond to problems. LaPlante and Neill (2006) call these "patterns," or familiar and named pairs of problems and solutions that are usable in different contexts. Patterns involve a conflict/problem, a typical solution (sufficiently general to be applied to recurring problems in different contexts, in varying ways), and positive and negative consequences. These are, of course, retentions.

One general form of problem (a meta-problem) is where the conventional solution generates more negative consequences than positive benefits – an "antipattern," involving "dysfunctional approaches to problem solving" (p. 4). Their approach is derived from prior taxonomies of antipatterns by Koenig (1995) and Brown *et al.* (1998). Identifying and understanding the existence and the types of antipatterns is a general prerequisite for beginning to identify or diagnose the particular or specific problem at hand.

LaPlante and Neill (2006) ground their typology of antipatterns in research on negative personality types (such as aggressives, indecisives, negativists, clams, bulldozers, and superagreeables with no follow-through perhaps due to conflict avoidance; Bramson, 1988) and on group process and managerial motivation theories. They describe over twenty types of management antipatterns (caused by individual supervisors or general management) and over twenty-five types of environmental antipatterns (caused by salient organizational strategy or culture, or broader socio-political influences). Similar to unusual routines, management antipatterns are "dysfunctional behavior[s] of individual managers, or pervasive management practices that inhibit success" (p. xxi). Further, the baker's dozen of context or foci of these antipatterns range from communication and finances to personnel and technology. Many antipatterns have multiple foci (and may even occur in clusters, or "swarms," of antipatterns; p. 11). For example, the management antipattern of "plate spinning" involves honesty, personality, and process, whereby "an insincere manager can distract his critics from the real problems by dispatching employees on a series of meaningless and time-consuming tasks" (p. 123). From the crazy systems and unusual routines perspective, this involves work and delay circuits. LaPlante and Neill characterize each of these antipatterns by a name, a central concept, the dysfunction and its symptoms, an example, an explanation, a "band-aid" or short-term fix (though they do not consider how band-aids can create larger and longer-term problems), a self-repair (guidance for the perpetuator), refactoring (the individual, institutional or cultural changes needed to resolve the situation), and identification (a short assessment tool for diagnosing the existence and type of antipattern).

Diffusion of innovation theory and socio-technical systems theory

An organizational innovation is at least as much a human process as a technical process (Rice, 2009b; Rogers, 2003). Organizational structures and systems are not entities existing apart from the human actors, but rather are generated, affirmed, or modified through the actions of organization members (Poole *et al.*, 1985, pp. 76–7). An organization's response to an innovation (structural or procedural change, technology) is affected by both intrinsic characteristics of the innovation, and characteristics of the organization into which it is introduced (Rogers, 2003). An innovation is likely to be a highly equivocal situation; as the organization members struggle to make sense of it, they may argue about it, or fall back on earlier decisions. To the observer, these pre-existing patterns appear to be scripts which guide or constrain the current interactions among the members (Weick, 1995, p. 71). Organizational members may perceive (correctly or incorrectly) certain advantages or disadvantages to its adoption. The innovation may seem compatible or incompatible with existing practices, beliefs, or organizational values; it may seem appropriately, or unnecessarily, complex. Once introduced into an organization, members may adapt the innovation to purposes the designers did not foresee, reinventing it as something substantially different from its starting point in the organization (Johnson and Rice, 1987; Rogers, 2003). The results of these complex processes are, unfortunately, not always beneficial for the entire organization, some of its members, or some of its clients. First-level consequences are typically intentional, beneficial, and near-term, while second-level consequences may be unintentional, negative, and delayed (Rogers, 2003). Since human behaviors are neither consistently rational nor entirely goal-directed, and since human agency is both enabled and constrained by the social systems in which people find themselves (Banks and Riley, 1993, p. 171), it is not surprising that an innovation can yield a mixture of harms and benefits.

Thus, as advocates of a socio-technical system approach to implementation have noted, the successful adoption of an innovative information system depends largely on jointly optimizing both the social and technical aspects of both the system and the implementation process (Hirschheim, 1985, pp. 167ff.). Systems analysis has traditionally been the domain of technical experts, trained in methods for identifying management's, users', and sometimes customers' needs and translating those into system features and constraints. On the other hand, implementation research has traditionally been the domain of social science experts, trained in methods for identifying relations among measurable variables and effects associated with systems and implementation policies (Lucas, 1981). An extension of this approach considers strategic aspects of implementing information systems, applying economic and political economy analyses (Keen, 1991; Scott Morton, 1991; Strassman, 1983).

There has been, as well, a growing awareness that both technical and social aspects are contextual and interrelated, often leading to contradictory, unintended, or paradoxical implementation obstacles, uses or outcomes (Ehrlich, 1987; Gattiker, 1990; Hirschheim, 1985; Johnson and Rice, 1987; Markus, 1984; Pasmore, 1988; Pava, 1983; Rice, 2004; Rice and Schneider, 2006; Sproull and Kiesler, 1991; Zuboff, 1984). A powerful, unstated, and often unknown assumption about information systems design is that the new, routinized, standard, efficient procedures will not only perform the technical tasks, but also remove threats associated with the prior processes. Thus there is no explicit consideration in either the technical or managerial procedures associated with the new system about the rise and maintenance of distortions, cover-ups (Argyris, 1985, p. 339), or URs. It is reasonable, then, to also expect a new ICT, however well or badly managed, to impact both job tasks and the social system – whether by accident or by design – in both positive and negative ways, both intended and unintended.

The introduction of a new network technology into an organization has the potential to profoundly change the communication flows within the organization, and thereby profoundly change group processes. Change in the organization's communication system can facilitate and stimulate change in work methods, structures, meanings, and relationships (Rice and Gattiker, 2001). The rules for organizational behavior are fixed by neither custom nor power, but can be altered in their enactment as organization members get their work done. Organizational structure (resources and behavior rules) both constrains action and is itself created by actions (Poole *et al.*, 1985).

As an example, Pentland and Feldman (2008) analyzed the implementation of a common system for two formally separate university continuing education programs – one on labor education, and another on human resource management. The labor program used a mix of custom mainframe software and manual analysis while the HR program used off-the-shelf PC integrated software. Both had to interface with the university accounting system, with difficulty. So the university chose a standardized commercial software package (an evolution from their HR current software), on a server, with better access and updating, consolidated accounting information and enrollment and registration information, allowed task rotation and coverage across staff, and management to get reports. In spite of these advantages, and good design elements developed through committee discussions, obstacles emerged. Eventually the labor program moved to a stand-alone PC system while HR used only some features of the networked program, and there was no unified university-level accounting and reporting. The outcomes were not due to technical failures, but to differences in the university's continuing education programs, such as identification, protection, boundaries, and control over seminars and data. The results were not, thus, necessarily "irrational." The underlying cause, Pentland and Feldman (2008) argue, was a disconnect between the technical design (the artifacts) and the participants' work processes. Schultze and Orlikowski (2004) reported on how the implementation of a self-serve information system in a bricks-and-clicks dotcom (a general broker in the small group health insurance market) increased the difficulty of maintaining relationships with customers and the agent's information load, affected the nature and quality of shared information, made it difficult for sales representatives to provide consulting to customers, decreased the frequency of interaction between the sales representative and their customers, and required sales representatives to use their social capital to foster agents' adoption of the system and to resolve errors caused by system dysfunctionalities. Overall, it created challenges to the company's business model.

Although practitioners often spend a lot of time attending to the details of the technology, networks are best thought of not as collections of computer hardware and software, but rather as the potential and actual patterns of communications among people. Networks are emergent communication processes, and both affect and reflect communication behaviors (Contractor and Eisenberg, 1990). The organizational changes that may be induced by a new communication technology are not easy to predict. It is not a given that simply adding a technology to an existing organizational environment will have a profound or lasting effect on the organization, and certainly no guarantee that any such effects will be positive or equal for all members of the organization (Johnson and Rice, 1987).

While some outcomes arising from the use of information and information systems in organizations may be negative, or are unintended and unexpected, in other cases they may be explicitly serving strategic self-interests at the expense of the larger organizational needs (Feldman and March, 1981; Zmud, 1990). In general, our reliance on large-scale systems requires a good degree of blind faith in their benevolence (see Giddens, 1990); we may be unaware of the full cost of this reliance.

Scholars have, of course, identified many dimensions of social systems in organizations. Of particular interest here are group processes. Because communication is at the heart of a group, a new communication technology has a significant potential to alter that process (Eveland and Bikson, 1989). For example, *process gains* from a communication system can include greater available information, critique and stimulation, and organizational learning; *process losses* can include overload, inability to recall relevant information, free-riding, domination, and pressures to conform (Nunamaker *et al.*, 1991, p. 46; Steiner, 1972).

Organizations may evolve dysfunctional structures (Giddens, 1984, p. xxxi) which resist well-intentioned problem-solving efforts, or even evade identification as problems. Deming (1986, p. 315) estimated that over 90 percent of the variation in any system is attributable to the system, not to the people working in the system. Another way of stating this is that all workers perform within a system that is (largely) beyond their control. He also argues that system variation does not vary randomly across workers; that is, variation comes from several (or many) potentially identifiable sources.

In sum, there are good reasons to look for changes in the organization when an ICT is introduced into a work environment where the predominant channels have been face-to-face, telephone, and print text (Rice, 1987; Rice and Gattiker, 2001). We can expect that the communication technology and social system will interact in complex ways, that the outcome is neither technologically determined nor organizationally determined (Bowers, 1995, p. 203), and that the effects of the ICT introduction into the organization can simultaneously be positive and negative, and vary from subunit to subunit. It would therefore not be surprising to find that a new ICT might simultaneously create, destroy, exacerbate, or mitigate URs within an organization.

Organizational routines theory

Definitions and conceptualizations of routines

A considerable literature considers organizational routines as a fundamental aspect of organizational economic behavior (see Lazaric and Becker, 2007). An organizational routine is (1) a set of interdependent executable capabilities, (2) recurrent (by a collectivity of the same or different people, at same or different times), (3) involving repetitive processing of similar information over multiple instances, (4) according to a set of rules or policies, (5) learned in an organization, (6) subject to selective pressures, (7) contextual (whereby the routine is more or less appropriate), (8) generally not deliberative (that is, increasingly tacit, implicit, or automatic, but may also include intentional choice), and (9) containing constituent actions that function as a unit (Cohen *et al.*, 1996; Felin and Foss, 2009; Guennif and Mangolte, 2002; Hodgson, 2008; Kesting, 2004).

More abstractly, routines may be characterized by their location on four primary dimensions (Cohen *et al.*, 1996). The first is explicit/implicit (tacit): the more implicit, the less able to be articulated or applied to other procedures. The second is local/distributed: the more local, the more specific and explicit the representing symbol and the location of storage, the lower requirement for joint activation of multiple components (such as organizational members), and the easier for one person to completely describe the routine. The third is context independent/dependent (situated): the more context dependent, the more the routine is activated by and associated with, and relevant and effective in, a particular context (including other organizational members/roles and their knowledge). Thus what might seem routinized for one might seem deliberative for another. This helps to explain why URs are so difficult to identify by those embedded in them. The fourth is search (preparation) intensive/knowledge (deliberation) intensive: routines may be more focused on preparing for action or more on applying knowledge to perform the action; alternatively, both preparation and deliberation themselves may be more or less routinized.

Routines are conditional, and stimulated by triggers into coordinating repeatable behavior, but they are *not* the behaviors. In this sense, routines per se are not "predictable;" indeed, they are often quite informal and depend on tacit knowledge (Cohen *et al.*, 1996, p. 23). They are, however, relatively enduring, persistent, and consistent, with similar outputs depending on similar inputs. Because of the procedural and enduring aspects, routines can become obsolete, or dysfunctional, but still be repeated in response to given triggers or cues (p. 23). The interactions and routines are shaped, supported, reinforced, or constrained by the social, physical, and organizational environment. Thus, the concept of *routines* provides an alternative foundational approach to neo-classical decision-making (rational, intentional, fully informed, individual-based decision-making).

Conceptualizations of routines typically apply two perspectives (Guennif and Mangolte, 2002): one focusing on technical and cognitive aspects of the firm (Nelson and Winter, 1982), and another on social aspects, especially the tension between individual effort discretion and organizational norms or policies (Leibenstein, 1966).

According to the first conceptualization, organizational routines are the necessary skills and capacities to quickly, in a programmed fashion, respond to a situation, without a large disjuncture between decision and action (and thus little deliberation). Routines, therefore, imply both how to perform the action (routine in action) as well as how to determine what action to take (memory or repertoire). Both thus presume existing knowledge, whether tacit or explicit. Repertoires of routines are where innovations can occur, and where organizational coordination of the separate actions must occur. Activated routines produce messages or signals to others in the organization about what to do next, which in turn stimulate other routines in action. Organizational coordination across these relationships creates a potential cognitive coherence of the repertoires (Leibenstein, 1966, p. 5). Based on the technical/cognitive perspective of routines, there are at least five components of coordinated performance: (1) an initial message stimulating a (2) repertoire that implements a (3) routine in action, which in turn produces (4) one or more other messages, leading to an (5) overall interdependent flow of messages, repertoires, and actions.

Nelson and Winter (1982) grounded their conceptualization of routines in evolutionary terms, involving variation, selection, and replication, with routines serving as organizational memory or, metaphorically, genes. Routines begin with individual skills and tacit knowledge used in a coordinated sequence of behavior that meets objectives given a context – that is, the technical and cognitive perspective. Felin and Foss (2009) argue that while this approach was related to prior work on organizational behavioral theory and the notions of bounded rationality, programmed procedures, satisficing, and individual-level processes (Cyert and March, 1963), much later work has paid more attention to collective, unintentional, and unobservable aspects of routines (similar to our perspective on URs). The shift from the individual to the organizational (collective) level typically ignores motivations, ability, and social pressures, conceptualizing these issues away by referring to an *organizational truce* that suspends such individual and social differences and discrepancies, allowing routines to organize actions and choice.

As humans attempt to operate within bounded cognitive processing and rationality, it is adaptive to develop routines for common and familiar situations. Routines help reduce cognitive demands on actors, so that they not only can conduct the given task better and faster, but also attend to other, less routinized tasks. A social form of cognitive load is the demands, central to organizations, of coordination and collaboration. Other organizational or environmental influences, including culture and politics, affect both the development and selection of routines as well as responses to discussions about those routines; they may also include competing routines. Routines also emerge due to contextual conditions. For example, cognitive functioning occurs more easily with lower levels of conflict, so actors achieve the organizational truce by agreeing on a routine, a more or less standard way of accomplishing the task, so that debates about the approach do not come up every time the task appears. Routines may be shaped and maintained through a number of devices: individuals' memories about an action's role in an overall pattern; local sensemaking through shared language and norms; physical artifacts, arrangements, written procedures; organizational practices including personnel training and rotation, archives, exemplars, organizational structure; and broad cultural and symbolic language, from codes to war stories (i.e., similar to culture) (Cohen *et al.*, 1996).

The second conceptualization is grounded in Leibenstein's (1966) concerns with performance, trust, and organizational conventions (Guennif and Mangolte, 2002). Organizational members have more or less *effort discretion*, which, in the aggregate, affects organizational performance. Principal–agent theory explains the tension here between performing at the level and form desired by the principal, and the level and form provided by the agent. The role of effort discretion in the variability and change of routines is discussed below.

Pentland and Feldman (2005) provided a conceptual and methodological framework for organizational routines by distinguishing among *performative*, *ostensive*, and *artifacts* aspects. Performative aspects are the actual collective work activities, sequence, and location; they are inherently improvisatory and divergent because of conditions, interpretations, and human agency. Ostensive aspects are the script, or abstract or generalized pattern of the routine, or the rules for action and the underlying norms and values. Ostensive aspects of a particular routine may have many fine-grained variations, with multiple interpretations and understanding, and are to some extent created through the performance over events or time. Because understanding is contextual and subject, any particular organizational routine has multiple ostensive and performative aspects.

Finally, artifacts are the physical evidence of the performative and ostensive aspects, such as machinery, physical space, written protocols, standard operating procedures, work instructions, constraints and facilitators. One way to foster dependability, consistency, and predictable expectations for a routine is to emphasize or impose the use of the artifacts. In this sense, people are able to refer to those repeatable and understandable sequences of actions as the "routine." Thus artifacts both represent and influence both the ostensive and performative aspects of organizational routines. Artifacts may represent performative aspects through activity tracking, or ostensive aspects through a policy statement. And artifacts may influence, or attempt to influence, ostensive and performative aspects.

But, as the artifacts themselves are frequently subject to participants' understanding (interpretation and sensemaking), they do not fix either the ostensive or performative aspects (though some aspects do, such as removing software features or requiring specific inputs). In the case of ICT, choosing different features, capabilities and action sequences (adaptive structuration, reinvention; Johnson and Rice, 1987; Majchrzak *et al.*, 2000) generates variety in both the ostensive and performative aspects of a routine. The human may have a different understanding than the designers or the artifact, and impose variety on the routine, creating workarounds (discussed below, pp. 133ff). More subtly, facilitation and constraining are relative to specific actions or subsets of routines. So, for example, the entire routine will generally be facilitated/constrained by larger technologies and routines, and not solely by the embedded technology. These artifacts are thus not, themselves, the ostensive or performative aspects of the routine.

Focusing on artifacts, and assuming routines are bureaucratically straightforward, leads to software and system design that assumes formulaic uses and easily implementable and followable rules. Pentland and Feldman (2005, 2008) state that routines based solely on artifacts, and those that have been ignored by participants because their understandings and practices were not included in the development process, are *dead routines*. Rather, organizational routines are generative systems, producing *live routines* involving both ostensive and performative aspects, with associated artifacts.

Perceptions of each of the performative, ostensive, and artifact aspects may differ and change. The ostensive aspect may appear simple or stable (to participants or researchers) while the performative aspect seems quite complex or variable, and vice versa. The performative, ostensive, and artifact aspects interact, and may diverge. These divergences, as discussed throughout this book, may be beneficial or harmful, locally or more globally. Divergence between ostensive and performative aspects may support or indicate greater flexibility and change, but also provide opportunities for factionalism and conflict, in turn leading to decline or innovation. Convergence between ostensive and artifact aspects may indicate appropriate training, motivation, and understandings, or authority and control of principal–agent linkage. Ostensive and artifact aspects may be closely aligned due to legal mandates (such as wording or procedures allowed or required), or artifacts may serve as an externalized form of consensual understanding of what is "meant" by the ostensive aspect. But, as discussed in Chapter 8, ostensive and performance aspects may drift far away from the artifacts over time without actors realizing it.

Another way of reading Kafka's and Singer's work is that the underlying challenge is to discover or assert which is the consequential reality, the source of rewards and punishments – the actual performance, the ostensive aspect, or the artifact? In many of Kafka's stories, these diverge, and no one knows or is able to decide which one predominates, allowing the "system" to punish or immobilize anyone attempting to take any action or engage in sensemaking of the various signals. Convergent and stable routines thus serve an important role as an organizational truce: the routine is a (potential and temporary) resolution to conflicts about power and action (Pentland and Feldman, 2005), allowing people to make sense of inputs, take action, and identify outputs and their consequences.

To the ostensive, performative, and artifact aspects of routines, Becker and Zirpoli (2008) add *collective dispositions*, involving knowledge and memory, triggered by context or input, as the means for developing an understanding of the causal mechanism generating the recurrent interaction pattern (Hodgson and Knudsen, 2004). Analyzing dispositions requires more than just observations of the behavior; rather, it demands a deep understanding of collective practices and understandings. For example, the emergence of some behaviors as recurrent interaction patterns (routines) is due to a collective disposition to attend to organizational costs, rewards, resources, and constraints (the inputs or triggers) and follow the less difficult, uncertain, or conflictful approach (the disposition). This disposition may in turn increase divergence between ostensive and performative aspects of the routine, or adapt one to the other, thus decreasing the routine's contribution to overall positive performance (whether locally or globally), or generating workarounds and URs. While the specific form of the aspects of the routine, and the divergence, may not be generalizable across organizational activities, collective dispositions may be. Chapter 5 highlights how some dispositions (valued scripts) foster URs.

Benefits of routines

General outcomes associated with these recurrent interaction patterns are increased coordination, reduced demand on cognitive resources, reduced error and waste, reduced task-related information search, greater accountability and feedback focus, quality (consistent high level), flexibility and adaptability (through ability to recombine modules of the routine), and learning (using feedback from comparison with a consistent baseline, minimizing noise and flawed understanding of causal relations), increased certainty, store developed and shared knowledge, decreased conflict through organizational truces and improved coordination of action (Becker, 2004, 2005; Turner, 2005). Alternatively, rigid and stable organizational routines can be seen as stifling adaptation to environmental changes, and innovation. Thus routines theory is also concerned with variation and change in routines.

Variability in discretion, effort, and performance of routines

Given the nature of routines and the tension between repeatability and social performance, what appear as formal procedures may evolve, mutate, be redesigned, or replaced, due to variability in interpretation, contexts, effort, and evaluation. But how might that occur, and how constrained are actors in both performing and changing routines?

From the technical/cognitive perspective on routines, each component of coordinated performance, of course, represents opportunities for errors, dysfunctions, misunderstandings, need for adaptations, control points, principal–agent discrepancies, manipulation, etc. (Guennif and Mangolte, 2002). Negative variations may occur in the actions without variations in the repertoires, and, more interestingly, actions may be replicated even though the repertoire has been changed. Cognitive coherence emerges only as long as there is no intra-organizational conflict arising from disparate interests and motivations involved in the particular interdependent flow – i.e., the truce (Nelson and Winter, 1982), though, more accurately, multiple truces, through multiple relationships, processes, and levels in the organization. The more general argument is that there is no straightforward or unique relationship between organizational inputs and outputs. For our purposes this means that routines do not determine behavior, are not necessarily replicated each time, and may diverge and evolve, thus conceptually allowing the development of local URs.

Based on the social aspects conceptualization of routines, typically members operate at some sort of compromise, or normative, level of effort. Importantly, they also come to expect others to do the same, forming a *social habit* or *effort convention* (Leibenstein, 1987, pp. 75–6), another form of organizational truce. This is different from the *truce* notion that organizational participants suspend their differences and motivations to maximally and repetitively perform the routine, because this form is a truce about what level of, and variation in, effort, motivations, and interests are jointly acceptable. Management and professions influence the effort convention by incentives, work conditions, socialization, modeling, and sanctions; members of one's social network influence the effort convention by inheritance, habit, modeling, cohesion, social pressure, and perhaps professional norms and union principles. A group norm for effort convention is less susceptible to sanctions than individual effort discretion, so groups have a considerable say where along the level of effort discretion its members perform. Thus, in addition to the familiar principal/agent discretion process, management also must have sufficient trust and cohesion from relevant groups to apply incentives or sanctions aimed at maintaining a desired effort convention.

Social habits and effort conventions may be dynamically constructed, sometimes with unintentional consequences. For example, achieving high performance through performing consistent routines may unintentionally and indirectly reinforce constraints. For example, in the case of waste pick-up, good crews that perform consistent routines strengthen customers' expectations for good and consistent service, and their associated timing and placement of waste containers, which generate constraints on, and negative feedback about, later unplanned or necessary changes in the crews' routines (Turner, 2005). Thus it may be more adaptive to vary among a small number of effective patterns, to develop expectations of both quality and change, therefore maintaining the possibility of responding to changes or improving the routine without negative evaluations.

Guennif and Mangolte (2002) integrate the cognitive/technical and social/effort conceptualizations of routines to develop an explanation of organizational routines, performance, conflict, and cooperation. The repertoire level of routines includes both practical/cognitive knowledge as well as the effort conventions. An interesting implication is that the technical skills required for any routine in action are also always associated with rules and conventions for social relations involved in accomplishing the action. Thus "even when a set of duly codified official rules and procedures exist, the productive behavior of the organization members can never be reduced to these rules" (p. 19) due both to the tacit nature of some knowledge relevant to the repertoire and the routine in action, and the variability and discrepancies due to effort conventions and diversions from the truce state. These two interact, such as when tacit knowledge allows greater variance from the truce state. "Routine is thus inscribed within a social dimension" (p. 14).

Weick (1995) argues that organizing reduces differences and equivocality, by generating recurring behaviors, cognitive categories, and a framework of actions (retained routines); thus, organizing is generalizing. But, because humans must continually adapt to changes in the environment while accomplishing their routines, and elements of routines are socially defined and subject to variations in representation, then both the routines and the generalizations are intrinsically unstable (Feldman, 2000; Tsoukas and Chia, 2002, p. 573). Because of the social foundations of routines, replication of routines requires not just transfer of information, but practices as well as relationships and structures. Thus the implementation, adaptation, and repair of routines may be particularly difficult in the absence of their associated relationships and structures (Hodgson, 2008). That is, routines are context-dependent. One example of this is that the activation or proper functioning of routines may require complementary actions, resources, or other routines. Thus routines are necessarily under- or even mis-specified when designed in general, and applied in different contexts in particular (Becker, 2004). Therefore those attempting to implement a routine may also need specific repair or maintenance skills, such as interpretation and judgment. More fundamentally, routines represent the encoding of past inferences, so if either the inferences had weak validity, or the response derived from the inference was weakly operationalized, the resulting routine will be flawed if not dysfunctional (Becker, 2004).

This means that actions associated with a particular routine are not clearly distinguished or defined by the boundaries of the routine (what Tsoukas and Chia, 2002, more generally refer to as an instance of a category). Rather, there is much ordering and variance (instability) in typicality within a category, around prototypical core instances. So a category, or recurring set of behaviors, can change as different instances become more or less prototypical, due to adaptive and improvisatory behaviors. Indeed, the non-prototypical instances (i.e., divergences from the formal routine), especially as they are closed to the category boundaries, must be interpreted, assessed by convention, jointly constructed, and based in prior knowledge. A category boundary may be extended, through practice and understanding, to include what was earlier a non-instance of the category, to a non-prototypical instance of the category. Thus there are shadowy, shifting areas of routines and procedures, open to adjustment, adaption, and redefinition.

So exceptions and non-routine behaviors require interpretations and category shifts that may transform those into expected and routine behaviors, if only locally. At the same time as the elements of the routine are being adjusted and re-categorized, humans reflexively interact with their own thoughts, create new meanings, innovate, and apply linguistic representations, thus generating new descriptions. This process may be fostered, or suppressed, more in some units and organizations than others. Due to these two kinds of interactions (external and internal), the reinterpretations of the routine may range from minimal to radical; each set of interactions, and adjustments to them, generates additional interactions, and potential adjustments to them. As people interact with others and interrelate their actions, they create a new pattern and categorical boundary, embedding those changes into a large network of routines, routinizing them.

Routinization implies performing the same sequence of behaviors under the same environmental conditions, without much deliberation – but both "behaviors" and "conditions" are rife with ambiguity and variance (Cohen *et al.*, 1996). However, the key is the generating mechanism (the set of condition-action rules applied), not the specific (variable) behaviors. Indeed, depending on the condition-action rules, a wide variety of behavior sequences could meet the requirements of a given routine. So, URs can develop when a routine is equally applied but allows wide variation in behavior, or when there is a large gap or even inconsistency between procedures and goals. For example, a standard operating procedure is an artifact, a representation of a routine, not the routine (contextualized action pattern) itself. Indeed, (1) not only do contextualized action patterns diverge notoriously from formal and explicit standardized policies and procedures, and (2) following the exact standard operating procedures will bring most tasks and even organizations to chaos or a standstill, but (3) it is quite common for newly promulgated (improved and explicit!) procedures to simply be ignored. Further, interpretive and semantic variability in communication about both behaviors and conditions is typically so great and unrecognized, that an individual may be applying either widely different rules and not know it, or be applying the same procedures in widely different or invalid ways and also not know it. Ordinary sets of rules or procedures cannot cover all relevant possibilities, and individuals are bounded rationally so they typically do not know or apply all the rules or the contingencies anyway, and even more so when multiple individuals are involved in a collaborative or coordinated activity. Thus URs may be an organic byproduct of inherent variation in established but weakly bounded routines.

Change in routines

The stability and patterning of routines, implies, in the extreme, that they do not so much change as develop defects (variation or mutation) and are selected out, in a gene-like evolutionary process which itself is a higher-level routine (Nelson and Winter, 1982). Guennif and Mangolte (2002) propose that *repertoires* and *routine decisions* provide stability through a set of possible *routine actions* more specifically appropriate for each context.

However, most conceptualizations of routines do allow for change and adaptation. Because they are processual, routines naturally decay, requiring maintenance but, as described above, also generating variation, resulting in improved, degraded, and dysfunctional routines. The processual nature also means that different routines operate at different speeds, over different life cycles and periods; thus they may interact in incompatible or reinforcing ways (Becker, 2004), representing the more general process of unsynchronized feedback loops, discussed in the systems theory section (pp. 109–10).

Allowing more active and intentional change in routine is Feldman and Pentland's (2003) concept of *performative* routine. Here, the extent to which using a routine meets the actors' goals determines whether the routine is used identically, or whether it is adapted. As with systems theory, adaptation of the routine occurs in order to maintain homeostasis. If routine actions continue to meet the goal's range of acceptance, actors continue to apply the routine identically. In this, more action-based approach to routines, routines emerge iteratively from action, slowly replacing the process of, or need for, controlling action. Yet this change comes about in a variety of ways, and not always according to the processes or goals of the formal routine.

Routines may be changed (or prevented from doing so) during repetition in both *undeliberate* and *deliberate* ways (Kesting, 2004). Undeliberate change means that adaptations of a routine occur as part of the attempt to accomplish, through repetition of actions and learning how to perform the routine better, a familiar goal – as opposed to a deliberate, planned redesign of the routine. Stability of goal through repetition of actions typically does not require or involve validation or deliberation during the repetition. So as long as the results are not observably and significantly discrepant from the intended goals, the routine will not be analyzed, variations may occur, and the routine may change. Assessment of the variability and change is limited to only that which can be observed, within one's domain and time frame – that is, not "objectively" and "externally" observable – and significance is contextual and actor-defined.

Deliberate change includes both conscious refreshing of an existing routine action as well as altering or replacing that routine action with a new action. While most business activities are more or less routine (at least at the repertoire level), the small percent of exceptions requires the bulk of managerial attention, deliberation, and rationality (Felin and Foss, 2009). An intriguing implication is that organizational differentiation and advantage comes from individual choice in resolving these exceptions, not in rigidly processing the routines, as those solutions provide the basis for developing new routines. Thus it may be beneficial to spend much more time and energy (both pragmatically and theoretically) on learning how to respond to exceptions and convert those insights into routines (or, as Johnson and Rice, 1987, argue, fostering reinvention).

However, many factors work against deliberate change of routine actions: limited actor processing capabilities; others opposing the change because it may create negative consequences for them; inertia in programmed behavior developed through the initial routine; design and initiation of the new action inspiring greater responsibility than performing the repetitions of the new action; cultural or organizational biases rewarding shirking responsibility for possible failures or disadvantages of change; future and collective benefits taking the back seat to short-term and individual benefits; and past experience indicating that changes to routines do not always lead to improved or expected outcomes (Kesting, 2004).

Changing a routine involves costs, such as increased cognitive demand involved in designing a new routine, the learning curve associated with the action, and managing the uncertainty associated with incomplete knowledge of and experience with the routine. If the apparent costs (including the number of repetitions to achieve the desired effectiveness and efficiency, and the level of performance attained) of continuing the current repetition are less than the apparent costs of switching, rational actors will maintain the repetition; this argument is similar to transaction costs analysis. It may be especially rational not to change the routine action if the routine is repeated infrequently (so that the eventual payoff is far into the future while costs are present). Alternatively, one might switch to a new routine that is less effective, but much easier to learn, if it will not be repeated many times, again as a way to reduce transaction costs. Therefore "it is not always *rational* to change a routine action even when there exists a more attractive alternative" (Kesting, 2004, p. 14). According to Pentland and Feldman (2008), resistance to changed routines (such as new technology) is the greatest when design is exogenous, the intended goal is to change familiar patterns of action, the artifact(s) is conceptualized as the routine, and when functional events primarily involve human interactants rather than automated procedures (see Chapter 8 for many related concepts).

Workarounds

In general, one trigger for change in (or bypassing of) routines is an interruption of a routine, either by the absence of the expected or the presence of the unexpected. Increased interruptions may lead to search for or adoption of new, external routines. Also, the same trigger may occur in different contexts, so the activated routine may be inappropriate, suboptimal, or harmful (Becker, 2004). More specifically, an alternative or response to, and a bypassing of, formally performing routines, and possibly a source for new routines, is the *workaround*. Workarounds are "work patterns an individual or a group of individuals create to accomplish a crucial work goal within a system of dysfunctional work processes that prohibits the accomplishment of that goal or makes it difficult" (Morath and Turnbull, 2005, p. 52), or "informal temporary practices for handling exceptions to normal work flow" (Kobayashi *et al.*, 2005, p. 1561; see also Gasser, 1986, for an early discussion of the concept).

Workarounds are different from errors and mistakes, deviance, and shortcuts. Unlike an error, a workaround attempts to achieve the desired outcome (though a workaround may generate subsequent errors), but not by the intended procedure. A workaround is not technically a mistake, because it is intended and not necessarily of lower quality than the formal "correct" procedure. Indeed, a workaround may be developed over time by multiple participants, resulting in a more elegant and insightful procedure. While workarounds deviate from formal procedures, they are not fundamentally intended as deviant behaviors; their central motivation is to accomplish what appears, or is rewarded, as the main, valued, goal, within the group's functional norms. However, workarounds may create negative or destructive consequences, similar to deviant behaviors. Workarounds are more general than shortcuts, which are specifically intended to reduce the time required to accomplish the goal (Halbesleben *et al.*, 2008) but – we know from much personal experience – may cost more in the long run, and create other blocks and subsequent workarounds.

The primary stimulus for workarounds are *workflow blocks* (Halbesleben *et al.*, 2008). Workflow blocks may be either intended or unintended. General sources of intended workflow blocks include changes in policies, work design, technology, or management control. An intended block is meant to improve outcomes by preventing errors or mistakes, such as occupational safety procedures; so working around intended workflow blocks courts known risks. Healthcare organizations have adopted medical and administrative technologies, reporting systems, work process redesign, and quality initiatives. These intentionally include workflow blocks to prevent certain actions that had been identified as increasing the possibility of errors or patient harm. Blocks are especially onerous in conditions of high workload, as the time required to learn how to properly respond to the block, and to stop (or reverse) the current procedure, takes away from accomplishing the current task and getting to the next pressing task. So the presumed long-term and collective benefits to patients and institutions in general do not easily outweigh the practitioner's immediate time demands, cognitive demands, or personal experience in performing a task.

The more problematic, however, are unintended blocks. Practitioners may easily identify these as inappropriate, invalid, and creating costly delays, and feel justified in developing workarounds. New policies, laws, or regulations may be perceived as too general, limiting, or arbitrary, and not informed by the actual worker's experience (e.g., not fully informed by a socio-technical systems perspective). Practitioners, in accord with group norms, may develop workarounds for newly implemented formal protocols or guidelines, which, even though they required considerable development and testing, may not seem applicable to the person's situation. The new workflow design may simply be inadequate or incorrect (Vogelsmeier *et al.*, 2008), creating bottlenecks, incompatible subprocesses, incomplete relations among a sequence of subprocesses, unsatisfactory alteration of familiar work practices, etc. New technology may have difficult features, over-restrictive constraints, inflexible procedures, or prevent previously informal arrangements, or may not be accompanied by redesign in associated work processes. A changed routine may require related, but not considered, changes in people's roles, such as requiring new or higher-level authorization and permissions, another form of potential workflow blockage. The possible confusion from, additional steps in, or obstacles to, communicating with the person may encourage practitioners, with multiple time demands from other patients, and increasing needs to coordinate the actions of multiple health practitioners, to arrange a way to work around people, roles, or processes.

Many errors occur in hospitals, leading to injury or adverse drug events, with a good percentage of them preventable. New medical information systems may alleviate some problems, but generate other kinds of errors. Some of the technological responses to reducing error include workflow blocks, in the form of computerized warnings, required processes, or action locks. However, these create disruptions, distracting staff from patient care, leading to errors. So some users devise workarounds, ways of avoiding or bypassing these workflow blocks. Edmondson's (2004) study of twenty-six nurses in eight hospital units found a continuous flow of small process failures throughout the day, both making it seem a natural part of the workday but also making it impossible to take the time to determine the cause, especially because most of the problems were initially generated from other units or locations. Nurses tended to impose a quick workaround and move on, not fixing the underlying system process, fostering a mistake-free persona, not generating learning, allowing the system problem to surface again, and creating problems for others.

Short-term solutions to process-related problems tend to deal with symptoms, or local processes (i.e., first-order problem-solving or learning, reactive control), but not the larger system interdependencies (or second-order problem-solving or learning, or preventive control). Often, reactive control is necessary simply to get the process moving again, and accomplish immediate objectives. But these will not prevent future instances of the same problem, which require changing assumptions and developing new processes. Thus, the underlying problems reoccur, while the short-term workaround solutions may impede the normal functioning of both the local and the more systemic processes (Ghosh and Sobek, 2007).

As an example of that cybernetic systems feedback principle, workarounds are attempts to bypass a block in order to meet the goal criterion, but do not change the more general relationships that generated the problem in the first place. This not only creates a layer of continuing unnecessary costs, delays, and frustration, but the workarounds may decrease overall performance and safety. But second-order problem solving is limited by other demands on time and attention, the non-involvement of managers in the problem-solving process, the difficulty in being vigilant about possible implications of the workarounds, insufficient slack resources, work empowerment, and cooperation from others who are not necessarily willing to work on what appears to be someone else's problem (Edmondson, 2004; Vogelsmeier *et al.*, 2008, p. 118). Vogelsmeier *et al.* (2008) studied how over forty nurses developed workarounds following the implementation of a portable electronic medication administration record cart in five nursing homes. The workarounds (1) allowed the nurses to accomplish their tasks, but (2) increased medical risk, and (3) allowed the blocks to reoccur. The ironic outcome of implementing the new system to improve safety checks was that when it did not fit with actual practices, the workaround sometimes avoided the safety check altogether, making the process less safe than before the technology. Halbesleben *et al.* (2008) analyzed a variety of healthcare workarounds in five nursing homes stemming from unintended workflow blocks that in turn fostered risky, difficult to detect, and hidden workarounds. In both studies, a locally beneficial UR wreaks global disadvantages.

Workarounds in healthcare settings (and elsewhere) may also emerge in response to attempts to repair or improve a larger system, as a way of hampering, bypassing, or disabling that larger system. For example, a district administration and NGO collaborated to improve the ineffective and wasteful public Indian healthcare system in one local center by monitoring nurse attendance and providing subsequent financial punishments or rewards. Initially, this monitoring/ sanctioning/reward system worked very well, substantially reducing absence and low effort. However, within a year and a half, the program had been completely vitiated by local health administrators and nurses who worked out ways of increasing claims for "exempt days" (Banerjee *et al.*, 2008).

Workarounds may create additional subsequent (both formal and informal) workflow blocks, and thus more workarounds, or may decouple the users, and local processes, from the larger formal system. Workarounds have other kinds of consequences, including decreasing employee satisfaction, making interdependences more difficult to identify, creating more contexts for subsequent errors, and increasing the willingness to engage in other workarounds. To the extent that they do work in the short-term, workarounds may become routinized and embedded, requiring and reinforcing prior and subsequent workarounds. Worse, because they are local and undocumented, they become invisible.

Meta-routines

Meta-routines are "a standardized problem solving procedure for changing existing routines and for creating new ones (Adler *et al.*, 1999)" (Ghosh and Sobek, 2007, p. 6). Routines may be *operating* routines (standard patterns in a given context) or *modification* routines (a meta-routine that changes operating routines) (Turner, 2005). Meta-routines process other routines, to some extent requiring that the input routine must be more explicit than implicit, and more local than distributed. Thus routines are both action patterns for solving problems, as well as means for governance and control (Cohen *et al.*, 1996). So the development of new, or alteration of existing, routines, requires not only a change in the routine, but, depending on the consequences, also a change in the meta-routine. Thus the development and emergence of new routines typically invoke greater conflict than the application or variation of existing routines. Indeed, the stability of routines avoids conflict, even at the cost of slipping into inertia. This inertia may stem from local resolutions of conflicts (truce), in that sense being a "better" routine than what might be involved in exploring alternatives. That is, the goal of the meta-routine may be how to minimize conflict rather than optimize performance. This more general or social meta-routine is based in social norms and scripts rather than typical organizational performance. Such inertia, however, means that local learning, to the extent that it occurs, does not result in discovering better rules or routines (double-loop learning). Thus routines (action capacities) become embedded, inaccessible, and impervious, subject to retention and replication within organizations, with local or global positive or negative consequences. A meta-routine may enable a UR, and a meta-routine may itself be a (particularly pernicious) double-loop UR.

Organizational and process improvement approaches – such as TQM (Cole, 1999; Deming 1986), Six Sigma (a business strategy using quality management methods intended to minimize defect levels; Harry and Schroeder, 2000), the Baldrige Award process, and the Balanced Scorecard – are examples of large-scale meta-routines intentionally designed to improve organizational routines. For example, TQM seeks to reduce variability in work processes, but first in designing work processes to attain quality and customer satisfaction (internally and externally). TQM includes statistical tools such as cause-and-effect diagrams, control charts, and check sheets, and management tools such as affinity diagrams, and process decision program charts. These tools are used in the meta-routine of *plan-do-check-act* (Deming, 1986). Six Sigma also seeks to reduce process variability through its meta-routine of define, measure, analyze, improve, control. More generally, effective meta-routines have three primary characteristics. They stimulate the validation of current contextual and perceptual knowledge, to reduce bias and opinions; foster collaboration and joint resolution, which creates, validates, and makes explicit collective knowledge; and encourage joint validation of the new understanding, confirming individual understanding and identifying differences (Ghosh and Sobek, 2007).

Total Quality Management in general (in the form of the Malcolm Baldrige Award), and the Excellence Model in particular, offer two main categories of performance measures, with nine elements (each with different percentage weightings and involving thirty-two sub-criteria, each with a set of rating questions): enablers (leadership, people management, policy and strategy, resources, and processes) and results (people satisfaction, customer satisfaction, impact on society, business results) (Paton, 2003). While both approaches require self-assessment, the Excellence Model is primarily self-diagnostic, not aimed at competing for excellence awards. For our purposes, the *processes* element of the *enablers* category is where an explicit attention to identification, resolution, and evaluation of URs should be added to the framework. See Ghosh and Sobek (2007) for an analysis of beneficial outcomes in hospital departments that had implemented meta-routines designed to improve quality management and organizational learning, compared to negative processes and conditions in those that did not.

Table 4.1 summarizes this overview of routines, workarounds, and meta-routines.

Developing a preliminary model of unusual routines

Complexity of unusual routines

Despite the disadvantages of URs, they can be both difficult for organization members to perceive and highly resistant to change. Such problems can defy attempts at organizational improvement. While feedback may indeed be necessary for systematic organizational improvement – and poor feedback may indeed be a cause or characteristic of URs – the act of providing feedback alone will likely be insufficient to cure an organization of URs (see Chapter 7). URs would seem to be cases in which the organization is incapable of double-loop learning, which is to say that it cannot "detect and correct errors in the operating norms themselves" (Van de Ven, 1986, p. 603). Over time, the ability of the organization to perceive its errors may decrease while its tolerance of those errors may increase (Singer, 1978). As one analyst puts it, an organization is "capable of absorbing considerable shocks and attempts to change it without actually changing" (Spender, 1998, p. 248). As discussed in Chapter 8, deliberate attempts to change organizational dynamics may even have the effect of further entrenching the existing patterns (Molinski, 1997).

A UR which has over time become routinized is likely to be highly resistant to change. At the individual level, routinized practices give

Table 4.1 *Aspects of routines, workarounds, and meta-routines*

Concept	Definition and components	Variability	Change	Outcomes
Routines	Incentives, constraints, imitation => habits => trigger routines Message stimulates repertoire, activating routines and associated behaviors, and subsequent messages Order, stability, repetition, interdependence, patterns, rules Technical/cognitive: Tacit and explicit knowledge Procedures Social: Motivations and interests, effort discretion, context, social embeddedness of routines Dead routines (artifacts) Live routines (ostensive, performative)	Influenced by social, physical, organizational environment Minimized by organizational truce, cognitive coherence around routines Variations around prototypical core instances Within effort discretion Encoding from past inferences Adaptive structuration, reinvention	Decay, defects, mutations, obsolescence, dysfunctions Selection Performative change relative to actors' goals, aspirations Peripheral actions get interpreted to belong within boundary of routine Routine's boundary gets expanded or narrowed Undeliberate (aspect of performing, without validation) Deliberate (intentional, with validation)	Retention, replication Change in routines in action Change in repertoire Repertoire may change but routines in action still repeated Repertoire may remain but routines in action change Learning to meet or change aspirations facilities by routines above minimum criterion

| Workarounds | Workflow block or interruption in routine – information, resources

Procedures, actions, digressions imposed to avoid risk, prevent errors and mistakes

Intentional, unintentional – design, roles, technology, organizational processes | Reactive, informal, temporary bypassing of dysfunction, interest, or problem in performing a routine

Esp. high workload, multiple constraints, conflicts between individual or professional norms and organizational constraints, inappropriate procedures imposed to avoid risk, prevent errors and mistakes | Bypass immediate block | Obstacles: individual abilities, group interests and norms, programmed behavior, fragmented responsibility, short-term vs. long-term costs and benefits | Reinforce single-loop over double-loop learning

Ignore or reinforce underlying system problem

Socialize toward workaround norm

Workaround become routinized, embedded, invisible

Increase patient, customer, worker risk

Generate improved processes | Costs and benefits different for different stakeholders, time periods |

Table 4.1 (*cont.*)

Concept	Definition and components	Variability	Change	Outcomes
				Organization does not know of problem or solution Decouple interdependent processes Fragment attention Generate subsequent blocks and workarounds for other units, customers, cycles
Meta-routines	Repertoire and routines for control and motivation of repertoires and routines, and for learning about and changing repertoires and routines Double-loop learning routines Validation of current routines Generate public collaboration and collective knowledge Joint validation of new routines	Potential for variability beyond threshold of meta-routine but with in effort convention Adjustment toward goals, homeostasis Adjustment of goals, nature of homeostasis Evaluation of routines and their effects	Change as ongoing process Evaluation of change, both process and outcomes	Process learning Empowerment Organizational evolution

organization members a sense of continuity in their daily activities (see Giddens, 1984, p. 282). At the collective level, the routine is a part of the shared organizational reality (Zucker, 1991, pp. 85–8). It seems clear that managerial intent may be insufficient by itself to create change, yet organizations do, in fact, change, and sometimes change radically.

Two related questions can be posed regarding URs: how do such dysfunctional processes arise within organizations, and what forces might be strong enough to change them once they exist? It seems plausible that they might result partly from symbolic uses of information by organization members (Feldman and March, 1981), that is, uses of information which serve cultural or socio-emotional needs more than instrumental needs of the organization. Perhaps URs are the manifestation of a fundamental tension between decision rationality and action rationality (Brunsson, 1985); perhaps they actually are not organizational problems that can be solved, but rather, organizational predicaments that must be coped with (Farson, 1996). Perhaps they persist because they serve power politics within the organization (Davenport *et al.*, 1992; Zmud, 1990), or self-interested gaming (Bardach, 1977). Or perhaps they can arise unintentionally, a kind of "evil twin" of self-organizing systems (Contractor, 1994; Contractor and Seibold, 1993) in which deviations from optimality are amplified rather than dampened, and the normal functioning of the system generates harms, perhaps at another site. And even if such routines can stymie rationalist efforts to affect them, might a change in an ICT (especially a new communication channel, because it both supports and reconfigures interactions among organizational members) yet perturb the organization's socio-technical system enough to mitigate them, or create new ones?

Parameters and components of unusual routines

While specific types and implications of unusual routines are particular to the organizational context, it is possible to outline some of their primary components.

Subroutines
Both clients and organization members may find themselves ensnared by "Kafka circuits," discussed in Chapter 1: work, delay, and error

(Singer, 1980), or, more generally, subroutines. Based on Chapters 2 and 3, we add the *blame subroutine*. Both blaming and crediting are judgments about outcome, agency, competence, and responsibility. Both are fundamentally social, possible only in the context of existing relations. But while crediting presumes a shared moral setting, blaming imposes a distinction between moral settings (Tilly, 2008, Chapter 1). Fear of failure and tendencies to blame instead of analyze create an "authority-responsibility double bind: A mismatch occurs between the responsibility expected of people to do the right thing, and the authority given or available to them to live up to that responsibility ... Error, then, must be understood as the result of constraints that the world imposes on people's goal-directed behavior" (Dekker, 2005, p. 201). Placing blame on others is often the only apparent way to adapt to feelings of loss of control over problem resolution (Argyris, 1985, p. 182). Blame subroutines are especially prevalent, and even honored, in some kinds of settings, such as political organizations. There, "criticism is a major activity. Blame, not praise, is the vehicle of evaluation. There is no one except yourself whose task it is to praise your successes, while there is at least one group whose task it is to blame you for your mistakes ... representatives become speculators in failure rather than in success ... A strategy of caution and passivity develops. Avoiding change is more likely to be rewarding than initiating it" and members are more likely to assume that constituents are opposed to change than they really are (Brunsson, 1985, p. 161).

Meta-routines

Just as functional routines and URs may co-exist, there may be functional meta-routines and unusual meta-routines. For example, similar causes of URs and barriers to feedback about them may operate at a higher system level, fostering dysfunctional feedback about, and sustaining, the single-loop dysfunctional feedback, which in turn sustains the first-level UR. In order to maintain a coherent interdependent flow of repertoires and actions, a meta-routine – whether individual actions or repertoires – may be necessary to control and motivate individual behavior, that is, to develop and maintain the truce (Guennif and Mangolte, 2002). This meta-routine cannot, of course, manage all possible variations or discretions, and, further, its extent must remain below some cost, efficiency, and effectiveness threshold. (This monitoring and maintenance meta-routine is related to the familiar and generally more macro-organizational concepts of transaction costs and principal–agent relations, discussed in Chaper 3.) So the discretion and variability of each actor above that meta-routine threshold adds another component between each repertoire and routine in action. Theoretically, any particular repertoire may generate a range of actions to the same stimulus message, as long as they are beyond (below) the scope of the meta-routine. Further, the actor may invoke a different repertoire to generate a routine in action in response to the stimulus message, if that variation is also beyond the meta-routine threshold, and outside the "truce" relations. Thus there may be considerable slippage between an official routine and a meta-routine, providing fertile ground for a first-level UR. More broadly dysfunctional or fragmented organizational substrates will routinize unusual meta-routines. Unusual meta-routines may in turn alter, or routinize, dysfunctional causes and feedback barriers of that substrate.

Scripts

Organization members may make collective sense of a new or problematic situation by identifying a "script" (either the ostensive aspect or artifact of the routine) to which it belongs. A script is a meaningful pattern of previous interactions, what one analyst calls "behavioral grammars that inform a setting's everyday action" (Barley, 1986, p. 83). The interactions of the actors, particularly in an equivocal situation, are guided by finding a relevant script; by following the script, perhaps unintentionally or even unconsciously, they attain a shared understanding (Weick, 1995, pp. 70–2). Over time, their cumulative actions create, then reproduce structure, and reaffirm its meaning (Poole *et al.*, 1985, pp. 76–7).

By no means are all organizational scripts components of URs! No doubt many scripts offer substantial savings of time and effort in productive organizational functioning, or at least contribute a beneficial degree of stability to interactions. Moreover, it seems reasonable to expect that a given script could be beneficial in one context, yet harmful in another. But our focus here is on the intrinsic characteristics of URs, and scripts do appear to be inherent components of URs, in the way they link organizational structure and individual actions (Barley, 1986, p. 83), however peculiar or dysfunctional the actions may seem to a third-party analyst. This is to say that the interactions in a UR, as with general routines, will be patterned. When scripts have become institutionalized (see Zucker, 1991, pp. 85ff.) (alternatively, retained), acts which fit the scripts are seen as objective and meaningful while acts which deviate from the scripts, even when the acts are constructive, appear idiosyncratic at best. It seems reasonable to expect that the scripts' degree of institutionalization would account for at least some of URs' resistance to change. Scripts differ from each other in their details, but share in potentially producing three potentially negative outcomes: undermining group legitimacy, maintaining the status quo, or diverting the group's focus. Scripts may generate particular management antipatterns (such as *fruitless hoops, metric abuse, Mr. nice guy, warm bodies*) or environmental antipatterns (such as *deflated ballon, divergent goals, fairness doctrine, worshiping the golden calf*) (LaPlante and Neill, 2006, pp. 9–11). In this way they underlie work, delay, error, or blame subroutines.

Symptoms
As Chapters 1, 2, and 3 describe, URs may show system-wide symptoms of denial, manipulation, non-responsiveness, rigidity, or suspicion or secrecy. These dysfunctionalities are no longer simple errors specific to particular transactions but have become characteristics of the (sub)system, or have in fact become the way the organization conducts its business. Many public bureaucracies and companies have become the butt of jokes, the object of contempt, or the cause of considerable grief, because of these traits.

Consequences
The potential for a new ICT to disturb the existing technical system seems clear. As noted above, there is a great deal of evidence that this event will also be influenced by, interact with, and impact the existing social system (Johnson and Rice, 1987). There will be changes in what and when people know, what and when people care about, and what and when they are interdependent with (Sproull and Kiesler, 1991, p. 3). We would not be surprised to see changes in formal reporting lines, formal hierarchy, motivation, information flow, and formal or informal power, for instance.

The specific outcomes are difficult to predict. There are several qualities of URs which can moderate the effects of the ICT. While the net effect of the UR to the value chain or entire organization is by definition negative, there may be localized benefits to a particular actor or subunit – one way in which a UR becomes impervious to change. Over time the UR becomes "invisible" and taken-for-granted by organization members, and even reinforced and valued by one or more subsystem. A new communication system may reveal URs and their real costs to the organization members, or, just as well, conceal them by providing a rational gloss over what in truth is a persistent irrationality. To put the visibility problem a bit cynically, an ineffective solution may suffice until the problem becomes severe enough to ignore.

Apart from the question of visibility, the new system may outright create, extinguish, exacerbate, or ameliorate URs. When URs are created or exacerbated, we can expect to find process losses; when the routines are extinguished or ameliorated, we can expect to find process gains (Nunamaker *et al.*, 1991; Steiner, 1972). Gains may result from bringing more information into the group, from critique and stimulation within the group, and learning by group members. Losses may result from overload, free-riding, domination, pressures to conform, or coordination problems. Observing or measuring these changes in a field situation is likely to be tricky business. Particular gains and losses may be localized to particular organizational actors or subunits; local process gains may precipitate higher-level process losses; and both gains and losses may occur at different times. The big picture is likely to be complex.

Organizational substrate

Particular organizational features will enable or inhibit the growth of URs. In a sense, organizational culture provides the medium in which particular scripts gain currency, in which particular interactions become normal behavior, or in which the dysfunctionality of URs becomes invisible to the participants. Both the technical systems and the social systems contribute to this organizational substrate. Two aspects of these systems need further comment: organizational values and subunit coupling.

Organization values as support for unusual routine scripts
To be recognized and accepted as legitimate by the actors, a script must be supported by some value or belief contained in the dominant

ideology of the organization. In an educational institution, for instance, the value placed on inclusion and the mistrust of positional authority support a script calling for every possible stakeholder to be brought into a decision process. In a less egalitarian culture such a concern might be thought irrelevant, wasteful, or damaging. In an educational institution, the value placed on diversity and the enthusiasm for generating new perspectives make principled objections seem noble. In a hierarchical organization such acts might play as a sign of disloyalty to the leaders and the organization's goals. In an educational environment participants might feel the gravity of their deliberations merits another semester or so. In a profit-making firm the shared perception of market pressure underlies a script of expeditious decision-making and steadfast execution.

Scripts superficially resemble the "implementation games" described by Bardach (1977), but differ in a couple of ways. Games are strategic moves in implementing (or stalling or preventing implementing) a policy decision which has already been made; scripts are guides for the discourse that defines a decision opportunity (and thus, as Weick points out, are part of sensemaking). Games subvert the professed values or intent of a policy; scripts, to be viable, must be seen, at least by some organization members, as consistent with professed organizational (or relevant unit) values.

Subunit coupling

Another organizational feature that influences URs is the degree of subunit coupling. Coupling is usually considered as the degree of interdependency among subunits (see, for instance, Weick, 1979, p. 111), all of which lie within the organization's boundary with its environment. For our purposes here it is more useful to think of the organization as a "family of quasi-autonomous but interacting systems of activity" (Spender, 1998, p. 250). Coupling, then, is a measure of subunit autonomy or boundary hardness (or, as Johnson and Rice, 1987, assume, the boundaries of unit discretion).

In a complex organization, accomplishing work – whether the work is creating an artifact or serving a client – usually requires coordination of task sequences within a number of functional units (Gasser, 1986, p. 210). The condition of loose coupling can generate a good deal of ongoing work simply in coordinating and adjusting the units' activities, or *articulation work* (p. 211). Unusual routines may even result from attempts to mitigate URs; "groups concerned with different aspects of the perceived problem may work on solutions to the problem which prove to be incompatible" (Turner, 1990, p. 372). When the units are loosely coupled, the losses caused by URs can be more diffused and the routines can be more invisible to the organization members, even if not to the organization's clients. Put another way, when subunits are loosely coupled they can more easily optimize their internal processes even when this creates a UR at the level of the value chain in which they are embedded, because negative feedback will be slower and/or less informed.

Moreover, loose coupling may inhibit the sharing of knowledge across the organization, thus decreasing the potential value of this "public good" (Spender, 1998, pp. 243–6) in two ways. Information held by one subunit may simply be unavailable to another, either because of technology or practice. In addition, the meaning of information may be incommensurate between the units, even when shared (Simard and Rice, 2007). Weick holds that tight coupling has the potential to hurt organizations by increasing the possibility of system accidents (1995, pp. 130–1). Here we are arguing that loose coupling can allow URs to grow and persist, by allowing subunits to develop buffers against each other and by limiting the force of corrective feedback between subunits.

Five propositions

All this suggested to us a number of propositions about a new ICT and related changes in URs, and about the dynamics of URs within an organization's culture.

Proposition One: if a new ICT mitigates URs it does so not simply as a more efficient channel (the first-level effect) but rather as an innovation the organization must process (the second-level effect).

Rationale: the ICT may greatly facilitate communication within the organization; it may even tend to loosen the hierarchical and temporal contexts of the messages (Rice and Gattiker, 2001). In some sense this is an improvement in the quality of communication, and an optimist might argue that this efficiency gain would mitigate existing URs. The pessimist would point out, however, that more communication does not necessarily mean better communication, and that a new communication system may also create new possibilities for such strategic uses of information as manipulation, gatekeeping, and distortion. If the system does precipitate a change in URs it is not simply as a more efficient channel, but rather as a significant event within the organization which occasions social system change (Barley, 1986, pp. 81, 84; Rice, 1987).

Proposition Two: loose coupling between subunits in a value chain allows URs to resist change.

Rationale: loose coupling can benefit an organization by facilitating adaptation and experimentation. Loose coupling can also allow subunits to optimize their own internal processes without regard for interdependencies along the value chain. A change-resistant UR can arise when the subunits optimize internally at the expense of other subunits in the value chain. A common example of this is when functionally interdependent subunits neglect to coordinate their activities; loose coupling weakens the incentive to address the problem in the value chain. Moreover, loose coupling can attenuate any corrective feedback between units which does exist. In short, loosely-coupled subunits in the value chain may achieve their individual homeostasis by buffering against each other even when they impose costs on each other, on the entire organization, or on organization clients; such costs are negative externalities of the subunit optimization.

Proposition Three: visibility alone is insufficient to mitigate URs when they provide localized benefits for a subsystem.

Rationale: an optimist would hold that awareness leads to improvement, and that by increasing the flow of information a ICT will promote awareness. The pessimist would point out, however, that human rationality is bounded. As one analyst puts it, "while organizations can be considered to undergo forms of learning, they do not always move readily towards 'intelligent behavior'" (Turner, 1990, p. 377).

Even when organization members are well aware of the existence of a UR, they may not want it to change, or may be unmotivated to attempt to change it. One possible reason is that they are satisfied that their own subunits have optimized internally; another is that they are inured to the existence of the UR and pessimistic that the effort to change it would be worth the result. This follows the logic of expectancy theory (described in Pace and Faules, 1994, pp. 83–4): motivation is low when the perceived effort is high and the anticipated reward is low. From a rational point of view, the organizational rewards and punishments may seem misplaced. (Reformers lament that "no good deed goes unpunished.")

Proposition Four: a UR can resist change because it glosses a contradiction in organizational values, or because its script affirms an ideological tenet of the organization.

Rationale: once again the optimist would argue that by facilitating information sharing, the ICT will bring problems to light and tend to build consensus. Once again the pessimist would point out that technical systems inevitably are subverted by the social systems they serve. The loss in efficiency caused by a UR may seem obvious to analysts, organization clients, and even to a number of organization members. Nonetheless, its benefits at the social system level may create an ideological constituency that defends the UR against change. A routine that is problematic to one group may well seem sensible to another (cf. Turner, 1990, p. 372).

Whatever its costs, a UR may benefit the social system in significant ways. Ambiguity in organizational values can help maintain cohesion (Eisenberg, 1984); the UR may mediate a value conflict for organization members, albeit at the expense of clients or customers. For instance, a UR can be created when a group decision process attempts to maximize buy-in by seeking compromise, or to resolve conflict through log-rolling. (Log-rolling is a derogatory term for the practice, among politicians, of trading support for each other's pet initiatives.) In a less pessimistic vein, it may sometimes make good sense for an organization to maintain somewhat contradictory goals (Boettger and Greer, 1994); for example, an educational institution may attempt to maximize each student's intellectual potential while minimizing per capita costs to keep tuition low. In this case, a UR may simply be the cost the organization must pay to optimize a system of inconsistent objectives, or locally consistent objectives held by globally opposed stakeholders.

Proposition Five: a cultural environment which places a high value on inclusion will tend to support double binds.

Rationale: double binds (Wendt, 1998) frequently afflict vertical communication in an inclusive culture. For example, management's messages about trust and participation in decision-making may create double binds. Even though the content meaning may be egalitarian and inclusive, labor may perceive the relational meaning as hierarchical command and control. A "vicious circle" of interactions

Table 4.2 *Conceptual rationales associated with each proposition*

Core concepts	Proposition
Unusual routines	1, 2, 3, 4, 5
ICT as innovation	1
Loose coupling	2
Resistance to change	2, 4
Visibility (of unusual routines)	3
Localized benefits	3
Scripts	4
Ideological tenets	4
Contradictions in beliefs, values	4
Double binds	5

may evolve which reinforces managers' petty tyrannies and subordinates' resentment (Ashforth, 1994, pp. 770–1), even when such roles are contrary to professed organizational values. There is some reason to think that, by loosening the hierarchical context and increasing the flow of messages, the ICT may alleviate this sort of UR, which can exact high costs in terms of misunderstandings, animosity, and wasted time.

Still, URs built around double binds may actually contribute to maintaining the boundaries between groups, thereby generating social system benefits for one or more parties. For instance, the formal boundary between management and labor may be demarcated with such structures as contracts and bargaining units, while group identity is maintained through suspicion of the other's motives and intentions. Similar boundary maintenance can exist between other functional subunits in the organization, stymieing attempts at coordination.

Table 4.2 links the conceptual foundations to the research propositions described above.

Conclusion

In sum, our review of prior work on organizational dysfunctionalities and our own personal adventures as members and clients/customers of complex organizations suggest a multi-level analytical model for making sense of experiences that have frequently struck

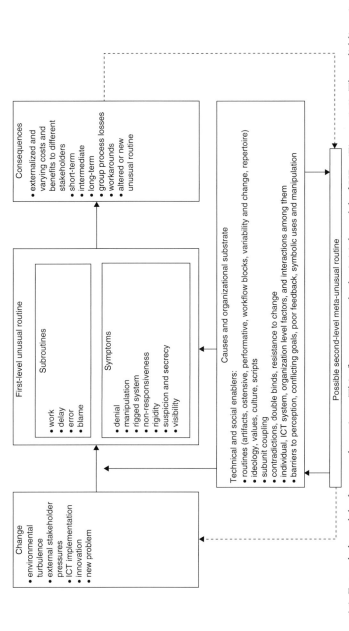

Figure 4.1 Extended model of unusual routines. This figures extends the initial model of URs (Figure 1.1). The solid lines indicate the interaction of the organizational substrate with the innovation or organizational change, jointly influencing the development of a UR; the dashed lines indicate a feedback path of the meta-routine of a second-level UR into both the innovation or organizational change, as well as the organizational substrate itself.

us as largely – at least initially – nonsensical. Because the organizational practices we are attempting to understand are both problematic (infrequent for any particular actor, yet pervasive across systems, and with negative consequences for at least some actors, i.e., *unusual*) and durable (embedded as well as proceduralized, i.e., *routine*), we expect to see both negative consequences and equilibrium-producing features.

To explain the persistence of URs we have looked into organizational dynamics. Our belief is that underlying cultural features of the organization must provide some support for URs, and have indicated this as the *cultural substrate* in Figure 4.1, which includes the set of causes of URs from the prior chapters. Absent such support, we would expect organizations to simply address nascent URs as problems to be dealt with, and to have some amount of success in correcting the problems or at least make rational trade-offs in changing the practices involved. In itself, this would be a rational actor's effort to identify and fix problems, and – granting the well-known limitations on both human and organizational rationality! – one would expect to see a higher degree of success than the literature and our experiences have confirmed.

Figure 4.1 also includes the possibility of an innovation of some sort disturbing the organization's equilibrium. Our hunch was that such events may at least highlight the existence of URs, perhaps by generating new processes that would reveal embedded dysfunctions, and might possibly create the opportunity for mitigating them. The circular flow in that figure reflects our observation that as innovations become incorporated into the organizational environment they are affected by the environment. Along those lines, the propositions described above were our expectations for the complex contingencies involved.

The next two chapters will describe a field study which took advantage of a large-scale innovation in the computer and information technology at a college to assess and elaborate this model, and provide results concerning the propositions in particular and unusual routines in general.

5 | *A detailed case study of unusual routines*

This chapter and Chapter 6 describe how each of the five propositions played out in a lengthy field study at an educational institution (Cooper, 2000), based upon our working model of unusual routines introduced in the preceding chapter. While the initial intent was to focus on the effects the implementation of a computer-mediated communication system (one kind of ICT) might have on URs, the early data collection suggested that the study would provide broader insights into UR dynamics in decision processes and operations. The study utilized depth interviews with a stratified purposive sample of organization members, and such qualitative methodology often does lead to pleasant surprises in the knowledge the study generates. That is to say, the study convinced us that the model had broader application than to ICTs alone, and had particular analytical value in understanding the relationship between problematic routine behaviors and organizational culture. It is important to emphasize that in no way was this intended as an assessment or critique of communication at the site! Indeed, we expect that the URs and interaction scripts surfaced in the study may be all too familiar to our colleagues at other institutions.

Method

The research site

At the time of the study, the organization had just begun a major end user computing initiative to implement a shared database of student records, and to provide email to all faculty and staff. Up to that point, college records had been maintained on a mainframe computer by an information technology (IT) department. To obtain needed information from these records, administrative units requested a report from the IT unit. A common complaint was that these reports were out-of-date by the time they are received, particularly budget figures. (See Gasser, 1986, pp. 213–14 for similar examples of *computer slip*.) Units frequently devised their own recordkeeping systems as a work-around to the centralized IT function, and with most workarounds, these systems were unique to each department. There had been no way to share this locally-generated information across units, other than printouts or telephone inquiries.

Inclusive decision-making was an important organizational value for the university, and was clearly evident in most initiatives. Some issues spawned task forces or study groups, most often at the college president's directive. The membership of these ad hoc work groups was carefully chosen to broadly represent various constituencies with an interest in the issue. Other issues were considered in an elaborate college governance system which had been in place for more than a decade at the time of the study. All constituencies on the campus were represented on a number of standing committees, and all organization members had voting rights in the general meetings. The charter of this permanent body specified that its decisions were advisory to the president and board of trustees and therefore not binding, and there was some disagreement about how much weight the governance body's decisions actually carried with the executives.

In all these decision processes document sharing, document editing, or other group work tended to be paper- and face-to-face meeting-intensive. In short, there was a great deal of collaborative work being done, but without much use of electronic communications to facilitate it.

Data collection

Given the exploratory nature of the study, the data collection employed semi-structured interviews with organization members. These interviews asked the informants about their personal use of computer-mediated communication (hereafter referred to as ICT), their department's use of ICT, about aspects of their daily activities which they perceived as frustrating or negatively impacting their job performance, and about organizational values which the informants saw as affecting decision processes.

The second author had worked in higher education for a number of years and had often been involved in group decision-making and the writing of policy documents. Over time, he had formed personal impressions of interaction patterns which often appeared in those collaborative activities, yet struck him as problematic in their effects on the decision process. These suggested to him five categories of interaction scripts (digressing, trivializing, reframing, scapegoating, and expanding; related to some of Bardach's (1977) implementation games) which might be associated with URs, and were used as prompts in the interview. He read the brief descriptions and asked the informants if they were reminded of group decision processes in which they had participated. The names of the scripts, in italic typeface, were solely for the interviewer's convenience in taking notes and were not read to the informants! Table 5.1 provides the interview guide.

Table 5.1 *Interview guide*

Involved in the [ICT] implementation?
If so, describe involvement.
Do you use email, or any other kind of computerized communication?
Does the XYZ Department use email, or any other kind of computerized communication?
Recognize any scripts? (Any context at the college, group or interpersonal.)

Digressing:
"Nostalgia" – Consideration of a problem is sidetracked by reminiscences of times when the problem was non-existent or less pressing, or speculation how a former leader would have handled it.

Trivializing:
"I Have a Concern" – A minor objection or concern (in comparison to the potential benefit of the proposal under consideration) stops further consideration of a particular course of action. Put another way, a small objection blocks a promising idea.

"The Microscope" – Discussion narrows to a small detail or aspect of the question. Time is used up in consideration of minutiae, rather than the central problem.

"Every Proposal is Wrong" – An objection or concern (sometimes trivial) is attached to each of a number of proposals under consideration. No proposal is decisively eliminated, and none gains a consensus.

Table 5.1 (*cont.*)

Reframing:
"*The Larger Issue*" – The question at hand becomes tied to another, broader issue, and discussion gravitates toward that issue.
"*Change the Agenda*" – The issue is reframed so that the discussion moves away from the initial question.

Scapegoating:
"*Kick the Dog*" – A weak consensus builds around problem definition, but not around a concrete solution or course of action. Blame is placed on a person or department not present at the meeting and over whom the group has no control.
"*Piling On*" – Problems are attributed to a person or department which has already received criticism regarding another issue.

Expanding:
"*We Haven't Heard All the Voices*" – An actor objects that some party was not adequately consulted or advised about the issue. The legitimacy of the group process is undermined.
"*Nobody Asked Me*" – An actor objects that he or she was not adequately consulted or advised about the issue. The legitimacy of the group process is undermined.
"*Everybody's a Winner*" – Disagreements over problem and/or course of action are resolved by inserting every party's language in document.

Can you think of other patterns, in discussions at the college?
Can you think of things that happen at the college that are negative, counterproductive or dysfunctional in some way, yet continue to happen repeatedly?
Are there any core beliefs or values at the college which interfere with discussion or collective decision-making? (at any level: college-wide, departmental, small group)
Can you think of times when someone's words seemed inconsistent with what you thought they really intended?

Sampling

Informants were selected to represent the major academic divisions of the college and levels in the administrative structure. The intent was to obtain a purposive, stratified sample (Miles and Huberman, 1994, pp. 27ff.) of the organization members across the subunits, based on the supposition that position within the organization might affect the informant's experience both with URs and with the system implementation. When the interviews within these strata revealed critical events or key players, snowball sampling was used to obtain data from the individuals directly involved in the ICT implementation, or individuals who seemed to play some key role in a UR.

The organizational chart suggested three major functional strata to be sampled, each containing a number of defined subunits: administration, faculty, and operations. There was a good degree of embedded complexity since each functional stratum contained members of different union bargaining units, and because subunits within a particular stratum varied considerably from each other in the degree to which they had adopted the new system at the time of the study.

Analytical method

In the early stages of the data collection, it became apparent that there often were sharp differences in the informants' perspectives on the interaction patterns we call URs. For instance, some informants saw the elaborate group decision processes as problematic, both in the large amounts of time and effort required to come to closure and in the perceived quality of the decisions emerging from them. Other informants, by contrast, felt that although such deliberations might become tedious they were vital to maximize the inclusiveness of the group. At first glance the perspective difference seemed to be between administrators and faculty – a group conflict endemic to academic institutions! – but as the data collection went on it appeared more as individual differences in orientation toward the product of the interaction (i.e., the decision), or toward the process (i.e., the deliberations) – in other words, between the content and the relational dimensions of interactions.

As is the case in much qualitative research, the analysis in large measure emerged from the interview data. Coding the interviews for references to URs, subroutines, and indicators helped to reveal their dimensions and dynamics. The details of the coding are omitted here for the sake of brevity. Space limitations likewise prevent a detailed exploration of the interviews, but the balance of this chapter is intended to give the reader a sense of how indicators of URs and their subroutines surfaced in them.

Proposition One

If a new ICT mitigates or exacerbates URs it does so not simply as a more efficient channel (the first-level effect) but also as an innovation the organization must process (the second-level effect).

The system as just a new computer: the first-level effects

Many informants expected the new ICT to produce first-level changes in such procedures as distributing class rosters to faculty and reporting grades to the registrar, but anticipated little impact on the organization beyond that. A senior faculty member and department chair, expected the email capability to make little difference in his/her subunit's operations.

Int: Does anybody in your department use email?

I really don't know. I know none of us have access to it on our own computers [i.e., at work], so if they use it they use it at home.

Int: Are there any plans that you know of?

Yes. We got new computers in the summer and we're wired or almost wired, and they tell us we'll get it shortly.

Int: Do you have any thoughts on what you personally or the department as a group might do with email?

I don't see any great advantage to email. I think we probably could talk with publishers, book reps, other faculty in other colleges, set up meetings and conferences. I don't see internally – I don't know, maybe because we don't have it, you know, we haven't gotten to use it, but – um, you know, we're so close to each other, I mean, I don't see where email is any great benefit to improve our communication.

More than just a new computer system: second-level effects on the social system

Some informants did see the ICT implementation as at least an opportunity for, if not a catalyst of, second-level changes in the social order of the organization. An interesting example of such changes in the interactions among organization members surfaced in the interview with an upper-level administrator who had been heavily involved in the planning of the new system and had already noticed second-level change beginning in the social interactions.

The first stage of the system implementation consisted of adapting a commercial software product, marketed to higher education institutions in general, to this specific institution. To this end, the college began a wide-ranging effort to solicit input from organization members at all levels about both their existing work methods and new functionality they might want the system to deliver. It became the task of the project team to fit the practices and preferences of the organization into the capabilities of the software. In a sense, the new computer system was simultaneously a template which could to a limited extent be adapted to the existing social system, and a force in itself which pressured the social system to change in particular directions. (This is a bit stronger than Barley's (1986) observation that technology implementations are *occasions* in which restructuring *can* take place, and a common analysis of ICT implementation by socio-technical practitioners and researchers.) This informant saw the implementation as actually compelling the social system to change, and seemed to intuitively recognize this structurational dimension of the implementation work: the committee was tasked with optimizing the functionality of the ICT, and simply took it as a given that there would be changes in the social system as a result.

We have not gotten into discussions of, "well – this is going to cause a change in this group's job description; we need to talk to Human Resources." We're not interested in doing that. That's not the point of this. That's Human Resources' problem; they need to deal with the way the jobs change after the jobs have changed. So we're not changing people's jobs ... we're simply saying, "this is the system."

Beyond the expectation of long-term second order effects, this informant also noticed immediate changes in the interaction patterns among organization members. The implementation work brought together people from different functional units which had tended to be only loosely coupled, an effect also noted in Aydin and Rice's study of a university healthcare unit (1992).

First, this has been the most startling, wonderful kind of experience. We had a group of people sitting around a table who had never sat around a table before ... really didn't know each others' functions ... The human resources, payroll, and the finance people really thought of themselves as a unit unto themselves and were surprised by the input they got from people who were on those implementation teams who came from educational services, because they thought they knew everything about it. So that was another big change.

Besides simply bringing about face-to-face interactions among people from different units, the design work also required that certain issues be settled expeditiously and that the solutions be uniform across the institution. Although the selection of codes, field names, and symbols in a database might seem a relatively trivial technical detail in a system implementation, it generated a surprising amount of controversy in that the need for uniformity forced a tighter degree of subunit coupling than had been typical at this institution (as also found by Aydin and Rice, 1992). The effort spent in resolving such questions is an indicator of the degree to which such tight coupling went against the grain of culture.

[B]ut that [conflict over codes for departments] was another one that was a lengthy discussion, and part of it is just understanding that in an integrated system you can't just not take into account what's going to happen within the other departments and the other areas of the college.

...

[T]he jurisdiction over a code is a very important thing but there has to be an agreement to maintain it, and so all of those discussions which are things that they tried to have us do with regard to the mainframe, but it was always fragmented, and this has brought about a real communication amongst the people, and we're not fragmented half as much as we were.

From an administrator of a unit that had already implemented the ICT, there were also some early indications of changes in the norms for communicative behaviors, such as increased responsiveness to messages, follow-up to meetings, density of communication interactions, and awareness of external information resources.

An interesting example of a blame subroutine surfaced in the interview with a member of the information technologies group. This informant's duties included performing maintenance and set-up work on desktop computers. S/he had, in the past, often received criticism from end users that the department had failed to perform the work the client had requested, criticism the informant viewed as sometimes unwarranted or even unethical. With the email function of the ICT becoming available at the college, this informant began using email to document the maintenance requests, which was a noticeable change from the informality with which much interdepartmental communication had been handled in the past (also noted in Romm's studies of political uses of computer-mediated communication systems, 1998).

Int: What use does your department make of email for business?
   Business? ... I use it as a great defense mechanism.

Int: Defense?
   I get it in black and white. I get my ass chewed off a lot around here because of lying. Users tell me that they want one thing, we go and do it, and they say that's not what they want. And so I make a lot of things come in black and white now.

Int: You mean, requests for your assistance or your services?
   Yeah. Requests for certain modifications, systems to be redone, things of that nature. So I use it as a defense system. I get it in black and white, and certain people don't like to do that in black and white. I've been bitten in the ass a lot of times, and I've learned from it, and so I use it for that. I use it when I want to get my point across, and I want it out in black and white.

In this informant's view, one dimension of the problem was that there were often simple misunderstandings between end users and computer support personnel about the details of such technical work, fostering delay or error subroutines. Beyond that, however, the informant felt there were times when clients falsely accused his/her department of incompetent work, interactions characteristic of blame subroutines.

Int: So your experience was – you used the word, blame. I'm getting the sense that you would do what people said.
   Yes.

Int: And then they would accuse you, or blame you, or fault you.
   Yes.

Int: For it not turning out the way they liked, later on.
   Yes. Exactly. Saying, "This isn't what I really meant," or "This isn't what I told you." And that's when it comes to the point where it's actually a lie, in my book. So I use it a lot for that.

The system as a catalyst for policy change: a major second-level effect

Some informants saw a relationship between the ICT implementation and policy changes occurring at this time. The change in the college's grading policy is the most dramatic example of such second-level change the informants attributed, at least in part, to the new computer system.

For several decades the college had used a somewhat non-traditional system of reporting course grades and calculating students' cumulative averages. The grading system had been controversial for some years prior to the ICT implementation, with many philosophical and practical objections to the existing system, yet proposals to adopt traditional grading had repeatedly been voted down in the college governance forum and the grading system had remained unchanged. About six months into the deployment of the new system, the college president made a speech to the college community to announce that because the state had altered its funding formula in such a way that the nonstandard grading system would significantly disadvantage the college, the board of trustees had made an executive decision to change to a traditional grading system. The president was forming a special commission to draft the specific policy for that system, which then would be presented for discussion in the governance forum.

There were several striking differences from the earlier initiatives to change the grading system. The impetus for the change was an event in the organization's environment, while earlier debates had arisen internally, driven by some parties' dissatisfaction with the old grading system. The decision to change had been made at the executive level by the board of trustees, rather than proposed in the collegial governance system and voted on in that body. The commission charged with drafting the language of the new grade policy had an expeditious timetable in which to complete its work, in contrast to the open-ended discussions and committee work characteristic of the earlier proposals in the college governance.

Int: I want to make sure I understand. At Governance Day you watched a videotape of the college president, and the college president said the grading system is going to change, by such-and-such a date, I guess?

Got to. He said, these are reasons why it has to change, and we've got to start talking about it and got to start making decisions about what we want to do.

Int: And the reason why is …?

There's a couple reasons. One is [the new ICT] … [I]t would be very difficult for [the new ICT] to adjust to our [current] grading system. Another is – if I can recall now – the state has some performance-based budgeting, and so the way they measure performance is based upon grades.

The rapidity of the change and its general acceptance by the college community was striking, given the previous resistance of the old system to change. As this quote illustrates, a number of informants felt that while the state funding formula made adoption of a traditional grading system inevitable, the ICT implementation was at least a catalyst in this major change.

Much more than just a new computer system: second-level effects on value chains

Although a bit unorthodox, it can be useful to think of sequences of operations in an academic institution as value chains. Students often must make their way through a sequence of procedures within their academic institution as they matriculate, register for classes, or qualify for graduation. Typically these procedural steps require contact with a number of different subunits within the school. As noted above, these subunits may be quite loosely coupled with the result that costs are externalized on the students in the form of work, delay, or error subroutines. (Or, if – sadly – the result is a deficiency in the student's academic performance, the cost may be externalized on his or her later employer or graduate school.)

The head of a large academic service unit expected the new ICT to change the procedural steps of the value chain including his/her unit. At the time of the interview, the unit sent students out to a specialized department for testing of their reading and computational skills, but s/he anticipated the ICT would make it possible to perform this testing within the unit. On the surface this may seem to be a simple first-level gain in efficiency, yet this informant intuitively recognized the potential for second-level change as the system altered the control

over and availability of this, and other, procedures, effectively altering subunit boundaries in the process.

[A]ll of a sudden as things come on line, newer people and people across
the organization laterally are going to have the capacity to do things that
were more restricted to one or another office, so we might deliver the testing right in our own office for example, rather than sending [the students]
to the testing office.

Another informant who worked on the design of the human
resources and payroll functions of the new system also observed how
the new system was the catalyst for changes in subunit boundaries,
such as greater decentralization, a potential threat to some departments, such as administrative services, which had controlled access
to financial information. This suggests that a general organizational
inertia may be an accumulation of subunit-level change resistance.

A high-level administrator, not directly involved with the implementation, made a very interesting link between the distribution of
power in the organization and the distribution of knowledge.

The technological systems that we talked about earlier, that will make
some things less secret, that information will really be public and shared,
rather than held and controlled as power by people on lower levels, sometimes, of the organization. All of those things, I think, will help. I think
the technology, the good budget, the pattern and participatory bargaining,
a very clear performance evaluation system that's viewed positively, that
rewards initiative and performance. All of those things would help.

It is quite interesting to note that s/he envisioned new flows of
information *upward* with the implementation of the new ICT, and
looked forward to a broader sharing of information replacing the current proprietary, localized control over information. Typically, organizational studies presume or conclude that power is concentrated in
the upper levels of the organization (see Morgan, 1986, pp. 280 ff.).
While there may be some basis for that generalization, it is worth noting that when certain knowledge is confined to the "shop floor," certain kinds of organizational power are likely to be vested there, also.
This quote from a practicing executive in an educational institution
reminds us that it is often more accurate to say that (at least some)
power is concentrated where the knowledge is concentrated, and not
necessarily where the organizational chart suggests authority lies.

Another administrator hoped for double-loop learning occasioned by the new ICT. This informant viewed the practice of holding meetings as a work subroutine:

Well, I think there's just too much time spent in a given week, sitting in meetings in this room or the trustees' dining room, or wherever, when the only reason you're meeting is because it was on the schedule. I mean, essentially what you get at the meeting you could have gotten in your email. And because of people who aren't there, you don't know what they think about it. And if they could respond to the group through email, then everybody would have everybody else's reactions.

I'm not saying do away with meetings, but I'm just saying that I think we need to look seriously at how to make better use of all this networking we've done. I mean, what did we spend? How many millions of dollars on a fiber optic network and an email system, a computer on every desk? It's not that I just want to sit at my desk and do email all day, I don't mean that either. But I think that we should use that facility to inform us.

I mean, every once in a while this phrase, the "learning organization," comes up. And I think that's the first step to being a learning organization: learning how to use information technology to get the information you need to learn. And I don't think we're doing that well enough. I think we've got the physical infrastructure in place ...

Int: Why is it, do you think, that we're not doing that if the plumbing, the infrastructure is in place?

We're too busy going to meetings.

Proposition Two

Loose coupling between subunits in a value chain allows URs to resist change.

The difficulty of managing a loosely coupled structure

One problem administrators face in an academic organization is that of matching resources to needs. A particularly difficult boundary management (Johnson and Rice, 1987, pp. 165 ff.) problem involves obtaining or allocating resources *outside* the administrator's span of control which are necessary to managing activity *within* his or her responsibilities. Two dimensions of special interest here include (a) the way subunits can interact as if loosely coupled when their functionality is highly interdependent, and (b) the ways institutional values and politics can preserve URs.

An administrator who worked in the enrollment and registration unit described an example of this kind of problem. His/her unit generated enrollment data as classes filled up, and s/he was hence in a good position to assess the fit of resources (in this case, open sections) to demand (in this case, students wishing to register for classes). The decision to open new sections where there was unfilled demand, however, was made elsewhere in the organization.

We send regular reports to all of the division chairs, division administrators, and department chairs, tracking what level of activity there's been in their class[es]. We send it on two different levels … [Redacted], from recruitment services, will do a daily enrollment report which will track, in essence, program by program. So for people who are on top of this – and some are and some aren't – they'll look at this very closely … We open new sections, potentially.

Int: When you say, "we," who's the we?
Um … it would ultimately be the division that would initiate it, but we would be the ones that would spur that, feed them the information that they need to do that …

Int: Your unit generates the intelligence about where there's the greatest demand and where there's slack demand, and where you need more resources, in this case meaning more open sections.
Exactly.

Int: You yourself don't create new sections.
Correct.

Int: But you send the information that there's a potential need or a potential surplus over to the division, which means to the academic side. They actually make the decision.
Correct.

Int: You don't have direct control over that.
No. We don't.

It is not problematic in itself that this informant's unit identified undersupplied courses but could not generate more sections; resources are always insufficient in (especially public) universities. Also, certainly this information could, in principle, stimulate an appropriate response in another subunit within the organization. However, this was not always the case, even when the mismatch between demand and supply was chronic for certain courses required for students to graduate. What does seem problematic at the conceptual level is that the subunit which created the supply/demand intelligence and the subunit which opened new sections were so loosely coupled. That the mismatch was a systemic and even regular occurrence, and not an exceptional situation, indicates this is a UR.

[Redacted] generates reports on a section by section basis, so people can track ... each individual section and know from that, basically, when they may need to open new sections ... [T]hat's the intelligence that they need to determine what they should be offering next year. They should be looking at how quickly are these filling up, are we forcing people into extension centers because there's no more on-campus sections. I look at those also, in what have traditionally been problem areas and gatekeeper areas.

And, again, to give you an example of what this dilemma is, we've had an ongoing issue over English 121. It's probably the most illustrative one I can give you. English 121 is what we call a gateway class. Basically, everyone's got to take that. We've had a real problem over the years monitoring the number of sections of English 121 – and there's like sixty, seventy sections that we offer – and having enough for our students to get in.

Int: You usually don't have enough sections?

We generally run out ... We run into logistics issues, we run into political issues – and they're significant.

Int: Political?

Well, we've had some very, very serious ongoing debates ... in terms of holding off because they were looking to increase the number of full-time permanent faculty. And we were saying, "hire adjuncts," and they were saying, "we can't get enough competent, qualified adjuncts to do those sections."

Int: Let's see if I understand you specifically. They did not want to put more adjuncts in the stable or on call, because they felt that would undercut their stated need for full-time positions.

Correct. Correct.

Such a UR externalizes its cost onto third parties (in this case, students who cannot obtain the courses they want), and can be quite resistant to change.

Loose coupling and change resistance

Informants whose jobs involved transaction processing often voiced frustration with routine procedures that were problematic for them, yet resisted their best efforts to change them. An informant who worked in the registrar's office described a longstanding difficulty s/he experienced with late registration of international students. A few points are worth noting in this passage. First, the costs of this UR were externalized onto the students in the form of a error sub-routine involving their registration and financial aid. Second, despite personnel changes and repeated efforts to resolve it, the problem persisted. Third, the informant, in non-technical language, attributed the problem to loose coupling between the subunits involved in this process.

Int: You indicated that there's some difficulty with the international studies students.

Yup. We swear that there's a virus in the files ... It makes no difference who is in charge at international studies. They just can't give us what we ask them. And it's just an oddity, I have no idea what it is. It's not that hard. We're very clear. We've been writing down what we need and when we need it, and it's really the timeliness that's the problem. We should not have students going abroad who haven't registered yet, and that happens ...

Int: Now, the management has changed a couple times ...

That's what I'm saying! That's why I say it has to be in the files. It's not the people [laughs].

Int: Have you checked the water cooler? [laughs]

[laughs] It's a very odd situation, very odd. And the thing that happens is that if a student has not registered and has not been formally accepted into the program they don't qualify for financial aid which in the case of international students comprises loans. And without those loans most of the students cannot afford to be in a foreign country. And so there's all of this last-minute stuff that is really mean to the students

...

The fact is that financial aid is in a tizzy, because now they're here [the students], they want their loan papers approved, and they've [financial aid] never seen them before. So there's all of this stuff that is just done so poorly

...

And that one is just a puzzle, and it truly is as if there's something in the animal of international studies that just doesn't allow itself to see itself as part of the institution.

Another administrator saw loose coupling creating coordination problems across the entire organization:

Well, it would be a lot easier if people who worked here knew what other people did. And I think that's a big part of the problem. Accounting really doesn't know what goes on in the division office. Receiving really is not aware of what goes on in a division office. I'm really not aware of what goes on in community development.

If we had an understanding of what the other areas did maybe we would be more cooperative, because there's a lot of territorialism, there's a lot of, "that's not my job, I'm not going to do it" ... So I think if we understood what the other people did a little better it would make everybody's life a little easier. Payroll wouldn't insist on ridiculous deadlines, accounting wouldn't insist on doing things in a certain way if they knew how it affected us.

These examples illustrate the wide array of change-resistant functional problems which can be related to loose subunit coupling and high levels of subunit autonomy. It is also interesting to note the blame subroutines which had arisen as a consequence of those longstanding problems. While increased communication is often suggested as a palliative for such coordination problems among subunits, it is not always clear exactly what kind of communication would be most valuable or how more of it would alleviate those problems. (Chapter 7 discusses feedback problems in greater depth.)

The system implementation and subunit coupling

An administrator in the IT group provided an interesting example of how the system implementation had begun to precipitate a tightening in subunit coupling. A number of points are worth noting in this passage. The new shared database required a higher degree of coordination among subunits than had been the norm, and activity related to the implementation was bringing some conflicts to the surface. It appears that the mechanism for defusing these conflicts had in the past been a blame subroutine with the blame directed at the mainframe IT department, which the new system was going to replace with end user computing.

A good example – I know it's going to come up soon – is, as we go around to different departments and explain what it's [i.e., the new system] all about and how interaction has to go on between departments, and communications – which just is not there. One department is going to affect another department by what they're putting into different fields, and how they're going to cooperate on the database.

Int: That's because the data is shared, right?

Yes. And I just see how different departments say, "No, this is how we want it. We really don't care about them." And vice versa. "No, my department's more important than that department." Well, it's going to be interesting when Big Blue [i.e., the mainframe] gets finally pulled, which is very soon.

Prior to the implementation of the shared database, subunits were for the most part free to choose their own software packages since the electronic data generated within the unit were used only within that unit. The introduction of a shared database prohibited that degree of subunit autonomy, and we can see both the ICT implementation beginning to precipitate a localized tightening in subunit coupling, and a notable resistance to this change rooted in the high degree of subunit autonomy which had been previously been a norm in the organizational culture.

Int: When you anticipate departments fighting or failing to cooperate among themselves, are you talking about academic departments, operations departments?

All of them. For right now we'll go with operations … Let me use a specific, because we just went through this. Financial Aid likes their – and I just lost the word for the product they use – Profields, or something like that. Either way, they use a different standard database, but their stuff has to go into the [new ICT], so when their information is in there registration can pull up what they happen to need, and the bookstore can pull up what kind of financial aid they're getting.

Int: That's their database?

That's what they're using to track their information. And that has to be relayed over to the [ICT] for the rest of the college to use it. It's like, "Well, no. This works for us, and this is how we want to deal with it." So, it's a college issue.

Proposition Three

Visibility alone is insufficient to mitigate unusual routines when they provide localized benefits for a subunit.

How a blame subroutine can camouflage negligence

Certainly the tactic of shifting responsibility for an operational problem is not unique to the culture of this research site (and is a general characteristic of humans – see the discussion of cognitive dissonance and self-attribution bias in Chapter 8). Of interest here is the way the evolution of a blame subroutine can institutionalize a problem and preserve it, even when the problem is chronic and well recognized. An administrator who had worked in the mainframe computer department (which the implementation was replacing with end user computing) described an example of a highly visible, yet chronic, problem. In this informant's eyes, the department unjustly suffered, in the form of a blame subroutine and a work subroutine, when some faculty submitted grades after the deadline.

Grading always had to be in by a certain amount of time. Now, it didn't matter that we didn't get the scan sheets [i.e., the optical scanning form on which faculty reported grades] on time to go put them in. It was O[ffice of] I[nformation] T[echnology]'s problem that [student grades] weren't out.

Int: Now, you're saying OIT?
The old OIT, when we were on the mainframe. We used to get scan sheets – there's a perfect example – grading, from faculty. They had to be out by a certain amount of time, the report cards had to be out by a certain amount of time. So, many times we'd schedule – "Hey, we need this in by this date" – and half of them [i.e., the scan sheets] weren't even in.
So we'd go, "Hey, we got two weeks. All right. Let's reschedule that whole run again." The grading process was a long run. That was a full night run. It was like a five- to six-hour run, with backups and everything else that were being upgraded. So we'd schedule that. Let's run it again.
And of course, half of them didn't give it in, so we had another fifty come in. Boom. Let's run the process. Say, "This is the last week to get it in, because next week we have to do everything." All right, another twenty-five come in. So that's just an example, but it goes the same with other types of reporting we had to do over there.
Just because the end user didn't have it in on time – it still meant it was OIT's problem.

This informant's department was penalized in two ways by this UR. First, it bore the cost of a work subroutine, in making multiple runs of the term grade job. Worse, it was the target – unjustly, in this informant's view – of a blame subroutine which evolved around this chronic operational problem.

How a delay subroutine can protect a perquisite

Some informants expressed frustration that participants in a group process would sometimes appear to deliberately sidetrack the discussion. The head of a large educational service unit viewed group time spent laboring over the details of a decision as a necessary task, but distinguished this from what s/he saw as tactics designed to stall the decision.

Some people can't focus on the big issue; they get to it by picking at the smaller parts of it. You just have to provide time for that. It's part of the dynamic of the group, whether that's departmental or part of a larger group. Sometimes those details are important.

Int: Have you been at meetings where you felt that time was being wasted over lots of detail?

No, my frustration in meetings is when you've got an agenda, and you think you'll go through these things one, two, three and all of a sudden you swing out to a tangential topic of some kind. And people who don't want to talk about the agenda item use it as a diversion. Somebody raises a hand to get off the topic and somebody else takes it some place else.

That happens and I find that more frustrating than working on details … [It's] like being inside a pinball machine. I like to have as few and short meetings as possible and you should have some action intended for the meeting, whatever it is you came for and get it done. I go to too many meetings and you think, "What did we do besides sit there for an hour?"

Int: Let me read you a different description [of a hypothetical group dynamic]. "The issue is reframed so discussion turns away from the original issue."

Informer: Yeah, that tends to happen a lot.

Int: Can you give me examples of where you experienced that?

It happens in division chair meetings. It will happen sometimes in governance and committee meetings … There are times when people come to meetings with alternate agendas.

How "good" decision-making can lead to an error subroutine

Like the grading system, the college's general education policy had been the subject of controversy for a considerable period of time prior to this study. Perhaps it is in this issue that the product/process distinction briefly mentioned above is most visible. Informants differed sharply in their assessment of this policy and the organizational system which resulted from it. Those favoring it spoke approvingly of the collegial decision process which generated the policy; those critical of it cited its complexity and questioned its educational effectiveness. The general education system had been in place for more than a decade at the time of data collection. A number of the informants had been at the college during the time that the system had been designed and implemented, and thus could reflect both on the system itself as a product and on the process that generated it. At the time of the interviews, the issue of the college's general education system had come up anew because of the state's desire to facilitate transferability of credits.

To an informant who became a full-time administrator but had earlier served as faculty, the existing general education system was obviously flawed, despite the support it had enjoyed among faculty. This informant was clear in his/her dissatisfaction with that system, and the process which generated it.

I sat on that original general education committee. That was a very long time ago. That whole general education model was born out of a desire to please everybody, so we ended up with this non-model model, this – you know, you can't make a horse out of a camel, which is exactly what we tried to do. We limped along with it for years and years and years.

To this informant, a seriously flawed system came out of the attempt to maximize the buy-in of the faculty.

But basically, in the beginning everyone felt their course should be designated [i.e., have the broadest applicability to the general education requirement] because everyone thought their course was important. So we ended up with the designated general education [courses] and the non-designated general education. And the non-designated was simply an effort to give a positive label to all those people and all those courses that didn't fit into the designated. And nobody – I served on that committee, I felt like I was in the twilight zone – nobody wanted to hear that maybe underwater basket weaving didn't meet general education requirements. They didn't want to hear it. And so this model was created that I don't think served us well over the years. It's not clear in the catalog, students didn't really understand it, transfer institutions didn't really understand it.

In stark contrast, the professor who chaired that committee looked back on that process as successful collective decision-making. To this informant, the major challenge facing the committee was to satisfy the concerns of all parties at the table.

Well, one of the first big leadership experiences I had here was … with the challenge of creating the college's newest general education policy. It was my job to bring the college into compliance with what was then the [state's] new general education policy … There were economic concerns, about "what was going to happen to my courses?" There were political concerns, in terms of shifts of enrollments from one place in the college to another place in the college. There were just layers and layers of things that people were worried about when we started to tinker with the general Ed policy of the college.

To this participant, the general education system the group was charged with designing had the potential to significantly disrupt the existing social order of the college, particularly with regard to power and resource allocation. The chief concern of the decision process, therefore, was to satisfy the concerns of all at that table; the process was successful because this was done.

Int: And the concern there was that some departments' enrollments would be drastically diminished.
    Right. But nobody's was.

Int: That was a concern.
    That was one of the concerns.

Int: Were there others, in arriving at that solution?
    Well, yeah. That would have created realignments of power in terms of SCH's [student credit hours] among departments. Then there were the economic questions. If your – if a course in your department didn't get a

certain status in the listing, then you might not need all the faculty you have. I mean, there were real economic concerns.

And then there were the philosophical concerns. What is general education, really? So all of those things – political, economic, philosophical – they were all flying around all the time. And would have to be hammered out on a – almost on a course – not almost: on a course-by-course basis ... We were trying to address all of what we recognized as serious concerns that people brought up to us in the process. So we were trying to respect what was at stake, from many points of view. So, I guess we did.

Despite this informant's favorable assessment of the general education system and the process which generated it, another interviewee expressed considerable frustration with the system itself, and its resistance to change. General education policy fell under the purview of a free-standing committee, apart from the governance structure, and so appeared quite buffered from feedback about its decisions.

Let me give you an example ... [W]e have a system for general education ... very atypical to what might be found at other colleges and universities, and we use terms that are nonsense terms, like non – what is it? – one general education course is called a "designated" general education [course], and there's a "nondesignated" general [education course] – which is a nonsense term. What's that about?

...

And there's all this discussion about general education. And then you have this General Education committee, and it seems to be autonomous. People get on there, some people don't even know how they get on there, but they keep going, and they seem to be dictating how general education happens [here]. And no one seems to be able to do anything about getting that committee changed or influenced. And it's almost an amazing kind of thing, it has a life of its own. And yet, here everybody is always complaining about the general education system that we have, yet no one seems to be able to make that change.

Proposition Four

A UR can resist change because its script affirms an ideological tenet of the organization, or because it glosses a contradiction in organizational values.

Inclusion, collegiality, work subroutines, and delay subroutines

As noted above, it may sometimes happen that inclusion, despite its merits as an organizational value, fosters delay subroutines in decision processes. This suggests another interesting paradox: a larger decision-making group may be a better enactment of some important organizational value, but actually do a poorer job at its task of making a decision. A department chair linked the openness and inclusion values to delay subroutines:

Well, I think when you're in college environment there are people who believe fundamentally in an open environment, and who believe in collegiality as a fundamental precept of the environment that we live in. And so if anything the belief in an open environment, an open discussion, operates against decision-making because ... we want to involve everybody, we want to make sure that nobody's left out, and we want to make sure that everybody has been able to present their point of view. So then decision-making in a college environment is very time-consuming.

Int: Time-consuming?
   Yeah. It's just not easy to make decisions in a college environment because of the commitment to openness and discussion and collegiality.

Another senior faculty member commented on the way an emphasis on inclusion can lead to group process losses. Even though at another point in the interview this informant was highly critical of a particular upper-level administrator for moving meetings along too fast and allowing too little time for open discussion, s/he still seemed vexed at the way committee meetings can spend a good deal of time belaboring details.

You see it all the time. Nit picking. How many times do you sit at a meeting that you agree on a concept of something and spend the next hour and a half trying to get it down on paper? People are complaining about should a comma go there, or should an 'n' go there. You have that. Also overanalyzing of things. The demand of being on a committee is to look at all these kind of things and it happens at all levels. I've seen progress come to a halt with only 2–3 people, all the way up, to where small details are blown out of proportion.

Of particular interest here is her/his point that collegiality requires that every comment be given equal consideration in the discussion, even comments that are off-topic or of little value in advancing the discussion. In this way, the rigorous enactment of an organizational value may protect a work or delay subroutine, without any compensating benefit of avoiding an error subroutine. Put another way, the group may suffer the process losses of *information overload* or *coordination problems* without enjoying the process gain of *objective evaluation* (Nunamaker *et al.*, 1991, p. 46). It is reasonable to see such a decision process as having a far greater symbolic benefit to the organization (through the ritualized enactment of a key organizational value) than functional benefit (by efficiently reaching a good decision).

At my own department level sometimes we get so hung up on these little points that we don't make decisions ...

Int: Is that damaging to your department?
   It can be at times. It's frustrating because you want to get policy made and you leave and you go, "What did we just do for those two hours?"

Int: And the answer is?
   Nothing ...

Int: How is it that the trivial concerns forestall making a decision that needs to be made? How come someone doesn't say, "That's trivial, let's move on?"
   Because at my department level, everyone has a right to say whatever they want. And, no one has the right to say, "Let's move it on" ... It's a democracy. We make no decision, but we talked a lot about it.

Int: So it's taboo for someone to say, "Don't you think that's kind of small?"
   Yeah. That would not be respecting your colleague.

While this passage describes a sort of rigorous egalitarianism fostering delay subroutines, other informants saw the enactment of collegiality as a gloss over power. A newly-tenured faculty in the sciences described an example of this delay subroutine in his/her department, concerning a curriculum issue. Since collegiality was enacted as consensus, a pressing decision on course content could be stalled until all faculty members agreed.

We have, let's say, three or four faculty members who primarily teach A[natomy] and P[hysiology]. And even though we follow the same basic curriculum as far as syllabi and objectives go, obviously everybody has the latitude to interject their own material ... And so we'll encounter situations where we're working on objectives, and there'll be discussions as to whether we should cover a particular topic. Three faculty members will say it absolutely needs to be in, and one faculty member will say, "I don't see that it needs to be there," or "I don't have the time to get to this." Or, "I won't be able to cover it."

So now the problem is that you're trying to reach some level of consistency, because people [i.e., students] are moving on to the nursing program. And so, in the lab, for instance, where our [teaching] assistants have to teach an agreed-upon curriculum for all the faculty, they're working off what are called lab lists, the anatomy that the students need to know. If we can't get all four faculty members who teach anatomy to agree on what needs to be on that lab list, those guys can't teach it. So the problem is that there are times when we want something to be on there, and there may be a person who doesn't want it to be, sometimes for nostalgic reasons. That blocks that decision.

Int: And then you just can't move forward with it?

And that can be very frustrating, and it doesn't go anywhere from there. The [teaching] assistants can be frustrated because three people are telling them yes, it needs to be there, the fourth person is not. It's very difficult to get all those people in a room at one point, so we have yearly meetings to try to do just that, and my strategy, my approach now has been to float some of these things out there and let them sit for six or eight months until they become someone else's idea. And what oftentimes happens, then, is that what may generate opposition from one or two individuals early on, as they've had the chance to ruminate over it, think about it for a while – you often see a very different response a few months later.

Yet another situation that can occur is that, for a variety of reasons, people join a decision process after it has begun. One informant described the problem this can create for the group leader, when the latecomers reopen issues that the group has already resolved. The leader must then strike a balance between conflicting imperatives: the need to affirm the inclusiveness of group (a core organizational value), and the need to avoid redundant discussions (a work subroutine).

Well, I think you don't like to embarrass people but often people come into various portions of a decision-making process and they're totally out of synch ... I mean, often what they do is they'll bring up something that has parts to it. Part of it was discussed six months ago and put to bed very, very fairly, but half of what they have to say might be interesting. It's like a new comment. And I think, again, the leadership has to decide what to do with that, and it has a lot to do with the person, the stake, the expertise they're bringing. It has to do, too, with where you are in the decision-making process. I see a lot of that in higher education institutions.

Representation and process losses

An important dimension of inclusion, mentioned by some informants, was that of representation. At the research site, this value meant that decision groups ought to physically include members of all groups with even a minor stake in the decision. A junior faculty member described an instance of an objection being raised to the legitimacy of a decision group on this basis.

We had a little problem with the structure of this committee that I'm on, and someone said, "Look this is not adequately representing the faculty across the board, therefore how you can make these decisions?" That's why we had a forty-five-person subcommittee to make sure that everybody was represented, and no one felt left out.

It would seem that a rigorous enactment of representation in a large organization is likely to create problems both in the functioning of a decision group, and in individuals' ability to participate in such groups. This informant described a problem of overload, and a related delay subroutine, in committees.

Int: What's your sense of the word "representative?" What does that word mean to you?
Probably the textbook definition is fair, accurate sampling of the group. Somebody from that division, from that department. The problem is that when you get so big, it becomes ineffective. And the minuscule and minor complaints surface, and that hinders the process.

According to this informant, an open-door policy had not fully satisfied this cultural value.

*Int: Now, if the door was open for people to attend, and they didn't, why
would there be a perception that people were excluded?*

You know, somebody said that exact same thing to me as we left that
meeting. "They're open meetings, anybody could come." I think the problem is that there are too many damn meetings on the campus. There's no
time for everybody to be on a committee, there's this, there's that, there's
the other thing.

In many ways, it appears that meetings can benefit an organization more as an enactment of inclusion and collegiality than as a
practical method of making decisions. An administrator with considerable work experience in for-profit companies seemed puzzled
that the organization would invest so much effort in meetings when
the gain seemed primarily symbolic. Other informants shared this
perception that oftentimes meetings became work subroutines in
themselves, giving an appearance of activity but generating little
useful output. As one put it succinctly, "It's like steering a car with
no wheels."

Respecting all stakeholders, and an error subroutine

A senior faculty member in the humanities described an interesting
problem in his/her department meetings. Another value current in
academic environments is that policy decisions must equally protect the interests of all identifiable stakeholders, even while ignoring
compelling differences in the relative weight of those interests. This
informant related how that value often led a group to focus more on
the outlying cases impacted by the policy than on the essential context
of the decision. At the outset, this prolonged the deliberations. In the
end, the group might be unsuccessful in finding a way to account for
the exceptional cases, and create a workaround to the policy. Here,
again, there are indications of work and error subroutines.

Like when the faculty get together in my department, we're affecting thousands of students, or we're affecting eighteen to twenty adjunct faculty,
and what we're so afraid of doing is causing disruption in their lives. We
want to look at it as closely as possible. Sometimes we get too narrow and
we spend too much time on an issue that could affect maybe two or three
students. At most.

The vision is that there's a great deal of desire to come up with the perfect
decision. We want to come up with something that will not harm anyone,

and there is the desire to come up with the perfect decision. And what ends up happening is that you start to focus on the exceptions. And you don't look at – you spend an inordinate amount of time on it. It prolongs the decision-making process. Does it change it? I don't think so, most of the time. We will write, "There will be an exception to this policy. Here is how to change it."

Int: Besides delaying, does it ever lead to a bad decision?
Sometimes it leaves it too broad, too general. It becomes too encompassing and therefore has no meaning.

An administrator voiced a similar observation about a standing committee s/he served on. The committee had spent a great deal of time deliberating about the college's policy on smoking, and in the end adopted a recommendation which many, including this informant, felt would be ineffectual.

We have met on that issue [the policy on smoking], and that issue alone, for almost two years.

Int: So, what do you do?
We go there and discuss surveys and people's opinions, and make no decisions.

Int: Do you ever generate a recommendation?
I think we finally did.

Int: Finally?
I think we just made a recommendation, but it's so watered down. We try to water our recommendations down so much so that they make everyone happy, that they're no longer meaningful. I find quite often a meeting [here] is a meeting to compromise and make everybody happy. And you just can't make everybody happy. There's got to be some winners. There's got to be some losers. Here, we want everybody to be a winner. We all can't be winners. And it's not in the sense of winner and losing, it's just that sometimes your opinions mean something, sometimes they don't.

Student-centeredness, and a work subroutine

Another example of a UR linked to an organizational value surfaced in the interview with a newly-tenured faculty in the sciences. While this informant in no way denigrated the organizational value of student-centeredness, s/he made note of an elaborate work subroutine (and, technically, an error subroutine) which had evolved around enacting that value. It seems likely that this routine will be familiar to most academicians.

If a student is unhappy about a particular grade, and wants to take a very unrealistic concern to the nth degree, they have the opportunity to do that because they're the student. A student who's got a 40 on everything that they've ever scored, who knows in writing that a passing average must be 65, being allowed to go from department chair to division chair to dean to a hearing, potentially. All of which is a tremendous waste of time, recognizing of course that the student needs to have a forum.

   If they're being treated unfairly there needs to be a process in place. But at the same time, if it's clear that things have been handled entirely professionally, for the best interests of the student, there's no reason why just because the student is a student or a customer, that the student should be allowed to just continue to get away with something like that.

   To this informant, the meticulous enactment of student-centeredness had also fostered an error subroutine in which the course grade may sometimes be an unreliable measure of a student's performance.

We'll have students … who will come in and say, "Well, Doc, I've passed every other course I've ever taken here. I've got a 4.0. I can't understand why I'm just getting a B in anatomy," or "I'm just getting a B in organic chemistry. What is it that's happening now that's giving me this problem?" And so, these oftentimes are the students who want every advantage. They'll complain to the department chair or the division chair, "I don't understand why it's so difficult."

   There's some level of, we're here to please the student, we're here to do what's best for the student, but the student is allowed to push that beyond what is realistic, beyond what is necessary, beyond what is in some cases professional. It encroaches on that student–professor relationship. And because that can happen across campus, the students have learned by habit that they can try these things, do some of these kinds of things. They may have learned that in high school and it's worked for them. They whine to their professor, their grade changes.

The problem of dominance and power relations in open meetings

While the college's governance system was designed to offer every organization member the opportunity to participate in decision-making, and it did appear to be an important symbol of this organizational value, a surprising number of the informants saw problems in its routine functioning. Nunamaker *et al.* (1991, p. 49) noted that group process losses sometimes tended to rise as the group size increased, and it may be that the problems informants mentioned were simply endemic to a decision group which, at least in its charter if not the actual attendance at its meetings, was as large as the entire payroll of the organization.

A number of faculty informants indicated they did not always feel free to express their views candidly at meetings because of pressure, not from administrators, but from their peers. Here, again, is a paradox: although the meetings were clearly an important symbol of openness as an organizational value, some participants did not perceive them as safe places in which to speak. (This problem resembles the process losses Nunamaker *et al.* called *conformance pressure* and *domination* (1991, p. 46), and Dutton's analysis of how avowedly participatory online discussions can end up stifling participation (1996).)

A senior faculty member in the humanities described how a structure intended to promote open discussion actually inhibited it. It is worth noting that this informant had been tenured for a good number of years, yet still felt some degree of intimidation from his/her colleagues.

I've had a person in my department say something in [the general meeting of the college governance] that that person thought, and was called on the carpet afterwards by one of the more senior faculty.

Int: Wow.
   Oh, yeah.

Int: So much for free speech, eh?
   Oh, also on votes. "Why did you vote that way?"

Int: You're kidding!
   Show of hand votes? [whistles]. So I usually sit behind the person who wants to watch me, I sit directly behind the person. So if they really want to watch me they have to turn all the way around – and they do.

Sadly, this informant saw no venue in which the participants could be free in sharing their perspectives about controversial issues.

And there is no forum to hear all the voices. There is no place because of the tenure structure, and the politics of the department, and everything else. There's no place to have that discussion that feels safe to people.

A junior faculty member in a different academic department also noted this degree of risk in expressing oneself in a public space.

I guess it's because I think people are – it's sort of like politicians are afraid often to cast votes even if their vote's in favor of something they believe in, because they may be afraid that those votes might be used against them in some way. I guess it's just the fear of going on the record about something.

This sentiment was not confined to the faculty ranks, nor was it based only on a fear of a specific reprisal. An administrator described a reluctance to risk a loss of face in the general meeting:

There's just so much resistance to change and the new people and the younger people. I mean, when I became the director of [names department], I was the youngest director here. And I was very intimidated to speak up, because you've got these big bullies who know what's going on, who'd be, "Looka here little miss, I've been here a lot longer than you and I can tell you that it's not going to work, what you're saying" … Somebody really let me have it … I never saw governance as a place that I can be honest.

While a number of informants described this problem in the governance meetings, it did not appear to be confined to that structure. The head of a large academic unit saw this process loss diminishing the effectiveness of its internal meetings:

One of the dynamics which I think is a very unfortunate one is that junior staff, junior people, can often feel their career is going to be affected and on the line if they cross a senior person who has tenure, might even be in a position to influence their career one way or the other … so that there's a reluctance to sometimes come right out in the open with how you feel about something if that's going to cross somebody whose investment is in a different outcome. A very unfortunate dynamic.

A new faculty member in another department put it succinctly: "I'm not tenured. I don't want to rock the boat."

To state the problem concisely, if perhaps a bit cynically, the large decision groups often seem to benefit a complex organization more as ritualistic enactments of openness than they do as processes which generate gains in stimulation, synergy, or objective evaluation (Nunamaker *et al.*, 1991, p. 46) through actual freedom to openly share ideas. Given that such large groups consume considerable time and effort, they sometimes can better be understood as work and delay subroutines fostered by symbolic purposes than as collaborative decision-making.

Ideology and change resistance

At first glance it might seem that change resistance is rooted in whatever personal advantages or privileges the status quo confers. While localized benefits do appear to be one dimension of change resistance in URs, another dimension is the connection of current practices to underlying beliefs. This linkage of operational procedures to ideological tenets seems to create a powerful inertial force in an organization. The head of a large academic unit described the way even minor procedural change could be blocked in large group decision processes.

Well, I'm being pretty candid here because of confidentiality, but it's like if you – when you operationalize your beliefs, your principles of your profession into certain practices, the notion that the practices in place are immutable, and if you alter the practices in any way, even if you modernize them, to certain people you inherently and implicitly violate the beliefs.

That's not a true statement, a logical statement. So that any modernization or alteration in how you deliver your service, which might even be an enhancement of that service, automatically in some people's thinking, becomes a violation of the tenets and beliefs that underpin your profession or your service. And some folks will argue that line, which is just patently not true.

...

Any change has a suspect purpose to it, and it's all a grand scheme ... it's almost a suspicion rather than a comprehension that some of these things might be for everybody's benefit. Some are not, obviously. Not all change is good change. There's an inability to discriminate, and then to differentiate that you can change some things and still preserve the best of what you're doing and your basic principles.

A mid-level administrator likewise lamented that there were a number of institutional practices which had become, in his/her words, "big sacred things." In this informant's eyes, certain practices needed to be re-examined but open discussion was impossible. The organization thus might be capable of single-loop learning, but not double-loop learning.

A staff member described a work subroutine in a standing committee of the governance structure. This informant sat on the committee charged with resolving policy issues concerning educational standards. The work subroutine resulted when the specific questions referred to the committee became tied to the broad educational philosophy of the college, an area beyond the scope of the committee. This passage illustrates the way discussion of comparatively narrow operational or procedural issues can become linked to broad questions of institutional values and ideology, and thus become impossible to resolve even as their consideration uses up a great deal of time. While URs may become change resistant because subunits which are functionally related are only loosely coupled, URs may also result when subunits or issues which are functionally unrelated become tightly coupled.

Yes, I've been in meetings where we go over and over and over the same things and don't get anyplace. That was happening last year in educational standards, because everything that came back to us was educational philosophy. If we recommended a change, we were really talking about changing the philosophy, and we really thought we should discuss the philosophy before we made changes that changed [the philosophy] without knowing we changed it.

   ...

Because we were coming around to the philosophy thing and we're gonna say this is what our philosophy is, we cannot change, should not change A, B, C and D until we looked back at the philosophy. So, there was a lot of getting nowhere even though it was airing things.

A senior faculty member recounted a similar situation in faculty association meetings, but saw it instead as a positive feature of the discussion. In this informant's perspective, the delay in considering the scheduled agenda item is offset by the benefit of time spent discussing important philosophical issues. Perhaps this informant's view of that turn in a decision group reflects the high value faculty, with their primary university role as educators and analysts, place on raising questions and defining issues.

Again, most of the meetings I go to are faculty association meetings. And at those meetings we discuss a number of policies – grading, [the new ICT], things like that. It often turns out that something like grading policy gets tied to a greater issue, like some more broad policy of how the faculty relates to the students, where the first issue is really a subset. Sometimes the original discussion needs to be postponed until the more broad issue has been resolved. That happens a lot in an open debate situation. Where there's a problem or a concern and someone raises it, this type of discussion really focuses or brings more clearly to mind, what the major issues really are.

A faculty member in the arts recalled his/her first impressions of department and division meetings at the college. This informant, like others, saw a connection between shared beliefs (or perhaps a nostalgia for the idealized past when beliefs were widely shared) and change resistance in the organization at that time.

[This has been] my seventh year here. And when I arrived, I was one of the few new people on this campus. Everybody else had been here for an eternity. And one of the things that I noticed was that in our department, we always ended up talking about the way things were rather than the way things could be … Even within the division meetings, it was constantly, "Well, we've always done it this way. It's important for us to look at it this way. It's important to think about it this way." So, yes – I was very struck by the inflexibility of many people.

Int: Inflexibility?
[The belief that] it was very special, and it was the way it should be, and this is what makes us unique, and so why would we look at it differently?

Given the tight linkage of core beliefs and operational practices, this informant seemed a bit surprised that such a large policy change as the grading system could eventually occur, the work subroutine notwithstanding.

Again, I go back to the idea that in the past there was not that much room for change, and it was because of those core values. Even when we started talking about the grading change, we went into the idea of educational philosophy and that seemed to hold us up for quite a bit … But we did change.

Contradictions, opposing perspectives, and ideological myths

In some interviews there were indications that URs had evolved as
ways for the organization to cope with contradictions in values. (These
dynamics reflect Eisenberg's (1984) point that ambiguity in values or
beliefs can sometimes benefit an organization.) A number of informants mentioned "student-centeredness" as an essential organizational
value, but differed quite sharply in how that value ought to be enacted
in the daily operation of the college, with some questioning whether
this value was anything more than an ideological myth.

A junior faculty member in the arts seemed to be an especially keen
observer of this aspect of the organizational dynamics. Perhaps, as
a newcomer to the college, s/he had not yet fully acculturated to the
organizational environment, so that any contradictions in the belief
system were still identifiable, if not downright vivid. This informant noted a difference in the administrative perspective and faculty
perspective on the nature of student-centeredness. The college had
recently begun offering a small number of courses in a short, intensive semester. This informant expressed reservations about the educational benefit to the individual student of such courses, but noted that
these courses had proven quite popular.

Is it best for the enrollment? Yeah. How can a three-week term be best for
the student? All of that stuff is in your short-term memory ... You're gonna
forget more than what you remember.

So, I'm not so sure that the decisions are in the best interests of the students. Or are they more in the best interests of FTE [full time enrollment],
which is really the lifeblood? If you offer a course that's finished in three
weeks, will you get people to take it? Absolutely.

...

What accountability for the people who leave? We should have a high
accountability. Do we just cram in what is usually offered in fifteen weeks?
I don't understand that. "Here's a chapter, read it. We're gonna talk about
it tomorrow, we're gonna have a test about it on Wednesday, then we're
gonna start the next one and have a test on Thursday." ... I don't see how
it's beneficial in the long run to the students. It's beneficial to the institution, but not to the students.

An administrator also saw contradictions in core institutional
beliefs and their enactment. The informant saw one particular belief

in particular as supporting change-resistant URs that imposed costs on students:

I think there is a core belief that [the research site] is somehow different than other places, and somehow better. And while I think [this] is an extra-ordinary place – I love being here, and I worked at [another college] for ten years ... I've got to tell you something. I didn't see any difference between the quality of the student coming out of [the other college] than I do the student coming out of [here].

This informant felt the belief in the organization's superiority pre-served a number of work and error subroutines that imposed costs on students, despite the professed organizational value of student-centeredness. In this informant's description, when work or error subroutines in value chains involving students were called into question in the form of a comparison to corresponding practices at other educational institutions, the critique that the local practices were deficient (in the language of this study, were URs) was fre-quently rebutted by the professed belief in overall organizational superiority regarding student-centeredness. In essence, supporters of the status quo took a position along the line of "we're differ-ent because we're better." (As described in Chapter 8, this seems a clear case of an organizational-level drive to reduce cognitive dis-sonance.) An observer might expect that such a deeply held value as student-centeredness would generate considerable discussion in the general meetings. Yet, this informant felt there was something of a taboo against openly problematizing some work and error subrou-tines s/he saw violating that value.

Proposition Five

A cultural environment which places a high value on inclusion will tend to support double binds.

Inclusive decision-making and its discontents

As noted above, inclusion appeared to be one of the strongest organ-izational values at the research site, manifest as a tradition that major policy decisions and documents will be collective works. It is diffi-cult to over-emphasize the strength of this value in the culture of this organization, and it seems this is true of higher education in general. The co-chair of the college's most recent accreditation self-study summarized it concisely:

And if there was one thing you learned [here], that was where it all began and ended. When [the other co-chair of the self-study] and I did [the accreditation report] we had one goal, and that was to make sure that everyone was valued, included, affirmed.

However admirable this value may be in itself, it seemed to put leaders of decision groups in a double-bind situation. They must guide the group toward the efficient completion of its task, while simultaneously enacting the inclusion and collegiality values sufficiently to maintain the group's legitimacy within the organization's culture. The comment of a senior faculty member illustrated how high the expectation could be:

A good discussion leader steers the discussion back on track. So, if you're having a discussion about, say, something like setting a policy or making a rule or something like that, if the discussion starts to wander away from the central issue and gets sidetracked on a little detail – or maybe really off on a tangent – that discussion leader has to drag the discussion back, and has to know how to do it so that nobody feels like they've been tossed out on their ear.

Int: That would seem to me to be a difficult task.
Maybe. But that's what committee chairs are supposed to do. That's their job, and if they can't do it they shouldn't be committee chairs. It's as simple as that.

Informants often identified the college governance as the place where they had seen UR scripts played out. Governance occupied a special niche in the belief system of the organization because it was the structure through which all organization members could participate in collaborative policy decisions. Decisions made in governance were, by its charter, advisory to but not binding on the executive management of the college. Still, organization members expected college executives to take the recommendations adopted in governance very seriously.

Inclusiveness was a key feature of the governance structure. Standing committees within governance had specified quotas of members from the various constituencies of the college (i.e., faculty, staff, administration, and students) so as to guarantee representation on them. Moreover, all members of the organization, including students, were invited to participate in monthly college-wide meetings called governance forums. The large group meetings were open to all who chose to attend, and a good deal of time was devoted to open discussion of policy issues before votes were taken on them. In sum, it would seem fair to view this collegial decision mechanism as an almost idealized enactment of the strong organizational value of inclusion.

Why was it, then, that so many organization members considered its actual workings as problematic, in one way or another? A senior faculty member pointed to a process loss related to group size (similar, but not identical, to the loss Nunamaker *et al.* identified as *air time fragmentation* (1991, p. 46)) and hinted at the difficulty the group leader might face in trying to avoid it:

Well first of all, the more people you have the more agendas you have of people, and the more people want to talk, and not necessarily discuss what is the central issue or even the issue that is at hand, or anything that's relevant. So I mean, you have to expect that people want to talk and you have to let them talk. You can't be autocratic about it. But sometimes that discussion veers off to something else that someone may raise. They'll say, "What about this? We didn't consider that." And are those germane to really what decision has to be made, or even what the problem is?

A junior faculty member observed a delay subroutine in a standing committee of the college governance:

And given that it was a detailed project that involved probably twenty to twenty-five committee members, it often happened that in the course of trying to reach that detailed document someone would raise an issue or make a point that was within his or her own area but which wasn't in anybody else's. And so it seemed that we would spend a lot of time giving that person a chance to air their idea or their question or their problem in ways that struck, I think, a lot of people as being kind of off the point of the larger goal that we were trying to reach. I think that happens with some regularity at the college.

But a delay subroutine may not be simply the unfortunate byproduct of an institutional value (in this case, a simple process loss related to group size). It is also possible that a long, drawn-out discussion may be in some parties' strategic interest in a controversy. As Proposition Three suggests, a UR may persist because it does benefit certain actors. A junior faculty member raised the possibility that the inclusion value sometimes was used, via a delay subroutine, to prevent change and maintain the status quo:

And I also think that there are frankly some people interested in keeping the process going for as long as possible because that means it will never get changed and they don't want the grading system to change. I'm not thinking of anybody here specifically, but I know that that attitude exists in the college community and so the longer this debate goes on without a resolution the happier they are.

Int: So you're saying that it may be that for some people talking, and talking, and talking about it is a strategic maneuver.
It's a strategic maneuver to avoid resolution.

Another informant, a senior faculty member who had become a full-time administrator, described a work subroutine that could arise around representation as the enactment of inclusion:

Everyone wants to be able to give their two cents on an issue, on the question before it moves anywhere – and that usually has to do with who's been involved, who's had an opportunity. One of the objections, for example, to the committee that was going to look at [educational] practices was that it was a voluntary thing, "Who wants to do this?" A lot of people volunteered. There were some areas where no one volunteered.

So the issue now became around should there be equal representation on it? It's voluntary, anyone who wants to, can. "Oh, but some people didn't, and they will be left out, and shouldn't they be involved? And shouldn't we give them another opportunity?" And after a while your eyes glass over and you say, look, you give them the opportunity, they don't want to do it, tough. If it doesn't come out to their liking, that's it. Again, the guardian of total involvement.

This informant clearly was vexed by delay subroutines created as the college's inclusion value was enacted in the college-wide governance. While s/he appeared willing to trade off a certain degree of inclusion for relief from the process loss its rigorous enactment generated, that remedy would open the group up to criticism from others who would rather trade off the delay in moving the decision along for the sake of maximizing inclusion or openness.

The problem of leadership in an inclusive organization

This tension between the need for efficiency in group decision-making and the need to satisfactorily enact this fundamental organizational value posed a challenge for group leaders. A number of informants, when asked about problems in group processes, faulted the leaders of those groups for the work or delay subroutines in those processes. Other informants, however, complained that college administration dictated policy and failed to adequately involve faculty in decisions. Perhaps it is ironic that the commonly used phrase, "strong leadership," can simultaneously have such different meanings, and that inclusion can foster blame subroutines.

The comments of a junior faculty member on a recent revision of the policy concerning incomplete grades offer some insights into this culturally-induced double bind. It is interesting to note that the informant seemed aware of the conflicting expectations.

And that's when you get in a situation, again, a catch-22. You need strong leadership, but you need strong leadership that is open to suggestions. The vice president has written a policy on incomplete [grades]. That wasn't given to any committee, it didn't go through [the governance] steering committee, but [s/he] wrote it. [S/he] went around to other colleges, got their language, used part of our [existing policy's] language, wrote it, and said, "Here it is!" That's strong leadership.

But, what it shouldn't be is, "Here it is, here's the policy." Rather it should be, "Here it is, let's talk about it." We'll spend a day – one day, that's it – talking about it. You go back, consider it, next time we'll meet we'll have a discussion. We'll vote or come up with alternative plans. That's part of the process, it's not, "Duck! Here comes the next policy."

But again you've got to have something there, and it sounds like I'm contradicting myself, but you need to have somebody saying, "I'm in charge, this is the way it's going to be." But not sitting up there as the benevolent dictator saying, "Here is the new policy. Adopt it!" Let's have a discussion about the policy. And I don't know if that's happened.

A senior faculty member in the humanities was quite blunt about his/her perception that the group decision process in the governance meetings was often no more than a gloss over the exercise of executive power:

I don't think that the upper-level administration is frank and honest. Decisions are made and we're made to think that our input has influence in making those decisions. There are times when we're misled. The grading change was an example. I was told before the conversation became public that the grading system was going to change. And that it was a done deal.

Int: Told by whom?
By an upper-level administrator.

By no means was the discontent with collective decision processes universal among this study's informants, however. The head of a large department within educational services spoke very positively about both governance and other collegial processes. It is interesting to note that this informant saw the discontent as rooted in a fundamental disagreement about the appropriate role of these collective processes in policy formation. This informant saw the collective process as advisory to the college executives, and was satisfied that those executives seriously considered that input. Others, in the view of this informant, expected the collective process to culminate in a referendum, with the majority vote binding on the executives.

A senior faculty member in the sciences saw the organizational context as requiring a kind of ritualistic behavior by all parties for the sake of enacting the institutional value of inclusiveness – albeit at the cost of generating work subroutines:

I don't think [the college president] lies and I certainly would never accuse [the academic vice-president] of doing that ... But again when [the president] responded yes to Prof. L, that we would not change the grading system if the faculty votes no, I didn't believe [it]. They spent a lot of money on installing [the new ICT] on the basis of the grading system and other things that would go along with that, and it was clear that it was going to be implemented.

I was on the committee [which reviewed the grading policy] the previous summer and it was pretty clear that no matter what we came up with the school was going to do what it wanted to do anyway. One could say that was lying and misleading. I would like to think that [the president] was engaging the faculty, and that's very generous. But [s/he] had to do something and that was the way of doing it. My experience is that I was wasting my time but somebody had to be on the committee.

So, when you say lie, there are techniques one needs to use when one is a leader and if the troops are politically sensitive or experienced, they will

Table 5.2 *Examples of subroutines in the case*

Subroutine	Example from the case
Work	• elaborate grade appeals • elaborate system planning documents, subsequently ignored • extensive face-to-face meetings • formation of additional subcommittees • group editing of paper forms • group lacking appropriate decision power • incompatibilities in formats of shared data • need to validate the representativeness of committee • policy review requiring reexamination of core values • procurement paperwork and interdepartmental handoffs • student testing during admissions process • unproductive meetings as symbols of inclusion
Delay	• consensus required for department's curriculum revision • continuing to add representatives to decision group • deliberate diversion from meeting agenda • extensive discussion, from everyone, as enactment of collegiality • inclusion, and personal agendas • indecision in transferring data to new system • miscommunication between users and tech support • non-responsiveness to messages • prolonged discussion of issue as a tactic to forestall decision • revision of general education policy • revision of grading policy • slow response to demand for courses
Error	• bad fit of course availability to demand • belief in institutional uniqueness precluding change

Table 5.2 (*cont.*)

Subroutine	Example from the case
	• dominance in open meetings
	• idiosyncratic general education policy
	• inefficient distribution of computing machinery
	• late registration of international students
	• poor linkage of course sections to number of full-time faculty
	• miscommunication between users and tech support
	• missed deadlines for payroll information
	• overweighting exceptional cases in policy decisions
	• permanent linkage of current practices to core values, "sacred cows"
	• attempting to please all stakeholders
Blame	• agenda-driven meetings seen as managerial control
	• claims that information was not shared
	• conflict between operations and academic units
	• executive decisions seen as illegitimate power
	• group decision process seen as gloss on executive power
	• late reporting of grades
	• scapegoating mainframe computing department and tech support

recognize that this is a charade and what is going to happen is going to happen despite the input. But this is a very reasonable way to make everyone feel good to have their input, keeps the waters smooth and the interaction open and friendly. Therefore it's acceptable to people.

In short, this informant believed the relational benefit of the process (through engaging organization members) outweighed its cost (in generating a work subroutine). Further, the informant viewed the college president's actions in a double-bind situation as evidence of leadership skill, rather than ethical deficiency.

Conclusion

Table 5.2 summarizes examples of the primary URs identified in the fieldwork of the case. The table should not be understood as a measurement of the communication climate of the research site, or as critique of interactions at the site. For us, perhaps the biggest discovery from this field study was the intimate connection between organizational culture and unusual routines, with their associated interaction scripts. The next chapter will show how we incorporated these elements into a revised model.

6 | *Summary and discussion of the case study results*

This chapter extends the discussion of the propositions to more general properties of unusual routines within complex organizations. Each proposition is represented by just one or two of the salient examples from the full case. The chapter concludes with a substantially reworked model of UR dynamics, indicating what we see as the relationships among innovations, organizational culture, and URs.

Proposition One

If a new ICT mitigates or exacerbates URs it does so not simply as a more efficient channel (the first-level effect) but also as an innovation the organization must process (the second-level effect).

The interviews revealed a number of URs with associated subroutines, some of which the system implementation seemed to be impacting as a second-level effect. Perhaps the change in the grading system is the clearest example. Arguably, the past debates over the grading system can be seen as a delay subroutine, in that the issue was never decisively resolved either in favor of retaining the existing non-traditional grades or in favor of a change, despite extensive discussion time spent on the issue. To some informants, the grading system had become a "sacred cow," resistant to change regardless of substantial criticism. While the new ICT was still in its early implementation phase at the time of these interviews, a major change in the grading system was made in a surprisingly short time frame. A number of informants saw the ICT as a contributing factor in this change.

Another second-level change which surfaced in the interviews was a tightening of subunit coupling through the implementation work. While not a UR in itself, loose coupling can be seen, as noted above, as a dimension of the cultural substrate which supports URs. The implementation work necessitated a degree of procedural rationalization which effectively tightened subunit coupling among certain administrative functions and might thereby mitigate delay and error subroutines, but also increase the potential to generate new subroutines in the boundary maintenance activity (for related examples, see Aydin and Rice, 1992; Johnson and Rice, 1987).

Paradoxically, while the decision to install a new system may have been motivated by the desire for first-level gain in efficiency, an organization may benefit (or suffer) most from the second-level restructuring of the social system.

Proposition Two

Loose coupling between subunits in a value chain allows URs to resist change.

The interviews surfaced a number of work and error subroutines that appeared to negatively impact the organization's clients, the students, in a number of situations (see Table 5.1). The error subroutine in matching the availability of a required course to the student demand preserved the academic departments' control over their course offerings and scheduling but its cost was externalized onto students, a third party to the conflict between administration and faculty. In this instance, loose coupling appeared to protect the UR even when that routine was recognized as a problem.

Perhaps the problem of international student registration is the most intriguing, since this UR seemed to generate no obvious benefit for the subunits involved. In this case, both the students and the administrative units were caught in an error subroutine that proved highly resistant to change. This example suggests that there can be a high degree of organizational inertia built into the social system even when there is little localized benefit.

Paradoxically, a high degree of subunit autonomy, often regarded positively as a dimension of organizational empowerment and flexibility, can also function negatively as a cultural substrate of URs' change resistance.

Proposition Three

Visibility alone is insufficient to mitigate URs when they provide localized benefits for a subunit.

Two points emerge from the contrasting views of the general education system and the decision process which led to it. Critics saw this decision process as seriously flawed for the same reason the supporters saw it as a success: the chief concern of the process was to satisfy the interests of the participants in the decision. (We should note that this group is not necessarily coterminous with the group of stakeholders, parties who were affected by the decision!) To the critics, this preoccupation led to the interactions we call an error subroutine, in that the general education system which came out of this decision process created difficulties for students with regard to course selection and transferability. To the supporters, the decision process maximized the acceptability of that system to the faculty and avoided disruption of the social order among academic departments. In sum, the process optimized the benefits of the outcome for certain internal stakeholders, but in so doing externalized its costs onto others who had not participated in the decision. This system created, or at least preserved, localized benefits for the academic departments. Paradoxically, maximizing buy-in at the inception of a policy may inadvertently maximize organizational inertia when the time comes to re-evaluate that policy.

Proposition Four

A UR can resist change because its script affirms an ideological tenet of the organization, or because it glosses a contradiction in organizational values.

To put it in a critical frame, the enactment of participation through large meetings seems to often be flawed by a number of process losses. The resulting paradox here is that while open meetings can be an important symbol of inclusion and openness as fundamental organizational values, they are not necessarily perceived as safe spaces in which to voice controversial opinions, particularly opinions which touch on organizational values. This situation reflects the use of information as symbol and as signal (Feldman and March, 1981). The dialogue in these meetings serves the organization well as an enactment of values – i.e., as symbol – but relatively poorly as a way of progressing toward good decisions – i.e., as signal. Neither are the representative committees perceived as efficient ways to reach decisions, particularly when the participants deliberately block mundane operational changes by invoking fundamental organizational values, or become mired in attempting to clarify organizational values about which there is no real consensus.

Even though such process losses seem to degrade the functioning of a decision group in a variety of ways, it may be quite difficult to change a process when operations are linked strongly to values. As Proposition Four suggests, URs can persist because their scripts affirm an ideological tenet of the organization, or gloss contradictions in values.

Proposition Five

A cultural environment which places a high value on inclusion will tend to support double binds.

In the current higher education environment, colleges face frequent challenges which necessitate expeditious and intelligent decision-making. Simultaneously, the deeply ingrained values and beliefs of those institutions require maximal inclusion of participants, representation of various constituencies, and airing of divergent perspectives in at least quasi-egalitarian decision processes. It would appear that, among other contradictions in ideological tenets mentioned in connection with Proposition Four, there was particular disagreement about the proper decision-making authority of these group processes. In short, one root of the double bind in an inclusive organization is contradictory beliefs about the very meaning of inclusion as an organizational value.

This condition can make the leadership of decision groups a daunting task: is it best to move the process along, or to maximize inclusion? Either choice is likely to become problematic, in one regard or another. The paradox is that organization members often wish for their leaders to keep groups efficient by mitigating work or delay subroutines, yet also criticize leaders for limiting group size, discussion time, or the scope of the group's decision-making authority – choices which those leaders might reasonably make to mitigate work, error, and delay subroutines.

Discussion

ICT implementation and unusual routines

At the time of the data collection, the system was just beginning to diffuse through the organization. The informants included both early adopters and others who seemed likely to be laggards in the use of the ICT. There were no signs that the new ICT exacerbated existing URs, but some indications that URs were created in the implementation itself. A few informants mentioned work subroutines in which they had prepared extensive descriptions of their departments' procedures as part of the system planning, documents which seemed to them to have been ignored as the system was actually implemented. A few administrators complained that their departments lacked computing machinery powerful enough to use the system's features, while higher-power computers had been allocated to faculty units which had less pressing need for them. (Another informant, in the IT department, corroborated that many computers sat on faculty desktops, unused.) This can be viewed as an error subroutine in the implementation, in the sense of faulty allocation of resources which weakens the initial purpose of the change.

Most of the observed change, however, was mitigation of existing URs along the lines described in proposition one of this study. The system did in fact generate some first-level efficiency gains early in the implementation, thereby mitigating some work and delay subroutine in accounting and purchasing functions. The more profound changes observed in this study, however, are the second-level changes which were beginning to occur in the social system at the time of the study. A number of informants described changes in the people they communicated with inside the organization. Some described changes in norms for communication, particularly in responsiveness to messages; this can be seen as mitigation of localized delay subroutines (perhaps, more specifically, shadow costs and media transformations). The new system, even in its planning stage, was the catalyst for a major change in grading policy. The grading policy had been the subject of criticism for many years, and the resolution of this issue can be seen as mitigation of a global delay subroutine in the college's response to its external environment. In short, there is reason to see the system implementation as the starting point for a period of substantial change in the social system of the organization.

A considerable tightening of subunit coupling was evident among certain functionally interdependent departments, such as registration and financial aid. As suggested in Proposition Two, this tightening of subunit coupling seemed to be mitigating error subroutines fostered by their previous lack of coordination. A number of faculty described change within their academic departments in the sharing of information about curricular issues, and in the discussion of those issues; these are signs of mitigations of work subroutines in the interactions with their colleagues.

Unusual routines beyond the ICT

The fieldwork surfaced a great deal of information relating to the general features and properties of URs, as well. It seems that the mitigation of URs occasioned by a system implementation tends for the most part to be localized at the subunit level, not globalized across the organization. Perhaps this is simply because educational institutions, as a way of organizing (Weick, 1979), tend to be very loosely coupled so that change in general tends to be isolated at the subunit level. A deeper explanation, however, is that there are a great number of other forces contributing to change resistance, beyond the condition of loose coupling. Some of the URs described by informants generated a localized benefit for a subunit, and externalized the cost. Put in general terms, there can be organization members with a stake in maintaining a UR, but not a countervailing group with an equal interest in mitigating it or an equal power to alter it. As Proposition Three suggested, even when the URs are recognized as problems, the localized benefits they provide may protect them against mitigation, fostering single-loop inertia.

In some cases the URs glossed a controversy over organizational values or beliefs, or, more often, served as ritualized enactments of them. Despite the frustration organization members experienced because of the associated work or delay subroutines, the strong connection of these subroutines to their cultural substrate gives them a high degree of resistance to change, as Proposition Four suggested. It seems reasonable to expect that a new ICT will not mitigate such routines simply by being a more efficient communication channel, and probably not even as an innovation that weakens organizational inertia as the organization processes it.

Rather, the potential of a ICT to mitigate URs with deep roots in the cultural substrate would seem to lie in its potential to evolve from an occasion for structuration (i.e., a catalyst of mainly single-loop learning) into a technology (or process) of structuration (i.e., an enabler of double-loop learning). For instance, communication through the ICT might come to be accepted as a legitimate enactment of collegiality and inclusive decision-making. Such an evolution might ultimately relieve the double-bind problem facing group leaders in an inclusive environment, described in Proposition Five. Clearly such a profound change would be stressful for any complex organization.

Validity challenges

There are (at least) two possible confounds in analyzing the effects of the ICT implementation in this particular case. Indeed, one of the challenges in studying a naturally-occurring field experiment is safeguarding the internal validity of the study while enjoying the real world complexity and richness of the data (Krathwohl, 1993, p. 445). First, several informants noted that there had been a substantial turnover in personnel at the college in the last five years, and attributed the changes they had observed in interaction patterns to the change in people. Second, a number of informants felt that the college president had developed a very effective style of leadership, and attributed many positive changes at the college to the work of that executive.

It is certainly reasonable to see both of these as factors in the changes observed at the research site. It is doubtful, however, that they directly account for much more of the observed change than the ICT implementation. Newcomers to an organization can bring new ideas, skills, and beliefs with them, but they also experience a thorough acculturation to the existing practices and values of the organization. In an academic institution, in particular, the tenure process creates a strong incentive for newcomers to conform to the existing norms. Executive leadership indeed has a powerful impact on the direction of organization, and plays an important role in change processes. Still, in a non-autocratic social system it seems questionable to attribute the persistence or mitigation of URs directly to the actions of a single individual, since URs are collective interaction patterns supported by collective belief systems.

A revised model of unusual routine dynamics

The case study prompted some revisions to our model of UR dynamics, and some clarification of the terminology describing them. Figure 6.1 reflects these revisions at the conceptual (not detailed) level. The major change in the model is the distinction between the single-loop learning path, which concerns mitigations and exacerbations of URs, and the double-loop learning path, which concerns change in the organizational substrate and the enactments of organizational beliefs and values. For both single-loop and double-loop learning, the organizational substrate (technical and social enablers, and other causes) affects the extent of single-loop or double-loop learning inertia.

In this model, an organizational innovation (or ICT implementation, environmental turbulence, external stakeholder pressures, new problem, etc.) initiates a process of essentially single-loop change in URs. This effect is moderated by the general barriers noted in Table 3.1 and Figure 4.1, here specifically emphasizing inertial forces within the organization, such as localized benefits of the URs. The change in URs, if any, may consist of either exacerbations or mitigations. Across a complex organization the impact of the innovation on URs tends to be both localized and varied. This path has been labeled *occasion for structuration*, since the innovation acts as a catalyst for localized structurational processes which may or may not produce change in URs. In the model, the UR is embedded in the organizational substrate; this represents that the dimensions of the organizational culture underlie and support both the single-loop inertia and the UR.

Table 6.1 provides aspects of the single-loop path from the case. It is important to note that this figure is intended to incorporate additions to our UR model from the case study but is not intended as an exhaustive classification of phenomena relating to URs.

The dashed lines in the revised model (Figure 6.1) represent the potential process of double-loop change. As mentioned above, this path is a structurational process involving dimensions of the organizational substrate and the enactments of organizational beliefs and values. There is another set of inertial forces that moderate this change, including interaction scripts, which were seen in the fieldwork to oppose deep change under the guise of supporting locally or globally held values (whether cynically or sincerely). The double-loop path is labeled *technology of structuration* (in line with Barley,

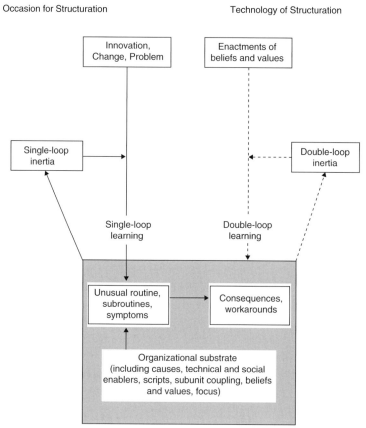

Figure 6.1 Dynamics of single-loop and double-loop learning in unusual routines.

1986), in that the ICT becomes an integral part of this change. While it appears that a variety of organizational innovations might serve to catalyze single-loop change in URs, the double-loop change in the organizational substrate and the enactments of beliefs and values is inherently a communicational process. Thus, an innovation in the communication system of an organization has a unique potential to catalyze double-loop change (as argued by Rice, 1987, and Rice and Gattiker, 2001). Table 6.2 lists aspects of the double-loop path from the case. Again, these items are those that surfaced in the fieldwork of this study; in other organizations some or all of these items may not exist, and others may well appear.

Table 6.1 *Working taxonomy of the single-loop process from the case*

Concept	Indicators
Causes: Single-loop inertial forces	• externalized costs • localized benefits • loose coupling
Unusual routine: Scope	• local (within a defined sub-unit or task group) • value chain (crossing sub-units, along a value-added process)
Unusual routine: Subroutines	• work • delay • error • blame
Consequences: Process losses due to unusual routines	• air time fragmentation • conformance pressure • coordination problems • domination • information overload
Consequences: Process gains from mitigating unusual routines	• objective evaluation • synergy

Implications for other theories of organizational communication

The case analysis has implications for some of the theories described in Chapter 4, especially sensemaking, innovation, socio-technical systems (including group process losses), as well as critical organizational communication theory.

The findings reinforce Weick's notion of sensemaking, and the relevance of sensemaking to organizational communication. Unusual routines are created and maintained in the interactions (the interacts and double interacts) among organization members. Large decision groups, such as the college governance at the research site, are prime examples of such collective sensemaking. Thus it is not surprising to

Table 6.2 *Working taxonomy of the double-loop process from the case*

Concept	Indicators
Double-loop inertial forces	• context switching • deception • interaction scripts • manipulation
Organizational substrate – beliefs	• institutional superiority • institutional uniqueness • in-use vs. espoused
Organizational substrate – values	• collegiality • consensus • inclusion • principled objections • subunit autonomy
Organizational substrate – focus or balance	• process (relational) quality • decision (content) quality

hear informants identify the governance structure as the location of a number of URs.

The case study also offers some insight into the dynamics of sensemaking. In URs the sensemaking appears not as an ongoing collectively rational process but rather as significantly fragmented or only locally-interactive processes, resulting in flawed or even failed consensual sensemaking. One might view URs simply as faulty sensemaking, but this would tend to beg the question of why there are times when the collective rationality appears so dim and other times the collective rationality is comparatively bright. Perhaps it would be more useful to view URs as the artifacts of stalled sensemaking processes, in that participants often are aware of the nonsensical aspects of their interactions yet continue to engage in those interactions (or, are unaware and thus continue). The case study finds that the stalled sensemaking which preserves URs may be restarted by change in the organization's communication system. Yet, as discussed early on in this book, ordinary experience seems to indicate that only isolated actors – whether managers, employees, organizational representatives (such as retail clerks or technical support), customers, clients, vendors, etc. – experience, identify, complain about, or do anything about, most URs. The fundamental issue about URs is that the system does not learn, and that there are potentially multiple locations or subsystems in the system where this learning does not occur.

The findings reinforce as well as extend the application of structuration theory to organizational dynamics. In the terminology of structuration theory, URs are features of the (socio-technical) system which themselves are sustained by the structures (that is, the practices and resources) in the system. Exacerbation or mitigation of URs entails change in those structures. Clearly URs resist change because of their basis in the accepted practices within the organization, and change because of changes in those practices. The analysis of the case finds that values and beliefs are of at least as much consequence in the production and reproduction of structure as are material resources and practical actions. Perhaps a key insight of structuration theory for the study of organizations is that prior actions constrain the possibilities for present actions, which themselves constrain future actions. (This is not meant to gloss the companion insight of structuration, that prior actions also enable future actions!) There is some evidence in the case study that the constraints that prior actions place on future actions often consist of the values and beliefs they define. In addition, the case study suggests that the communication system of the organization is central to its structurational processes, at two identifiable levels. Change in that communication system can at least constitute an occasion for structurational processes. Further, the communication system may itself become a technology for ongoing structuration within the organization.

Proposition Three notwithstanding (that localized benefit can sustain a UR or subroutine), this study tends to challenge some of the current thinking in the critical study of organizations. Much of that work (e.g., Deetz, 1992, pp. 221ff.; Deetz, 1995, pp. 113ff.; Huspek, 1994; Natale *et al.*, 1994) either affirms or accepts as axiomatic that organizational dynamics always involve the dominance of certain parties over others. In contrast, this study suggests that many of the most problematic interactions involve a lack of coordination – or even awareness – among subunits. While critical theory posits that a loss to some actor is necessarily the result of a gain to another, URs sometimes seem to generate losses for all the actors, even if those losses are not equal, or may generate both losses and gains while those who gain may know neither the presence or location of the losses. While critical theory attributes the dominance of certain actors to their possession of power within the social system, URs often appear to be behavior loops in which nobody has enough power to break out of them.

The concept and model of URs show some promise in explaining problematic interaction patterns which are quite common in organizations, yet are not fully explained by the theories from which they draw.

Practical implications

While the case study was designed as an academic investigation, a number of ideas surfaced which may be of value to practitioners, whether rank-and-file members of an organization who struggle to make sense of change (or make sense of inertia) in their work environment, or managers who wrestle with the task of guiding organizational change in positive directions. These ideas can be clustered around a few main points.

It is important to think about communication systems as part of the social system of the organization, and not just part of the technical system. This, of course, is a foundational principle in organizational structuration theory, diffusion of innovations theory, and socio-technical systems theory. Certainly an organization may initiate change in its communication system with the intent of gaining some benefit in its technical operations, but it is unlikely that the social system will be untouched, or that the social system will not influence the course of the change in the communication system. A practitioner would be wise to consider both the potential impact *on* the social system, and the impact *of* the social system. There will likely be changes in who communicates with whom (both inside and outside the organization), about what topics they communicate, and in what time frames they communicate. Further, while a new communication system can indeed be an opportunity for positive change in the social system, it should not be taken for granted that all social system change will be positive.

Dysfunctions such as unusual routines do not arise only from violations of organizational values; they can also arise from the enactments of those values. Organizational values (especially shared values, or consensual sensemaking) are most often spoken of in a favorable light, and indeed there is much good they can do in terms of shaping relationships, interactions, and practices in the everyday functioning of the organization. However, when problems evolve in those relationships, interactions, and practices, their implicit linkage to organizational values can make it difficult for organization members to make the operational changes needed to remedy the problems. (See also Chapter 8 for examples of dysfunctional and harmful organizational values fostering as well as representing URs.) Moreover, organization members may inadvertently create bad (i.e., having negative consequences) enactments of good (i.e., having positive intent) values by making poor or dysfunctional sense of ambiguous situations. In sum, organizational values can support dysfunctional interaction patterns, and make them resistant to change.

As a core organizational value, inclusion can have unintended negative consequences for decision processes. Inclusive or participative decision-making has much to recommend it, both in an ethical sense and a practical sense (Hirschheim, 1985). It may become problematic, and even a paradoxical tool of divisiveness, however, when this value is rigorously enacted as a requirement for consensus on decisions, or a requirement for complete representation within the decision group. Executives or group leaders may find themselves in double-bind situations as they try to move the group toward a decision. The group's focus may be diverted away from its task, and placed on the adequacy of its inclusiveness.

Value chains may contain unusual routines when the costs of transactions are not imposed where their benefits accrue, or when corrective feedback is not applied at the point where negligence occurs. Some of the URs identified in this study generated a localized benefit for one party or one subunit, at the expense of another. A UR is likely to be strongly change resistant when accountability for the dysfunction is misplaced, or lacking (as in the workarounds discussed in Chapter 4).

A change in one component of an organization may create (or suppress) the opportunity for change in other parts. A change in the communication system of an organization has a unique potential to foster deep change. Organizations, as collective entities, may resist change just as vigorously as individual humans do (Chapters 7 and 8). Managed change can be surprisingly difficult to initiate when it is resisted by a variety of inertial forces, many of which are cultural rather than technical. Once change is underway in one subsystem, however, change may become easier in others, not because of functional links between the systems but because some of the organizational inertia has been overcome. Ironically enough, evolutionary or incremental change can sometimes be more difficult than revolutionary or major change.

Directions for future research

This line of research suggests many possibilities for future work. While the single-loop path of change in URs was observable at the research site, the double-loop path was nascent at most. Longitudinal study is needed to validate that part of the model. Another obvious task is to check the reliability of the UR model developed in this study by applying it to organizations other than educational institutions. At the very least, it would be interesting to compare and contrast the respective organizational values and beliefs. A related question would be whether the cultural substrate and other social system features which proved so central to URs in this study are as crucial in a organization devoted, say, to manufacturing physical goods. It is plausible that technical system features may move to the foreground at such a site. Put another way, there may be some contingent relationship of URs to the essential business activity of the organization.

Another useful line of inquiry would be to identify particular combinations of values that may foster URs. For instance it appears that at the research site the values of principled objections, individual differentiation, and decision by consensus produced work subroutines in decision processes (see Table 5.1). It seems reasonable to expect that there are analogous bundles of values and URs which can be identified through fieldwork at other organizations. Again, this sort of negative synergy is probably highly context-sensitive.

There are other interesting dimensions in the relationship of URs to organizational values. As a number of informants noted, group decisions at this site traditionally operated on a consensus basis, as an enactment of inclusion. Other organizations may also value inclusion, but enact it quite differently. When decisions are legitimately made on an authoritarian (hierarchical influence) or democratic (majority rule) basis, different UR dynamics are likely to play out. An intriguing axiological question concerns the nature of the values themselves. The case analysis has, for the most part, treated URs as unreasonable enactments of reasonable values. Nonetheless, it is conceivable that they may also be reasonable enactments of unreasonable or unethical values (Chapter 8).

The revised model presented in Figure 6.1 takes a broadly systems-theoretic approach to explaining UR dynamics. However, based in the emphasis on sensemaking and communication interaction, it also represents a critically-oriented view of URs as the products of unresolved dialectical processes. In this approach, the highest level dialectic would be between the process (or relational) quality and the decision (or content) quality. Process quality encompasses such dimensions as inclusion, stakeholder recognition, participant satisfaction, sensemaking and egalitarian climate. Decision quality, in contrast, encompasses such dimensions as efficiency (in time or resources), organizational gains, decision rationality, and clarity (as ambiguity reduction). The systems-theoretic approach employed in this study, however, yields system-level insights into dynamic change in URs, and in our view provides the better explanation of that change. Moreover, a systems analysis is not inherently constrained by the need to identify pairs of opposing forces. Still, an overtly dialectical analysis could be useful in surfacing the aspects of conflict in URs. In either case, this project suggests that URs are rich subjects for study.

Conclusion

Perhaps the most intriguing general insight from this study is the most paradoxical. In complex organizations, seemingly irrational behaviors (i.e., irrational with regard to their cost/benefit ratio) can in actuality be rational, in that they provide sufficient benefit from their affirmation of some cultural value to outweigh the costs they impose. Indeed, those costs may be quite substantial. For instance, when an organization ignores or rebuffs feedback (as in a number of the cases described in earlier chapters), this would seem irrational on the face of it. However, the nature of the cultural substrate in that particular organization may be such that the cost/benefit calculus does make sense to at least a substantial proportion of the organization's members, or at least when the dominant coalitions have least to gain, most to lose, or hold values that are most challenged, from feedback. Another possible explanation lies in the displacement of the cost of a UR (again, as in a number of the cases described earlier). While the cost of a given UR to the organization's clients or to a particular organizational subsystem may be quite high, it may not appear to be so to the organization as a unitary entity, or, at least, to those subunits that have the practical ability to mitigate the UR in question. Indeed, they may see only benefits, and no costs. This situation may be conceptualized as *organizational pollution*. Yet another possible explanation might be that the inertial forces created by firmly-established URs simply make it extremely difficult, or effectively impossible, for the organization to change in a constructive way.

An awareness and analysis of unusual routines should deepen the understanding of those behaviors generally explained simply as manifestations of limitations on human rationality. It may be that the limit is not so much on human actors' rationality, per se, but on the overall beneficence of, and variations in, different rationalities in the context of organizational behavior.

7 | *Individual and organizational challenges to feedback*

A seemingly straightforward solution to preventing, avoiding, mitigating, or resolving unusual routines would be to vigorously institutionalize feedback from users and participants, both internal and external to the organization, which would then be analyzed and used to adapt or correct the problem. Certainly task and performance feedback is a central concept in organizational management. Feedback is presumed to foster organizational learning and improved productivity through identifying problems in past performance, providing ways to resolve those problems, reinforcing organizational goals, and helping employees improve their interpersonal competence through providing credible information about their impact on others (Ang *et al.*, 1993; March, 1991). Job feedback may be explicitly about individuals and their absolute performance, or socially comparative, relative to others. Errors provide opportunities, through feedback, for organizational learning, especially if they reveal underlying causes and lead to implementing positive changes (Tax and Brown, 1998). Garvin (1993) compiled a list of definitions of organizational learning that ranged from "the detection and correction of error" (Argyris and Schon, 1978, p. 2) to "encoding inferences from history into routines that guide behavior" (Levitt and March, 1995, p. 517) to "the process of improving actions through better knowledge and understanding" (Fiol and Lyles, 1985, p. 808).

If the causal relationship between intention and consequence were, in actuality, this straightforward, one might expect that the few surviving URs could be explained as instances of malice or negligence. However, apart from issues of practicality and cost (which total quality management, organizational learning, and customer relationship management theories all argue would be well-justified long-term investments; but see Paton, 2003, discussed in Chapter 8), this approach vibrates with difficulties, especially if the feedback processes themselves are flawed or dysfunctional, as discussed in detail here. The following aspects of individual and organizational feedback are potential causes, manifestations, and obstacles to resolving, as well as consequences of, URs.

Feedback challenges inherent in human communication behaviors

Desperately seeking feedback

One challenge has been to clearly conceptualize organizational feedback itself. Research has shifted from considering feedback as something a recipient receives passively to conceptualizing two forms of active feedback seeking: *eliciting* (direct) and *monitoring* (indirect) (Ang *et al.*, 1993; Fedor *et al.*, 1992). These provide different forms of information, and may be differentially appropriate, such as when high-skill training depends on informed, formal feedback. Eliciting gets only what others want to share. Monitoring acquires other information, but requires making inferences about that information and its source from non-verbal cues and others' comments. It would seem more valuable when the costs (perceived and actual) of asking directly are high, such as in public situations or low-trust climates. Also, feedback itself may generate uncertainty about its meaning, contingencies, etc. So monitoring may precede eliciting, to determine costs and appropriateness of eliciting. Characteristics of the feedback source will also influence elicitation of feedback, such as a less confrontational communication style, greater credibility, and a more favorable personal relationship with the feedback seeker. Individual traits fostering feedback seeking include self-esteem and intolerance for ambiguity. Face-to-face and even public socially comparative feedback may be sought when positive performance evaluations are expected, as a way to manage one's public impression (Ang *et al.*, 1993). Face-to-face communication seems appropriate for providing and discussing sensitive and confidential information as in significant feedback However, such content may cause loss of face and status, especially in attempting to provide negative feedback to superiors, or when a low-performing subordinate requests feedback, which may reinforce negative evaluations from the superior. So computer-mediated and non-public feedback seeking may be appropriate for some forms of feedback, to the extent it reduces undesired social cues. However, as

Culnan (1989) discussed (see Chapter 3), mediated feedback systems have their own limitations and constraints.

Discourse and language

Meaning both is constructed through and, in turn, constitutes relationships. Markham (1996), referring to the literature on social constructionism and the subjective, negotiated, and interactive nature of meaning, emphasizes that ambiguity and multiple meanings are inherent in social, and thus organizational, life. Interactions across different construals (perceptions, practices, and processes), and within and across different levels (individual, group, organization, culture), inherently create many opportunities for slippage in meaning within and across feedback cycles (and, as discussed in Chapter 4, organizational routines). Further, trying to communicate about the problem may be well nigh impossible unless these underlying perceptions, practices, and processes are identified, explained, and understood (Ballard and Seibold, 2003).

Feedback is thus also highly subject to power relations, as powerful actors or situations can constrain, reinforce, or deny possible meanings through embedded formal and informal structures and mediating technologies (Rice and Gattiker, 2001). One paradoxical implication is that as discourses become more systematically distorted and naturalized, and the initial rationales for them become irretrievable, the act of raising objections to them or even promoting awareness of them becomes considered more and more irrational. Thus members become "largely unaware that they participate in the co-construction of a complex system of systematically distorted communication and discursive closure" (Markham, 1996, p. 413).

An organization may intentionally couch goals and objectives in vague, ambiguous, and even contradictory discourse, as a way of reducing rules and limiting expectations, in order to encourage autonomy, or innovation (Eisenberg, 1984; Markham, 1996), or, unfortunately, avoid responsibility or loss of face (Argyris, 1990). This ambiguity about goals and values allows more members to construe the goals and values in ways that motivate and include them; the resulting diversity supposedly fosters identity cohesion. But this strategic ambiguity may interact with the surrounding environment of organizational power relations (and the need to ground fantastic ideas in practical applications for clients) to instead generate complex control structures. Hidden in the ambiguity may be real expectations, made explicit – and punitive – only afterwards, when they are not met, indicating a hidden system of control, generating URs. Extensive ambiguity about how to accomplish one's goals may in actuality reduce organizational identity and commitment, as roles and task significance become unmoored, and increase frustration, wasted effort, and recurring problems through lack of clarity. Indeed, asking for more explicit direction from a management structure wishing to foster creativity through ambiguity may itself be punished because it contradicts the prevailing "free-wheeling" discourse. And unintended or harmful ambiguity may go unquestioned or unexplored (Markham, 1996). Members' responses to this ambiguity may routinize and further embed paradoxical and contradictory organizational control systems that decrease creativity and innovation, while also reinforcing some kinds of work and professions as inherently contradictory and tense. These "communicative responses to painful workplace experiences thus bind them in the cycles they seek to escape, and a powerful system of control is reinforced and concretized" (Markham, 1996, p. 391).

Even supposedly explicit knowledge is not necessarily understandable in different operational contexts or communities (Heaton and Taylor, 2002, p. 213). Further, in this view, what is "implicit" is the expert community's underlying assumptions about this constitution of communication, which thus enables and shapes both the communication and collaboration within, and how it relates or presents itself to, other communities. That is, the tacit knowledge about how to communicate within and across communities shapes the explicit knowledge within and across communities (Alavi and Leidner, 2001; Wenger *et al.*, 2002). Thus knowledge, and its manifestations in text, are both the product and the process. The same (read: explicit) "text" mediating different processes in different expertise communities has different meanings. Thus URs involve both product (content and outcomes) and process.

Further exploring the communicative aspect of URs, we might also think of some of them as organizational clichés. Clichés are combinations of symbols that, through routinization, formulaic expression, and fixed sequence (Tovstiadi and Beebe, 2006; Van Lancker-Sidtis and Rallon, 2004), have become a sign. That is, they have a largely fixed meaning at both content and relational levels (Watzlawick *et al.*, 1967) in spite of (perhaps even contradictory to, as in irony, sarcasm, or satire) the component symbols, yet this meaning is highly situational and culturally specific. They serve as a sign of some common, frequent, useful set of occurrences and their communication components. Clichés thus simultaneously increase symbolic complexity while simplifying sign complexity. They are highly pragmatic when familiar but confusing and nonsensical when interpreted literally or out of context (Tovstiadi and Beebe, 2006). URs to some extent display the same tension: increasing certainty and predictability through the routine while also increasing complexity and misunderstanding through the unusual. Thus, at an even more general level, URs and clichés are simplifying stereotypes, projected by the user onto a complex reality, with benefits and costs, utilities and errors. URs, clichés, and stereotypes simplify things for some people, while others pay the cost in terms of increased complexity, or in trying to decipher the component complexity. Considered as clichés, URs are organizationally and culturally specific retained meaning, ready to be used to bracket experience and reduce equivocality. However, unlike the ideal sensemaking process (Weick, 1995), they serve to prevent alternative sensemaking, and indeed, in order to work well, must exclude qualifications, personal variations, and adaptive form. Like clichés, they thus represent significant challenges to cross-context communication such as feedback.

Contextualizing meaning by layers

Bateson and others (Bateson, 1972; Watzlawick *et al.*, 1967) proposed two primary levels of communication meaning: *relational* (command) level communication forms the hierarchical context for interpreting *content* (report) level communication (though Bateson implied other levels of cognition). The theory of Coordinated Management of Meaning (Cronen *et al.*, 1979) extended this hierarchy of meaning, and helps to frame some concepts that are useful in understanding the communication aspects of feedback about URs. According to this theory, communication and human action are managed through rules to achieve proactive goals rather than through reactive consequences of environmental events. But rules vary across time and across people. Moreover, these "intrapersonal rule systems come together to create

interpersonal (consensual) rules that guide production and interpretation of communicative behavior" [in communication episodes]
(Brenders, 1987, p. 331). Thus people can (but may not) transcend
the cultural repertoire of episodes, and make sense of a particular
interaction episode that may differ from each participating person's
cultural or personal episodes.

An episode exists within a hierarchy of meanings contextualized
by *constitutive rules* (which make sense across levels of abstraction)
and constrained by *regulative rules* (which limit allowable variations in response within levels of meaning). The general hierarchy
ranges down from archetypes and life scripts to propositions (reference and predication) and streams of behavior (the significance
of that speaker making a particular statement to that listener at
a specific time, such as "insult," "asking," etc.). The hierarchy
of meaning contextualizes lower-level meanings by constitutively
relating them to more and more abstract meanings. Some people
have less well-organized hierarchies; some may use all or fewer of
the levels. Communication, then, is the non-summative meshing
of the individuals' (and groups' and organization's) rules – maybe
even unknown to the participants. Brenders (1987) critiques this
model, however, noting that meaning involves both recognizing the
conventional use of an expression (use of language rules) and the
speaker's intended illocutionary effect. In particular, he argues that
the hierarchy of meaning helps to disambiguate, rather than strictly
determines, meaning, although speakers and listeners alike have
varying abilities to accomplish these goals.

One implication for attempting to resolve URs is that participants may either not know, or be unable to know, which level of
meaning best represents either the intended process or the UR.
For example, in some episodes from the case study, the relational
level (symbolic meaning) was positive, but the content level (task
operations) was negative. Further, they may have insufficient or ill-
matched expertise in communicating these with others, especially
those elsewhere in or outside of the organization. Put bluntly,
the meanings may be coordinated, but faulty or harmful in some
way. Misunderstanding the hierarchical relationship intended by
the feedback would make it difficult to effectively resolve a UR,
while mismanaged hierarchical relationship in the feedback could
reinforce, or constitute, a UR.

Reflexive loops, paradoxes, and undesired repetitive patterns

Not all meaning systems or situations may follow strict hierarchies, however, leading to *reflexive loops* and *paradoxes* (Cronen *et al.*, 1982). In these situations, content and relation may be simultaneously the context for and within the context of the other. There are one-stage loops (the content *is* the relation) and two-(or more)-stage loops (where content or relation redefines or discounts the other). For example, repetitive feedback that is unwanted, misunderstood, or defended by someone embedded in a UR can be interpreted as a problem in itself that appears unresolvable. There may be a reciprocal influence between the levels even when a clear hierarchy exists, especially in iterative interpretations where the accumulated content redefines the context. A change in the higher-order concept can change subordinate units of meaning, but higher-order concepts are not immune from changes in lower-levels of meaning. A contextual force that cannot change in response to changes in the next lower level "could be symptomatic of an unhealthy system incapable of renegotiation of growth" (p. 97), such as a UR. A particular content may emerge as the context to interpret a whole pattern of interaction (divorce, aging, organizational crisis) in which all the other prior and subsequent actions are recontextualized based on a single episode. (Chapter 8 discusses several aspects of both over- and under-sensitive organizational and social response to threats.) The development of context may begin as a fully reflexive loop, and then be clarified through a sequence of lower-order messages. So, initially, confusion among participants would reign as to context, and thus as to acceptable content, but this is not simply a "mistake." Indeed, in situations that allow and foster emergent context, reflexive loops are endemic. Conversely, reflexive loops may be ignored precisely because the situation is presumed by some of the participants to be non-emergent, thus vitiating the meaning and purpose of feedback, and reinforcing the UR.

Social action, then, involves tacking back and forth between levels involving a weaker force (upward implicative) and a stronger force (downward contextual force). One implication of this argument is that three or more levels of meaning are required to analyze reflexive relationships, because the higher-order level must be contextualized itself (Cronen *et al.*, 1982). If meaning is transitive, either of the social perceptions can be the context for another, and it still makes sense (for example, a committed relationship and a confirming response during conversation). Thus, meta-rules may exist that define which social perceptions can be the context of which others (i.e., which are transitive and which are intransitive). Higher-level social organization and personal experience provide information on meta-rules on how two levels of social perception can be related. Thus a reflexive loop may be problematic in some contexts or for some actors, but not others. In the case of a UR, the evolved procedure may makes good sense to the internal unit and be rewarded, but generate negative subroutines and sanctions for other units, who seem to the first unit only to be jealously complaining about the reward structure.

Indeed, this "reflexivity is a natural and necessary feature of human systems of meaning" (p. 91), but some reflexive loops are problematic. There may be *strange* loops – those that cause problems – and *charmed* loops – those that do not. In strange loops, confusions exist about the course of action. One illustration would be asking what the problem is – which is generally considered to be the very first step in a rational decision process – when it is not clear what the context is. "Thus, it is impossible to decide what the context is, impossible to decide what [the content] signifies, and impossible to decide whether asking what is wrong is an appropriate response" (p. 105). Such communicative problems are common and detrimental to organizational life (Stohl and Schell, 1991). Chapter 8 discusses how Argyris applies this kind of analysis to organizational defensiveness and double binds.

Resolving such paradoxes requires asking the meaning of the message in order to clarify other levels of the relationship. This may or may not be available in the individual's repertoire, or acceptable to the other participant. Effects of strange loops (especially double binds) are more limited if the strange loops can be sealed off from higher-order levels, to avoid higher-level strange loops. If unable to do this, the "individual possesses no stable point of focus from which the 'I' ... can consider that pattern of interpretations and actions that constitutes the 'me'" (Cronen *et al.*, 1982, p. 107). So, for instance, it seems crucial not to question the identity or purpose of the organizational representative in attempting to identify or resolve a UR. The irony is that a strategy which successfully copes with a strange loop at one level may exacerbate it at another.

Confusions will persist when the participants have no strategy for resolving intransitive loops, and when significant others block efforts to resolve or seal off these intransitive loops. Individuals may then attempt to separate levels of meaning or convert strange to charmed loops according to their own hierarchies of meaning independent of the others' hierarchies, cementing misunderstandings, and enmeshing higher levels of meaning in these unresolved strange loops. Clearly this is one recipe for URs. Cronen *et al.* describe three examples of possible episodes relevant to URs: these include the *enigmatic episode* (weak links of life-script, antecedents or consequents to possible speech acts, range of responses is unknown, valence toward the consequence is likely negative), *value expressive rituals* (strong links of antecedents, life-script, episode, consequents, with positive valence, range is low) and *perfunctory ritual* (weak link to life-script, neutral valence of consequent). So a UR may be obscured or unresolved if an enigmatic episode of a client meets with an organizational representative's value expressive ritual, or a perfunctory ritual if the job is not personally significant.

One problematic episode that both represents a UR itself as well as reinforces URs is the *unwanted repetitive pattern* (URP) (Cronen *et al.*, 1979). An example is when both participants want a friendly conversation, but usually end up in recurrent, hostile, polarizing duels, patterned in ways that the participants can identify, and yet stable across topics. Walton (1969) noted the existence of these repeated, patterned disruptive communication episodes in organizations.

Spitzberg (1993) and Stohl and Schell (1991) describe a general dysfunctional group process, called a *farrago* (meaning "mixed fodder for cattle"), characterized by displaced feedback, in particular decision-making procedures that become complicated and compromised due to preventive actions designed to avoid or accommodate one or more members, typically someone established enough to be professionally secure but not high enough to be responsible for the group's performance. (This concept is similar to Argyris' (1986) skilled incompetence, below.) The person creates obstacles and intrusions sufficient to weaken and damage the entire group's communication processes. Attempted responses, however, are parried, leading to greater inertia as to solving the problem. The group treats the individual as a culprit and a source of problems, but not a scapegoat or a victim. However, the individual continues to demonstrate a high degree of competence on group tasks. As a consequence, issues become redefined against the backdrop of the member; subsequently, the group expends a great deal of energy talking about that member. Members become so worn out that they fail to deal with task issues, and priorities become confused. Members leave such meetings angry, depressed, or frustrated with the individual and the group. But, Spitzberg emphasizes, interventions that focus solely on the member will not eliminate the problem. This is because the dysfunction cannot be located within any one individual or one group meeting. Instead, it occurs over time, actors, and contexts, involving anticipatory interactions, interactions during meetings, and interactions during post-meeting debriefing sessions. Group properties that foster a farrago include an overt policy of participative decision-making, ill-defined lines of authority, ambiguity of rules, high task interdependence in multiple domains (so interactions and deviations circulate and create sequential consequences), and weak socialization practices (Stohl and Schell, 1991). As in family systems dysfunctions, the focal individual's dysfunctional behavior is dependent on other members' willingness to play to the norms, rules of courtesy, disclosure, etc. The group may end up, ironically, incorporating the terminology, worldview, and behaviors of the offensive member. In this way, some URs may develop as a response to failed feedback, while reinforcing the failed process.

Skilled incompetence and the contradictions of competence

The concepts of the two-level communication hierarchy – relational and content – may help explain some problems in providing feedback about URs. For example, the valued norm of getting along with others (the relational meaning of an episode) may not always be an asset, because it may suppress conflict and resolution (the content meaning of an episode), as illustrated in the farrago. Argyris calls this *skilled incompetence*, where "managers use practiced routine behavior (skill) to produce what they do not intend (incompetence)" (1986, p. 74; 1990). This skill can become institutionalized, such as in the form of constant meetings where no difficult decisions are made (for example, due to a valued norm of inclusion, as in the case in Chapter 5), leading to an organizational culture that cannot abide straightforward content, to despair and attributions of failure by others, and even to disasters. At the client/organization interface, following relentlessly pleasant scripts for responding to client frustrations may trivialize the unusual (i.e., a significant complaint) into a routine "service encounter" (Chapter 3).

An even deeper problem in producing competent communication is that interpersonal communication is not necessarily "competent" or even easily characterized as to the relevant form of competence. As Spitzberg put it, "our daily interactions are rife with hassles, insults, complaints, guilt-inducing messages, predicaments, hurtful comments, deception, conflicts and problems about which we feel we cannot communicate" (1993, p. 139, referencing many studies). Competence plays three roles in the development and dynamics of relationships:

(1) an ability that facilitates relationships or gives advantage;
(2) a mediating role as an inference influencing others' response; and
(3) a self-inference, influencing individual motivation and behavior toward and in relations.

If competence is an ability, an actor must be able to choose among goals and objectives. If one's communication is goal-directed, but one is faced with ambiguous, incompatible or incompetent goals, then dialectical motives arise. If competence is an attributed quality, the receiver of a message must make sense of competing attributions of motives and situations; that is, must engage in dialectics of inference. For instance, raising meta-level feedback about paradoxes and proposing potential metarules for resolving a UR is not an acceptable role for customers, and such attempts are usually inferred by the organizational representative as customer incompetence (in terms of expertise, social norms, or simple intelligibility) (Chapter 3). True communication competence, then, requires constant negotiation of these dialectics.

Feedback challenges inherent in organizations

Were the difficulties in individual meaning management and competence not obstacles enough to even recognizing – much less resolving – URs, organizational settings provide yet more challenges and complexities.

Reporting errors through feedback, and errors of reporting feedback

The nature of errors

Errors may be defined as a decision/behavior unintentionally resulting in undesirable discrepancy between real and expected state, with avoidable potential/actual negative consequence (Zhao and Olivera, 2006, p. 1013). Errors are different from suboptimal results, failures (which may be an expected or even acceptable outcome), or violations (intentional). Edmondson (2004) makes the distinction that while workers may become aware of a problem, and problems are less sensitive topics of discussion, they are often unaware of errors (especially their own), and errors can be interpersonally threatening to discuss, suppressing awareness by others.

Errors may be categorized into three types of primarily cognitive-based error (Zhao and Olivera, 2006). *Slips* are appropriate intentions not well implemented, and are often due to distractions or problems in procedures or design. *Rule-based mistakes* include:

(1) incorrectly applying otherwise well-known procedures in situations that either are familiar, or seem so; and
(2) correctly implementing a procedure which is inappropriate for the actual goals, due to an incorrect assessment of the problem, a biased selection of rules, implementing familiar but improper rules, or not having sufficient time to assess the situation or appropriate procedures.

Knowledge-based mistakes occur when one is unable to correctly or completely assess a problem, fully or correctly identify causal relationships, or have sufficient information, due to organizational procedures and rewards that make appropriate rules aversive and reinforce inappropriate rules (Reason, 1990). Rule-based mistakes would seem to inspire URs through dysfunctional feedback while knowledge-based mistakes would seem to generate workarounds, but more general URs could generate all of these kinds of errors. The frequency of detection varies across different types of errors, and the frequency of occurrence of different types of errors varies across work environments. For example, more slips and rule-based mistakes occur in service jobs (Stewart and Chase, 1999).

Edmondson (1996) summarized prior literature to identify two different ways of conceptualizing errors and accidents – related to the individual, or related to the system – and proposed a third group level, where these two intersect and interact to enable or prevent errors. At the individual level, people may make errors and have difficulty in identifying or reporting them due to inadequacies in behavioral capabilities or educational training, which can hinder one's ability to perceive unexpected phenomena (Rumelhart, 1980). Behaviors or procedures that are very well learned become somewhat automatic, leading to inattention, error, and selective perception (Norman, 1981; Reason, 1984), creating "secondary errors of not noticing" (Edmondson, 1996, p. 68). Emotional states can also affect attention and cognitive processing, creating errors.

At the system level, the nature and design of systems create conditions for errors as well as their consequences (see especially the discussions on complex and automated systems in Chapter 8). Perrow (1984), in particular, argued that systems with interactive complexity (processes that cannot be reversed, and which involve multiple, non-linear feedback, so that one's actions cannot be linked to subsequent consequences) and tightly coupled system components (leading to direct and possibly rapid effects of one component on others) are most likely to enable accidents. As with the literature on complex systems errors (Chapter 8), Perrow challenges the easy explanation of operator error. Standard organizational practices may indeed encourage errors. Familiar responses may only treat symptoms instead of the underlying problem (which can stimulate moral hazard in the principal–agent relationships as well as systemic reinforcement of the problem), and culture and hierarchy may suppress the reporting and learning from errors (due to the familiar association of errors with individual blame and incompetence, Michael, 1976).

Analysis at the group level, or how social behavior affects performance (including errors), has two primary traditions: social, affective, and unconscious influences, and cognitive, goal, and structural influences. For example, group norms, social relations, and group identity can shape group processes, motivation, knowledge-sharing, and performance (Alderfer, 1987; Argyris, 1985). Alternatively, more material conditions, managerial and leadership style, team structure, and task design also influence performance – and errors (Hackman,

1987). These factors are especially salient in hospital settings, with multiple professions, structures, and interdependencies (Edmondson, 1996).

Many organizational accidents result from an accumulation of small failures, creating a condition beyond the boundaries of usual system monitoring and correction (Reason, 1997). Group and organizational norms may foster a lack of attention and reinforcement of risky attitudes and behaviors. One example is what Vaughan (1996) called the *normalization of deviance*, in which these behaviors become taken-for-granted and enable the accumulation of errors.

Because of the frequent, complex, and changing interactions among people in service delivery, errors and failures will be common occurrences. Further, due to the mix of activity interdependencies, and constant uncertainties in some kinds of work, a series of small failures, and interactions among them, can generate interruptions in service and loss of attention, leading to co-worker, customer, or patient dissatisfaction, and more errors, what Tucker (2004, p. 152) calls *cycles of failure* (see also Heskett *et al.*, 1997). In providing services in healthcare institutions, many people can intervene (or fail to) at up to ten general stages leading up to administering medicines to patients, and these may be fairly loosely coupled, making it difficult to assign responsibility, and thus to generate a causal explanation (Edmondson, 1996). The fact of potentially very harmful errors in hospital procedures and medication itself is tragic; but studies have found as high as 1.4 medication errors per patient per hospital stay. Much more striking is that when systems are implemented specifically to predict and track errors, the rate can go up as much as 4,000 percent (Evans *et al.*, 1992) – meaning that most errors in many organizations are never even detected! In a detailed observational study of eleven nurses in six hospitals, and surveys of nurses and managers in forty-eight hospital units, Tucker and Spear (2006) recorded 8.4 operational failures per eight-hour shift, while managers estimated the nurses experienced 5.7 operational failures per shift.

Barriers to identifying and reporting errors

Identifying errors faces considerable psychological and organizational barriers (Singer and Edmondson, 2008). But detecting and realizing that an error has occurred does not necessarily mean that the causes or consequences are perceived, understood, either at the time of detection or later, or reported. Learning from errors seems particularly difficult for organizations, throughout three phases of error reporting proposed by Zhao and Olivera (2006). First, someone has to detect and realize any of these types of errors, based on an action, an outcome, or a limiting function, independent of whether the causes and consequences are perceived or understood. Second, those involved will assess the situation based on cognitions (cost–benefits to self, group, organization, potential victims) as well as emotions (fear, shame, embarrassment, guilt). Third, participants have different behavioral responses, ranging from reporting (straightforward, rationalization, blaming) to non-reporting (covering up, dealing with it by oneself, ignoring). Indeed, employees and customers tend not to report their errors (Tax and Brown, 1998). People hesitate because reporting involves complex trade-offs between potential costs (from effort to threat to one's reputation) and benefits (from learning to reinforcing one's values) (Zhao and Olivera, 2006). Other barriers to reporting errors (Singer and Edmondson, 2008) include:

- concerns about self-esteem, confidence, and public embarrassment decrease motivation to report errors;
- group emphasis on conformity;
- insufficient psychological safety;
- organizational rewards reinforce success, not failure;
- organizational structures may hinder upward flow of negative information;
- particular hesitancy to respond to potential failure if high stakes, opposing interests, and ambiguous situations; and
- personal willingness to report errors.

Edmondson (1996) analyzed preventable errors in administering drugs to patients in two hospitals. The two hospitals differed systematically in error frequency as well as in how likely those errors were detected, or led to learning about preventing such errors. She concluded that strong manager and co-worker norms against errors (ostensibly a valid norm) can suppress the identification, reporting, learning, and thus preventing of, errors. Thus in some cases, the teams most needing to reduce their errors may be least likely to detect and discuss them, meaning they will not improve, and may not know it. Suppressing feedback about this feedback creates ongoing cycles of defensiveness, or learning (Edmondson, 1996). A paradox is that leadership cultures that suppress the noticing and reporting of mistakes officially appear as higher performers (i.e., fewer errors or failures formally noted) but are less likely to learn from their actual mistakes, while open cultures may end up appearing more error-prone and thus possibly subject to sanctions, although they provide a richer context for resolving and reducing failures (Edmondson, 2004). Another barrier to feedback is that the ordinary functioning of hospitals favors the development of quick workarounds (see Chapter 4) rather than allocating time and resources to uncover the underlying causes.

Another problem in dealing with errors is that people predominantly focus on single-loop perceptions, treating the "error" simply as an "error." Rather, the embedded process fostering the making of errors is part of the routine (i.e., an error subroutine). So not encouraging or responding to feedback is itself a larger error, as it prevents learning about the dysfunctional process. In schizophrenic family systems, homeostasis is possible only through prohibiting acts defining the nature of the relationship (Palazzoli *et al.*, 1978).

Based on an analysis of nurses' experiences with operational failures in hospital settings, Tucker (2004) found that most such failures were due to insufficient or erroneous supply of materials or information across unit boundaries, what she called a *system error* or *workflow error* (a form of what Zhao and Olivera (2006) call a knowledge-based error). This is performing a task that appears correct at the time based on expected subsequent conditions, but is later identified as incorrect, a waste of time or unnecessary, and caused by insufficient information or resources at the time (p. 155). Tucker's system error becomes a more systemic UR when the unexpected change in, or insufficient awareness of, the other information or procedures is generated by an external or some more general process, rather than being an idiosyncratic, one-time mistake in communication or procedures. Nurses spent 9 percent of their time on failure resolution, and most of these operational failures were systematic rather than random or idiosyncratic. Of the instances coded as operational failures by the researchers, 44 percent had not been identified as such by either nurses or managers – they were, instead, considered "as if the situations were expected parts of their work routines ... without any indication that they could be avoided with some system improvements and redesign" (p. 162), and 52.6 percent were considered as failures only by the nurses. The 194 operational failures created three categories of nine impacts (on nurses, patients, and the hospital):

- complexity: *additional tasks* required to solve the initial failure, *direct time* spent on resolving the failure, *indirect time* spent on activities related to the failure but not to the resolution;
- patient care efficiency: *work interruptions* caused by either the failure or the resolution, *direct delays* due to waiting for the resources whose absence constituted the failure, *indirect delays* between resolving the failure and finally completing the tasks;
- interaction with environment: *subjective risk* (here, to the patient's safety), *number of people involved* in resolving the failure, and *tangible and intangible losses* (p. 157).

These operational failures represented a cost of almost $100/hour per nurse. The high impact failures cost on average over $400/hour per nurse, taking more than five additional tasks, the assistance of two other people, and thirty-four minutes to resolve, and another forty-two minutes to then complete the original task.

However, the nurses tended to figure out workarounds or temporary solutions (single-loop learning) to most of these failures, without correcting the underlying processes that generated the failures (double-loop learning). The ironic long-term disadvantage of these fairly rapid repairs is that their organizations do not have the opportunity to notice these failures, and thus learn from them (Tucker 2004; see also Tucker and Edmondson, 2003). While some operational failures may be noticed, in the sense that they require some resolution and thus associated time, interruptions, costs, and delays, they may often not be perceived as "actionable" systemic flaws either capable or worthy of being a target of process redesign or improvement. Thus, over time "failures become an expected part of the work routine" (p. 162). This is also somewhat due to nursing norms of individual responsibility, time pressures to tend to patients, and individual capability of overcoming hospital practices. Perhaps more importantly, most operational failures stemmed from other departments (due to necessary interdependencies), over which individual workers had no control, and possibly not even awareness. Organizational administrators beyond the nurse were very unlikely to experience or perceive these local operation failures, thus neither being aware of them, able to develop accurate perceptions of their costs, or be even responsive

to the occasional reporting of such failures. This is particularly salient given the predominance of other departments spawning the failure, because cross-boundary resolution requires higher managerial
involvement. Individual nurses simply do not have the necessary
authority (formal as well as interpersonal) to provide this kind or
level of feedback.

Timing of feedback

Time frames are also relevant to how feedback and systems operate.
The timing of feedback may take a variety of forms (Widen-Wulff and
Davenport, 2005). In *routine* timing, actions are episodic, reciprocal
(answers provided to questions), and within a predictable time frame.
Ad hoc timing emerges in difficult cases, especially for novices who do
not know who knows, so feedback is unpredictable. *Regularly scheduled* feedback contexts (such as meetings, referral to experts) take
on the form of ritual or normative timing. Under *compliance timing*,
responses are generated sequentially by the completion of a prior process; so the timing is not routine, but the triggers and response timing
are. *Pragmatic* timing is highly contextual, as it requires judgment
about what to share, when, and with whom, given time constraints
and cost–benefit considerations. *Formative* timing concerns more
general, broad feedback contributing to overall organizational awareness (such as board meetings).

Other temporal components of feedback systems include *initial
condition* – small initial changes might become amplified over time;
accelerating cycles – loops pick up speed, negatively or positively,
and changes become unstable; *interaction* of the source of the change
with other systems to create synergistic effects, with varying effects
depending on the subsequent system; and the system's *cycle time* –
when does the cycle begin, slow down, reverse, and are the effects
immediate or delayed (Goodman, 2000). Some schemata or routines
may have been initially adaptive, but those conditions no longer pre-
vail; that is, "The environment of the complex adaptive system has
changed at a faster rate than the evolutionary process can accommodate" (Gell-Mann, 1994, p. 299).

Thus the consequences of feedback cycles may depend on the cycle's
timing (Goodman, 2001). For example, a change in an initial variable
affects a change in a second variable, which in turn affects a change in

the first variable. A positive loop would increase the rate of each of the consecutive changes, accelerating local and overall effects. Further, effects of feedback depend to some extent on the timing of the change. For example, new organizational policies and structural changes may initially improve continuous improvement teams, which in the long run reduces short-term problems, reducing the demand on problem-solving teams, which can then respond faster and develop higher-quality solutions. In the long run, most short-term problems may be avoided, so that problem-solving team members may transfer to continuous improvement teams. But the opposite might occur as well. Organizations might allocate disproportionately more resources to solving short-term problems, occupying all the efforts of the problem-solving team, reducing overall response time and effectiveness, and hampering any long-term process improvement (Goodman, 2001).

Learning by doing rather than by learning

Relying on client or user feedback seems to assume that relevant information is not already available – that is, problems in use are due to information unavailable during design. But von Hippel and Tyre's (1994) study found that two-thirds of the problems encountered in using new machines that attached integrated circuits to large circuit boards could have been solved with information that was in fact already available at development time, and two-thirds of that was actually known by developers but not used. But the relevance of specific information can change during, and after, the design process. Indeed, the other third of the problems involved information that became available from the environment only after introduction of the system (and a quarter of that came from people working on other aspects of the production process and other systems affected by the initial system). Thus a major source of problem identification and feedback is a particularly intriguing subset of unintended consequences, what they call *interference finding*, where using a new system in the field actually precipitates symptoms that did not, or could not, occur in the development lab. Sometimes this is due to assumptions of developers and test users as to what might present sources of problems, and what is not relevant. Usually, however, identifying such problems is much more likely in the actual using/doing, because many complex interactions only occur then, and they would be difficult to predict or even conceptualize during design. The use environment itself may change in the context of use, so the appropriate design solution would then also be different, especially when problem solvers are autonomous or the use context has great variance (von Hippel and Tyre, 1994).

Learning from feedback or memorizing responses?

Organizational memory processing

Organizational memory is information about prior decision stimuli and responses that bear on present decisions (Walsh and Ungson, 1991). Although individuals actively construct memory via cognitions, the understandability of problems and solutions is constructed through sharing interpretations (as Weick would argue, through double-interacts negotiating shared understanding). Organizational memory plays a crucial role in how organizations learn (Huber, 1991), thus contributing to the resolution, but also creation, of URs. Levitt and March (1995; citing Cyert and March, 1963) propose that behavior in organizations is usually driven by routines. Organizational members seek to match tasks with currently existing practices and procedures rather than make new choices about how a task should be completed (Chapter 4). These routines evolve from past experiences rather than from anticipated future events, a process similar to Weick's sensemaking. With this routinization of tasks and processes as a primary form of organizational memory, organizations become "history-dependent" (Levitt and March, 1995). Organizational memory includes the routines established by the organization, but also includes unrecorded procedures and protocols as well (Huber, 1991). Therefore, organizational memory is the history and routines of an organization and more, much of which is stored in the heads of organizational members (Simon, 1991, p. 128).

Thus one difficulty with organizational memory is that information about the triggering stimulus is typically retained only by individuals, even if the organization's response to this stimulus is retained as a set of formal procedures or designed into a system (i.e., through routines). While subsequent interpretations constitute organizational memory, they may not include the initial context, or the causal "why" of interpretation. These partial sources of information may be too equivocal or may even overload short-term memory, and thus not become part of organizational memory. In these instances, individuals use personal biases/heuristics derived to compensate for limited cognitive capacities. Even at the organizational level, there is much filtering via interpretative schemes or frames. Both of these processes may obstruct or distort some of the situation's stimuli and causal mechanisms and therefore responses (Walsh and Ungson, 1991).

The resulting organizational memory is distributed through five *retention bins*: individuals, culture, transformations, structure (roles, rules, and norms), and ecology (physical environment and layout). External archives (former employees, competitors, government, financial service firms, media, historians) are another retention bin (see also Dixon, 1993, p. 11). Each of the retention bins differentially emphasizes more or less of the actual decision stimulus and organizational response. Organizational conversion processes (training, budgeting, planning, administration, manufacturing, etc.) also represent remembered information. One form of conversion, standard operating procedures, or routines, represents schemas that both facilitate and constrain interpretation and behavior, making it difficult to question the system as to how to correct the problem.

Further, some retrieval processes are largely automatic, such as from transformation, structures, or ecology bins, and not easily managed consciously. As routines theory argues, this speeds short-term problem solving, but decreases the consideration of exceptions, and disregards some information. Controlled retrieval is conscious, making analogies to past decisions, and limited by participation in the organization, such as through socialization, decision-making, or other activities (Walsh and Ungson, 1991). In the language of reflexive loops, this creates a paradox, as the content becomes the context for the relational-level communication. Thus one source of URs is automatic retrieval when controlled retrieval would be appropriate.

Learning through memory
While organizational memory typically fosters single-loop learning and the status quo, adaptive processes *can* be embedded in standard operating procedures. Double-loop learning *can* be formalized, thus reducing transaction costs for routine transactions. However, such changes would be more robust if they are embedded in and legitimized by tradition, and facilitated by support networks. The point

here is that often the content level of organizational memory must be critiqued, not the retention bins or retrieval processes themselves (the relational level).

Of course, individuals may misuse organizational memory, though this may be motivated by automatic retrieval processes inherent in transformation, structures, and ecology bins. So successful awareness and change may require that current retention bins be filled with new decision stimuli and behavioral responses, through, say, training, simulations, crises, redesign. The organization's culture may be a source of information misuse, by imposing automatic retrieval and unassessed memory. But non-routine responses are not inherently preferable. They may replace appropriate automatic retrieval when the risk of automatic retrieval is overestimated. And cognitive limits, personal heuristics, overgeneralizing past experience, inappropriate analogies and simply poor procedures can generate incompetent uses of organizational memory. Finally, organizational memory can be intentionally or ideologically abused. The potential for political control and dependency makes organizational memory a "tempting tool" (Walsh and Ungson, 1991, p. 77). Structural position and transformations in turn can control the acquisition, retention, and retrieval of memory (Pettigrew, 1972). Thus intentional redesigns of transformation processes will also affect, perhaps even prevent, acquisition and retention of certain types or sources of memory. As noted in Chapter 4, changing routines is thus inherently conflict-inducing, here because different stakeholders will have different resources, position, and expertise associated with these memories.

Thus, URs may be the repository of, or the consequence of, incomplete, mismatched, incorrect, or biased organizational memories. Because organizational representatives are a crucial source of organizational inputs, trained assessment of decision stimuli is especially critical there. But those positions must also have access to power to alter internal retention bins and processes, and have considerable tenure in order to be able to contextualize organizational memory, or see new things in an old light. These positions should also include newcomers and visitors, who can see completely new things, see old things in a new light, and question automatic retrieval processes. As a norm for management practice, the appeal of this observation is apparent. The difficulty for the practicing executive, of course, is determining which "new insights" might actually be superior to current practice.

There is no guarantee that a change – while symbolizing organizational learning – will not itself create or perpetuate URs. The real-world possibility that new might be worse is inescapable.

Even presuming the individual, social, and organizational factors suppressing the identification and reporting of errors were overcome, subsequent learning may still not necessarily improve performance (Singer and Edmondson, 2008) because of:

- difficulty in observing the changed performance;
- insufficient provision of underlying rationales for conflicting positions;
- learning curve and initial error costs decreasing performance early on, while benefits may occur in the longer term (see also Johnson and Rice, 1987);
- costs and risks of learning, to the organization, the task or service, and the individual;
- multiple dimensions of performance, each differentially influenced by learning from the error (for example, for hospitals, patient health, research, teaching, and economic efficiency);
- the possibility that some of the dimensions may never be perfectible and are meaningful only within a particular context, while evolution in the organization and its environment changes the criteria and meaning of sufficient performance (Winter, 2000).

Rational but unreasonable, even schizophrenic, systems

If one assumes organizational interrelations and feedback flows are linear, then rational decisions seem appropriate, and incapable of generating chaos (DeGreene, 1990). However, chaos can be externalized, or created, by over-emphasizing internal equilibrium, or by promoting first-order equilibrium over higher orders, or by limiting hierarchical contextualizing of content by formal relational order, or even by confusing relations and content (creating paradoxes and recursive loops) such as fostering skilled incompetence through emphasizing cordial relations over resolving difficulties. Conceptualizing organization as a linear equation defines its boundary conditions in such a way as to make changes either predictable or unlikely. On the other hand, organization as a non-linear system, especially if it is in a far-from-equilibrium state (such as with respect to clients' behaviors or expectations), is so sensitive to initial conditions that a small change can lead to qualitatively different conditions, in unpredictable ways. Personal interactions may also be non-linear systems, managed through linear organizational routines. Thus, small behaviors such as individuals or events – some mix of "rational" and "symbolic" history – can generate chaos, or at least URs, in organizational systems (Mees, 1986).

Organizations may attempt to respond to feedback by changing their response to problematic behaviors, but this creates new behaviors that generate new information (both environmental and internal). This new, additional information must now be processed and interpreted, creating many more sources, kinds, and content of feedback, generating even more choices for change. Further, if feedback or control is inaccurate, delayed, repressed, misinterpreted, or if the acceptable range of variation is too narrow, then external variations can lead to deviation amplification and chaos (Mees, 1986).

Under such equivocal conditions, organizations may rely on automatic retrieval or organizational memory from a few, formal retention bins in an attempt to make sense of the new, depending on their retrieval capabilities and strategies, leading to conflicts and tensions between different perspectives (Walsh and Ungson, 1991). Thus organizations may attempt to manage complexity and crises through linear, but divergent, routines. Organizations will naturally strive to re-establish stability, but that does not necessarily require internal change. Homeostasis can be achieved through suppressing or avoiding certain environmental information (such as behaviors from "irate" clients) through enacting only reinforcing portions of the environment, or through *buffering* and *transformational shields* (Miner *et al.*, 1990), *strategic manipulation*, and *catatonic non-responsiveness*. This in turn may generate later external deviations and stronger instabilities (e.g., higher complaints and product returns, product recalls, software incompatibilities, consumer boycotts, liability litigation). It may also reduce an organization's ability to adapt, especially second-loop learning about possible ways to respond, adapt, and innovate (Nonaka, 1988).

In schizophrenic systems, homeostasis is possible only by prohibiting any defining of the nature of the relationship (Palazzoli *et al.*, 1978, p. 38). So organizational representatives, when confronted by a client with a UR, will likely deny their location in this new relationship, preferring to externalize or buffer the UR. One form of disconfirm-ation is to pick one particular word and manipulate it to disqualify or avoid defining the relationship ("that's not part of my job"), or use one of the words out of context to reduce its meaning ("full service doesn't mean we do everything!").

Vicious circles

Social systems often differ from individual intentions, and sources of the effects of systems behavior on individual actions are difficult to identify. As Cohen and Bacdayan (1994) suggest, one reason routines persist is that their component procedures are distributed through-out an organization, and are not easily identified or discussed. The resulting side-effects may be desirable or undesirable. Trying to avoid the negative side-effects may end up fostering and reprodu-cing them, a *deviation-amplifying feedback loop*, or a *vicious circle* (Masuch, 1985, p. 14, italics added; Chapter 4, this volume). Based upon whether system feedback is *self-reinforcing* or *self-correcting*, and whether it is *deviation-amplifying* or *deviation-counteracting*, four kinds of vicious circles may occur. Self-reinforcing, deviation-amplifying feedback creates undesired change, and possibly cri-sis. Self-reinforcing, but deviation-counteracting feedback develops desired change. Self-correcting, deviation-amplifying feedback nur-tures undesired permanence, or stagnation; while self-correcting, deviation-counteracting feedback generates a desired permanence, or stability. Of course, one actor's vicious circle may be another's gain.

Masuch (1985) describes several organizational pathologies as examples of vicious circles. In a *pathological status system*, status is initially provided to induce performance, but, as it is difficult to take back, the social system increasingly needs other status indicators to differentiate among actors, and eventually the status differences dis-appear, and have no stimulating effect. An example of a *pathological communication system* is when the formal communication system designed to reduce rumors and manipulation becomes upward infor-mation biased, which is responded to by counter-biasing attempts, which in turn generate increased upward bias to counteract the coun-ter-biasing attempts, reducing the overall value and significance of official information, and eventually generating reliance on rumors and manipulation. *Pathological growth* is a common phenomenon in the literature and practice, whereby administrative units grow into bureaucracies, which, because of their self-perpetuating nature and coordination overhead, in turn place limits on organizational improvement. Being embedded in external systems can expose organizations to *pathological conflict*, such as when regulatory bureaucracies trigger counter-bureaucracies, eventually sapping all energy, ending escalation by both parties.

Combinations of and interactions among action loops can create even greater dysfunctionalities. *Explosive clusters* involve two or more positive feedbacks, with at least one deviation-amplifying (for example, bureaucrats reproduce, and make more work for each other). *Monitored clusters* occur when one or more deviation-amplifying circles combine with one or more negative feedback loops (such as an expanding loop interacting with one or more diminishing loops), leading to stagnating vicious circles (for example, the growth of an organization's bureaucracy/formalization continues expanding until it has insufficient additional resources to counter the continued growth of apathy caused by the bureaucratic conflicts). For another example, increased organizational formalization reduces everyone's "elbow room," including management's. To the extent that the local union is aware of this, it may sponsor increased formalization (work to rule), thus reducing management's ability to control unions because of even less elbow room (Crozier, 1964). This blocks a return to a more rational state (i.e., the "escape route"), because the subsequent "self-correcting circle obscures the effect of the first (vicious) one" (Masuch, 1985, p. 22). Members become aware of worse, but not better, alternatives, leading to a suboptimal condition. Thus an inadequate understanding of the first circle generates irrational action and potential conflict. The second feedback appears to solve the problem but really only treats the symptom. A third feedback stabilizes this while also preventing improvement. One consequence is the increasing vocalization of dichotomous but misleading perceptions of "us" and "them." Vicious circle *implosions* occur when several different loops are activated by an initial change, each one then generating negative changes in the other loops (for examples from universities, see Cyert, 1978). Thus, "if vicious circles persist in strategic situations, some misperception must be present" (Masuch, 1985, p. 24). In particular, participants early on need to search actively for the hidden initial cause. However, this is unlikely, given participants' cognitive dispositions (Chapter 8), the complexity of multi-level social systems, and the self-sealing nature of vicious cycles. Another example is a *conflict spiral*, when the substance of a continuous and circular inter-action is repeated contentious communication, which involves threats or costly or unfavorable consequences on the other if the other does not comply (Brett *et al.*, 1998).

Examples of feedback loops creating the opposite of the intended outcome are provided in *crowding motivation theory* (Frey, 1994). People may be willing to donate or volunteer their resources (such as giving blood). Organizations or social policy may presume that paying people to do this will increase such behavior. The ironic result, how-ever, is that intrinsic motivations (pleasure, altruism, etc.) for donat-ing (which induced the initial donations) are crowded out by extrinsic motivations (pay, promotion, etc.). Further, financial rewards may end up generating a lower amount and quality of blood, as now some may be motivated to lie about their health in order to gain the income, while volunteer blood donors may come to resent that their effort is not similarly rewarded, feel that they are being taken advantage of by self-interested opportunists (Titmuss, 1970), and stop giving. A related example is *government crowding-out theory*, which considers the extent to which government's borrowing to increase expenditure or cut taxes crowds out, through higher interest rates, investment from the private sector (Andreoni and Bergstrom, 1996). Frey (1994) pro-poses a countervailing *crowding in* effect, whereby remuneration may in fact foster greater and higher quality contributions. The distinction seems to depend on whether extrinsic motivations are perceived as controlling or acknowledging. Rewards that seem to be controlling displace the locus of control outside of the person, while rewards that acknowledge and appreciate the intrinsic motivations may strengthen the intrinsic motivations, and thus contributions.

Defensive routines and mixed messages

Argyris (1985, 2002) distinguishes between *espoused theories* – what people say is their theory of action – and two kinds of *theories in use* – what they actually do, which, unfortunately, typically involve conflicting rationalities (Argyris, 1988, p. 262). People then trade off, typically without knowing it, local situational rupture for long-term systemic rupture. Alternatively, a problem can be solved locally, while the underlying systemic bypassing still remains, which can recreate the local problem later on (e.g., workarounds).

Of the two general theories in use, Model I is by far the most prevalent, and seems consistent across race, gender, culture, education, wealth, organizational type. Its four governing principles are: (1) be in unilateral control; (2) strive to win and not lose; (3) suppress negative feelings; and (4) act rationally. People try to act in ways consistent with these, but are typically unaware of this. Following the theory-in-use Model I, in turn, requires *defensive routines*, "any action, policy, or practice that prevents organizational participants from experiencing embarrassment or threat and, at the same time, prevents them from discovering the causes of the embarrassment or threat" (Argyris, 2002, p. 213). Organizational defensive routines differ from individual psychological defenses because they are learned through socialization, taught as strategies, supported by the organizational culture, and persist over time independently of changes in personnel (Argyris, 1988, p. 257).

Use of defensive routines prevents questioning the use of defensive routines, leading to increased misunderstanding, mistrust, self-fulfilling prophecies, escalating error, subsequent cynicism, avoiding taking responsibility, and avoiding doing anything that might involve "losing" or feelings of threat or embarrassment. Thus they are counterproductive by inhibiting learning, including learning about how to reduce, resolve, or prevent the initial threat as well as by preventing learning about why organizational members did not learn about the problem and its explanations (Argyris, 1985). These behaviors lead to *organizational bypass* and *cover-up*, which reinforce individuals' Model I. Bypass strategies come in two forms. The first is to be straightforward and direct, but in judgmental and rigid ways that make it difficult for others to respond honestly, so the underlying problem is bypassed. The second is to "ease in." This is a covert form of taking action to control others while leading others to think one is not attempting to control them, and indeed appearing to save the other's face, so that one cannot be held responsible for the subsequent defensive response, and making the white lies and easing-in strategy undiscussable (Argyris, 1985).

What makes these processes particularly difficult is that the bypassing is often sincerely or unconsciously intended to maintain respect for others' feelings and status, and that typically individuals are not aware that they are creating defensive actions which in turn trigger organizational defensive loops. Then, later attempts to deal with the underlying problem, threat, or defensive routine are seen by many as autocratic, uncaring, and thoughtless (Argyris, 1985, p. 10). Organizational practices make this situation worse, creating a *generic "antilearning" pattern* (Argyris, 2002, p. 206), in which firmly held or assumed causal claims or goals are stated abstractly, so it is difficult to know how to accomplish them, and difficult to test their validity or assess their accomplishment. This is one of the negative dimensions of strategic ambiguity, noted earlier, although this can hardly be called strategic, as few know they are actually doing this.

One kind of organizational defensive routine is the *mixed message*, with four rules: (1) design and communicate an inconsistent message; (2) act as though it is not inconsistent (the communicator may not know it is inconsistent); (3) make both of these undiscussable (including the lack of awareness); and (4) make this undiscussability undiscussable (Argyris, 1988, p. 214). Mixed messages can spawn a remarkable set of consequences. First, they generate rules that require inconsistent actions. Second, they generate incomplete or incorrect attributions that also cannot be discussed, so organizational members cannot correct the distortions or errors, which thus increase them over time, reinforcing the mixed messages, undiscussability, and nontestability. These defensive routines themselves become unmanageable and uninfluencable. The defensive routines escalate and become embedded in the organization (Argyris, 1985, p. 74). Thus defensive routines are both one form of, and a way of reinforcing, URs.

This situation leads to double binds on the part of both management and subordinates. This mutual double bind generates mistrust and suppresses communication, creating self-fulfilling processes attributed by the other side (Argyris, 1986). Thus both superiors and subordinates hold good and bad feelings toward each other. The implication is that to overcome what they do not like, people must be able to discuss it, but this violates the undiscussability rule which is part of organizational defensive routines – a form of skilled incompetence. Table 7.1 summarizes the basic components of organizational defensive routines.

Table 7.1 *Development of defensive routines*

Initial motivations	Initial response to a salient problem	Resulting processes	Implications
Cooperative Constructive Caring Model I principles: control the encounter's purpose, maximize winning while minimizing losing, minimize negative feelings, and maximize rationality. However: Model I Theory-in-Use leads to: concerns about other's intentions; readiness to test validity of concerns; desire to maintain image of honorable motivations.	Basic defensive routines include: (1) keep premises and inferences tacit (to avoid losing control), (2) advocate your position in order to be in control, (3) unilaterally save your and others' face – that is, do not surface fallacies, errors, or abstract claims, use non-directive questioning, over-protect individuals, and cover up that one is acting this way so as not to upset the other (Argyris, 1988). Aware that responding to the initial concerns may be perceived as threat, conflict, discourteous.	The use of mixed messages is undiscussable and that undiscussability is undiscussable, to protect self, other, and the organization. Mixed messages are used to respond to mixed message to avoid threat, conflict, and discourtesy.	Distance and polarization between participants, and between participants and the organization, due to the tension between a sense of personal responsibility to discuss issues in order to solve problems, and the inference that those in power will defend their (hidden) interests and sanction anyone raising those issues. This creates a personal sense of dishonesty or dissonance, as well as reduced self-responsibility, low status, group-think, win/lose decision processes, gaming the system.

Respond to threat by bypass-ing the causes of the threat; avoid pain to self and others; over-protect self and others; thus preventing learning.
Send mixed messages, a way for both parties to save face.

So actors develop attributions and causal explanations in the form of concluding what the other's motives are. These explanations are built upon culturally understood meanings as well as meanings the participants impose, and about which par-ticipants then develop theories to justify the imposed meanings.
The attributions are not publicly tested, as that would require discus-sion of motives and attributions.

Resolutions become nearly impossible, as that would require making many undis-cussable topics and processes discussable. So, mutual dou-ble binds. Organizational members become resigned, and this acceptance of "the way things are" becomes normative, natural, and invisible.
Participants invoke the ini-tial honorable motivations, which are in principle not blameworthy, as a defense.

Table 7.1 (*cont.*)

Initial motivations	Initial response to a salient problem	Resulting processes	Implications
		Thus defensive reasoning is used to protect from learning about one's own reasoning. The participants are not only not aware of their inferences, but certain they are not engaging in this process. Thus the process is self-sealing.	"Solutions" bypass the issues, the defensive routines, and the participants. The responses maintain or escalate the errors. Organizations may implement new procedures or apply different but pre-existing ones, to be able to control if the issue comes up again. Participants learn these new rules, and respond to or critique the rules rather than take responsibility for learning about their role in the initial problem.

Note: Summary of Argyris (1985, Chapter One; 1988).

As a specific example of mixed messages and conflicting goals, even in an organization avowedly committed to TQM principles, there may be substantial mismatches:

(1) between what is proposed by the organization as the principles guiding measurement and what employees perceive those principles to be;
(2) between what measures are prioritized in different units;
(3) between the frequency of use of measures reflecting the guiding principles and the ranking of what the employees actually consider the best available measures of quality; and
(4) between the collecting of information about tasks in order to improve performance quality, and the actual application of that information to learning and improvement (Lehr and Rice, 2005).

Further, the very nature and use of measures, used as intentional feedback processes, depends on underlying assumptions and theories about feedback and measures, such as organizational learning, Weickian sensemaking, TQM, and critical theory (Lehr and Rice, 2002, 2005; Paton, 2003).

Conclusion

No doubt the constructive use of feedback is vital to a healthy system of human interactions, whether the system we are considering is a particular organization or a complex web of interactions between an organization and its clients. But just as necessary conditions ought not be mistaken for sufficient conditions, feedback cannot be assumed to be the generic remedy for URs. Much of the difficulty in conceptualizing URs as a class of analytic problems stems from the way feedback can be not just a contributor to, but a structural component of, a given UR. As Box 7.1 summarizes, the literature identifies a number of problematic aspects of feedback, both as human communication behavior and as organizational feature. We are left with something of a sober realization: limited or defective feedback is insufficient as a complete explanation of URs, and more feedback cannot be expected, in and of itself, to mitigate unusual routines.

Box 7.1 Summary of individual and organizational challenges to feedback

Feedback challenges inherent in human communication behaviors

Contextualizing meaning by layers: meaning of feedback embedded in, and (mis)constructed through, hierarchical levels of rules about content, context, and relationships.

Desperately seeking feedback: different forms, sources, relationship, and medium of feedback affect nature of its content.

Discourse and language: meaning of feedback (even if apparently explicit) highly contextual and socially constructed, thus subject to power relations; may be intentionally ambiguous; unusual routines and related feedback may be similar to clichés.

Reflexive loops, paradoxes, and undesired repetitive patterns: some relations and processes do not follow clear hierarchies of levels, resulting in reciprocal, reflexive, transitive, strange and charmed, double-bind, ritualized, unwanted repetitive.

Skilled incompetence and the contradictions of competence: one level may impose constraints on other level in ways that foster negative outcomes at the first level, such as skilled incompetence, and dialectics of inference.

Feedback challenges inherent in organizations

Defensive routines and mixed messages: divergence between espoused and used theories in organizations creates a complex system of defensive routines, mixed messages, confusion, mixed levels of feedback, double binds, and undiscussable problems.

Learning by doing rather than by learning: much relevant feedback information already exists at problem site, but unused, but some created only through the problem itself, with ripples of errors and feedback resources.

Learning from feedback or memorizing responses? Routines are manifestations of organizational memory, fostering better processing but also hindering adaptation and learning; individual learning difficult to transform into system-wide feedback; different retention bins provide different kinds of memory and are differentially accessible; feedback itself may be routinized, with similar advantages and disadvantages; many obstacles to learning from feedback.

Rational but unreasonable, even schizophrenic, systems: feedback may stimulate oscillations or chaotic organizational responses, amplify deviations, heighten biased enactments, preventing and distorting second-loop learning.

Reporting errors through feedback, and errors of reporting feedback: different kinds and sources of errors, at individual, system, and group level, accumulating and normalizing ongoing errors; many barriers to identifying and reporting errors; emphasis on single-loop learning.

Timing of feedback: feedback may be scheduled or contextual, temporally mismatched with problem, having fixed or varying timing, and focused on short-term or long-term, leading to different effects.

Vicious circles: difficult to identify distributed components of unusual routines and interdependent cycles; feedback may breed vicious cycles and organizational pathologies, including feedback biased in ways that reinforce, or repress learning about, or transform into new negative forms of, the underlying problem.

8 | A multi-level and cross-disciplinary summary of concepts related to unusual routines

Because of the pervasiveness of the underlying phenomenon of dysfunctional feedback throughout individual, group, organizational, technical, and social relations, there are, of course, many related concepts. Unusual routines may be the general, underlying process of which many of these are specific forms, identified in specific conceptual and practical contexts. So this chapter reviews a wide range of related concepts. Scott Adams' comic strip *Dilbert* is probably the best archive of examples of these and related URs in organizational settings (www.dilbert.com).

Cognitive and social processing errors

Personal heuristics

Dorner (1989/1996) generally explains some reasons why we make faulty decisions that can lead to unintended consequences. First, human thinking is slow and cognitively bounded, leading us to economize on thinking. So, we tend to take action, or possibly plan and gather information and then take action, rather than "formulating our goals in concrete terms, balancing contradictory partial ones, and prioritizing them" (p. 186). Talking about thinking, actions, and problems does not mean better performance. We tend to focus on one or few variables instead of the complex interrelationships, reducing time and effort demands. We focus on one or a few rules to govern complex interrelationships, thus diminishing strategic thinking. We extrapolate linearly over some indefinite time, ignoring possible diversions, changes, and non-linear relationships. We ignore side effects and long-term interactions and repercussions. We conceptualize new situations in terms of prior, traditional approaches. And we seek to ignore consequences of actions. Human cognitive processes filter out and remove details from memory. It is especially difficult to conceptualize and retain prior temporal patterns. Many of these attributes are explored below. Humans in general are highly skilled at both effortlessly making, and maintaining faith in, our inferences (Argyris, 1985, p. 59), decreasing our motivation to actually evaluate those inferences.

Second, psychological processes and tendencies affect our thinking (Dorner, 1989/1996). It is well understood that humans – and organizations – do not understand well. (The irony in that comment is intended!) That is, there are significant human cognitive processing constraints, significant organizational habits and bureaucratic dysfunctions, and pervasive limits on obtaining and distributing relevant information within organizations, each of which limits "rationality" and fosters, as well as encourages, deviance and unintended consequences. Relevant concepts here include *bounded rationality, satisficing,* and *the garbage can model of organizational decision-making* (Cohen *et al.*, 1972; March and Olsen, 1976; March and Simon, 1958). The central research area for understanding our cognitive and psychological biases is *personal heuristics and biases*, individual tendencies that contribute to paradoxical and preferential positions (Gilovich *et al.*, 2002; Kahneman *et al.*, 1982; Tavris and Aronson, 2007), which can be parsimoniously paraphrased as when "people answer a hard question by substituting an easier one" (Sunstein, 2005, p. 36). While they may be typically quite effective, and have a good basis in cognitive evolution, they also foster predictable and systematic errors.

Cognitive dissonance

Dissonance may well be the most salient processing error relevant to URs. Cognitive dissonance is the sense of anxiety or conflict resulting from a perceived incongruity between one's actions and beliefs, leading to an inherent drive to reduce this tension and anxiety by reducing the dissonance. People respond somewhat to cognitive dissonance by changing beliefs or actions, but more often they postjustify or reinterpret the situation to make it more consonant. If, for example, someone experiences significant pain, effort, or embarrassment to obtain a goal, they will be more satisfied with the outcome than if they did not, because that self-justifies the apparent tension or conflict by maintaining the self-identification of being a rational, good, honest, reasonable person (Tavris and Aronson, 2007). Classic studies such as Milgram's (1974) obedience/shock experiments or having students simulate roles as prison guards or prisoners (Haney *et al.*, 1973; Zimbardo, 1971) found that those imposing harm on others increased the perpetrators' denigration or projected guilt of their victims. Humans' processing of cognitive dissonance is shaped by our deeply rooted but false beliefs: (1) that we accurately perceive all aspects of our environment, and thus (2) that everyone else sees the environment as we do. Thus we tend to believe that disagreement must be due to the other person's misperceptions and biases (Tavris and Aronson, 2007, p. 42). So, not only do we often arrive at incomplete or wrong conclusions, we maintain them even when provided disconfirming evidence. A central problem here is that "Introspection alone will not help our vision, because it will simply confirm our self-justifying beliefs" (p. 44).

This drive to reduce cognitive dissonance leads to a wide variety of self-justifying, over-amplifying, misleading, and defensive behaviors. Essentially, if we are confronted with information on our own behaviors that create a salient discrepancy, we adjust our attitudes and beliefs to reduce the apparent discrepancy rather than, say, acknowledge the discrepancy and change our behavior or self-identity. And we do this the more we are personally invested in the issue at hand, and more interested in maintaining the psychological and social status quo (Tavris and Aronson, 2007, p. 223). "[W]e tend to cling tenaciously to our schemata and even twist new information to conform to them" (Gell-Mann, 1994, p. 303).

Partly due to our drive to reduce cognitive dissonance, we attempt to preserve a positive sense of our competence, emphasizing expectations of success, downplaying uncertainty or doubt, fostering self-protection at expense of system goals (Dorner, 1989/1996). We emphasize our sense of control, thus over-emphasizing planning and information gathering. We see new problems as existing ones, thereby increasing our sense of competence and security. We attempt to solve only problems we think we can solve, avoiding others. And we tend to think only about current problems, thus discounting and ignoring possible future side-effects.

Unaware self-justification, however, blocks out and reinterprets evidence, leading us further into the errors, attitudes, and behaviors that created the dissonance in the first place. While maintaining our self-identity is important, the self-oriented approach to reducing dissonance creates deviation-amplifying feedback loops. Soon, we are doing things and holding beliefs that early on would have been entirely unacceptable and even foreign to us. Soon, our actual memories are entirely consistent with our self-justifications. That is, we don't usually "lie" but, instead, come to believe explanations and events in the way that most justifies our beliefs about ourself, and that most reduces the dissonance between that and what "happened" (p. 70).

When we find new information that confirms our beliefs, we more positively evaluate and believe that information – what is called *confirmation bias*, involving both selective perception and self-justification. However, the drive to reduce dissonance through self-justification instead of evaluating the evidence generates *attribution bias* – that an error, bad behavior, or mistake is due to the circumstances or someone else, and not to our own abilities or beliefs (Tavris and Aronson, 2007, p. 63). *Categorizing* is a natural and fundamental human disposition, leading to stereotyping, and in-group/out-group distinctions. There are many evolutionary and daily benefits to categorizing, such as faster decision-making, information processing and retrieval, identifying real distinctions, avoiding danger, and predicting behavior (p. 57). But when categorization is based on faulty information, cognitive dissonance reduction also leads us to increase and reinforce our categorizations rather than exposing them to evaluation and accuracy. So, ironically for those with an underlying faith in reason, information, feedback, and challenging or trying to present counter-evidence often serves to increase, rather than diminish, the confidence and rightness of the belief or behavior (p. 61). One implication here is to try to avoid (by oneself and by others) attempts at justification, and instead consider the processes involved and how to prevent them in the future.

Sometimes only very strong, irrefutable evidence may have any effect at all, such as DNA testing to exonerate wrongly convicted people. Even in these cases the original prosecutors, police, and judges rarely admit they were wrong and there are very few policies for compensating or even apologizing to those victims. One of the long-term ironies here (as with procedural injustice, discussed in Chapter 1), is that each innocent person subjected to unfair interrogation and conviction, as well as (some of) those who become aware of these cases, becomes less supportive of authorities in general and police activities in particular. That is, the larger self-reinforcing deviation-amplifying loop is to generate more people who are likely to disapprove of, and break, the law.

One very strong self-reinforcing justification is one's confidence in the attitude or belief. Research is quite clear that there is almost no relationship between confidence and accuracy. Nonetheless, strong confidence leads us to continue even more briskly down the wrong path. A corollary misleading belief is that vehemence, loudness, or ferventness of one's opinion (commonly termed "passion") is evidence of its accuracy. Most people, unfortunately, are unable to experience much awareness of any of these components, leading them to dismiss or avoid counter-evidence from research or victims, and seek out and generate more self-justifying examples (Tavris and Aronson, 2007, p. 125).

Related to self-confidence in perception, but somewhat more ambiguous than dissonance reduction, is the apparently increasing tendency to "invent metaphors and images and arguments to justify our choices, or cope with a state of affairs, and then forget that the word is not the thing; that our discourse about something does not necessarily change it" (Thompson, 1988, p. 133). This is made worse by the increasingly mediated nature of experience, through images, words, sounds, digital representations, and personalities. People also seem inherently unable or unwilling to live in excessively simple or understandable situations; we may be driven to "build worlds for ourselves that are slightly beyond our understanding" (Starbuck, 1988, p. 71).

The most general form of self-justification to reduce dissonance is simply to deny that there is a problem in the first place. This drive is generated both by a belief in the near-perfection of our primary processes (such as, in the case of police and the courts, interrogation and conviction), as well as by, in the United States, a cultural fear of being seen to have made a mistake. Note that it is not necessarily a fear of making the mistake but of others knowing that we have made it, because then someone may think we are stupid, and our public identity (or face) would be threatened. A challenge, critique, or even question about one's attitude or belief (perceived or actual, from others or oneself) is often taken as a critique or rejection of one's self – as a person – rather than the behavior or attitude or decision. Thus, shaming and blaming – whether intended or not – often serve to further reinforce the self-justification, removing awareness even further from the underlying problem or process (Tavris and Aronson, 2007, p. 171). Couching (by others), or perceiving (by oneself), a question about a problem in terms of personality or one's nature serves both to reduce the other's dissonance as to their role in the problem, as well as to increase one's self-justification and denial of the evidence. This is one reason, for example, for underestimating personal risks (such as for health behaviors such as smoking or drinking) (Sunstein, 2007, p. 232). Paradoxically, greater self-esteem induces even greater attempts at dissonance reduction, including stronger negative evaluations of the other, because what might appear as negative attitudes or behaviors are even more contradictory to the highly positive self-image (Tavris and Aronson, 2007, p. 199).

Errors in logic and logics of errors

Approaching individual error processing from a different perspective than personal heuristics, Elster (1983) challenges assumptions about rationality as the basis of choice and decision-making, and explains a wide variety of irrational behaviors, desires, and beliefs. Given his definition of action as "the outcome of a choice within constraints" (p. vii), he argues both that people may choose their own constraints, and that constraints may shape one's preferences. Both of these present problems for standard theories of rational choice.

He argues, for example, that a variety of states that are presented as outcomes of rational choice are essentially byproducts of irrational processes; that is, the outcome is shaped by causal factors irrelevant to the actual preference. These include "willing what cannot be willed," "self-management technologies," some kinds of commands, "trying to impress," "faking," intentionality in art, the basis of power, self-defeating political theories, and the projection of meaning. Fundamental to his framework is that there are two kinds of rationality explaining behavior. The first is rationality in the sense of one's action based consistently on one's consistent beliefs and preferences (*thin rationality*, emphasizing autonomy). One criterion for a set of consistent beliefs is that not only should they not be contradictory, but they are all believed. That is, there is a second-level belief about the first-order beliefs. Behavior based on the first level when the second-level belief is not held, or is contradictory to the first level, is conceptually irrational (p. 5). Under thin rationality, the action itself may be irrational, and there may be many factors affecting beliefs and preferences that are essentially irrational (p. 3). The second is rationality in the sense of evidence linking belief and outcomes (*thick rationality*, emphasizing judgment).

Preferences may be rational or irrational on the basis of *time*. Presuming that there are good reasons to discount the future at a particular rate, one can either discount the future even more than one believes is appropriate because one is impatient and thus engages in an irrational decision (this is different from simply preferring a greater future discount), or one can change the future discount over time, thus irrationally changing the basis of an earlier decision. Elster notes that some may delay and group several future choices in order to select the greatest reward, but this may also reduce flexibility and even foster compulsive behavior (1983, p. 8).

Of course, distorted and illusionary beliefs, even generated by self-interest, do not necessary guarantee achievement of those interests. Indeed, they may actually harm those self-interests. For example, the behavior following from those (self-interested) beliefs may be assessed by others as evidence (engaging in self-interest) against the rationale for fulfilling the belief. Alternatively, positive social outcomes may accrue from individual illusory beliefs; if everyone correctly understood the probabilities of success in risky or highly competitive activities (such as acting, the arts, or professional sports), few would actually engage in the extreme time and effort needed to achieve them. While such errors or mistakes may be useful, that is, help to accomplish desired outcomes, they are nonetheless causally misleading and harmful for intentional planning or design.

Thus, some URs may not be susceptible to change to the extent that embedded participants who tried to will an awareness of how their actions were self-centered and insincere might be too self-centered and insincere to achieve the state. An inversion of this fallacy is *willing awareness of the unwilled*. Consider satire: to be effective the perpetrator must willingly repress the appearance of willfulness but it can be successful only if both the actor and the audience are aware of this intentionality. The perpetrator must be intentionally satirical, while the target cannot be intentionally satirical; rather, the target's unawareness of the alternative interpretations of the behavior strengthens the point of the satire. That is, perfect satire should be invisible to the target of the satire, but completely obvious to the audience, and the art of the intentionality, as expressed through the language and subtlety of the satire, should be completely transparent.

At a more societal level, Gaskins (1992) argues that certain aspects of modern culture have become increasingly reflected in public discourse – institutional, legal, scientific, professional, and everyday communication – culminating in a powerful strategy of reasoning that he calls *argument-from-ignorance*, generating or reflecting a "widening gap between legitimacy and evidence" (p. xvi). This argumentation fallacy is known as *ad ignorantiam*, asserting that something is true because it has not been shown to be false, or that it is false because it has not been shown to be true (Weston, 2009, pp. 73–4). Many contemporary debates are fundamentally adversarial, shifting what might be a productive discussion into public assertion contests. Partially this is due to inherent uncertainties (even, or especially, in science), possibilities for multiple interpretations (such as in case law and philosophy), the responsible use of qualification, increasing blurring of formerly distinct boundaries (such as cultural interactions related to globalization), continuing change (such as in technology or social norms), and our post-modern mistrust of authority, universal principles, and the common good (Gaskins, 1992).

The essential question is "just how much – or how little – are we entitled to infer from the lack of information?" (p. 2). The general scientific approach, derived from Karl Popper, is to consider all positive statements based on even extensive information as tentative, pending evidence of refutation. This is opposed to the argument-from-ignorance approach, which allows statements of strongest support in cases of least information, because there is no disconfirming evidence (most simply stated as "I am right, because you cannot prove that I am wrong", p. 2) which then also "requires some kind of decision rule (usually unstated) about how the parties to a discussion should proceed in the face of uncertainty or indeterminacy" (p. xv). Examples include legal rules about how one must bear the burden of proof (what Gaskins illuminates as who must bear the "risk of non-persuasion"), and programming rules about default operations. This also implies that sophisticated parties understand that an effective strategy involves shifting the burden of proof in light of ignorance about the underlying phenomenon. He argues that many realms of public discourse are adopting (usually without awareness) aspects and rhetorical strategies of the legal/judicial approach as a way to deal with the increasing uncertainties and indeterminacy in other realms.

This strategy of shifting the burden of proof may well be implied or involved in some aspects of unusual subroutines, especially error and blame subroutines. That is, the representative of the entity associated with the UR may be, due to ignorance and in fact using that ignorance as the basis for judgment, shifting (or applying) the burden of proof – that is, a particular claim as to the nature or source of the problem – to the original claimant or to other components of the UR.

Gaskins (1992) identifies a variety of ignorances. The central consequence of such forms of ignorance is the ability, and need, to generate continuous adversarial discourse that critique the opposing position in unanswerable ways, shifting the burden of proof. Sudden shifts in who must bear the burden of proof are highly consequential, even revolutionary, because all subsequent discourse must follow different paths.

Predictable surprises, worst-case scenarios, and the precautionary principle

One organizational and social phenomenon following from human and systemic error processing biases are *predictable surprises*. These are not just a case of the *hindsight bias*, the retrospective belief that an event was much more predictable than it actually was beforehand. "A predictable surprise arises when leaders unquestionably had all the data and insight they needed to recognize the potential for, even the inevitability of, a crisis, but failed to respond with preventative action" (Bazerman and Watkins, 2004, p. 4). But there is a continuum between very predictable surprises and unpredictable surprises. Characteristics of predictable surprises (pp. 5–8) include (1) at least some leaders were aware of the problem and that it needed to be solved, (2) people understand that the problem is worsening, (3) resolving the problem involves significant near-term/immediate costs and long-term/delayed benefits, (4) costs are certain but benefits are uncertain (the combination of (3) and (4) makes it very difficult for leaders to justify taking action), (5) tendency to maintain status quo prevents preparation for predictable surprise (i.e., current system functioning and absence of present crisis prevents making changes to prevent future possibility), and (6) a powerful minority (special interests) benefits from status quo even at cost to the collective interests.

Bazerman and Watkins describe many factors contributing to the emergence of predictable surprises. Of those, the following seem most relevant to the concept of URs. Information may be categorized as too sensitive to share (due to fears of status loss, revealing confidential sources, limited upward and integrated sharing). Responsibility is ambiguous or diffuse (reducing or removing incentives to act). Roles and structures may generate conflicts of interests, or principal–agent divergence between individual and collective goals. Consensus about a decision or strategy may be illusory (e.g., groupthink) whereby lack of active opposition is seen as positive support which in turn allows participants to repudiate blame and responsibility later on. Dissent may be suppressed explicitly through a spiral of silence, and implicitly through excessive control of responsibility so that others bear the costs without recourse. Special interests can manipulate a system for their own interests. Organizations embedded in the market system need to meet quarterly dividend expectations, which heavily discounts the future. As discussed below, individual benefits conflict with the collective good (social dilemmas and social traps), leading to free-riding and the tragedy of the commons (Hardin, 1968). When the predictable surprise does happen, higher-level stakeholders direct blame to individuals or specific groups, rather than to the systemic flaws or processes.

Distinct from predictable surprises, *worst-case scenarios* represent a potential range of negative outcomes that may not be deterministic or even hypothetically predictable. But they suffer from the same problem of being difficult to envision, and thus plan for or prevent. As Cerulo (2006) concludes, humans have a strong tendency to use ideals as both representatives and definitions of concepts, and thus the basis for future comparison, interpretation, prediction, and generation of specific instances. (This is a form of availability bias, the vividness effect, discounting the future, and the substitution of metaphor for action.) The further away from the concept, the more fuzzy, ambiguous, or irrelevant. So "best-case examples of a concept are overemphasized and highly detailed" (p. 9). But these concepts are also derived from the group or community cultural repertoire. So people suffer from a drive toward positive asymmetry, "the tendency to emphasize only examples of the best or most positive cases" (p. 10).

Thus we seem to have a blatant disregard for, even an inability to conceptualize, the worst possibilities, through three cultural practices: (1) eclipsing (worst cases are invisible, via banishment, physical exclusion, shunning), (2) clouding (possibilities are only vaguely defined, via impressionism, shadowing), and (3) recasting (convert a possibility to something positive, rhetorically or prescriptively) (Cerulo, 2006). This positive asymmetry influences all kinds of quality assessments/measures. One implication is that measurement scales might only measure levels of the good, without considering the bad, whether within the same measure, or as a separate dimension. In addition, consequences of the label of "worst" are influenced by cultural and social factors, such as the durability of the label, the relative power of the labeler and the labeled, and the context of the labeling (for example, whether criticism is tolerated or not). Positive asymmetry will dampen early warnings about the emergence of a UR.

Posner (2004), like Cerulo, bemoans the inattention to potential threats, in particular global catastrophes (in four categories – natural such as asteroids, scientific accidents such as nanomachines gone wild, other unintended man-made catastrophes such as severe ecological damage, and intentional catastrophes such as bioterrorism). He points to a wide variety of factors hindering our perception, analysis, and response to such risks. These include cultural factors such as scientific illiteracy, science fiction, and heavy discounting of the future, psychological factors such as those in Box 8.1, and economic factors such as global decentralization and innovation.

The other end of the individual and social bias continuum from insufficient engagement with social risks (such as predictable surprises, worst-case scenarios, and catastrophe myopia) is immobilization or hesitation to take action from fear of them, represented by the *precautionary principle*. This asserts that "regulators should take steps to protect against potential harms, even if causal chains are unclear and even if we do not know that those harms will come to fruition" (Sunstein, 2005, p. 4). This can be seen either as very prudent, protecting against possibly devastating, long range, and irreversible harms, or as very fearful, vastly overestimating risk, suppressing innovation and progress, and creating other costs and harms. Both possibilities involve, from Sunstein's perspective, a failure to attend to factual information and related probabilities, due to an array of psychological and societal heuristics and processing limits (such as those in Box 8.1). A particularly insidious implication of making such decisions (such as restricting certain kinds of rights in an atmosphere of fear about possible terrorism), is when the consequences of either short-term costs or of discounting long-term benefits are borne by different social groups or actors than those imposing the decisions, or than by those supporting those decisions based on the personal heuristics and social factors. The unequal distributional consequences are more likely if the restricted groups are socially categorized as "outgroups," and thus stereotyped, by the supporting groups (p. 209). More centrally, Sunstein argues that strict adherence to the precautionary principle is inherently paradoxical and irrational; because it ignores risks relating to not taking certain actions (*substitute risks* and *opportunity benefits*), it does not apply itself to its own application, and, to be consistently applied, leads to paralysis.

Related to the general idea of perceptions of and responses to threat is what Edmondson *et al.* (2005) call the *recovery window* – the period between an organizational threat and either its prevention or a subsequent major accident. As the error has already occurred, the recovery window provides the possibility of resolution of the error and prevention of the negative consequences. Organizations respond to this recovery window in different ways. During the recovery window, the organization needs to first identify and assess the threat, and then develop preventions or solutions. But organizations do not naturally respond well to this opportunity, partly because threats can be quite ambiguous, and solutions may not be identifiable or feasible. Further, organizations may not be aware that there even is a recovery window, for any particular threat. An analysis of the Columbia shuttle disaster found that organizational responses contributing to the failure to take advantage of the recovery window were active discounting of the risk (applying prior assumptions and transforming the unusual to the familiar), fragmented discipline- and location-based analyses (lack of information sharing, isolation of minority opinions, duplication of effort), and postponing action in favor of observation (hesitancy because of uncertainty or existing strong beliefs, resignation) (Edmondson *et al.*, 2005). When organizations do become aware of the threat, they typically respond in one of two ways. The first response category is a *confirmatory response*, which essentially discounts ambiguous threats (without testing the optimistic assumption behind the discounting) while delaying actions. The second is an *exploratory response* which favors over-responsiveness combined with organizational learning. The confirmatory response apparently is the normal, default response. Thus organizational leadership must consciously and proactively foster an exploratory response approach. This argument differs from the threat-rigidity theory (Staw *et al.*, 1981) by focusing on why social entities discount ambiguous threats, instead of how organizations tend to replicate organic responses to threat by shutting down communication channels and relying on programmed behavior.

Box 8.1 summarizes many of the individual heuristics and psychological traits from across disciplines representing or explaining concepts potentially involved in URs.

Box 8.1 Individual processing heuristics, with example application to unusual routines

Affect heuristic: whereby fear, anxiety, and regret, for instance, strongly influence decision-making, even when unrelated to probabilities or available information. *Example*: fear of management disapproval from reporting errors.

Attribution bias, or *ego-biased interpretation of events*: self-serving (individual and group) attribution of blame (to others) and credit (to self). *Example*: blaming service problem on customer.

Availability heuristic: generating an inaccurate probability assessment, by basing decisions on available (more noticeable, recent, frequency, vivid, retrievable), familiar and salient instances (which may vary by ideology, region, and medium) instead of baseline information. *Example*: attributing cause of unusual routine to most observable person or process.

Cognitive dissonance: the tension induced by having conflicting ideas or beliefs, which may generate a threat of irrationality and chaos, and the related drive to reduce cognitive dissonance, through a variety of biased processing of information. *Example*: routinizing dysfunctional process as way to justify being engaged in it.

Failures of foresight: being unable to attend to or accurately interpret a series of discrepant events and danger signs (Turner, 1976).

Example: possibly due to barriers to perception, cannot imagine dysfunctional consequences of current unusual routine.

Hindsight bias: where people, upon knowing the outcome, retrospectively interpret an event as much more determinant and causal than they perceived during the event (Fischoff, 1975), facilitating easy blame of others who should have known or seen better. *Example*: explaining low-probability automation system problem as operator error.

Loss or risk aversion: when people heavily discount future benefits and opportunity costs while emphasizing present costs; thus this is especially relevant for future benefits that are difficult to determine or explain, and unfamiliar risks. Avoiding future risk, however, can also generate significant costs to the status quo. Contributes to the *precautionary principle*. *Example*: contributes to social dilemma of emphasizing present and local benefits over future and collective costs.

Omission bias: a version of loss or risk aversion – avoiding small costs, risks, and harm, which prevents taking actions to avoid greater costs and risks. *Example*: encourages workarounds.

Optimism about a benign nature: opposite of pessimism about the harmfulness of human decisions, in spite of the clear danger, toxicity, and risk of natural entities, chemicals, and processes. *Example*: minimizing potential unintentional consequence of complex technology.

Positive illusions, and the *third-party effect*: leading to denying or undervaluing risks to self, while over-estimating relevance and import of present actions, discounting the salience and contribution of other groups, or leading to blaming others. *Example*: displaces concerns about and blame for unusual routine.

Predispositions: such as being fearful of specific risks, leading to strong accessibility and affect heuristics. *Example*: in organizational culture of penalties for errors, reduces learning feedback.

Probability neglect: possibly suppressing any probability assessment – focusing on the worst case, regardless of its actual likelihood, especially when the risk engages strong emotions or the image of the extreme (bad) outcome dominates. *Example*: strong

> **Box 8.1** (*cont.*)
>
> consensual sensemaking about the negative consequences of changing shared values can foster dysfunctional meta-routines.
>
> *System neglect*: the inability to understand or accept that risks are inherent to systems, and, alternatively, that (even one-shot) attempts to change systems may generate their own, unpredictable, and interdependent risks. *Example*: underestimating unintentional and externalized implications of implementing new systems.
>
> *Vividness heuristic*: remembering and retrieving on the basis of the dramatic or vivid nature of the phenomenon, even if the actual evidence is non-representative or unavailable, leading to an overestimation of the actual frequency of the event. *Example*: strong reactions from other to raising issue fosters continuing undiscussability and defensive routines.
>
> Note: citations are provided only for those not mentioned in the chapter text, or for a specific example.

Social traps and dilemmas

Varieties of social traps and dilemmas

A *social trap* (also called a *social dilemma*) involves multiple and conflicting rewards, which influence individual and group decisions within social contexts (Barry and Bateman, 1996; Cross and Guyer, 1980; Platt, 1973), and lead to the more general and more problematic situation of multiple but conflicting consequences or outcomes. In particular, individual or short-term costs and rewards conflict with collective or long-term ones. The classic statement of this is that an individual's rational, reasonable self-interested decision over time decreases the welfare of everyone in the collectivity (Kollock, 1998). "When a large number of people make the self-interested choice, the costs or negative outcomes accumulate, creating a situation in which everybody would have done better had they decided not to act in their own private interest" (Liebrand *et al.*, 1992, p. 4).

One form of the social trap is when the aggregate demand on a common resource by individuals begins to damage, pollute, or deplete the commons itself (Edney, 1980, p. 131). Edney feels that such dilemmas are not fundamentally due to conflicting rationalities, but due to conflicting human values. Another perspective is that social traps can develop when individual actors do not know about, or don't care about, the long-term or collective consequences (Barry and Bateman, 1996, referencing Schelling, 1978). Social dilemmas are enabled because no one has an incentive to change their behavior, and sometimes because there is a "dominating strategy" which provides the best outcome for one person independent of anyone else's behavior. Most importantly, "A group of people facing a social dilemma may completely understand the situation, may appreciate how each of their actions contribute to a disastrous outcome, and still be unable to do anything about it" (Kollock, 1998, p. 185). Thus, awareness may not be sufficient to resolve a UR associated with a social trap.

Kollock distinguishes two main types of social dilemmas based on how costs and benefits accrue to each person – a social fence and a social trap. These dilemmas are due to externalities, or *uncompensated interdependencies* (p. 188). In a *social fence*, there is an immediate individual cost (the fence needing scaling), but a potential benefit for all (provision of public goods). Because the benefit is a public good, it is non-excludable – anyone can enjoy the benefit – so some system members can engage in *free-riding*, due either to greed, or a fear that others will not contribute and thus one will be a "sucker," generating resentment. Not having enough individuals willing to pay the immediate costs means the public good cannot be produced. In a *social trap*, if everyone takes the immediate benefit, the collectivity suffers a disaster (known as the *tragedy of the commons*). Here, the joint resource is non-excludable, but rivalrous – that is, use of the public good by some reduces the amount left for others, and, in particular, when the good falls below a threshold sustainable capacity, the public good becomes used up, unusable, or unavailable. Attempting to allocate the resource, or exclude some, involves additional costs. Variants of multi-person dilemmas involve *temporal lags* (there is a delay between initial action and consequent disaster), individuals having different *incentive structures*, some *members are not known or their behaviors are not observable*, costs are diffused through *third parties or unequally*, and one member has *little control over others' outcomes*.

Social traps can take on other, more specific forms (Cross and Guyer, 1980, pp. 19–32ff.). These include: the *time-delay trap* (the penalty is delayed enough that it is not considered in cost/benefit thinking); the *ignorance trap* (the attractiveness of the reward is sufficiently high that the penalty is inadequately considered); the *sliding-reinforcer trap* (a behavior which was once rewarding continues even though its consequences have become penalizing); the *externality trap* (an individual's action producing a reward for him/her produces a penalty for some number of others); the *collective trap* (a scaled-up version of the externality trap, similar to the tragedy of the commons); and the *hybrid trap* (a combination of the above types). Other permutations of social traps include *internal* (one-person), *missing hero* (one person is needed to act on behalf of the group), and straightforward *ignorance* of the negative consequence (Platt, 1973). Each of these social trap forms has its social fence or counter-trap version, in which aversion to a penalty is the reinforcer. For example, short-term negative consequences deter individuals from acting in ways that would have long-term positive benefits for the group, or avoid long-term negative consequences (Barry and Bateman, 1996; Messick and Brewer, 1983; Platt, 1973, p. 641).

Social traps may result from well-intentioned attempts to improve the collective. For example, misdirected or ineffective organizational diversity initiatives can activate social traps of constituency (social distancing of those who experience the consequences), temporality (short-term or long-term consequences), symmetry (equivalence of incentives and outcomes across groups), cognizance (extent of awareness of consequences and their temporality), and exclusivity (limited or dispersed control of consequences), leading to increased prejudice, intergroup conflict, and institutional bias (Barry and Bateman, 1996). Further, social traps may interact, creating nested and embedded traps. For example, collective processes themselves may enhance these social traps. Collective behaviors may be *locked-in*, reinforcing the very conditions that seed the social traps; under the *invisible hand* condition, there may be no collective causal or regulatory process, yet individual behaviors support a stabilized pattern; in the *invisible fist* condition, individual behaviors have the opposite consequence, amplifying the deviation beyond control; and *invisible chains* emerge when individual behaviors interlock to create difficult-to-change patterns (Platt, 1973).

It seems reasonable to think of individual behavior as purposive (i.e., goal-directed), yet, as the social trap/dilemma concept shows, such behavior guarantees neither maximal self-benefit nor maximal collective benefit. One explanation of this paradox is the concept of *contingent behavior,* or individual "behavior that depends on what others are doing" (Schelling, 1978, p. 17). One form of this is the *self-fulfilling prophecy,* whereby particular expectations by some actors (say, negative expectations about other actors) have characteristics that induce behaviors (by those other actors) that fulfill the initial actors' expectations (p. 115). Other social factors may also induce and complicate social traps (Liebrand *et al.,* 1992). People vary in the value they place on the relevant outcomes. Costs and benefits may vary across the actors. An in-group bias would support social traps that create more benefits for one's group. How payoffs are framed (e.g., are negotiation concessions giving up or gaining some benefit?) affects perceptions of costs and benefits. And information asymmetries and perceived benefits affect what information is shared at the organizational and the individual level, in turn making it more difficult to either identify or resolve social traps.

Social traps and unusual routines

Unusual routines are similar to social traps, in that rewards/punishments are often displaced from the actor (as in subunits optimizing internally but displacing costs onto a different subunit) or that rewards/punishments accrue at different levels (as when an organization-level benefit exacts a subunit or individual cost). However, while social dilemmas are the collective costs for individually-accrued benefits, or the loss of collective benefits from individual avoidance of local costs, URs also include collective benefits which impose costs on other individuals/subunits, and local benefits that impose costs on other individuals/subunits. The economic and psychological conceptualizations of social traps are much more detailed, as discussed above, but provide the bases for understanding the social trap and dilemma aspects of URs.

Organizational complexity

Organizational interactions are inherently complex, difficult to identify, and generate unanticipated consequences

Organizations are inherently complex, involving layers of interactions and feedback loops (Goodman, 2000); they are systems with loosely coupled subsystems and thus many possibilities for combinations and interdependencies (Anderson *et al.*, 1999, p. 234). Excessive complexity requires simply too many resources to coordinate, because there are exponentially increasing possible interactions and interdependencies, so that there is always an underlying (and, with increasing complexity, exponentially greater) level of actions, error, damage, waste, and chaos (Quevedo, 1991, p. 33). Because the content of organizational work and social activities relies on acceptable and shared meaning, there may also be simply too much semantic variation (such as multiple and mis-interpretations, over-time shifts in understandings and meanings, and natural flexibility in language) to keep within formal or even known bounds.

Thus it is very difficult to fully understand, and thus design or plan, the implications of even what might appear to be routine processes. Unintended consequences almost invariably accompany, or replace, intended ones, thus affecting subsequent action (Archer, 1995; Merton, 1936; Tsoukas and Chia, 2002). Because of multiple levels and subsystems involved in any complex and significant organizational or social problem, organizational processes designed to resolve problems often create other problems, or in the long run worsen the original problem (such as applying financial bureaucracy to better mange healthcare facilities, which has negative consequences of subverting ethical decisions, reducing the nature of care, and generating conflicts among stakeholders; Chambliss, 1996). A set of parallel policies appropriate to their individual units may, through interaction, generate unintentional and negative outcomes for all units, perhaps even amplifying their initial deviations, creating obstacles and even opposing outcomes to their initial goals, what Schulman (1989) calls *error-amplifying decision traps*. "Once these complex systems are set in motion, actions often 'escape' their purposes and result in unintended consequences" (Van de Ven and Poole, 1988, p. 49), so it is impossible to trace system behaviors to an individual's actions, as they create random, or counter-individual outcomes (Masuch, 1985). That is, change is not an exception, but ongoing organizational improvisation (Orlikowski, 1996).

One unit's internal change is another unit's external change, for tightly coupled subunits. Alternatively, internal, normal, and continuous changes at the organizational level may appear to be external and discontinuous changes for the subunit. "Interactions across levels may generate effects that run strongly against intuition. Outcomes at one level might or might not be echoed at an adjacent level" (Siggelkow and Rivkin, 2006, p. 793). Interdependencies among possible solutions, and between organizational levels, may prevent an organization-wide satisfactory solution from ever being considered, even though its components exist individually across each unit's solutions. Siggelkow and Rivkin's (2006) simulation model finds, for example, that, contrary to what organizational learning theory might predict, very frequent exploration by lower-level managers in firms with greater interdependencies among units leads to decreased exploration for a modeled firm as a whole. This negative outcome occurs because the more lower-level exploration, the more opportunities for removing from consideration proposals which otherwise (unknowingly by the selecting unit) might have positive externalities for other units and thus the organization as a whole, preventing those proposals from being considered by upper management. However, at moderate levels of exploration, and especially when units were not highly interdependent, organizational performance increased, and especially at finding more successful solutions further along the search process (i.e., options and possibilities were not foreclosed).

For any organizational entity, there may be gaps between a desired and the actual state. If the organization identifies such gaps, it may respond by redesigning or changing processes, attempting to maintain homeostasis (Goodman, 2000). However, the gap may not be defined; may occur but not be monitored/measured; may be measured and known but not followed by action; or may be measured and known but there may be a delay in initiating changes, reducing the effects of the change (Goodman, 2000). Partially this is because it is "difficult to think about dynamic events like feedback loops and time delays. It is easier to pay attention to immediate effects and visible changes" (Goodman and Rousseau, 2004, p. 7). Attempts to maintain homeostasis or achieve new goals may also result in organizational efforts that encourage units to change to benefit the organization as a whole, but, without much attention paid to the process of dealing with the gap, typically such changes generate benefits only to the unit (if at all).

These initial gaps between what is required and what is known generate unanticipated outcomes, which both create possibly dysfunctional feedback loops, as well as post-action interpretation, that can institutionalize the initial practices, including the gaps (Giddens, 1984; Vaughan, 1999; Weick, 1979). Units pursuing different locally beneficial outcomes may engage in both conflict and concessions, resulting in organizational (collective) outcomes that none of the units wanted (a form of social dilemma) (Archer, 1995, p. 91).

Increasingly decentralized and dispersed organizational structures diffuse accountability, also making feedback and overall understanding difficult. Local solutions may be better informed about their own context, but their interdependencies with the rest of the organization are unobservable and difficult to identify across boundaries. Accountability ambiguity allows upper-level members to intrude into operators' work, yet with less expertise and experience, while the consequences for this intrusion usually occur elsewhere and later, so learning is difficult (Rochlin, 1998).

Organizational complexity and rationality

Related to the notion that organizations are inherently complex, making implications of actions and feedback difficult to identify or understand, is the concept of organizational rationality itself (Taylor *et al.*, 2000, p. 114). Much of organizational behavior may not be clearly rational. Decisions and actions generating problems may not be rational, responses and solutions to those problems may not be rational, and attempting to identify and solve a problem through rational analysis may be inappropriate, all making it difficult to analyze and understand URs. Alternatively, the bases or criteria of some forms of organizational reality may create other forms of irrationality. For example, Ritzer critiques the "McDonaldization of society" because "rational systems inevitably spawn a series of irrationalities that serve to limit, ultimately compromise, and perhaps even undermine, their rationality" (1993, p. 121). (A question here is whether Ritzer means all rational systems, thus rejecting the possibility of rationality, or certain kinds of rational systems, thus implying locally inherent irrationality.) Internal rationalization often generates organizational benefits while externalizing the costs onto society (a social dilemma fostered by a particular economic system). Efficient processing can be quite inefficient because the individual process, which by itself is efficient, generates greater use by others, making the entire process inefficient; thus long lines are inherent to ordering through "drive-up" windows or in "fast food" restaurants. Dehumanizing work settings generate considerable hiring and training costs due to turnover and health problems. "Just-in-time" manufacturing, for example, requires more frequent deliveries, wasting fuel, generating pollution, cluttering roads with trucks, making other people late or pressured (Ritzer, 1993, p. 143).

Brunsson (1985) reflects much contemporary organizational theory and practice in arguing that the concept and assumption of "managerial rationality" is insufficient or even misleading, because motivation, organizational climate, social networks, and organizational ideologies are central to decision-making, and especially to action. However, he goes further: decision and ideology irrationality is both functional and necessary for organizational action. This is because, he says, the main purpose in most organizations is to foster coordinated actions, while also maintaining flexibility, and not overly reducing the range of people's actions. In order for organizations to implement processes for deciding upon and achieving significant and coordinated action, they tend to be more routinized, and less flexible, in turn making it more difficult to take and coordinate new or significant action, either internally or externally. He specifically rejects the notion of high-level individuals engaging in purely rational decision-making and problem-solving that lead to action which significantly changes organizations in order respond to turbulent environments. Relying on existing organizational routines and ideologies to handle environmental turbulence inherently limits the extent of change, while making such significant change would inherently threaten the very same routines and ideologies. Thus organizational action is the primary purpose and the primary challenge of organizing, not rational decision-making, per se.

To foster action, then, decisions must also involve expectations (cognition), motivation (emotions, desires, goals), and commitment (social links, accept responsibility). This is especially the case as organizations exist in highly interrelated systems of a small number of other organizations; such systems are inherently turbulent. Theoretically, each of these can be used as a starting point for facilitating action. But Brunsson's cases seem to indicate that (1) rational decision processes as motivations do not lead to much commitment or expectations, but, instead, create uncertainty about both responsibility and risk; (2) expectations do not provide a strong basis for commitment and motivation; (3) beginning with commitment was most effective, especially under conditions of lower conflict; (4) consistent, conclusive, complex, and persistent ideologies can strengthen motivation and expectations; (5) these same ideologies limit second-level change that does not itself match the ideologies; (6) but, if conclusive, it may be easier to note where they are no longer appropriate to the environment; (7) although ideologies that privilege consistency will suppress identification of these inconsistencies; so (8) the ideologies need to change before significant environmental change, in order to take significant second-level responsive action. Thus decisions and actions may be unrelated, one present without the other, and not in causal sequence. But to the extent that decisions are intended to produce action, it is important to incorporate motivation, expectations, and commitment links between decisions and actions. To the extent that each of these non-rational elements is stronger, the stronger is the basis of the decision for the action. Thus Brunsson argues for making rational use of irrationality, especially for radical change, because there motivation and commitment is crucial.

Organizational paradoxes

The nature of paradoxes

A paradox consists of "contradictory yet interrelated elements – elements that seem logical in isolation but absurd and irrational when appearing simultaneously" (Lewis, 2000, p. 760). With paradoxes, it is not necessary to choose between two or more contradictions or even mutually exclusive elements; all the elements are present and accepted, and occur simultaneously (Cameron and Quinn, 1988). Paradoxical arguments, considered separately, appear sound; together, contradictory or contrary (Van de Ven and Poole, 1988). Paradoxes are "interaction-based situations in which, in the pursuit of one goal, the pursuit of another competing goal enters the situation (often without intention) so as to undermine the first pursuit" (Stohl and Cheney, 2001, p. 354). For example, a tension central to the paradox of learning is between the old and the new; for organizing, it is between control and flexibility. Attempts to reduce this tension through defensive responses may produce an initially positive effect but in the long run create opposing and unintended consequences, increasing the

fundamental tension (Stohl and Cheney, 2001). One side of a paradox may influence the conditions of the other side's operation, may
create necessary conditions for the other, or the two may influence
each other over time (Van de Ven and Poole, 1988). Paradoxes can
occur in one or more statements, are self-referential, and can trigger
a vicious circle.

Other characteristics of paradox include: actors using either/
or logic, caught in vicious cycle; the problem is located in assumptions, and all subsequent reasoning will appear internally logical, so
the cause of problem is externalized; the problem is impermeable to
rational instruction – indeed, that generates defensiveness and not
only reinforces the vicious cycle but often creates another cycle; and
the problem can only be resolved through counterintuitive behavior,
reframing, and discovery, not instruction (Argyris, 1988).

Positive and negative aspects of paradoxes

Paradox has benefits – it allows multiple interpretations, creativity,
new ideas, synthesis, deeper understanding, motivates change, stimulates humor as well as surprise, and allows tolerance of inconsistency
(Siporin and Gummer, 1988). Paradoxes also have the potential to
stimulate the development of virtuous cycles and positive benefits,
especially from energizing through reframing (Quinn and Cameron,
1988).

But paradox also has dysfunctional and pathological consequences.
Paradoxes "create and sustain seemingly inescapable, lose-lose, double-bind situations ... the statements refer back to and thus reinforce
and recreate themselves" (Wendt, 1998, p. 324). "Pathology, such as
'double binds' or 'vicious circles' ... can lead to system disorganiza-
tion, decline, and dissolution" (Siporin and Gummer, 1988, p. 208).
People may respond by correcting the problem, leaving, or engaging
in defense mechanisms (such as denial or compensation), or engaging
in disruptive and deviant behavior (p. 209). Curiously, the individual
may benefit through silencing the underlying conflict, gaining sympathetic support, and manipulation of others. These behaviors may
also be rewarding for the actor's social group, such as avoiding an
issue or a group through scapegoating or isolating a deviant member (Hirschorn and Gilmore, 1980). Sometimes the rewards associated with the deviant behavior increase the linkage between the pain

and the symptom, and encourage the accretion of double binds. The reinforcement of this symptomatic deviance generates a secondary deviation, the adaptation of social relations to fit the deviant behavior. For example, the deviant gains attention, a sort of protection from the underlying problems, especially by viewing them as beyond the person's control (Siporin and Gummer, 1988).

Types of organizational paradoxes

Paradoxes are inherent to organizations. Putnam (1986) argues that not only is it fundamentally difficult for an organization to develop and maintain a coherent identity and consistent public messages, but organizational contexts and countless interactions among actors, role, and symbols provide a constant potential for incompatibilities across levels (such as verbal/non-verbal, literal/metaphoric, abstract/concrete, content/relationship). Paradoxes may be more likely and frequently perceived in the post-industrial environment, due to more information, complexity, turbulence, and competition (Cameron and Quinn, 1988). Putnam (1986) focuses on three categories of organizational paradox: contradictory message, paradox cycle, and system contradiction. Contradictory messages and paradox cycles are symptoms of system contradictions, and appear in communication patterns associated with organizational events.

A *contradictory message* presents mutually exclusive alternatives, but allows or requires the individual to choose only one. These may occur through mixed-message or message-behavior inconsistency. For example, a verbal message can contradict a non-verbal cue, and, to make things worse, the person may not be aware of exhibiting these contradictory messages. People in turn differentially interpret and respond to this contradictory message, so both parties can contribute to the contradiction. Managers often find themselves mired in message-based contradiction paradoxes, because they must manage inconsistencies between subordinates and upper management, what Tompkins and Cheney (1983) call a "zone of ambiguity" (Putnam, 1986, p. 156). If several interpretations are allowed, then this "zone of ambiguity" is embedded and becomes structured, putting managers in a problematic condition where subordinates are behaving inconsistently. An organizational member may choose to accept one of the messages and ignore inconsistency, but may be open to a charge of disobeying or misperforming. The member may accept both messages and try to operate within the contradiction, but this generates complexities if the action is part of an interdependent or integrative context. Finally, under unusual conditions, proposed by organizational change researchers, the member may attempt to transcend daily logic and the specific assumptions of the contradictions paradox and integrate the contradiction into an innovative alternative.

Paradox cycles involve exchanging contradictory cues in an ongoing relationship, which traps one or more of the actors in a dynamic pattern. Putnam (1986) distinguishes a paradox cycle from a vicious cycle, a deviation-amplifying loop, or a regenerative loop (Bateson, 1972; Maruyama, 1963; Wender, 1968), where feedback increases the behavior which fosters the feedback response – an interdependent loop. But those feedback patterns are not necessarily paradoxical in the sense of involving an internally paradoxical cycle. The classic example of a paradox cycle is the double bind (Watzlawick *et al.*, 1967). Here, the relationship itself between participants becomes binding: participants cannot exit, but also cannot comment on the relationship, and cannot confront each other. So misinterpretations rule, generating further behavior which is consistent for each individual, but inconsistent across the individuals.

Finally, the organizational system itself may generate constraints that are manifested in contradictory messages and paradox cycles, representing a *system contradiction*. Organizational objectives, goals, and structures may clash with constraining conditions (Benson, 1977). Tensions may arise between current and emerging structures, and the current structure responds by constraining or adapting the emerging structure, so contradictions occur in this interaction. As noted above, consequences of change and innovation are unpredictable. So people cannot stay fully informed or aware of even their own unit's activities, much less the long-term indirect consequences, and they may not be aware that practices *are* inconsistent internally, or with another unit's. Innovations may generate inconsistencies because of new procedures, rules, processes, and thus paradoxes and cycles, which then create a system contradiction (within units or across the organization). Systemic contradictions may lead to message paradoxes and oscillating behavior, such as "frivolity and dire seriousness, passivity and zealous activity, psychological withdrawal and intense involvement" (Putnam, 1986, pp. 164–5, based on a case described by Johnson, 1977). In turn, responses to message contradictions may foster awareness of system contradictions and thus present opportunities to change these practices, to reinterpret meanings.

Examples of organizational paradox

Molinski (1997) presents three paradoxes of *organizational change*. First, while change requires management, the process of management obstructs change. To diffuse, innovations may have to be seen as independent of specific managers, to avoid seeming biased or too specific. Second, change depends on commitment by leaders, but excessive commitment and too many projects can overwhelm organizational resources and distract employees from accomplishing their work. Third, promoting change requires persuasive and motivating rhetoric, but invoking existing central principles and language can limit openness to such change.

Stohl and Cheney (2001) identify four main types, and subcategories, of paradoxes of *organizational democracy* (participation) programs. *Structure paradoxes* include paradoxes of design (e.g., how to "order" participation by employees, while dealing with managers' perceived loss of power), adaptation (evolution of responses to environmental change while maintaining initial principles), punctuation (short-circuiting the process of participation to gain efficiency of the participation goal), and formalization (how to routinize an inherently informal process). *Agency paradoxes* consist of paradoxes of responsibility (how to subordinate empowered and knowledgeable individuals to the group), cooperation (mismatch between team participation and individual reward), sociality (excessive collaboration may reduce energy for internal and external participation), and autonomy (the collective principle of participation may reduce individual agency). *Identity paradoxes* are manifested by paradoxes of commitment (consensual process vs. support for diversity and alternatives), representation (wider participation vs. worker solidarity), and compatibility (high group participation values may conflict with organizational or cultural values). Finally, *power paradoxes* involve paradoxes of control (replacing organizational with group and concertive control), leadership (emergent local leadership vs. equality of participation), and homogeneity (goals of consensus and language of dialogue may suppress dissent). Argyris (1985) also analyzes some paradoxes of implementing increased participation and, in particular, as a way to balance corporate control and divisional autonomy. Executives may try to manage the corporate policy of decentralization with necessary involvement through mixed messages (aimed at communicating what might be a threat to decentralized autonomy in ways that they believe will reduce the threat), which generate further uncertainty and threat, stimulating defensive routines, all of which is undiscussable, in order to avoid immediate conflict or challenge, but about which people act as though these are not undiscussable. Long-run difficulties ensue. For a related example of two contrasting approaches to organizational boards of directors – *control and collaboration* – see Sundaramurthy and Lewis (2003), and of paradoxes of organizational restructuring, see McKinley and Scherer (2000).

Organizational quality management, and performance measurement in particular, creates opportunities for paradoxical conditions. Paton (2003) shows that quality management and performance measurement, designed and intended to be used to improve organizational quality, consistency, and performance, frequently leads to counterproductive behaviors, and especially so in social service/non-profit organizations. For example, the development of large number of performance measures creates information overload and high implementation costs, leading to a focus on some of the measures, so only some get measured, in turn leading to partial measurement and subsequent bias in practice toward those activities. As some other activities become neglected, over time new measures arise or old measures are reincarnated to include them. So a sort of measurement oscillation develops. Further, the multiplicity of measures also contradicts one of the criteria of good performance measurement systems, that of parsimony. Also, it is difficult to actually connect measurement with subsequent learning and improvement through an explicit causal relationship with specific activities or conditions, due both to an inadequate understanding of the internal processes as well as to multiple stakeholders being involved in the activities and measures (Paton, 2003, p. 43; see also Lehr and Rice, 2002, and especially Lehr and Rice, 2005, for a detailed analysis of this phenomenon). The assessing project team, or the focal department, can become more visible, and possessive or defensive about the award, nurturing interdepartmental tensions, or devolving into just "bearing" the measurement and process without actual commitment or learning. A focus on performance measures may also lead to a variety of dysfunctions, such as "tunnel vision, sub-optimisation, myopia, convergence to a norm, ossification, gaming and misrepresentation" (Paton, 2003, p. 41, referring to Smith, 1993).

Organizational deviance

Systemic and normal

As Vaughan (1999) notes, Weber had foreseen that negative consequences would follow from organizations becoming reliant on extreme legal-rational authority. Dimensions of these consequences include altered interactions between and among people and organizations, resulting in individuals losing power, but also in the form of organizational actions, such as mistakes, misconduct, and disaster.

Rather than the results of beneficent, rational, transparent, and intentional organizations, these forms of organizational deviance are systematically produced, what Vaughan (1999) calls *routine nonconformity*. The foundational assumptions are Merton's notion that all action systems generate consequences that are both indirect and in conflict with the intended goals, whether of the initial actors (people or organizations) or of others (as discussed earlier), and Durkheim's belief that the normal conditions inherent in all social systems systematically foster pathological behaviors (Durkheim, 1966/1938; Merton, 1940). Thus routine nonconformity does not include coincidence, chance, or operational breakdowns normally associated with material technology. This concept is very similar to URs, though much more bounded within organizational contexts and not explicitly considering second-level feedback problems.

As an illustration of the pervasiveness of even low-level organizational deviance, Litzky *et al.* (2006) summarize surveys showing that 60 percent of employees participate in some kind of theft, and 48 percent engage in some kind of improper behavior (from incomplete quality control to lying to customers to illegal financial activities). Those deviant behaviors induce subsequent organizational costs worth $20 billion, including lower product consistency, greater production costs, loss of inventory control, varying service quality and reduced service reputation, reduced profits, inconsistent pricing, less repeat business, litigation, damaged corporate reputations, and business failures.

Also arguing that organizational deviance is inherent, Moberg (2006) notes that organizations present a variety of contexts that raise ethical challenges. One context involves *psychic struggles*, such as *cutting corners* ("organizationally permissible but ethically questionable," possibly due to different reward systems and sources), *cover-ups* ("requests or demands by others to ignore their unethical behavior"), and *complicity* ("social pressures to engage in unethical behavior," from others as well as precedent, requirements for performance, and policies that are inherently unethical) (p. 308). A second context is *moral dilemmas*, requiring choice by different stakeholders (each with their own reasonable or principled needs or justifications), from multiple morally acceptable alternatives. Another context is *leadership ethics*, where one attempts to persuade others of one's particular moral view of a situation, which is in conflict with the others' or the organization's position. And a fourth context is *collective action*, where multiple actors must be involved in order to raise or change an ethics situation, by providing evidence, validity, or protection.

Primary factors generating the potential for routine nonconformity include: (1) the organization's environment, (2) characteristics of the organization (the familiar triad of tasks, processes, structure and tasks), (3) individuals' cognitive practices, and (4) the social relations among all three (Vaughan, 1999). *Increased uncertainty due to complex environments* tends to be associated with routine nonconformity due to the inability of assessing current situations and predicting actual implications, especially for new organizations, and, by extension, new processes and subsystems. More proactive approaches to managing environmental uncertainty involve power relations, which, whether through imposition of one structure over another, or even through compromise, tend to deflect, alter, co-opt, or confuse the organization's initial goals, assumptions, practices, and standards. Tendencies toward isomorphism (imitating or adopting more general industry-wide institutionalized innovations or practices, from bureaucracies to networks) may also lead organizations away from their specific situations, expectations, and understandings, generating unintentional and suboptimal practices.

Organizational complexity itself is of course a central cause of mismatched behaviors and unexpected outcomes. But so are dense internal relationships (which can enable deceit and self-interest), and *centralization and formalization*, which embed and diffuse practices without deep understanding of local contexts, and stifle adaptation and flexibility. For example, the more formal and hierarchical the structure, the more fragmented the understanding of interconnections, the more difficult to identify who or what is accountable, the greater chance for problems when processes cross structural boundaries, and the greater likelihood that meaning gets transformed across those boundaries. "Efficient" and "effective" systems may be so bureaucratized and uninterruptible that they become unable to learn about or correct their own errors (Crozier, 1964).

Performing *tasks* generates errors, due to differences in amount and frequency of skill, and workplace role (Hughes, 1951). Tasks may often be designed in ways that allow misuse of information, while making monitoring and accountability difficult. The tacit knowledge (Polanyi, 1966) and interpretive flexibility (Pinch and Bijker, 1984) required for implementing and using technology, and performing complex tasks, virtually guarantees that there will be unforeseen and unwanted consequences. Information technology affects structure, interactions, personal characteristics of actors, and both material and discursive aspects. ICTs do have many advantages, such as improving organizational structure, increasing flexibility, and overcoming constraints. But ICTs also have disadvantages, such as increasing time for consensus, and making it harder to detect the opportunistic behavior of others. So, for example, the very advantage of facilitating social interactions, and growth in scale and complexity of social networks, also leads to a "creeping crisis" involving unethical collective action, insider trading, fraud, and manipulation. "Illegal activities take on an aura of normalcy among actors and networks engaged in them through cultural and linguistic techniques leading to group-think" (Korac-Boisvert and Kouzmin, 1994, p. 68).

The very structures, processes, and tasks that are designed to coordinate and accomplish formal organizational goals also provide the means for shared support, for opportunities and mechanisms, and for cloaking, of misconduct. The interplay of occupational roles may actually concentrate, diffuse, or delegate both the risk and costs of mistakes. Some structures may facilitate, encourage, or cause crime, such as setting unrealistic goals and harsh consequences for failure, or early socialization and training in how to violate rules (Needlemann and Needleman, 1979). Indeed, the value systems, loyalties, social controls, and competition in some professions generate forms and acceptance of *normal lies*, or in organizational contexts, *professional deceit*, in the form of outright falsifications, omission, equivocation, or disclaimers (Ruane *et al.*, 1994, providing examples from the real estate business). Whereas a deviant lie is a socially unacceptable practice, a normal lie is a known falsehood rationalized and legitimated as a means to a good end. Healthy organizations need deception and distortion (diplomacy, tact), to create and sustain positive images, and allow focus. Managers exhibit contradictory impulses, so leadership needs tolerance of ambiguity, and the ability to manage dilemmas (Farson, 1996). These are different than normal lying or professional deceit, but help set the stage. Thus, a paradox develops: we learn that lying is bad, but also learn how to lie, and in what contexts those lies are acceptable. Further, socialization provides us with appropriate responses to normal lies – it may be best to ignore the lying part, in order to maintain social order and get the job done. *Professional deceit* may be not only tolerated, but fostered, through occupational rewards and entry requirements, occupational loyalties, social control styles within an occupation, and an occupation's level of professionalization (Ruane *et al.*, 1994). Like Vaughan (1999), Litzk *et al.* (2006) argue that individuals' deviant behaviors and outcomes are often due to organizational and management norms and reinforcements.

Employee mistreatment

Mistreatment of employees, by fellow employees, managers, and the workplace, also are pervasive and systemic characteristics of organizational processes. Litzky *et al.* (2006) suggest how some managers' actions may act as *workplace deviance triggers* (compensation/ reward structure, social pressures to conform, negative/untrusting attitudes, job ambiguity, performance, unfair rules, and violating employee trust). These triggers generate a wide variety of workplace deviance, such as harming production quality and quantity by wasting resources or working slowly, political deviance that puts others at a disadvantage such as favoritism and gossiping, unauthorized property acquisition or damage such as false expense accounts or theft, and aggression toward others such as sexual harassment or threats (Litzky *et al.*, 2006; Robinson and Greenberg, 1998).

Employee mistreatment is a form of organizational injustice, whether interactional (mistreatment by authority), distributive (unequal access to resources), procedural (unfair procedures that affect distributive process), or systemic (larger organizational unfair systems) (Harlos and Pinder, 1999). Providing feedback would seem both a natural and frequent response to perceived employee mistreatment, because "both victims and perpetrators must be able to talk about mistreatment, learn from mistakes, and avoid mistreatment in the future" (Meares *et al.*, 2004, p. 5). But the nature of that communication may vary, in at least four main ways: privileged, muted-but-engaged, angrily disengaged, and resigned. Communicating about mistreatment is often silenced, and some with more power have greater privilege to communicate about such topics. As attempts to communicate about or resolve a mistreatment fail or are ignored, the employee shifts through those four forms of communicating, ending in disengagement and resignation, with employees concluding "mistreatment as normal and inescapable" (p. 21), or not labeling the experiences as mistreatment. When organizations do not have clear definitions of or procedures for handling mistreatment, it is especially easy to dismiss and hard to articulate, allowing for superficial treatment, misleading others to think action occurs, or distraction and manipulation. That is, targets are unable to label their experiences, and thus unable to communicate about it. These kinds of organizational situations present a dilemma for employees: "if they work to resist mistreatment, they are placing themselves in a position where they are likely to face more mistreatment. If they react to the mistreatment by becoming disengaged, they are indirectly recreating the power structures and giving up on the chance of being heard" (Meares *et al.*, 2004, p. 21), and, eventually punished for that lack of commitment.

Workplace mistreatment is when "the individual perceives a deterioration in the employment relationship ... and that an organizational constituent is blamed ... serving as the basis for potential remedial action" (Olson-Buchanan and Boswell, 2008, p. 77). Under conditions of multiple interpretations about events with significant consequences, such as perceived workplace mistreatment, individuals will engage in sensemaking, including discussions with others. Assessing the extent and nature of mistreatment may depend on how it is characterized (personalized or policy-related), its severity, and the target's perception of the intentionality of the perpetrator. Further, various individual and situational factors (prior experiences, organizational climate, the other members involved) may moderate or suppress the extent and form of this sensemaking. Third parties may provide alternate, mitigating, or reframing explanations. Sensemaking may then help shape the form of response to the perception of mistreatment. Some kinds of reactions, however, such as "passive coping and denial of discrimination," may themselves generate subsequent negative physiological responses (p. 83). Behaviorally, the person may respond via remedial voice, lower productivity, loss of commitment, revenge (peer or public complaining), and quitting. Paradoxically, decreased commitment, involvement, and performance may be used retroactively to justify prior perceived mistreatment (p. 86). Withdrawing from work or engaging in remedial voice may generate backlash by third party others and the reported source of the mistreatment, leading to *blaming the victim* (Fine, 1983), retaliation, and punishment, as in many cases of whistleblowing. The person's network of relationships will also be affected, possibly negatively. All this uncertainty and stress generates more sensemaking. For example, lack of support by others for initial sensemaking that leads a person to conclude they were a subject of mistreatment, may lead the individual to further withdraw and avoid remedial voice, reinforcing the others' initial sensemaking.

Employee emotional abuse "is repetitive, targeted, and destructive communication by more powerful members toward less powerful members in the workplace" (Lutgen-Sandvik, 2003, p. 472). Precisely because it is repetitive, it entails the generation of a series of stages:

(1) The cycle begins when the target, for some reason, attracts negative attention. When a superior and a subordinate have discrepant views of the event, the superior's view succeeds, both because of positional power and because of control of discourse.
(2) Progressive discipline follows. The organization may follow the legal requirements of due process, but, if this takes the form of organizational sanctioned discipline, which may be intended to improve the target's performance, it actually ends up camouflaging the abuse. The target's response may reinforce the abuser's initial report of the target's incompetence. Thus abuse is reframed as progressive discipline, creating a paper trail for later justification.

(3) The next stage may achieve a turning point. The abuser may engage in repetition, reframing, branding, support-seeking, and more personal claims. The target may seek support and corroboration. But "when targets attempt to give voice to their experiences, abusers often reframe the former exchanges and describe the situation very differently than targets' experiences; this experience is central to muted group theory" (p. 484). Branding shifts the blame for abuse to the target.

(4) The turning point typically raises awareness of the situation to higher organizational levels, which are ambivalent. They may take no action, admit the situation but do nothing, promise action with little outcome, attribute the problem to a personality conflict, ask the target to work around the problem, suggest or require some change in target's behavior, minimize the target's complaint while building up the abuser's abilities and value, brand the target, retaliate against the target, and sometimes formally discipline or remove the abuser (Keashly, 2001).

(5) Depending on the organizational action, isolation and silencing of the target may follow. Others learn to suppress their own views, as well as the target's.

(6) The target leaves or is expelled, but the cycle renews. "Regeneration of the abuse cycle suggests that the problem does not reside in a specific problem employee but is an explicitly or implicitly supported norm of the organizational culture" (Lutgen-Sandvik, 2003, p. 493).

Malone (2004) identified five dimensions of reactions to *malicious envy* in the workplace: attacking the envied person, motivation, less commitment, negative self-thoughts, and self-promotion. Miner's (1990) survey found 77 percent of the respondents had observed an envious situation at work and 58 percent had been directly involved in that situation. Negative emotions such as envy affect outcomes such as performance, productivity, withdrawal, sabotage, intent to quit, dissatisfaction with supervisor, and job dissatisfaction (Bedeian, 1995; Duffy and Shaw, 2000; Vecchio, 2000). More extreme than malicious envy is sabotaging a co-worker (Solomon, 2002; Umiker, 1994; Williams, 1994), or what Malone (2002) calls *co-worker backstabbing*. These range from starting rumors, gossiping, turning others against a co-worker, talking behind someone's back, and character assassination; to pretending to support an idea, then undermining and criticizing it behind the target's back; and hiding the truth or lying while giving incomplete or wrong information.

Petty tyranny includes arbitrariness, self-aggrandizement, belittling, lack of consideration, conflict resolution through forcing, discouraging initiative, and non-contingent punishment. Ashforth (1994) presents a model of petty tyranny in the workplace that explains individual predispositions, situational facilitators, interactions between the two, outcomes, and how those can help sustain the behavior. Individual predispositions include beliefs about organizations (e.g., impersonal and formal relationships), about subordinates, about self (e.g., compensate for personal insecurity by overcontrolling; high self-esteem), about others, and about preferences for action (e.g., low tolerance of ambiguity). Situational facilitators consist of both macro-level factors (e.g., institutional values and norms, mass production and formalized procedures; performance measurement over content) and micro-level factors (e.g., power, both if low – for example, leading to attempts to enhance self-importance – and if high – for example, attributing others' success to own control). Interactions between individual and situational factors may lead to tolerance by others of petty tyranny, buffering one's identity from one's power role, and greater responses to stress if one has low tolerance for ambiguity but the position requires directing others. The ongoing managerial petty tyranny produces employee helplessness, work alienation, low self-esteem, low performance, and lower work unit cohesiveness. Paradoxically, these outcomes may in turn sustain tyrannical behavior, because (1) the exercise of power itself fosters some of the behaviors, (2) the effects of tyranny induce negative stereotypes of subordinates that justify continued coercion, (3) subordinates' disaffection may generalize to other managers and the organization, and (4) attending to these behaviors may come at the cost of long-term disruptions.

Technological complexity

Technology is inherently complex and difficult to understand or predict

The intended effects of an innovation may be clearly stated at the outset, and confined to the technical system; the emergent effects are likely to be more profound, less predictable, and to include the social system (Kiesler and Sproull, 1987, pp. 33–4; Rogers, 2003). A new technology is generally intended to produce both efficiency effects and social system effects (Sproull and Kiesler, 1991). The first-level efficiency effects are the most known and perhaps the most knowable, such as cost per unit of output. In practice, of course, many real costs are overlooked because they are difficult to capture (Keen, 1991, pp. 141ff.), but the key point here is that conceptually, if not operationally, this level of effect is relatively easy to understand.

By contrast, the second-level effects can be both more elusive and more profound. The unintended consequences of a new communication channel can evolve over a long span of time and extend far beyond organizational boundaries to the larger society. The telegraph (Beniger, 1986, pp. 17ff.) and telephone (Marvin, 1988; Sproull and Kiesler, 1991, pp. 6–7) both had social system effects far beyond their efficiency effects; many now expect the Internet will, too (Katz and Rice, 2002; Shirky, 2008). It is reasonable, then, to expect a new communication channel to induce significant changes in an organization's social system. (See Huber, 1990, pp. 245–59 for specific propositions about these changes, and Orlikowski, 1991 for a discussion of contradictory implications of ICTs.) Still, it may be difficult to anticipate the changes, or even to perceive the changes as they occur.

Technology often creates the opposite of its intended purpose, or at least outcomes that are different from and contrary to our expectations and intentions (Farson, 1996). For example, the residential washing machine raised standards for cleaning, so people spend more time cleaning; the automobile radically changed society, landscape, industry, safety, social relations, and level of concern for children. More broadly, *revenge effects* of an innovation/technology are "unforeseen results that create new problems or undo existing solutions to old problems, and which paradoxically aggravate the very problems it is trying to solve, and to the disruption of the pre-existing system, creating disequilibria and dysfunctional feedback loops" (Tenner, 1997, Chapter 1; see also Posner, 2004, Chapter 1).

Simply by becoming more and more complex, systems are becoming impossible to understand and thus monitor, diagnose, even fix – and possibly even more so for people working inside the system because challenging evidence and beliefs are less available to them, and global, interaction effects are neither conceivable nor perceptible (Dekker,

2005; Perrow, 1984). Further, socio-technical systems adapt, evolve, change over time, so initial specifications and designs are inherently misleading, over-optimistic, and over-constraining (Dekker, 2005, Chapter 9; Hirschheim, 1985; Johnson and Rice, 1987). Implementing a new ICT in an organizational setting brings changes to individual activities, work practices, and organizational processes. Similar to many analyses of system implementation, a study of the transition from a paper-based workflow to scanned digital document workflow, and the accompanying switch from a mainframe system to desktop computers, found many unexpected negative consequences and add-itional processes (Rice and Schneider, 2006). For example, finding information sometimes took longer than on the old system, both for the reasonable explanation that customer service representatives were not as familiar with where information was stored, but also for the unintentional fact that the system prompts would no longer allow the users to exit a screen (to look for associated information) with-out completing all fields, which was impossible without obtaining the associated information (see also Chapter 2).

A general problem is the increasingly complex, interdependent nature of computer hardware and software. For example, Seymour (1990, pp. 79–80) describes trying to solve a problem associated with updating a graphics card, made difficult to solve because "the company was packing, with this new card, a disk with driv-ers for *another* card – but *labeling* the disk as if it were the one for my card." Seymour identifies several reasons why such problems occur: adding on new, often unnecessary or more sophisticated fea-tures, often at faster cycles than training and user manual creation; increased complexity in both the program and its integration with other programs; and the pressure to rush new products to market before all problems are fixed or all support sources can become familiar with them.

The continual need for monitoring, managing, and upgrading computer systems also creates ongoing costs and even new com-plexities. A *computer fritter* is a computer-related activity that is not work doing the actual task, but either activities involving in *working at* the work, or peripheral and unrelated activities associ-ated with learning, maintaining, and exploring the computer – what Nash (1990, p. 211) calls "the generation of work that is intrinsic to the device itself." Digressing from the work to explore unrelated features, reformatting a document in ways that have no substantive value, going online to browse websites that come to mind while working or working at, and taking the time and expense to unnecessarily expand or use features are "pure" computer fritters. A fritter is, in one sense, a way to organize time; it may function to delay doing work by putting it off to another time, or by requiring additional preceding activities. Nash's (1990) typology of computer fritters include startup, operating system, upgrade, infection, and game fritters. The operating system fritter, for instance, involves learning how to use and manage operational details, including reading specialized magazines and online discussion groups. A subset includes the formatting, initializing, filing, and backing-up fritter (may be useful as a break and diversion from problems in accomplishing the actual work, but may also generate additional fritters, such as creating new directories, renaming files, etc.) "Each of the types of fritters relates to the other through a system of thought and action in which a decision to fritter in one way can implicate and trigger frittering in another" (p. 221). Computer fritters may be considered somewhat related to *shadow costs* and media *transformations* (Rice and Bair, 1984) and the more prosaic *tinkering*. But, to the extent that "working at" involves experimenting with and learning from the device or features, some forms of frittering are also necessary – and desirable – for fostering reinvention (Johnson and Rice, 1987).

System manipulation

Many computer systems are more reliable, stable, trustworthy, and informed than individual human expert sources, such as flight navigation systems, CAT scanning, and diagnostic interviews that allow more disclosure (Conger *et al.*, 1996). But because both the bases for processing decisions and the knowledge embedded in computer systems are not available to users, and indeed complex systems have many and changing sources for these processing decisions and knowledge, it is difficult to debate the assumptions and reasoning, allocate responsibility, and thus change or learning (Dutton and Kraemer, 1980; LaFrance, 1996). Users are more likely to place more trust in systems with more adaptive or designed interfaces, such as interactivity and discourse (Moon and Nass, 1996), yet those do not change the system's underlying data, assumptions, or reasoning. In the long run, our increasing dependence on computer systems may lessen the credibility of human sources.

Zmud (1990) argues that the very nature of organizational information systems makes some functions especially vulnerable to "strategic information behaviors" such as manipulation or distortion. This may happen in two primary ways (in the content of a message that a system transmits/stores/distributes, or in how a message directs operations of the system itself) and in a variety of system nodes (sensor, filter, router, carrier, interpreter, learner, and modifier). What are some of these vulnerabilities? Information overload can increase users' susceptibility to misrepresentation. Additional messages, and thus knowledge of and responsibility for interpreting them, are likely to be delegated. The context of messages will be diluted through representation in artifacts, leading to increased dependence on and trust in these artifacts, and, indeed, increased use of artifacts instead of people or complete messages to achieve strategic information goals. This also means that initial perpetrators will be more difficult to identify, increasing the likelihood of people attempting to manipulate information. So Zmud argues that it is not the technological complexity of computer systems per se that facilitates manipulation, but the pace, abstraction, and distancing possible in communicating through such systems.

Information systems and their associated interactions and interdependencies provide easy opportunities for manipulation and rigging. Consider what Pogue (2003) calls *stealth inflation*. He describes what at first appeared to be a simple mistake on his cellphone bill but which later proved to be a pervasive, hidden cost increase masquerading as "bonus minutes" which effectively inflated the monthly bill beyond a defined time limit. As a *New York Times* columnist, he asked anyone else who had had this experience to send him an email. He received more than 1,200 in the first four days! This flood of stories raised several issues. Because service billing is permeated by "mistakes," they are generally not perceived as "mistakes," but, worse, they could not really be mistakes. For example, one person noted that, after a service representative told him he would simply have to call each month to have the amount adjusted, he suggested she put up a sticky note on her monitor with his account number to remind her to correct it each month. She replied she couldn't do that because she "would have thousands of sticky notes attached to my monitor!" Thus, this is not an occasional or non-routine "error."

Technology generates normal accidents

Most advanced systems are so complex and interdependent that accidents are "normal." That is, they happen because of complex, unimaginable interactions among simple malfunctions, often involving the safety devices themselves, in organizations too inflexible and hierarchically structured to response quickly (Perrow, 1984). "Complex systems have a multitude of interactions, not simply cause-and-effect relationships. Causes may not be proximate in time and space to effects ... a seemingly more proximate cause ... may hide the effects of the earlier decision ... apparent causes may in fact be coincident interactions" and that may even heighten the influences that fostered the original problem (Hughes, 1998, p. 182; referring to Forrester, 1980). Some potential negative interdependencies exist continually, while others occur intermittently, as other systems change, and others emerge only under a specific combination of events (Roberts and Bea, 2001). *Artifact failures* are linked to accidents and man-made disasters, which result from multiple sources and multiple errors. "A variety of errors, slips, and false assumptions build up in the 'incubation period' prior to a large-scale failure, creating an accumulating set of latent preconditions ... until a trigger incident or precipitating event brings together the various forms of predisposing factors" (Turner, 1990, p. 366). These latent preconditions include unnoticed or misunderstood events due to erroneous assumptions, difficulties in handling information in complex situations, a reluctance to fear the worst, and disregarded, violated, out-of-date safety rules and precautions.

Normal accidents occur because some costs and benefits are not perceived or assessable by the user or consumer; when systems are tightly coupled; when the system components are highly redundant (because human operators are trained or limited to see only the components, and the failed components cannot be isolated from each other); or when ongoing attempts to cope and adjust are imperfect, thus building in interactions and failures (Perrow, 1984). Many other factors contribute to the emergence of normal accidents, such as these: (1) optimizing technical systems may increase reliability but also overload human limitations, and cognitive, social, and organizational aspects, to (2) the riskiest phases in most systems are startup and shut down (like takeoff and landing in air transport), so operators need more experience with those but repeated exercises are either too risky or expensive, and (3) system environments that have a greater diversity of interests concerning attribution of responsibility for and suffering of consequences from accidents provide both more sources of pressure to improve, as well as delaying and compromising reform. Complex interactions with tight coupling in risky systems result in a very small number of very consequential catastrophes. One problem is that the causal relationships among X and Y causing the catastrophe, in the context of many other conditions, cannot be observed, measured, or even identified, and thus used to predict and thus possibly prevent others. When catastrophes do occur, they are described as unique or unrepeatable, so we cannot always learn from accidents. Perrow (1984) concludes that we might be able to study failed systems but we cannot study these kinds of systems that have not yet failed.

Unusual routines are far more pervasive, common, small-scale, and do not necessarily involve either complex or risky systems. However, URs may accumulate, facilitating the emergence of normal accidents. An illustration is the institutionalization of NASA evaluation cycles that turned information meeting criteria for delaying launches into indicators of satisfactory launch conditions, leading to the Challenger disaster (Vaughan, 1996).

Automated systems and system error

Computerized technology, and in particular automated systems, are especially relevant to a discussion of the association of the inherent complexity of technology with URs, because such systems often are intentionally designed to embed error-protection subroutines, but may also be part of both organizational and technological systems that seed and even fertilize other errors, and propagate workarounds. Automation in particular may increase system complexity, produce data overload, reduce understanding and control, distance the organizational member from processes, performance, and consequences, create new opportunities for error, impose additional forms of mediation (i.e., interfaces and representations), remove some forms of indicators and evidence, reduce opportunities for recovering from errors, more tightly couple what had been independent subsystems, foster local workarounds that may generate negative internal interdependencies (Gasser, 1986), and generate crossover errors that occur simply because components are now close to each other (Dekker, 2005, pp. 152–7). Rochlin (1998) underscores the nearly universal unanticipated consequences of complex computerization, especially when the situations require synchronous interactions between the operators and the systems. The unintended consequences occur partially because the technical design increases the number of mediating steps between users and the actual processes, and reduces possibilities for discretion, slack, or buffers between uncertainty, decisions, and consequences, or learning through small mistakes.

Automating processes in order to remove "human error" does not necessarily remove or avoid error, and can both increase and institutionalize it (Dekker, 2005). At the very least, it may remove most signals about progress and change, imposing very challenging cognitive demands on human monitors. Vigilance becomes especially difficult for what not only appears routine but is routinized; human monitors not only become fatigued by attending for long periods to non-changing systems but also become complacent due to the smooth operating and invisible nature of all the subprocesses.

Systems are often designed under the myth that "new automation can be substituted for human action without any larger impact on the system in which that action or task occurs, except on output" (Woods *et al.*, 1997, p. 1927). Yet tasks and actors are highly interdependent; "even highly automated systems still require operator involvement and therefore communication and coordination between human and machine." Nonetheless, systems are rarely designed to include communication with the users, or connections to or awareness of other (social and technical) systems and tasks. Thus they cannot provide adequate feedback, creating problems in tracking system behaviors and impacts, and thus knowing when to intervene. Also, new complex systems create new context-dependent cognitive demands, load distributions, error pathways, and mismatches between user abilities and needs, and system capabilities, possibly allowing/requiring operators to manage the situation beyond recovery, creating a more risky and consequential situation.

A central phenomenon of technology complexity and system error is the *idiot's paradox*: high-risk/high-reliability systems are automated so they are supposedly easy to use, but, paradoxically, are operated by highly skilled operators who may end up causing more system failures (Rodgers, 1992, p. 233). But that inspires designers to automate even more tasks, which in turn create fewer but more consequential accidents, and more likely due to human error. The problem is that it is difficult to manage attention to two kinds of tasks – routine and non-routine. This creates three kinds of error in attention management: mistaking routine for non-routine information; misallocating attention between the two; and information overload. Paying more attention to non-routine tasks uses more attention and processing capability, while more attention to routine tasks decreases awareness of environmental conditions leading to improper corrections. Most such systems are designed not to turn all control over to the computer, so that operators have some control over what kinds of tasks to pay attention to, but many inputs are beyond the control of the operator.

Bainbridge (1983) early on exposed some of the ways that automation of industrial processes could ironically increase rather than reduce or eliminate problems in replacing or supporting human operators. While such systems are generally thought of as intending to replace human intervention, they still need considerable control and monitoring, and must allow for human intervention for startup, exceptions, and whatever can not be automated. Intervention requires both manual control skills (such as performing the minimally necessary actions) as well as cognitive skills (especially for diagnosing the cause of the exception and how to resolve it). Interestingly, the longer the system runs without exceptions, the more out-of-practice the operator is with the manual skills. An ironic implication is that manual interventions may be slower, need to rely on more iterative feedback as to their effectiveness, require more secondary actions to respond to the initial ineffective actions, and be less able to solve the underlying exception. Somewhat similar problems are associated with demands on operators' cognitive skills. Operators will have more difficulty in retrieving from long-term memory knowledge that has not been activated for some time, will be less likely to adjust and refine that knowledge through occasional use and feedback, and will be insufficiently grounded in an understanding of the system interdependencies and assumptions and current status. From a work satisfaction and task significance perspective, monitoring a well-running automated system becomes highly deskilling (with subsequent loss of personal status and identity), without opportunities to learn or improve skills needed to handle infrequent but highly consequential responsibilities. These conditions increase stress and decrease health levels, both contributing to greater errors.

Bainbridge (1983) went on to explain that the longer the system runs without interruption or problems, the more difficult for the monitoring operator to maintain visual and mental attention. One implication here is that while automatic systems may have been designed to consider this issue by building in audio or visual signals, those systems themselves are more abstract and remote from the operator, so they themselves may fail, but without being noticed. Additionally, automation involves multiple stages and streams of very rapid processing, beyond what operators can monitor in real time, requiring them to rely on more meta-level indicators. That is, more complex systems require greater potential monitoring and intervention skills, but more successful systems create conditions for intervention failures, and multiple audio-visual learning systems themselves create even more cognitive load on the operators just at the time that they must apply infrequently used understanding and knowledge. Interestingly, as complex systems build in more adjustment and feedback systems, signs of failure will become more and more muted. That is, rather than abrupt, explicit failure, each stage's failure can become masked, until the large interdependencies begin to fail and become noticeable, which is well past the time an operator can make focused interventions. Bainbridge (1983) concludes that many operators working with automated systems are given an impossible task, embedded in a situation rife with ironies.

New demands and new kinds of work generate new possibilities for errors, which could not be foretold by system designers, so cannot be signaled or prevented through use of the system itself (Dekker, 2005). The human factors perspective assumes that "errors" are real and can be reliably and validly measured. But even the categorization of an error involves subjective decisions, subject to measurement errors. Errors may be the cause of failure, the kind of failure (decision, perceptual, skill, physiological, communication, information processing), and a process (such as a departure from a standard procedure). Further, "error" may be a cause or a consequence, or both. An "error" depends on the stakeholder, internal or external role of the observer, type of measurement, location in a process, goal of the process, difficulties in achieving goals using standard processes, paradigm (errors as causes or consequences, individual or systemic), etc. One person's "error" may be another person's innovative workaround or solution. Indeed, the contexts of normalization must be understood in order to understand the sources and meanings of an "error" (Dekker, 2005, p. 54).

Many unanticipated problems and failures with automated systems are related to human–system interactions. Users have difficulties tracking the system's activities, leading to *automation surprises* for both users and designers. Systems create new context-dependent cognitive demands, load distributions, error pathways, and mismatches between user abilities and needs, and system capabilities for a variety of reasons (Woods *et al.*, 1997, p. 1927). New systems may help decrease workload in already low-workload conditions, but become distracting or harmful in pressured, critical workload situations. Systems may not indicate where or when to look for changes or disconfirming information, especially in rare or crisis situations, so users may not be appropriately allocating their attention, leading to breakdowns in attention to either (or both) the system and the situation. Complex systems may foster *mode errors* and *automation surprises*. A mode error occurs when what might be an appropriate action in one system mode might be inappropriate in another mode, and is made worse when the user is not aware of a mode shift. Automation modes are designed to autonomously process an interlinked series of activities, are becoming more interdependent in complex systems, and are responsive to more varied inputs (not just a single human operator), so modes can be changed through internal system decision, and a "single" mode error can generate a string of unidentified consequences, through both errors of omission and commission, all with increasingly lengthy feedback loops. These create automation surprises that are difficult to even detect, much less recover from. Indeed, taking action in such situations is just as likely to trigger "indirect mode transitions," where responding to feedback from one mode under the incorrect assumption of another mode, may generate internal parameters that activate a third mode – all while the user is assuming they are operating within the initial mode – and thus generating more unintended consequences. This of course makes detection, and resolution, even more difficult.

Automation often generates new roles and coordination demands. As this demand for coordinating the various automation processes as well as human interactions exceeds one's abilities, supervisors or users may exit the automation system, or the system may reach its autonomy threshold and return full control to the operator (called a *decompensation incident*, Woods *et al.*, 1997, p. 1931). This often occurs just at the time that the automation system is both generating and monitoring complexities that humans cannot process, while the operator is not even aware of the underlying crisis, is unprepared or unable to handle the situation, and is thus surprised or shocked to find out the seriousness of the underlying problem. Users come to rely on automation that is highly reliable for expected situations, but may fail in rare situations. Thus they may over-trust systems (a barrier to perception).

Working around errors, and system drift

Goodman (2000) provides a typology of progressing organizational errors, based on expectations, deviations, monitoring, and corrective action. If there are expectations but no negative consequences, this is a standard problem-solving situation. If there are no expectations, and a negative consequence, problem-solving errors occur (the means are not understood). Routine operations happen when there are expectations, but no deviations; but if there are no deviations but negative consequences, there is an error in process design or perhaps an external shock. If there are deviations, the monitoring/measuring systems do not detect them, but there are no negative consequences, this is a latent organizational error. If the monitoring system does not detect them and there are negative consequences, there is an error in measurement design. If no corrective action is taken, but with no negative consequence, this again is a latent organizational error. Finally, if no corrective action is taken, followed by a negative consequence, a primary organizational error occurs. There may be different antecedents of errors, and different linkage analyses, for each of these types of errors.

As one of many examples, Goodman describes a problem with canisters in one airline's jets becoming increasingly out-of-date, mislabeled, and thus incorrectly managed. The various and accumulating influences were outsourcing of maintenance, many sequential stages involving lack of verification and clearly going against procedures, differences in metrics across levels, interorganizational interdependence largely through people and thus loosely coupled, lack of a clear time dependence or time factor involved, and canisters sitting around for a long time. Each step was not necessarily causal, and only very infrequently operationally linked. At each step, the canisters were relabeled, more and more generally, so that their consequential meaning disappeared, eventually leading to serious safety risks.

It is easy and normative to explain errors/failures on the participant's not following procedures. But some analyses (at least of flight accidents) show that, first, procedure violations are not necessarily involved in accidents, and second, some procedure violations are in fact more effective and safer ways of accomplishing work goals (Dekker, 2005, p. 133). The latter instance can be considered a workaround that is superior to the formal procedure, and which does not apparently create other dysfunctions, but is not formalized into standard procedure at the organizational level. Increased procedures or directives to follow procedures do not necessarily improve compliance or safety; and some procedures seen as deviant at one time become the basis for new rules and procedures later on. Procedures are established under assumptions that they are the best way to achieve goals safely, that they are not in contradiction with other procedures, that there is enough time and other resources to do them correctly and completely, that the participants understand the situation clearly enough to know which procedure is appropriate and in what sequence, and that there is sufficient information available both about the situation and about the accomplishment of the procedure (Dekker, 2005, p. 134). It is rare that such assumptions are met independently, much less jointly. And following formal procedures may require additional skills, judgments, and processes not formerly needed, increasing time, cognitive demand, and effort. Following formal procedures explicitly may increase risk and failure (see Weick's (1993) discussion of the Mann Gulch fire disaster). This is especially true in novel and uncertain situations, precisely where formal procedures have the least basis (as in the threat-rigidity responses to organizational crises, discussed by Staw *et al.*, 1981).

So a central paradox is that actual procedures naturally generate the need to devise alternate procedures. Deviance from initial formal procedures not only becomes routine, but is necessary, to accomplish goals in actual contexts – through practical drift (Snook, 2000), fine-tuning (Starbuck and Milliken, 1988), and workarounds (Gasser, 1986).

"[R]eal practice is easily driven underground" because "informal work systems compensate for the organization's inability to provide the basic resources ... needed for task performance ... Actual practice ... settles at a distance from the formal description of the job. Deviance becomes routinized" (Dekker, 2005, pp. 143 and 145), especially through experience and informal networks. As discussed in Chapter 4, unfortunately, organizations rarely identify, learn from, or incorporate these local solutions. Further, local adaptation, without assessment and consideration of more global and longer-term implications, is also dangerous. Emergent procedures may improve local goal achievement and even safety, while leading to long-term divergence from organizational goals and safe operations of other subsystems, without the initiating unit being aware of these consequences of their adaptations.

Workarounds can also contribute to *system drift*. Safe systems can drift, over time, into error and failure, through quite regular adaptive processes (as discussed for routines in general in Chapter 4). Interestingly, systems that learn well from these local trade-offs may very well be more likely to drift into long-term failure (Starbuck and Milliken, 1988). That is, if short-term and local competitive forces determine adaptation, long-term competition and survival is heavily discounted: how much can one borrow safely (now) from safety (in the future)? Thus, generally failures are not discrete incidents; failures develop through normal practices, a gradual accumulation of decreased control. But organizational safety procedures are typically oriented toward finding failures, as incidents, and dealing with failures primarily as reactions to what are seen as failure incidents. So the tendency to locate failures as specific incidents, generally related to an individual's behavior, inherently prevents an understanding of the development and even encouragement of failures, as part of interacting social and technical systems. A paradox here is that failures are a product of over-time interactions within teams, organizations, and industries, yet are treated as individual errors (if at all), but can only be understood and prevented through collaboration and joint understanding (Dekker, 2005, p. xiv).

Open systems drift inside their *safety envelopes*, sometimes developing resilience and stability, sometimes crossing into failure (Dekker, 2005, p. 2). Dekker identifies three common aspects of failure drift. First, such accidents are associated with ordinary people doing their job according to instructions in normal situations and organizations, particularly in contexts of resource scarcity and competition. Second, these typically occur in organizations with power relations and scarce resources (fostering self-interested behavior), and with conflicting goals, such as safety and profit or development and maintenance. Third, progression toward failure is transparent and incremental, without prior signals such as smaller failures, and with only small stepwise divergences from initial conditions, fostering legitimacy and normalization. Put another way, subsequent processes may be maintained correctly, but linked to prior processes that are not, so failure occurs in the subsequent process and not in the prior process. Each adjustment of the formal criteria to a current situation makes local sense, but moves incrementally from the prior norm, so the system drifts toward failure (p. 22).

Ironically, looking for errors and failures (of the typical, event-oriented, and more frequent kind) may not only prevent, but also cause, subsequent failures (of the atypical, incremental, and highly unlikely kind). Indeed, reporting as required may prevent others from ever being exposed to evidence of an impending major failure (an interesting counter-point to the discussion about reporting errors in Chapter 7). Tragically, hindsight analyses may lead critics as well as professionals to proclaim surprise and shock about no one identifying these problems during the drift (Dekker, 2005, p. 24). Indeed, post-hoc explanations may be sources of ongoing failures themselves as they focus on larger perspectives that are neither perceptible nor beneficial locally.

Box 8.2 summarizes many of the organizational and social factors from across disciplines representing or explaining concepts potentially involved in URs.

Box 8.2 Organizational and social processes, with example application to unusual routines

Complexity of organizations: full range and implications of interactions inherently difficult to identify, understand, predict, due to interdependencies, multiple level feedback, responses to deviation from homeostasis. *Example*: difficult to identify nature, source, and level of causes and even problems.

Box 8.2 (*cont.*)

Discounting the future: strongly underestimating the likelihood of potential negative outcomes, leading to inefficient and costly short-term solutions, generating even greater costs later on, and especially underevaluating the distribution of those harms to other people. *Example*: reinforcing local unusual routines that generate externalities for others, the collective, and even the initial actors.

Discourses and logics of errors: different and shifting bases for not only defining errors or harmful behavior, but also of the rationales and arguments used to raise and evaluate those definitions. *Example*: responses to customer complaints as unjustified, it's not one's job, it's "the computer"; bypassing, bureaucratic rigidity.

Error generated by automated systems: due both to the largely invisible and uncontrollable interdependencies both built into the system and developed through proximity and oversight, but also between operators and the system. *Example*: not predicted but consequential interdependencies, especially with new systems (see Chapter 2).

Excessive organizational rationalization: locally or globally rational routines creating internal costs and constraints, and externalizing those onto others. *Example*: legitimation, aura of rationality.

Group polarization: when social interactions within a group of like-minded individuals lead to more extreme fears or positions than those held by the separate individuals (Moscovici and Zavalloni, 1969), due largely to the availability heuristic and probability neglect. *Example*: strong sensemaking with negative consequences, esp. in social dilemmas.

Inherent complexity and abstractness of technology: creating and allowing first- and second-level positive and negative, short-term and long-term, consequences. *Example*: allowing *manipulation*, forcing iterative and accumulative work and error *fritters*.

Moral panics: a particular form of *cascades* or *bandwagons*, whereby certain images or fears (typically about specific groups or specific mass behaviors, and often about taboo topics), rapidly diffuse both through word-of-mouth and media agendas, creating public overestimations of the frequency of occurrence of the object, and concerns about extreme or pervasive negative social consequences and threats to social values, without much basis in evidence, or possibly intentionally to shape and control society (Cohen, 1980). *Example*: potential response to challenges to embedded unusual routines, especially meta-routines.

Normal accidents: crises stemming from a very rare sequence of what might appear to be independent events, but which might be intermittently or contextually interactive, or inappropriately tightly-coupled. *Example*: inability of human actors to perceive or intervene constructively in very complex, low-probability sequences.

Normalization of risk into acceptable processes (Edmondson *et al.*, 2005) through: (1) downplaying the threat if the evidence is ambiguous (Goleman, 1985), (2) preferring confirming to disconfirming information (Einhorn and Hogarth, 1978), (3) escalating commitment to a path with prior investment (the sunk cost error) (Arkes and Blumer, 1985), (4) breeding over-confidence (anchoring to existing beliefs, avoidance of disconfirmation evidence and divergent opinions) (Heath *et al.*, 1998), and (5) developing a shared cognitive frame (Russo and Schoemaker, 1989), especially under time and budget constraints. *Example*: fundamental basis for development and routinization of unusual routines.

Organizational attributes and structures: structure (hierarchical, rigid, efficiency-oriented, formal channels, valuing channels over content; geographical dispersion), group design (coordination, support, authority and reporting relations, mandate/goal, distributed teams), climate (such as psychological safety), and culture (emphasis on certain kinds of evidence, especially relevant with ambiguous risk, may make it too difficult to raise questions; taken-for-granted beliefs in the specific technologies, arguments, consequences). *Example*: bureaucratic rigidity, both loose and tight coupling (with different implications for diffusing and identifying unusual routines).

Organizational deviance: harmful and generally unacceptable behaviors and processes allowed, reinforced, fostered, or ignored by organizational policies and culture. *Example*: unusual routine

Box 8.2 (*cont.*)

aspects of employee mistreatment, employee emotional abuse, petty tyranny.

Organizational paradoxes: inherent to organizations, interrelated, contradictory but internally reasonable, situations or pressures, providing potential for learning, but also associated with dysfunction and pathology, generating inconsistent messages and subsequent behaviors. *Example*: reasonable, justifiable, but conflicting goals such as efficiency and quality service.

Responses to threats/crises: confirming, exploration, rigidity (Edmondson *et al.*, 2005; Staw *et al.*, 1981). *Example*: denial, cognitive dissonance reduction, externalization.

Social amplification of risk: people's responses to the initial crisis event – and, especially ironically, responses designed especially to avoid such risks in the future – generate additional, often greater, costs and harm (Pidgeon *et al.*, 2003; Sunstein, 2007, p. 139). *Example*: workarounds.

Social traps and dilemmas: when individual self-interested, rational action conflicts with, deplete, damages, or dominates collective benefits and public goods, through a variety of processes and interdependencies. *Example*: unusual routine reinforces local benefits at collective or external costs.

Social/availability cascades or *bandwagons*: fear spreads through individuals responding to expression (interpersonally and via media) of emotion or salience by others, but little or no new information is provided by such influence; that is, they are not responding to increased information or understanding about the risk, but to the fact that others are responding to others. *Example*: initial response to system crisis can generate threat-rigidity response, closing down opportunities for learning.

System and error drift: over-time shift of assumptions, expectations, criteria, and attention. *Example*: requiring or allowing workarounds and divergence from procedures, accumulating into serious errors and putting operators into untenable situations.

Note: citations are provided only for those not mentioned in the chapter text, or for a specific example.

Conclusion

Across the disciplines, there is much evidence of individual, social and organizational processes that promote URs, are forms of URs, prevent identification of URs, and are outcomes or indicators of URs. At the individual level, an extensive array of personal heuristics and cognitive processing errors, especially cognitive dissonance, make it difficult for people to perceive, identify causal influences on, and take responsibility for aspects of what may be URs. Both individuals and social systems intentionally and unintentionally embed errors of logic in attempts to make sense of difficult social issues. These and other factors blind us to predictable surprises, create unrealistic attitudes toward worst-case scenarios, and impose over-constraining precautionary principles onto social risk. More conceptually, the tension between individual and collective, or local and global, costs and benefits plant seeds for the growth of social traps and social dilemmas. At the organizational level, their inherent complexity spawns a wide range of unintended consequences, and interacts with organizational rationality(ies). Indeed, organizational paradoxes are pervasive, generating challenging feedback loops and contradictions. Organizational processes can develop, maintain, and even reward organizational deviance (such as employee mistreatment and petty tyranny). Similarly, technological systems are becoming increasingly more complex, interdependent, inscrutable, automated, and unpredictable, leading to a continuum of unintended consequences, such as manipulation, normal accidents, systemic error, workarounds, and system drift. Foundational aspects of unusual routines are pervasive in various research literatures.

9 Recommendations for resolving and mitigating unusual routines and related phenomena

Based upon the analyses and reviews of the prior chapters, this chapter provides some recommendations (Box 9.1) for how to increase awareness of, attention to, discussion about, and resolution of factors and contexts that encourage unusual routines and related problems.

Encourage customer service feedback from all stakeholders

The literature on ways to strengthen customer satisfaction is vast. Jones and Sasser (1998, p. 19) suggest several approaches to continually monitor and improve customer service. These include:

(1) embed customer satisfaction indices (measure over time, and type of product/service, or customer);
(2) seek feedback through multiple channels and content (comments, complaints, questions);
(3) conduct market research (both before people become customers and when they defect);
(4) train, empower, and support frontline personnel to better listen to customers and to forward the problems and solutions to the organization; and
(5) develop strategic activities involving customers in the business.

Wexler *et al.* (1993) provide detailed recommendations of ways to instill and improve service quality, in the areas of service zones, integrating service and selling, encouraging demanding customers, nurturing complaining customers, managing recoveries from service problems or failures, generating moments of positive and negative experiences as well as truth, grounding the organization in vision and values, implementing a quality service change effort, and managing the people systems that provide the foundation for all the service components. Rather than following the "customer is always

306

Box 9.1 Recommendations for avoiding, analyzing, mitigating, and resolving unusual routines and related processes

- Encourage customer service feedback from all stakeholders;
- apply socio-technical systems theory, involve stakeholders from design through walk-arounds;
- reduce blaming and defensive approaches to cognitive dissonance;
- manage paradoxes and sensemaking;
- foster learning through feedback;
- heighten awareness of predictable surprises and avoid overreacting to worst-case scenarios;
- understand and resolve social traps and social dilemmas;
- discuss and resolve conflicting goals, vicious cycles, and workplace deviance;
- avoid simple and individual approaches to complex technology and system error; and
- apply and combine linkage and routines analysis.

---

right" aphorism to the point that customers become trained to expect the unreasonable and the organization puts its financial and ethical resources at risk, they recommend instead encouraging creative and demanding customers while nurturing complaining customers, having a consistent and explicit basis for responding, and empowering the representative to resolve those situations on that basis.

Wexler *et al.* (1993) clarify that customers may well be wrong, but the customer nevertheless is still the customer, so the problem should be resolved in a satisfactory way to the customer, representative, and organization (p. 186). As part of the "recovery process," the organizational representative should enable (we would add reward) the customer or client to provide information about the episode, and then move that back into the organization's service and operation systems. As does the quality management literature, they emphasize that since employees are also internal customers, experiencing how their jobs and processes work, and thus are well-positioned to provide insightful feedback about problems and potential improvements, they, like customers, should be allowed and enabled to complain.

Beyond conducting research on customer preferences, obtaining feedback about product satisfaction, and responding appropriately to complaints and problematic encounters, quality-oriented organizations should involve customers in sharing "interdependencies, values, and strategies over the long term" (Lengnick-Hall, 1996, p. 792). For example, as part of strategic quality management, organizations should conceptualize customers as the center of quality activities. Quality becomes a competitive advantage, not just a problem to be solved, so customers should be actively involved in the design, assessment, and even production of services. Because trust and relationships between customers and the organization is crucial, organizations should strengthen customer commitment not only through traditional forms such as warranties, etc., but also through improved self-efficacy in interacting with the organization. This approach broadens the conceptualization of customers as both input (resource and co-producer) and output (buyer, user, and even a product, such as health patients). It thus makes explicit the need to improve the quality of the entire system, within and across organizational boundaries. Representative of the system-perspective in quality approaches to customer satisfaction are recommendations such as designing the organization–customer relationship for "stability, symmetry, and mutual benefit" via clear communication of expectations and implications, because "customer resources need to know how their actions and capabilities affect system activities" (Lengnick-Hall, 1996, p. 800).

Beyond just conceptualizing "complaints" as "necessary and useful feedback and learning," organizations need to transform their internal procedures and culture to both seek and value external as well as internal feedback. Paton (2003), in addition to a variety of negative implications of performance measurement (Chapter 8), does identify three potential main benefits of performance measures: making problems visible, stimulating discussion about the activity, and developing relationships with stakeholders. There should be multiple channels, encouragements and rewards for both external clients as well as internal organizational members to provide such feedback, training for organizational representatives to foster such information in supportive ways while also not taking criticism personally, and management support for organizational representatives to take initiative in getting the feedback to the appropriate personnel (Barlow and Moller, 1996; Stauss and Seidel, 2005). Various sources agree that organizations that are successful at knowledge transfer tend to have a high-trust, risk-taking, knowledge sharing, change-embracing culture (DeLong and Fahey, 2000; Leonard, 1995; O'Dell and Grayson, 1998; Pfeffer and Sutton, 2000).

Service interactions provide sources of customer information in two ways: for use by service providers (possibly to modify behavior based on interaction feedback), and to help organizations make decisions (considering service representatives and contact personnel as organizational boundary-spanners), especially concerning the development of new services and modification of existing ones (Bitner *et al.*, 1994). Employees desire to provide quality service, but experience frustration with "lack of basic knowledge of the system and its constraints, inability to provide a logical explanation to the customer, cumbersome bureaucratic procedures, poorly designed systems or procedures, or the lack of authority to do anything" (p. 103). Rather, they need training, coping mechanisms, problem-solving skills, awareness of predisposing situations, and tools to interact with such customers. As noted above, organizations also need to "train" customers, so that they have reasonable role expectations; often the customer appreciates this new information.

A fundamental way to move customers up to higher levels of satisfaction is a "recovery process for counteracting bad experiences ... A company must train [frontline personnel] to listen effectively and to make the first attempts at amends when customers have bad experiences. They also must have processes in place to capture the information and pass it along to the rest of the company" (Jones and Sasser, 1998, pp. 18–19). An organizational implication of the research on customer service interactions is to manage so as to prevent dissatisfaction, but then also manage to respond positively to complaints. Thus, active solicitation of consumer complaints plays a dual role – both for correcting errors, and for reducing negative word of mouth (Halstead, 2002). In top service organizations, delivering seamless service involves these principles: continuously identify problems; those who receive a customer complaint own it; do not blame someone else; and the customer should not suffer from internal incompetence or misunderstandings. These principles are based on the awareness that no system is problem-free and that difficulties will arise but must be resolved (Dillard *et al.*, 2000). Seiders and Berry (1998) recommend two major classes of actions to reduce perceptions of *service unfairness.* The first is to *prevent unfairness perceptions from developing.* This includes identifying the kinds of exchanges most at-risk (those with the greatest potential for generating discrepancies with the three kinds of justice, those that are more severe or frequent, and those associated with the most negative emotion), developing reasonable policies, ensuring that all representatives and components are responsive to attempts at correction, designing components and training representatives to be able to adapt to both situations and responses, emphasizing respect and empathy for the customer's situation, and providing support for expectations and claims. The second set of recommendations involves *managing perceptions of unfairness.* This includes training for and reinforcing interactional justice by all organizational members with customer contact (and not relegating this solely to customer complaints personnel), providing appropriate and valid explanations (increasing psychological equity) and compensation (actual equity), and explicitly demonstrating accountability (taking responsibility, not blaming others, and avoiding bias against vulnerable customers).

Apply socio-technical systems theory, involve stakeholders from design through walkarounds

"Users" should be widely defined, to include designers, managers, complaints operators, and external clients as well as those organizational members who directly "use" a system, and those new to the organization or those leaving the organization. All of these should be involved in not only the design and implementation, but ongoing evaluation of an ICT, job, or procedures. Further, designers, implementers, and managers should emphasize the communicative and informational aspect of ICTs. The form and value of symbols used in reference to systems both reinforce and hide underlying influences on the development of URs (such as notions of computer accuracy, user-friendly interfaces, accounting criteria, or access to large amounts of information – more specifically, legitimization cues and ascribing normalcy).

Each organizational newcomer or new system user should be asked to identify problems they experience (of any kind, such as work, delay, error, or blame subroutines) and suggest solutions (of any kind, such as reducing barriers to perceptions) during their first months – and rewarded for doing so. *Newcomers* have novel, near-anthropological experiences trying to understand and survive the new tribe, before they have been habituated or have figured out ways to cope and impose acceptable sensemaking. Moreover, those leaving the organization should be asked to participate in an exit interview, again identifying any problems and solutions that they care to offer (such as routinized workarounds or instances of conflicting goals or simple exiting behavior). *Departers* have considerable experience and frustration in trying to make the system work and may be able to suggest changes without concern for personal consequences should they stay. In both cases, all comments should be about roles, procedures, resources, norms, expectations, scheduling, whatever – and not personal comments. That way, identification of problems and discussion of possible solutions are framed as ways of improving the system, rather than as personal attacks against individuals. Of course, organizations should involve current members in seeking out such insights and aspects needing change. These suggestions are, of course, explicit aspects of socio-technical systems approaches that aim to optimize the fit between technical and social systems (Chapter 4).

For example, at one of our former universities, once a year a small "red tape committee" with a person from each department and administrative office will get together and develop a list from their past year's experiences of anything that seemed like it did not work, needed changing, or just had to be removed; go around to every room and wall in the building adding to the list; and then have those things taken care of. This might require a request from maintenance and facilities for legal, safety, or union reasons, but if not, someone on the committee will just do it him- or herself. The "red tape committee" reports all the accomplishments to the faculty at the end of the year, which fosters motivation, public awareness, and well-matched initiation and completion cycles.

However, such attempts may easily be stymied. For example, the housing association one of us lives in tries to do something like this, with an annual "walk-around" by the association board members, to identify things that need fixing or cleaning up or would just make things look nicer. However, this plan suffers from two dysfunctional feedback loops. First, the walk-around occurs around March, but the board is newly elected each July. Each new board determines the budget for the year sometime in early fall. So anything identified in the walk-around as new will not have a budget item, so if it costs much at all simply cannot be done in that year. Instead, the walk-around should be done by the newly elected board, before the budgeting process. Further, the three months (April, May, June) between the walk-around and the new board's budget may not be a long enough time period to resolve all (or any!) of the problems, and anything not completed by the current board by the next election disappears as an agenda item. Finally, items identified by the walk-around that are not major enough to require a significant budget item (which would not happen until the following fall, but would likely not be on the new board's agenda) are usually allocated to anyone who volunteers to fix the problem. But, as they have volunteered, there are only three months, and the new board has no commitment to the list, if the volunteer does not do it, it does not get done, and there is no feedback from anyone about this lack of follow-through. So most of the problems are not fixed even though there is an explicit organizational process for identifying things that need fixing. Thus mismatched cycles and poor feedback sabotage this good intention and reduce the effort and time to a near-pointless exercise, one that is repeated each year, and one which primarily produces wasted energy, resignation, and cynicism.

Reduce blaming and defensive approaches to cognitive dissonance

Attempts to improve systems and solve problems must transcend blame (and, relative to cognitive dissonance, avoid blaming in the first place). Blaming ignores the system, and generates negative implications, including defensiveness, protection, silence, suppression of learning, categorization of failures as deviant, fear of punishment for openness, and decrease in identification and reporting of errors, leading to more failures (Dekker, 2005, Chapter 10). Accountability should be conceptualized not as accepting punishment, but as encouraging members to provide accounts. In a sense, processes must shift from focusing on rewarding or blaming an individual to emphasizing the collective benefit.

Concerning the problem of cognitive dissonance, this reinforcing, self-justifying feedback loop must be disrupted early, before people become deeply embedded, surround themselves with similar folks, and generate significant harm. Questions about or critiques of problems and processes should be surfaced early on. Otherwise, over time the self-justification processes will increase the perception of the extent of the damage and the denigration of the other, as well as the memory alteration and confirmation biases of the self (Tavris and Aronson, 2007, p. 209). Major ways out of the general reinforcing feedback loop of avoiding responsibility and succumbing to inappropriate avoidance of cognitive dissonance are: (1) exposing oneself to those who suffer the consequences of our attitudes and beliefs; (2) being aware that one may not in fact be correct; and (3) subjecting one's attitudes, beliefs, and practices to impartial evaluations based on evidence external to oneself (Tavris and Aronson, 2007, p. 105). Another strategy for escaping self-justification is to share mistakes in a group setting, where the norms against making mistakes and taking blame may be overcome, and the underlying processes may be described. The process of getting to the underlying process, and confronting biases and memories with evidence, probably requires independent moderators, as they would be less likely to have conflicts of interest or prior behaviors to justify – that is, the need to reduce dissonance. The scientific model – no personal ownership of the causal explanation, public disclosure, replication, subjecting hypotheses to rigorous evidence attempting to refute the hypotheses – seems one of the few approaches able to minimize self-justification, self-reinforcing dissonance reduction, and conformation biases. However, few institutions (or individuals, for that matter) seem aware of these principles, much less open to such light. A further way is to consider the proposal or insight separate from the source, and to couch the others' perception as coming from oneself or one's in-group. At the very least, a greater awareness of the process of dissonance reduction and self-justification might provide a vocabulary for perceiving and talking about these most human traits.

LaPlante and Neill (2006) follow their descriptive typology of managerial and environmental antipatterns with twenty general suggestions for helping to avoid and resolve antipatterns. They sound prosaic and common-sensical, yet are explicit principles and actions for refactoring identified antipatterns. Some of these concern an individual's approach to interacting with others (be kind; don't blame other people – e.g., break the culture of blame discussed earlier as well as avoid shifting responsibility; listen; negotiate; never attribute to malice what stupidity can explain; be a mentor). Some relate to intervening between the problem and the solution (learn to deliver bad news; do not shoot the messenger – which will quickly close off awareness of problems; let people learn from their mistakes; remember the law of unintended consequences). And some involve self-awareness and one's own responsibilities (do not worry for other people; just get it done; never give up; always set and meet expectations).

Manage paradoxes and sensemaking

Analytical approaches to identifying paradoxes range from examining narratives and discourse, asking questions that surface hidden conflicts, and applying multiple paradigms (Lewis, 2000). Escaping reinforcing loops caused by responding to tensions inherent in paradoxes requires what may appear as counterintuitive responses. These include acceptance (living with it), confrontation (talking about it), and transcendence (practicing second-order, rather than first-order, thinking) (Cameron, 1986; Putnam, 1986). When dealing with system paradoxes, it is important not to make negative connotations about the participating members of the system. Analysts of URs must get around the linguistic disconfirmations noted in Chapter 7. They must become inaccessible to reactions of pleasure or anger; that is, they cannot become "involved" (either actually or by labeling), or they will immediately become part of the game, the UR, at a higher level (Argyris, 1985). The goal is to positively evaluate the *system's* tendency toward homeostasis, but not critique *members'* tendency toward it (Palazzoli *et al.*, 1978, p. 149). Instead, try to locate all members on the same level, but conceptualize the motivations for the behaviors as trying to preserve the cohesion of the system as a whole, rather than as valuing one or other of the members. Otherwise, access to the system as a whole is lost and coalitions are formed, because of the primary characteristic of systems to attempt to maintain homeostasis. Indeed, a fear that equilibrium is in danger is a prime source of motivation for change, although usually toward reinforcing the current state (Palazzoli *et al.*, 1978, p. 58).

Managers attempting to deal with their paradoxical role of mediating between executives' and subordinates' responses to change may process three aspects of the paradox (Lewis, 2000). *Performance paradoxes* involve how subordinates respond to the paradoxical communications of both trust and monitoring, leading to fragmented and contradictory messages and behaviors. One approach here is to "split" the mixed messages or tension sources and discuss each separately, increasing members' ability to see them as complementary. *Belonging paradoxes* are about tensions arising from associated changes in work relationships, such as between team commitment and individual independence. For example, attempting to make sense of these tensions may generate *recursive cycles*, where taking action to pursue a goal raises fears about responses that prevent them from achieving the goal (such as raising questions of trusting new team members without signaling low trust in those others). Here, managers may introduce *collective reflection* (where people identify their own defenses, outside of the particular stimulating context, often moderated by an empathetic outsider), and *modeling* (within the team, describe hopes or expectations about team interactions). Finally, *organizing paradoxes* occur when "organizations tend to solve problems fostered by the constraints of one objective by introducing a new objective. Yet the new organizational objective may be just as constraining, albeit in new ways, thereby compounding issues" (Luscher and Lewis, 2008, p. 233, referencing Putnam, 1986). *Systemic contradictions* arise, with conflicting goals and policies, embedded and routinized in communication practices (Putnam, 1986). Managers may attempt to overcome or deny or ignore such paradoxes by giving out clear, explicit, singular messages. But these are of course confronted by their own conflicting prior messages, without allowing the opportunity to comment on the conflict. Overall, Luscher and Lewis (2008) recommend several strategies for coping with these paradoxes. One is to accept, but not submit to, the paradox. This means being aware of the inconsistencies and ambiguity without blaming others. The common agenda should not repress individual needs. Providing more information about the diverse perspectives in advance of discussions and meetings should also help. Sensemaking in conditions of paradox may be fostered through phases of circular questioning (Luscher and Lewis, 2008). It is difficult to solve a problem if the underlying issue is a dilemma, with choices having both high costs and high benefits. So reflexive questions may be used to critique implications and relate various options, stimulating double-loop learning, breaking out of binary choices into a reframing. This may uncover some of the contradictions and tensions, such as expectations from executives and from subordinates, who often hold contradictory goals or criteria.

Breaking out of harmful organizational frames and their negative consequences requires at least one of three conditions, according to Westenholz (1993): first, availability of discussion forums where adherents of different frames of reference can meet (necessary but not sufficient); second, having a few employees who are capable of paradoxical thinking argue for trying something new (however, they will typically be interpreted on the basis of existing reference frames, so this will not necessarily foster change); and third, unexpected, surprising actions that violate reference frames (but advocates must not benefit themselves at cost to others; even so, such actions may be likely interpreted with suspicion, fear of manipulation). Several other conditions, however, can prevent even those conditional possibilities for change. People may relapse into traditional frames of reference before a new understanding develops, especially if few others support the change, or if peer pressure maintains the prior frame. Even if reframing progresses, people may be reluctant to express new attitudes, and be fearful of being rejected by their former reference group. And even if people take action from the new frame, supporters may be isolated from other frames, either by their prior own group, or by other groups who still interpret action as though it were from the prior group.

Thompson (1998) does suggest, however, that some paradoxes are resolvable, through:

(1) conceptualizing what appears as conflicting ends of a continuum instead as independent dimensions;
(2) developing a shared vision through insights from diverse sources;
(3) using creativity to improve operational processes through consistent processes;
(4) establishing and re-evaluating clear criteria but design in flexibility in how to meet those criteria;
(5) using higher-order group cohesion to allow and value cognitive conflict (while avoiding affective conflict) in order to surface assumptions and needs;

(6) accompanying challenging goals by empowerment, minimal interference, and systemic accommodation; and
(7) developing criteria and evaluation processes for both individual and team performance, allowing minority opinions.

Possible solutions to paradox cycles include transcending the paradox by increasing the contradiction space or synthesizing the opposites (Barnes, 1981; Wilder, 1979), or admitting to or relinquishing the symptoms, say by either exaggerating them or behaving opposite to what one would prefer to do based on consistency within one's meaning system.

Foster learning through feedback

Winter (2000) advocates continuous improvement attempts to routinize multiple influences on increasing aspirations concerning explicit processes. Examples include quality management, benchmarking (taking advantage of vicarious experience), the balanced scorecard, and root-cause analysis. Foundational to the quality management approach are four main themes (Deming, 1986). First, focus on customer relationships (both inside and outside of the organization). Second, empower, involve, and train employees in management decisions and TQM methods. Third, continually gather and analyze statistical data about organizational processes, both to avoid finding out about problems too late, and also to emphasize the data instead of individual or department blame. Finally, develop an organizational climate that promotes unity and change, safety and support for discussing problems.

Indeed, this same approach should be applied to all organizational members, as they are also users and internal customers. And there must be a larger, more pervasive culture of seeking and sharing feedback, through and in spite of the various factors mediating feedback from customers and clients. For effective transfer of knowledge throughout the organization, leaders need to consistently champion the message of knowledge sharing for the greater good of the organization (Allen and Brady, 1997; O'Dell and Grayson, 1998).

Based on her study of nurses' responses to local errors, Edmondson (2004) recommends that in order to foster learning from feedback about errors and processes, organizations need to:

(1) develop and communicate a compelling vision, such as continuously improving the total system;
(2) foster a learning environment – encouraging and valuing reporting of errors and problems through psychological safety (which also means defining boundaries), including changing terminology from "investigations" to "analysis;" and
(3) provide management leadership and support for teams to identify problems and try and evaluate new approaches.

In the long run, learning from frontline staff experiences to not only identify and remove operational failures, but more importantly to improve general work systems, would significantly increase hospital safety and efficiency (Tucker *et al.*, 2008). Singer and Edmondson (2008) advocate a change in organizational learning mindsets. This involves moving (1) from advocacy (lack of listening, reliance on quantitative date) to inquiry (openness, tolerance for ambiguity, reliance on intuition and interpretation), (2) from confirmatory (reinforcing accepted assumptions) to exploratory (experiment to test assumptions) responses, and (3) from coping (defensiveness, view errors and inquiry as a threat, overly technical orientation) to learning (viewing problems as exciting opportunities, and team orientation).

Workarounds should be identified whenever possible, assessed as symptoms rather than solutions, and analyzed to uncover the workflow triggers and more general system problems as well as possibly more appropriate system and process designs (Roberto *et al.*, 2006). However, because workarounds "are dependent on the specific work processes, work context, and individual staff members involved" (Vogelsmeier *et al.*, 2008, p. 118) they may be difficult to identify, analyze, and apply. One response is to improve the measurement of potential workarounds, such as using the "Situation, Individual, Task, Effect" human factors approach, which develops descriptions of actual and ideal workflow (Charlton, 2002). Possibly norms and potential consequences of workarounds on downstream staff could be a more salient component of training and evaluation. Implementation of workflow changes should consider organizational climate issues, such as psychological safety, which influence the extent to which workers will discuss their concerns about such changes and suggestions for workarounds (Edmondson, 1999; Halbesleben and Rathert, 2008).

Heighten awareness of predictable surprises and avoid overreacting to worst-case scenarios

Concerning barriers to perceiving predictable surprises, Bazerman and Watkins (2004) suggest a variety of tactics.

(1) Proactively scan the environment for threats, though this requires resources and avoidance of selective attention.
(2) Foster individual or local incentives that generate collective costs, help overcome both individual rationality and collective irrationality; this may, however, be more difficult in decentralized organizations, especially when groups and managers are rewarded for benefiting their own unit, at cost of other units and the organization.
(3) Integrate information from multiple sources instead of fostering independent, unconnected evidence within organizational "silos," which are a natural outgrowth of increased specialization, and necessary for more complex issues.
(4) Identify and filter out noise, due to both conflicting and too much information (due in turn to insufficient resources and/or a rise in amount and diversity of threats); this is especially a problem when there are strong incentives for maintaining the status quo and avoiding being wrong.
(5) Balance leaders' caution with analysts' overreaction, which can lead to multiple false alarms, and subsequent discounting of warnings.
(6) Respond quickly; observe and evaluate the results.
(7) Implement the lessons into organizational memory; and change organizational cultures that foster delays, blame, and poor definition and measurement of criteria.

There are some contexts in which *difficulties in envisioning the worst* can be overcome (Cerulo, 2006). This is more likely when the communities are service-oriented, have permeable community boundaries, are grounded in formal knowledge bases (i.e., the scientific model of assuming that claims may be disprovable, based on evidence), and grant considerable autonomy to its members. These characteristics foster an *emancipating structure*, which not only allows, but fosters, deviance from perceptual conventions, pursuit of unanticipated problems, and development of creative solutions.

Examples include responses to SARS and the Y2K millennium bug, in contrast to the 1986 Challenger disaster and the FBI "Phoenix memo" providing early concerns about the terrorists who flew planes into the World Trade buildings and the Pentagon (Cerulo, 2006).

Exploratory, instead of the more typical *confirmatory*, responses by organizations to crises are more likely both to take advantage of the recovery window (the period between a threat and either its prevention or a subsequent major accident), and to develop procedures that reduce related accidents in the future (Edmondson *et al.*, 2005). These entail a number of suggested behaviors: challenge existing assumptions; exaggerate ambiguous threats in order to overcome obstacles, embedded assumptions and typical responses; proactively manage teams to engage in problem-solving (avoids putting costs and stigma on spontaneous individual and group initiatives); avoid confirming pre-existing beliefs; act rather than wait (rapid learning); foster openness and psychological safety; question whether causal explanations are unqualified, especially in conditions of uncertainty; go beyond formal, limited explicit experiments that preclude discussion of alternative explanation; and encourage dissent (identify confidence in prevailing views and consider effect of leaders' confidence, status, and influence, which will suppress opinions and reduce psychological safety).

Understand and resolve social traps and social dilemmas

A number of actions might reduce social traps or social dilemmas and promote cooperation: greater expectation of others' cooperation increases one's own likelihood of cooperating; pre-existing individual differences, such as social value orientations and trust; the extent to which one perceives their contribution might help achieve collective goals; the extent to which one feels their contributions to the collective may be observed by others; and feelings of personal responsibility (Liebrand *et al.*, 1992). "One interesting and potentially important way to escape from collective noncooperation is to coordinate the social dilemma [social trap] in a manner such that people feel committed, or actually promise to contribute, to the collective welfare" (p. 15). Unfortunately, in URs commitment to the collective need can actually help preserve the UR against efforts to mitigate it! Open communication may help to reduce some social dilemmas or traps, by making others' intentions more accessible, strengthening commitment to a discussed course of action, allowing participants to engage in moral persuasion, and improving group identity and cohesion (Barry and Bateman, 1996, p. 774, referring to Messick and Brewer, 1983). However, a UR approach notes that such noble intentions may mask the identification of subsequent processes and costs, thus generating divergences elsewhere in the social system. For other solutions or typologies of solutions to social traps and social dilemmas, see Cross and Guyer (1980), Dawes (1980), Edney (1980), Messick and Brewer (1983), Platt (1973), Rutte (1990), and Van Lange *et al.* (1992).

Discuss and resolve conflicting goals, vicious cycles, and workplace deviance

Boettger and Greer (1994) argue that organizations should handle complex inconsistent demands instead of eliminating them. Such an approach requires training systems that emphasize "goodness" and complexity management, and should also strive to identify internal systems that reward one or more sides for contradictory behaviors, but which cannot be acknowledged by one of those sides. However, an over-reliance on simple consistency in complex environments may lead to larger problems, such as ignoring honesty, ethics, and customer trust. When ambiguity is inherent in a process, or when it is chosen as a strategy for gaining flexibility and identity, it should also explicitly be accompanied by supporting second-level discourse about that ambiguity (Markham, 1996).

What are some ways to manage contentious communication and vicious cycles through communication? Brett *et al.* (1998) suggest five specific approaches. First, avoid reciprocating negative communication and one-upsmanship. However, not reciprocating may send an unintended message, that one is not listening, or one's position is too weak to propose. Second, avoid engaging in tit-for-tat as it tends to encourage conflict spirals. Third, apply Osgood's (1962) Graduated and Reciprocated Initiatives in Tension Reduction: announce a concession as part of a strategy to reduce escalation, invite the other to reciprocate a concession, then unilaterally perform the concession. This provides a de-escalating communication that can then be reciprocated; however, this may also serve to reward the initial obstinate behavior. Fourth, use mixed communications, such as reciprocating a contentious communication and also stating a noncontentious/cooperative communication. This gives negotiators a face-saving way to choose how to reciprocate and how to refocus the negotiation. However, there should be a sense of possible penalty for not cooperating. Fifth, label the process as contentious. This makes it difficult for the first party to disagree without seeming entirely intransigent, implying a willingness to refocus. Labeling and discussing a process may unfreeze participants, moving them toward a more effective process (Hackman and Morris, 1975).

Strategies managers might consider several ways to reduce workplace deviance:

(1) create an ethical climate (respond, model, display rates and costs of deviance);
(2) build trusting relationships (reciprocal psychological contracts between managers and employees, especially early on in the socialization process; empower employees; avoid monitoring and coercion);
(3) assess and discuss rules, rewards and punishments (fair processes, measurable and attainable goals, evaluations by self as well as stakeholders, team-based rewards, equal sanctions, clear expectations); and
(4) broaden the conceptualization of deviant behaviors beyond just non-supervisory employees to all organizational members.

Avoid simple and individual approaches to complex technology and system error

Possible ways to reduce errors associated with complex systems are to use non-redundant multiple/divergent stakeholders and communication displays, build in measures of resource scarcity and competition, and use the extent of resource scarcity and competition as indicators of potential safety risks (Dekker, 2005, p. 62). Systems should be designed to communicate their intentions, so that users have realistic and appropriate expectations. Note that this implies that a system is, in a way, a medium through which designers communicate their intention, and into which users must responsibly place their trust (Woods *et al.*, 1997, p. 1935, referring to Winograd and Flores, 1986). The greater the levels of system authority and autonomy, complexity and number of components, and coupling among components, the greater the need for communication and coordination among users and between users and system needed to foster observability or awareness. Note that rarely is just one "user" involved, and wider practices should be supported and improved by an ICT, not just individual tasks, in actual use contexts.

High-reliability organizations (Roberts and Bea, 2001) implement three general strategies for avoiding accidents. One is that they proactively try to find out what they do not know. They train organizational members to seek out anomalies, decoys, or false trails, and empower people to own problems and to take action to resolve them. They design systems (processes, people, and technology) to deal with the unexpected; this includes simulating accidents. Their organizational norms explicitly acknowledge that systems and their safeguards may not be perfectly, or even well, designed, and hence the organization builds in redundancy among people, communication, and media. A second strategy is to balance efficiency and reliability, which in other organizations creates paradoxical messages and conflicting goals. They "make it politically and economically possible for people to make decisions that are both short-run safe and long-run profitable ... rewarding the unsafe and not recognizing the safe leads inevitably to unsafe behavior and accidents" (Roberts and Bea, 2001, p. 74). Typically, organizational members are not rewarded for double-checking, and because this lack of double-checking is neither applied nor measured it cannot be managed. Further, accounting techniques must be developed to consider the full costs of accidents and low reliability. A third strategy is to communicate these larger, system-wide issues to all stakeholders. This includes how local actions affect other people and systems, what are the organization's consistent principles, and what is the central decision and communication system during crises.

Systems should be designed in ways that the various participants can learn more about the system and provide feedback about the system, through the system at the interface, as well as through complementary media. For example, Griffith (1993) shows that although managers frequently use systems to monitor subordinates' work in order to improve their "performance" or "quality," there is no technological reason such work monitoring features cannot be designed to be useful for and adaptable to the users themselves, thus including the system as part of the "team."

Woods *et al.* (1997) suggest several kinds of feedback that might be helpful in complex systems, without making the situation worse. Systems designs should improve communication among system and users, or connections to or awareness of other (social and technical) systems and tasks. Without these aspects, systems cannot provide adequate feedback, which in turn makes it difficult for users to track system behaviors and impacts, and thus know when and how to intervene. These should include information about when the system is having difficulty handling the situation, is taking extreme action, or is moving into the limits of system authority. But this requires sensing when a user or a system is still performing but having more difficulty doing so, or when they are reaching thresholds, while avoiding nuisance signals, false alarms, or distractions. New approaches to training for using automated systems should emphasize ongoing conceptual processes such as mental modeling and experimentation, rather than simply training on procedures, as not all situations can be known or simulated. Like most organizations, High Reliability Organizations have their share of accidents, but unlike most organizations, they exhibit what Weick and Sutcliffe (2001) call "mindfulness." This consists of (1) preoccupation with failure (avoid accumulation of failures), (2) reluctance to simplify interpretations (understand the underlying complexity of organizational reality), (3) sensitivity to operations (identify minor discrepancies, expect the unexpected, and support voicing concerns), (4) commitment to resilience (invest in approaches to recover rapidly from small errors), and (5) deference to expertise (value competence and experience) (p. 10).

Finally, understanding humans' roles in problems stemming from complex technology requires, according to Dekker (2005, p. 74), reconstructing the person's rationality during their operation of the system, involving their normal and often unnoticeable work context and points of view. Dekker assumes that people are making sense of their situation and experience – enacting their environment (Weick, 1995) – in order to take action and achieve goals, and do thus not typically perceive any divergence between their understanding and the "actual" situation. So analysis should focus not on why someone took the "wrong" action, but why they thought what they did was the "right" action – and especially when it *was* the right action. Usually, many factors influence these actions. For example, airport maps may be out-of-date, have variant versions, inadequate landmarks, disappearing clues in certain weather, context-dependent signs, etc.; so pilots following the official maps precisely may paradoxically create the accidents the maps are designed to prevent. One diagnostic approach is *naturalistic decision-making* (Orasanu and Connolly, 1993), which focuses on how people assess their situation at the time, shifting from retroactively explaining a "decision" to understanding local "sensemaking" in the context of uncertainty, ambiguity, and time pressure.

Apply and combine linkage and routines analysis

Linkage analysis

A socio-technical systems approach to analyzing variance interactions in organizational information systems was suggested by Bostrom and Heinen (1977a, 1977b). They argued that because information systems in organizational settings are socio-technical systems, interdependencies among processes (including non-computer-based tasks) will generate mismatches and downstream variances. So their approach was to create a matrix of all task processes, and identify which upstream processes affected which downstream processes (especially non-sequential relationships, where the output of one task might not have an effect until several tasks later). For each of these relationships, the analysis would then identify the extent to which the outputs and inputs are matched, or generate variance. The intersections of greatest variance would then be investigated to understand both the nature of the prior outputs and the intervening processes. In a way, this is applying cybernetic control analysis to either bring the system back within acceptable variances at the intersections, or gain double-loop learning to redesign the task processes and flows.

Goodman (2000) suggests a more general and conceptual *organizational linkage analysis* approach to identifying how errors develop and have significant negative consequences for other units in the organization, through both positive and negative feedback loops. It is not limited to physical consequences, is not focused on technology, and considers interactions among different kinds of errors. Linkage analysis considers interrelations among organizational levels or units, how activities and outcomes at one level or unit are connected (or not) to activities and outcomes at the same (horizontal) or a different (vertical) level, and conditions and mechanisms when activities and outcomes at one level affect activities and outcomes at another level or unit (i.e., not individual motivations or choices). Linkage analysis helps understand the overall complex change process by identifying *critical change pathways* – "a causal model that specifies the practices needed to build linkages between successful local changes and firm-level results" (Goodman and Rousseau, 2004, p. 8). More explicit linkage mapping may also generate more support for a proposed organizational change, partially by making assumptions and mental models more explicit and thus analyzable.

Organizational linkages are connections between activities, events, and outcomes, within and across units and levels (individual, group, and organizational), generating changes in one unit/level on another (either intended and positive, or unintended, or negative). While individual (unit/level) changes may positively or negatively affect other units and higher levels, it is also true that higher, system-level changes (technical subsystems, organizational subsystems, human systems, social subsystems) may have intended/unintended and positive/negative effects on lower levels. Linkage problems arise through the use of dissimilar measures across units, more interdependent organizational forms, more intermediary outcomes, more programmed or automatic activities, longer time periods (so constraints have more opportunity to attenuate the influence of changes), constraints (such as operations, communication, delays in reciprocal interdependencies), when actions of one unit generates negative outcomes for other units, more peripheral activities (as they are less observable, and their effects on core activities are difficult to identify), and interactions among these.

Goodman (2000) provides several tools for linkage analysis. Outcome coupling identifies the structural properties (outcome metrics) that affect influences of changes in one unit or level on change in another unit or level. Identifying different feedback systems uncovers loops created by additive, sequential, or reciprocal forms of organizational interdependence. For example, as reciprocal forms involve "multiple units interacting together in different combinations on different objects" (p. 35), influences of the changes in one unit on another are very difficult to assess. Understanding limiting conditions assesses the influences across units or levels, affected by the extent of intermediary activities or events, by the extent to which processes are automatic or routinized and thus create embedded effects, and by time lags between changes and effects. Analyzing compensatory process mechanisms (reactive problem-solving, focus of attention) helps explain linkages across units or levels. Finally, linkage analysis involves an understanding of the context of the social system.

Linkage analysis requires three main steps. First, identify linkages, based on interdependence, performance metrics across levels (affecting measurement intervals, criteria, causes and thus interventions), functional contribution of the unit to the organization, and time lags between change and observable results (involving the mediating and transformation processes connecting unit-level change to organizational-level outcomes). Second, identify the obstacles to those linkages. For example, in one case analysis, Goodman and Rousseau (2004) describe a negative feedback cycle between product development and manufacturing processes, and deviation-amplifying loops within product development. Third, develop processes to build those necessary linkages, such as shared multi-level motivation systems, both single-loop and double-loop cross-unit problem-solving mechanisms, and coordination and evaluation of horizontal and vertical linkages.

Routines analysis

Routines may also be analyzed at different levels: (1) a focal routine, (2) a repertoire of routines, or (3) the organization as an interdependent set of routines (Turner, 2005). Becker (2005) identified four somewhat overlapping components for analyzing organizational recurrent interaction patterns. These include:

(1) frequency of repeated sequences (requiring, of course, a definition of what is the same or variable behavior);
(2) fixed condition-action rules (requiring a way to assess the similarity of causal mechanisms defining what conditions generate cognitively and behaviorally what relevant actions to take);
(3) task variety and analyzability (standard organizational concepts); and
(4) content, process, and sequence, as well as variety and constraints. This last focus entails assessing:
   • content: what constitutes the action, actors, goals, artifacts, and context?

- process: what is the hierarchy of moves, related to both special-ization (different ways of accomplishing the tasks) and decom-position (different steps in the process)?
- sequence: what are the combinations or sequences of actions?
- lexical variety: how many steps and tasks are involved, and how does that vary from the mean?
- sequential variety: what is the range of combinations of those steps and tasks, and how does that vary from formal, expli-cit procedures, or across instances of the routine (Pentland, 2003)?
- combination constraints: what are the limits to the possible combinations, due either to interdependencies between actions, or from external institutions – e.g., technological, organiza-tional, cognitive?

Pentland and Feldman (2005) recommend the decomposition of an organizational "routine" into its ostensive, performative, and arti-fact aspects, and assess how these interrelate and diverge (Chapter 4). Based on their conceptualization of dead/live routines, artifacts, and ostensive/performative aspects of routines, Pentland and Feldman (2008) suggest several strategies for designing live, effective routines, including these: emphasize the ostensive (build up patterns of under-standing over time, from a variety of perspectives); understand the actors' perspectives and locations in paths of crucial functional events; be aware of equifinality of multiple actions producing the same narra-tive; consider how training and incentives reinforce patterned connec-tions between functional events; reconceptualize an organizational routine as incorporating user-based design points, not just decision and action points; constrain the routine through artifacts for func-tional events or key controls that must be stable, repetitive, consist-ent, high quality, mandatory, standardized, and auditable; accept and expect inherent variety, change, and unintended patterns and conse-quences in routines; and apply workflow management systems and business activity monitoring to describe actual action patterns instead of just the formal procedure artifact.

Another approach similar to linkage analysis, but applied to iden-tifying and analyzing routines, is to use an actor-based "narrative network" (Latour, 2005; Pentland and Feldman, 2008), which expli-citly represents the pattern of action of an organizational routine, including the variation possible in each performance of the routine, and the associations among the actors (human and otherwise, such as the artifacts associated with the routine) and the patterns of actions. Computational organizational analysis provides another way to model cycles and loops of routines (Carley and Prietula, 1994). As Anderson *et al.* (1999, p. 233) review, "the interaction of elements in a system produces surprising, emergent behavior that can be understood through formal models, even if those models cannot necessarily predict how a given system will evolve."

So the stability and implications of a routine and its effects depend to some extent on the level and scope of analysis, and which aspect of the routine, what time frame, and whose perspective, are invoked. Identifying, understanding, and repairing the relations among feedback loops in order to rein in URs does not necessarily require imposing a set of fixed rules or procedures. However, it does require making things more explicit, by describing what exactly is happening and not happening, identifying the interdependencies between local and more global routines, assessing the trade-offs of interdependent loops and/or better synchronizing them, emphasizing the need for actors to engage in interdependent and emergent sensemaking, such as through cross-functional teams (Anderson *et al.*, 1999) or roving liaisons, and identifying when process and feedback loops are mismatched.

Conclusion

Our most crucial suggestion is that all stakeholders (customers, organizational representatives, system designers, managers and executives, change agents, etc.) keep a holistic view of individual actors, their activities and local processes, interdependencies with other actors, activities, and processes, and the organizational context in mind. Tucker (2004) rightfully concludes that work and problem-solving processes must build-in awareness of interdependencies, as operational failures often are caused by some prior process, and consequences spread beyond the site of failure. This is to say that a UR is often the embedded and nearly invisible result of behaviors, decisions, omissions, and dysfunctional feedback from other locations. It is also to say that the attempt to resolve a UR in a given subunit, without due care for the value chains of which it is a link, is likely to create or exacerbate URs there and elsewhere. This is of course a fundamental implication of systems theory. A holistic approach means a systems approach, but without blind assumption of functionalism, to understanding URs, subroutines within routines, meta-routines, and units subsumed within routines. The overall system may be generally functional, with eddies of dysfunctionalities. But consequences of local actions seep out into higher loops, or are prevented from doing so. Local actors may be unaware of those consequences; other actors may be unaware of the cause or the source. A single dysfunctionality may in actuality precipitate a cascade of related, imitative errors, and efforts to address one UR in isolation are prone to failure or, worse, reinforce current or spawn new URs. That is, zooming in or out of a UR may reveal more URs not visible at the initial level; lower-level URs may be embedded in higher-level ones.

However, central to this holistic approach is the ability to identify the existence of a UR, or at least its symptoms, and being able to articulate the influences, components, processes, and outcomes of URs. Thus this book has attempted to describe a wide variety of manifestations of URs and their components, in the hope that being able to name and conceptualize the phenomenon is a necessary first step to understanding and analyzing it, which are necessary for resolving or mitigating it.

10 | *Summary and a tentative integrated model of unusual routines*

The allure of unusual routines

The impetus for this work was our puzzlement at the frustrations and disappointments so commonly felt both by organization members and by outsiders interacting with complex organizations. While both of us are academicians by trade, it seemed obvious that the imperfections we perceived in organizational functioning were not unique to our personal workplaces. This is an experience the authors had shared at various academic institutions and organizations, and many others outside of academe have described to us in ordinary conversation. Interestingly, very soon after beginning to describe the phenomenon, most people would immediately relate to the concept and begin to tell their stories of dealing with URs, although before then they would have had a hard time articulating the experience, its components or complexity, and certainly would not have called them URs. Neither of us expects that the real world should perfectly conform with our individual preferences (that would be a much poorer world, indeed!) or that organizational processes should be perfectly functional or reasonable (and the criteria for that would be impossible to agree upon) – but nonetheless we both wondered just how it is that so much of everyday organizational life and interactions with organizations could seem so nonsensical. In the broadest sense, our aim has been to try to understand a subset of the imperfection of human communication behaviors within and with organizations, imperfections that might possibly be resolved or mitigated.

We gave the intentionally oxymoronic name *unusual routines* to the object of our curiosity: systematic (not necessarily frequent, and systematic only in specific interdependencies or contexts) interaction patterns and processes, in an organizational context, which display dysfunctionalities, though not apparent to some or all participants, or create unreasonable costs, typically for someone outside the local process, yet are resistant to efforts to mitigate them, which may have one or more levels, and which may occur over short and/or long time periods. The relative permanence of these patterns and processes suggested the noun in that term: they are *routine* in the sense of being features of "how things are," manifest as repeated and systematic processes. Unusual routines are repeated and change-resistant precisely because there is some process that generates, reinforces, or hides the initial problem. Further, they become routinized, and embedded in and with specific routines.

The adjective perhaps can be misunderstood: by unusual we mean to suggest that a good case can be made to see them as problematic in some substantial aspect – unusual in the sense that at least some part of the outcome would seem unusual/problematic by at least some stakeholders, if they knew the outcome was associated with the UR. Further, while URs in general may be recognized as a fairly common experience in general, and any particular one may occur systematically (in some sense), the second aspect of the unusual here is that one or more of the people engaged in the routine rarely experience this particular routine because it may be activated only by an infrequent particular set of circumstances, or possibly frequently across people but infrequently for any particular person, contributing to the difficulty in identifying, understanding, and resolving.

Beyond the question of whether something that is systemic and pervasive can be unusual, another objection is more general: that is, that the term implies unusual routines are a small subset of organizational routines, which otherwise are primarily functional. The argument there is that in fact the classical tenet of functionalism and systems theory that all or most routines are functional and maintain equilibrium is a myth – indeed, completely functional routines may be the unusual phenomenon. So the adjective severely underestimates the overall pervasiveness of URs, and continues to maintain the rationalistic assumption of functioning routines as the norm. This is an interesting empirical question, and the result would likely depend on the granularity and the scope of analysis (in terms of the extent of ramifications throughout multiple system levels and time periods) (Becker, 2005; Becker and Zirpoli, 2008).

Our own view is that (1) many routines seem to work more or less well, within the understandable, though still improvable, constraints of humans, resources, and settings, although (2) optimal functioning (setting aside the definitional and values aspects) is not as frequent as most people might benefit from; (3) beyond the issue of expectations, optimal functioning should not be assumed either practically or conceptually; and (4) people, systems, and organizations may attempt to be rational but are significantly bounded and in some respects may be inherently or intentionally irrational, at least from the perspective of different actors and feedback cycles; nevertheless (5) the evidence from Chapters 7 and 8 indicates a wide range of failure of proper routines; and (6) there is a subset of routines that are unusual, in the sense of a particular process infrequently experienced by any particular person, largely unidentified as such, occurring sufficiently frequently and systematically in general to generate negative consequences whether local or distant, and both created and sustained through one or more dysfunctional feedback loops.

Our preliminary models

The Canadian sociologist Benjamin Singer provided us with a starting point, in his articles on feedback, errors, and crazy systems (1973, 1977, 1978, 1980). These are complex networks of interaction (among individuals, among organizational subunits, among organizations or other social objects) which display unpleasant dysfunctionalities in their operations. Singer presented a second level below these in the model, what he referred to as Kafka circuits. His three Kafka circuits – work, delay, and error – are much closer to one's immediate experience, and the term *circuit* suggests the feeling one has of being trapped or constrained by one's circumstances, but also a loop of energy and activity, probably not involving learning, but possibly a short-circuiting of the large system. Conceptually, we saw the circuits being created locally and accumulating globally into the organizational traits indicating a system gone crazy (but only, apparently, to some) – subroutines of more general URs. Other literature led us to identify particular organizational or personal costs we believed Kafka circuits imposed. We believed, along with Singer, that it might often be difficult for organization members to perceive URs, since they developed incrementally, and due to several described barriers. This might explain, at least in part, why there was little or no action taken to address them as problems. At this point we had an essentially static model of URs with accompanying subroutines, a descriptive

conceptualization primarily intended to catalog some of their characteristics (see Figure 1.1).

The cases of Chapter 2 pointed out the paradox that well-justified
implementations of sophisticated ICTs can foster a wide range of
problems and negative subroutines, due to a wide variety of causes,
and exhibiting a wide variety of symptoms (Table 2.1). The customer
service literature and cases of Chapter 3 introduced the notion that
organizations frequently fail in either allowing or seeking feedback,
with again a wide variety of individual, system, and organizational
causes, and a wide variety of short-term, intermediate, and long-term
negative consequences for their business, their managers and representatives, and their customers (Tables 3.1 and 3.2). This was evidence to us that the routine was a structural element in itself rather
than a summary generalization about people's behaviors, or due to
the typical ICT enemies of "resistance to change" or "uninformed and
untrained users," or the typical customer service enemies of "uncaring organizations," "difficult customers," "discourteous service representatives" or simply "the system." Two additional aspects of URs
were highlighted from these discussions. First, organizational actors
such as system designers and users can all behave rationally, and with
due regard for others' well being, and yet be effectively trapped by the
routine and its subroutines. Second, the local UR typically generates
costs or disadvantages to someone else, in another unit, the larger systems, or outside the organization (described in Chapter 8 as a social
dilemma); and those may in turn generate subsequent URs (described
in Chapter 4 as workarounds).

Chapter 4 then reviewed central theories necessary to understand
the development, (dys)functioning, persistence, and effects of URs –
systems theory, sensemaking theory, diffusion of innovation theory,
socio-technical systems theory, and organizational routines theory.
Routines theory provides a conceptual foundation for the general
topic of URs, although routines theory itself does not much consider
this phenomenon, and the other theories are necessary for elaborat-
ing the understanding. Table 4.1 summarized how the definition and
components of organizational routines, along with how they vary and
change (especially workarounds and meta-routines), and what kinds
of positive and negative outcomes seem to be associated with them.

With this background, we understood that the persistent and
systemic nature of URs – the characteristics which most clearly

distinguished an usual routine from a simple error or mistake – might largely be the result of feedback loops (their presence, absence, dysfunctionality, content, and timing), at two levels. Given that organizations are rarely monolithic and uniform with regard to everyday practices, our thought was that various factors including dysfunctional feedback affected the interaction among people, units, and processes, generating the initial UR. However, a similar range of causes may exist to affect the feedback about the problem, creating a second-level, or meta-unusual routine. We extended our conception of levels by embedding the subroutines within the routines, and showing particular elements of the organizational environment as foundationally supporting URs (see Figure 4.1). The other major addition was the notion of an organizational substrate which provided general support for URs, an environment conducive to the development and sustenance of URs. These are factors in the organization which themselves are not parts of URs and not confined to URs, but contribute to them. These complement other causes of URs, developed in Chapters 1 through 3.

Some of the developed concepts were used to derive five propositions about the mitigation of, and resistance to, URs, explored in the extensive case provided in Chapter 5 (guided by the questions listed in Table 5.1). This study was initially interested in URs associated with a campus-wide implementation of an ICT (an electronic mail network), but quickly uncovered much more general and widespread URs (summarized in Table 5.2). The study pointed us toward some specific conceptual additions to the model. We saw the espoused values of the organization as a key source of support for URs (Argyris, 1985): often a functionally problematic interaction pattern (i.e., one which increased costs or led to faulty decision-making) served as a symbolic enactment or unfortunate byproduct of some important organization value (such as inclusiveness) (Chapters 8 and 9). We also got a sense from the interviews that the interactants often invoked pre-existing scripts (digressing, trivializing, reframing, scapegoating, and expanding; similar to implementation games; Bardach, 1977) and saw these as simultaneously enabling the interaction in particular directions but also constraining the interaction in particular other directions. It also appeared that subunit coupling, relatively tight or loose, should be added to the model, as this construct offered a good degree of explanatory power, and reflects Weick's (1995) thinking on the

extent to which sensemaking can occur, and influence other organizational units. It also seemed useful to distinguish between single-loop
and double-loop change (Tables 6.1 and 6.2), as a way of understanding the persistence of URs (which single-loop change might alter only
superficially, and double-loop change might alter substantially, each
affected by different forms of inertia grounded in the organizational
substrate), while also reflecting an important concept in theories of
organizational learning and systems theory (Huber, 1991). So the
study helped us develop the revised model of Figure 6.1.

It might be thought that, once these components of URs were explicitly identified and understood, participants could then begin to mitigate or resolve URs by providing both single-loop and double-loop
feedback. However, Chapter 7 reviewed a wide range of individual
and organizational barriers to, or dysfunctional forms of, feedback
loops that both contribute to as well as result from URs (Box 7.1).
Chapter 8 showed that many concepts, from individual-level cognitive
and psychological limits, to organizational deviance, to social-level
approaches to risk and discourse about evidence, all reflect overlapping aspects of URs (Box 8.1, 8.2).

A proposed integrative model of unusual routines

We now revise our model one last time in this book (but encourage
further development of the URs model), incorporating the essential
elements of the earlier models, and generalizing it to consider the situation of a complex organization with existing URs processing a perturbation to its equilibrium (some sort of planned, intended change)
or dealing with some other disturbance to its steady-state functioning
(some sort of problem, existing UR, accident, crisis, threat, challenge,
opportunity, regulatory intervention, or large-scale management initiative). Our thought here is that URs tend to persist (i.e., are quite
stable, as organizational processes), absent such a disturbance in
the current state of the organization; while such disturbances might
heighten existing URs as well as generate new ones, but also provide
opportunities for revealing and resolving them.

The model (Figure 10.1) is circular, incorporating paths of both
single-loop and double-loop change in the organization. That is to
say, URs tend to create a substantial amount of inertia (hence their
change-resistance), due to their intimate connection to foundational

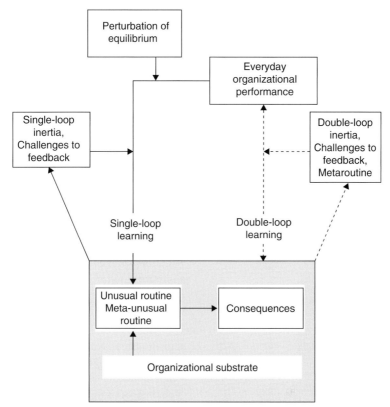

Figure 10.1 Concept-level integrated model of unusual routines.

aspects of the organization's culture, the inherent limitations of human beings as organizational actors, their developing embeddedness, and their reinforcement or obscuring through dysfunctional feedback. Espoused values and established interaction scripts are particularly salient dimensions of the organizational culture in this regard. Subsumed in the diagram are elements introduced in our developmental models. Table 10.1 provides some of the primary elements of the components in Figure 10.1.

Innovations, including (recursively) deliberate efforts to mitigate URs, are likely to produce only relatively superficial changes along the single-loop path. Those rarer cases in which some sort of substantive change occurs in the organizational substrate (via the double-loop path) are the ones in which there is the possibility of substantive

Table 10.1 *Primary components of general concepts in Figure 10.1*

Component	Elements
Everyday organizational performances	• denial • manipulation • non-responsiveness • rigidity • suspicion, secrecy • in-use enactments of beliefs and values
Perturbation	• change • crisis • environmental turbulence • external stakeholders, pressure • ICT implementation • imminent failure • innovation • new problem • unmanageable complexity
Single-loop inertia	• air of rationality • apathy, confusion • individual and organizational challenges to feedback • legitimation cues • normalcy • psychological and cognitive heuristics and limitations
Double-loop inertia	• externalization of costs/harms • fragmentation • individual and organizational challenges to feedback • localized incentives, self-interest • loose subunit coupling • manipulation of information or system • organizational and social processes • technical features of system

Table 10.1 (*cont.*)

Component	Elements
Unusual routine	• subroutines • symptoms • visibility • meta-routine
Organizational substrate	• goals • causes from individual, system, organization, and interactions • scripts • subunit coupling • symbolic value of practices • social and technical enablers • espoused beliefs, values • focus/balance on process/relations and decision/content
Consequences	• externalities • group process losses • positive and negative • short-term, intermediate, long-term • varying for different stakeholders • workarounds

change in the URs. However, as Chapters 7 and 8 reviewed, many obstacles, behaviors, and situations work against feedback achieving the desired results: second-loop awareness and resolution; avoiding reinforcing the initial, or creating more, URs through the feedback process itself; or even providing beneficial feedback at all.

The diagram is closed at the top, indicating that the everyday organizational performance of behaviors and operations tend to reinforce the change-resistance of existing URs. Single- and double-loop learning are shown where they are possible, when the organization is in a state of flux (i.e., consequential change). In essence, this is a model of a meta-routine (Chapters 4 and 8).

We see the normal state of a complex organization as essentially static from the perspective of second-loop learning, which is to say that most interactions within the organization lie along the left side of the figure. In this conception, the relationship of URs to the organizational substrate is crucial. Similar to Lewin's (1943) force-field analysis, we see an implict/potential cost/benefit trade-off occurring whenever some force has the potential to disturb URs. As long as the total perceived benefits outweigh the total perceived costs, for those who could resolve or mitigate the UR, our expectation is that the URs will remain stable. The more fundamental problems with URs, however, are that the "benefits" and the "costs" are often highly ambiguous or difficult to identify, distributed near and far, across different people and units, and thus they are highly subject to individual, organizational, and social processing biases. Thus not everyone even knows about the costs or about the benefits, and everyone is evaluating quite different sets of benefits and costs (depending to some extent on the substrate of espoused beliefs and values, and how they are enacted in use) without much awareness of the benefits or costs to others, and often receiving and reinforcing (perceived) benefits precisely because of (non-perceived and reinforced) costs to others. Perceived costs are reduced by externalization onto third parties, various workarounds, and (local) reinforcement of the UR from the organizational substrate. So there is probably very little actual cost/benefit analysis actually going on, and most of that is highly biased or under-informed.

Other factors foster inertia about URs within the organization. No doubt, stability is beneficial to an organization, and homeostasis is central to systems, but given that learning necessarily involves change, inertia (such as continuing to perform, especially efficiently, a formal encoded routine) is an organizational force foundationally opposed to organizational learning (Cohen *et al.*, 1996; Fiol and Lyles, 1985). Importantly, systems theory, and second-loop learning theory, emphasize homeostasis as requiring adapting to changing environments, not simply maintaining the same levels of the same processes (Barnett, 1997).

Single-loop learning is more easily generated than double-loop learning, but it consists of relatively shallow change in the organization, and, as noted above, due to both inertia and challenges to feedback, often simply reinforces the initial problem or creates, through local workarounds, other problems, often for other participants

(Edmondson, 1996). We see perceptual barriers, challenges to feedback, and workarounds as noteworthy contributors to single-loop inertia (and in the case of workarounds, they often reinforce organizational inertia without the organization knowing it, precisely through only local and informal learning). At both the individual and collective levels, the tendency for organization members to view daily operations as "normal" (as in many of the mini-cases described in Chapter 3) inhibits their ability to perceive a problem as problematic; whatever workarounds they might devise lessens the stimulus to do so.

Double-loop learning involves change in the organizational substrate, and hence is both more rare and more consequential to the daily functioning of the organization (Argyris and Schon, 1978), although it too (perhaps much more so) is vulnerable to inertia and challenges to feedback. Challenges to feedback, loose coupling among subunits and satisficing at individual, subunit, and organization levels make particular contributions to double-loop inertia by delaying, lessening, or preventing awareness across the boundaries. Active double-loop feedback can also just as well create or exacerbate URs as mitigate them. In short, feedback (in general) is not a panacea for URs (Chapter 7).

What satisfices at one place in an organization may well create costs at another; there were a number of illustrations of that cost-shifting in the large case study (Chapters 5 and 6). In turn, a satisficing response at a second location to the costs externalized from the first location may well create costs at yet another location. While loose coupling may permit subunits to optimize internally at the expense of other subunits, what degree of coupling (without useful feedback to the prior phases) does exist can induce a cascade effect of this sort, eventually settling at a condition which is tolerable (largely because it becomes seen as "routine") to most of the subunits. The net result may be a collection of subunits, each with a bearable load of URs, but an organization riddled with them to a damaging level; a cynic might comment that this seems to be the case with many public bureaucracies. It is hard to imagine, but theoretically possible from the perspective of URs, for the opposite condition to develop, too – that is, many units are performing at suboptimal levels (possibly because they don't have the imagination or will to generate local workarounds), but, because they are not spewing URs, the organization as a whole could be functioning quite well, especially if higher-level organizational goals and values are thereby nurtured.

In our view, individual venality, incompetence, malice, or lack of engagement are not root causes of URs – unless venality, incompetence, malice and lack of engagement are themselves repetitive, systemic, and reinforced or ignored, constituting a particular kind of UR (Chapter 8)! Rather, organizational actors are human beings, and hence finite, adaptable, sensemaking, and diverse in their awareness of the organization's functioning as a system; often their best attempts at managing their and others' daily life in the organization may create group processes and organizational procedures that not only generate but also reinforce URs (Chapter 8). Their responses to stimuli tend to be localized to their positions within the organization, and their satisficing behaviors (including workarounds) may thereby consist of cost-displacing or cost-creating actions without their realizing it.

Conclusion

While our primary intent in this work was to gain some insights into how organizations develop URs and why suboptimality and even acknowledged dysfunctionality often seem to be as good as things can get inside complex organizations, we have painted something of a dismal picture of organizations and organizing behaviors with this analysis. In light of so much force maintaining the status quo (or, rather, various status quos) within an organization, one might wonder just how anything might disturb the equilibrium enough to induce or even permit the identification, analysis, mitigation, or resolution of URs, especially meta-URs. We see a threshold level some perturbation must exceed before double-loop learning occurs, and expect the level is generally quite high. Most often it seems these perturbations come from outside the organization, in the form of regulatory intervention, fiscal crisis, legal action, customer complaints or boycotts, or market threat. The "Black Swan" event – low probability but high consequence – described by Taleb (2007) is an intriguing case, in that it is more likely to force a large-scale rethinking of the organization's functioning than would a deliberate, planned effort. Even a genuine crisis, though, may fall short of that threshold, inducing a system that is superficially different but has not really learned. Whatever the impetus, planned change efforts are subject to paradoxes and conflicting goals that may cause additional URs (Argyris, 1990; Chapter 8). However, Chapter 9 provided a variety of recommendations from the research and concepts in Chapters 7 and 8 about ways to resolve or mitigate the specific issues, with implications for the general problem of URs.

Essentially, it appears that unusual routines are the sometimes visible, sometimes invisible, artifacts of the staggering complexity of human interaction in complex organizations, which may well explain how efforts to improve organizations so often make them more complex, but not necessarily better. On the field of communication interactions, the unusual becomes the embedded routine, the skilled response becomes the awareness blindfold. On the field of organizational design, the innovative becomes the ineffective procedure, the reasonable becomes the irrational. The nature and unusual outcomes of organizational sensemaking seem highly dependent on the context of, the people participating in, and the subroutines of, the routine.

References

1888 Press Release (2009, March 28). "VIP corporate housing proves that employee relocation business is still thriving." Online, available at: www.1888pressrelease.com/vip-corporate-housing-proves-that-employee-relocation-busine-pr-108880.html

Adler, P. S., Goldoftas, B., and Levine, D. I. (1999). "Flexibility versus efficiency? A case study of model changeovers in the Toyota production system." *Organization Science*, 10(1), 43–68.

Alavi, M., and Leidner, D. E. (2001). "Review: knowledge management and knowledge management systems: conceptual foundations and research issues." *MIS Quarterly*, 25, 107–136.

Alderfer, C. (1987). "An intergroup perspective on group dynamics." In J. W. Lorsch (ed.), *Handbook of Organizational Behavior* (pp. 190–222). Englewood Cliffs: Prentice Hall.

Allen, M., and Brady, R. (1997). "Total quality management, organizational commitment, perceived organizational support, and intraorganizational communication." *Management Communication Quarterly*, 10(3), 316–41.

Anderson, P., Meyer, A., Eisenhardt, K., Carley, K., and Pettigrew, A. (1999). "Introduction to the special issue: applications of complexity theory to organization science." *Organization Science*, 10(3), 233–6.

Andreoni, J., and Bergstrom, T. (1996). "Do government subsidies increase the private supply of public goods?" *Public Choice*, 88(3–4), 295–308.

Ang, S., Straub, D. W., Cummings, L. L., and Earley, P. C. (1993). "Effects of information technology on feedback seeking." *Information Systems Research*, 4, 240–61.

Archer, M. (1995). *Realist Social Theory: The Morphogenetic Approach*. New York: Cambridge University Press.

Argyris, C. (1985). *Strategy, Change, and Defensive Routines*. New York: Harper Business.

(1986). "Skilled incompetence." *Harvard Business Review*, 64, 74–9.

(1988). "Crafting a theory of practice: the case of organizational paradoxes." In R. Quinn and K. Cameron (eds.), *Paradox and*

Transformation: Toward a Theory of Change in Organization and Management (pp. 255–78). Cambridge, MA: Ballinger Publishing.

(1990). *Overcoming Organizational Defenses: Facilitating Organizational Learning.* Needham: Allyn and Bacon.

(2002). "Double-loop learning, teaching, and research." *Academy of Management Learning and Education*, 1(2), 206–18.

Argyris, C., and Schon, D. (1978). *Organizational Learning: A Theory of Action Perspective.* Reading, MA: Addison-Wesley.

Arkes, H. R., and Blumer, C. (1985). "The psychology of sunk cost." *Organizational Behavior and Human Decision Processes*, 35, 124–40.

Ashforth, B. (1994). "Petty tyranny in organizations." *Human Relations*, 47, 755–78.

Aydin, C. E., and Rice, R. E. (1992). "Bringing social worlds together: computers as catalysts for new interactions in health care organizations." *Journal of Health and Social Behavior*, 33, 168–85.

Bainbridge, L. (1983). "Ironies of automation." *Automatica*, 19, 775–9. Reprinted in J. Rasmussen, K. Duncan, and J. Leplat (eds.) (1987), *New Technology and Human Error* (pp. 276–83). Chichester: Wiley.

Ballard, D., and Seibold, D. (2003). "Communicating and organizing in time: a meso level model of organizational temporality." *Management Communication Quarterly*, 16, 380–415.

Banerjee, A. V., Duflo, E., and Glennerster, R. (2008). "Putting a band-aid on a corpse: incentives for nurses in the Indian public health care system." *Journal of the European Economic Association*, 6(2–3), 487–500.

Banks, S. P., and Riley, P. (1993). "Structuration theory as an ontology for communication research." In S. Deetz (ed.), *Communication Yearbook*, vol. 16 (pp. 167–96). Newbury Park: Sage.

Bantz, C. R (1992). "Organizing and the social psychology of organizing." In K. L. Hutchinson (ed.), *Readings in Organizational Communication* (pp. 90–9). Dubuque: Wm. C. Brown Publishers.

Bantz, C. R., and Smith, D. H. (1977). "A critique and experimental test of Weick's model of organizing." *Communication Monographs*, 44, 171–84.

Bardach, E. (1977). *The Implementation Game.* Cambridge, MA: MIT Press.

Barley, S. R. (1986). "Technology as an occasion for structuring: evidence from observations of CT scanners and the social order of radiology departments." *Administrative Science Quarterly*, 31, 78–108.

Barlow, J., and Moller, C. (1996). *Complaint is a Gift: Using Customer Feedback as a Strategic Tool.* San Francisco: Berrett-Koehler Publishers, Inc.

Barnes, L. (1981). "Managing the paradox of organizational trust." *Harvard Business Review, 59* (March–April), 107–16.

Barnett, G. (1997). "Organizational communication systems: the traditional perspective." In G. Barnett and L. Thayer (eds.), *Organization – Communication, Emerging Perspectives V: The Renaissance in Systems Thinking* (pp. 1–46). Greenwich, CT: Ablex Publishing Corp.

Barry, B., and Bateman, T. (1996). "A social trap analysis of the management of diversity." *Academy of Management Review, 21*(3), 757–90.

Bateson, G. (1972). *Steps to an Ecology of Mind.* New York: Ballantine.

Bateson, G., Jackson, D., Haley, J., and Weakland, J. (1963). "A note on the double bind." *Family Process, 2,* 154–61.

Bazerman, M. H., and Watkins, M. D. (2004). *Predictable Surprises: The Disasters You Should Have Seen Coming, and How to Prevent Them.* Boston: Harvard Business School Press.

Bear, R., and Hill, D. J. (1994). "Excuse making: a prevalent company response to complaints?" *Journal of Consumer Satisfaction, Dissatisfaction and Complaining Behavior, 7,* 143–51.

Becker, M. C. (2004). "Organizational routines: a review of the literature." *Industrial and Corporate Change, 13*(4), 643–78.

(2005). "A framework for applying organizational routines in empirical research: linking antecedents, characteristics and performance outcomes of recurrent interaction patterns." *Industrial and Corporate Change, 14*(5), 817–46.

Becker, M. C., and Zirpoli, F. (2008). "Applying organizational routines in analyzing the behavior of organizations." *Journal of Economic Behavior and Organization, 66*(1), 128–48.

Bedeian, A. G. (1995). "Workplace envy." *Organizational Dynamics, 23,* 49–56.

Beniger, J. R. (1986). *The Control Revolution.* Cambridge, MA: Harvard University Press.

Benson, J. (1977). "Organizations: a dialectical view." *Administrative Science Quarterly, 22,* 1–21.

Bertalanffy, L. von. (1968). *General System Theory: Foundations, Development, Applications.* New York: George Braziller.

Bitner, M., Booms, B., and Mohr, L. (1994). "Critical service encounters: the employee's viewpoint." *Journal of Marketing, 58*(October), 95–106.

Black, N. (2004). *Two Sides to Every Coin … The Customer isn't Always Right!* Littleton: DNJ Books.

Blumberg, P. (1989). "Ignorance in the 'knowledge' society: the technically uninformed customer." In *The Predatory Society: Deception in the American Marketplace* (pp. 59–84). New York: Oxford University Press.

Boettger, R. D., and Greer, C. R. (1994). "On the wisdom of rewarding A while hoping for B." *Organization Science*, 5(4), 569–82.

Bostrom, R. P., and Heinen, J. S. (1977a). "MIS problems and failures: a socio-technical perspective, part I: the causes." *MIS Quarterly*, 1(3), 7–32.

(1977b). "MIS problems and failures: a socio-technical perspective; part II: the application of socio-technical theory." *MIS Quarterly*, 1(4), 11–28.

Bowers, J. (1995). "Making it work: a field study of a 'CSCW' network." *The Information Society*, 11, 189–207.

Bramson, R. (1988). *Coping with Difficult People*. New York: Dell Paperbacks.

Brenders, D. (1987). "Fallacies in the coordinated management of meaning: a philosophy of language critique of the hierarchical organization of coherent conversation and related theory." *Quarterly Journal of Speech*, 73(3), 329–48.

Brett, J., Shapiro, D., and Lytle, A. (1998). "Breaking the bonds of reciprocity in negotiations." *Academy of Management Journal*, 41(4), 410–24.

Brown, J., and Duguid, P. (1996). "Organizational learning and communities-of-practice: toward a unified view of working, learning, and innovation." In M. Cohen and L. Sproull (eds.), *Organizational Learning* (pp. 58–82). Thousand Oaks: Sage.

Brown, W. J., Malveau, R. C., McCormick III, H. W., and Mowbray, T. J. (1998). *Antipatterns: Refactoring Software, Architectures, and Projects in Crisis*. New York: John Wiley & Sons.

Brunsson, N. (1985). *The Irrational Organization: Irrationality as a Basis for Organizational Action and Change*. New York: Wiley.

Cameron, K. (1986). "Effectiveness as paradox: consensus and conflict in conceptions of organizational effectiveness." *Management Science*, 32(5), 539–53.

Cameron, K., and Quinn, R. (1988). "Organizational paradox and transformation." In R. Quinn and K. Cameron (eds.), *Paradox and Transformation: Toward a Theory of Change in Organization and Management* (pp. 1–18). Cambridge, MA: Ballinger Publishing.

Carley, K., and Prietula, M. J. (eds.) (1994). *Computational Organization Theory*. Hillsdale: Lawrence Erlbaum Associates.

CBC Marketplace. (February 20, 2005). "Insider interview: Paula Courtney on surveying customer dissatisfaction." Online, available at: www. cbc.ca/consumers/market/files/services/complaining/courtney.html

Cerulo, K. (2006). *Never Saw it Coming: Cultural Challenges to Envisioning the Worst*. Chicago: Chicago University Press.

Chambliss, D. (1996). *Beyond Caring*. Chicago: University of Chicago Press.

Charell, R. (1974). *How I Turn Ordinary Complaints into Thousands of Dollars: The Diary of a Tough Customer*. New York: Stein & Day.

(1985). *Satisfaction Guaranteed: The Ultimate Guide to Consumer Self-defense*. New York: Simon & Schuster.

Charlton, S. G. (2002). "Selecting measures for human factors tests." In S. G. Charlton and T. G. O'Brien (eds.), *Handbook of Human Factors Testing and Evaluation* (2nd edn, pp. 37–53). Mahwah: Lawrence Erlbaum.

Choo, C. W. (1998). *The Knowing Organization: How Organizations Use Information to Construct Meaning, Create Knowledge, and Make Decisions*. New York: Oxford University Press.

Ciborra, C. (1987). "Reframing the role of computers in organizations – the transaction costs approach." *Office: Technology and People*, 3, 17–38.

Cohen, M. D., and Bacdayan, P. (1994). "Organizational routines are stored as procedural memory: evidence from a laboratory study." *Organization Science*, 5(4), 554–68.

Cohen, M. D., March, J. G., and Olsen, J. P. (1972). "Garbage can model of organizational choice." *Administrative Science Quarterly*, 17, 1–15.

Cohen, M. D., Burkhardt, R., Dosi, G., Egidi, M., Marengo, L., Warglien, M., and Winter, S. (1996). "Routines and other recurring action patterns of organizations: contemporary research issues." *Industrial and Corporate Change*, 5(3), 653–98.

Cohen, S. (1980). *Folk Devils and Moral Panics: The Creation of the Mods and Rockers*. Oxford: Martin Robertson.

Cole, R. (1999). *Managing Quality Fads: How American Business Learned to Play the Quality Game*. New York: Oxford University Press.

Conger, S., Cooper, J., Schofield, J., and Stein, E. (1996). "Open peer commentaries on LaFrance, M. (1996). Why we trust computers too much." *Technology Studies*, 3(2), 179–95.

Contractor, N. S. (1994). "Self-organizing systems perspective in the study of organizational communication." In B. Kovacic (ed.), *New Approaches to Organizational Communication* (pp. 39–66). Albany: SUNY Press.

Contractor, N. S., and Eisenberg, E. M. (1990). "Communication networks and new media in organizations." In J. Fulk and C. Steinfield (eds.), *Organizations and Communication Technology* (pp. 143–72). Newbury Park: Sage.

Contractor, N. S., and Seibold, D. R. (1993). "Theoretical frameworks for the study of structuring processes in Group Decision Support Systems." *Human Communication Research*, 19(4), 528–63.

Cooper, S. D. (2000). *Unusual Routines and Computer Mediated Communication Systems.* Unpublished dissertation. New Brunswick: Graduate School, Rutgers, The State University of New Jersey.

Cronen, V., Johnson, K., and Lannamann, J. (1982). "Paradoxes, double binds, and reflexive loops: an alternative theoretical perspective." *Family Process*, 20, 91–112.

Cronen, V., Pearce, W. Barnett, and Snavely, L. (1979). "A theory of rule-structure and types of episodes and a study of perceived enmeshment in undesired repetitive patterns (URPs)." *Communication Yearbook*, vol. 3 (pp. 225–40). New Brunswick: Transaction Press.

Cross, J. G., and Guyer, M. J. (1980). *Social Traps.* Ann Arbor: University of Michigan Press.

Crozier, M. (1964). *The Bureaucratic Phenomenon.* Chicago: University of Chicago Press.

Culnan, M. (1989). "Designing information systems to support customer feedback: an organizational message system perspective." In J. DeGross, J. Henderson, and B. Konsynski (eds.), *Proceedings of the Tenth International Conference on Information Systems* (pp. 305–13). Boston, December.

Cyert, R. M. (1978). "The management of universities of constant or decreasing size." *Public Administration Review*, 38, 344–9.

Cyert, R. M., and March, J. G. (1963). *A Behavioral Theory of the Firm.* Englewood Cliffs: Prentice Hall.

Daft, R. L., and Lengel, R. H. (1986). "Organizational information requirements, media richness and structural design." *Management Science*, 32(5), 554–71.

Davenport, T. H., Eccles, R. G., and Prusak, L. (1992). "Information politics." *Sloan Management Review*, 34(1), 53–65.

Davidow, M. (2003). "Organizational responses to customer complaints: what works and what doesn't." *Journal of Service Research*, 5(3), 225–50.

Davidow, W., and Malone, D. (1992). *The Virtual Corporation: Structuring and Revitalizing the Corporation for the 21st Century.* New York: HarperCollins.

Dawes, R. M. (1980). "Social dilemmas." *Annual Review of Psychology*, 31, 169–93.

Deetz, S. A. (1992). *Democracy in an Age of Corporate Colonization.* Albany: State University of New York.

(1995). *Transforming Communication, Transforming Business.* Cresskill: Hampton Press.

DeGreene, K. (1990). "The turbulent-field environment of sociotechnical systems: beyond metaphor." *Behavioral Science*, 35(1), 49–59.

Dekker, S. W. A. (2005). *Ten Questions about Human Error: A New View of Human Factors and System Safety.* Mahwah: Lawrence Erlbaum Associates.

DeLong, D., and Fahey, L. (2000). "Diagnosing cultural barriers to knowledge management." *Academy of Management Executive*, 14(4), 113–27.

Deming, W. Edwards (1986). *Out of the Crisis.* Cambridge, MA: Massachusetts Institute for Technology, Center for Advanced Engineering Study.

Dillard, C., Browning, L. D., Sitkin, S., and Sutcliffe, K. (2000). "Impression management and the use of procedures at the Ritz-Carlton: moral standards and dramaturgical discipline." *Communication Studies*, 51(4), 404–14.

Dixon, N. M. (1993). *Organizational Learning* (Report 111–93). Ontario: The Conference Board of Canada.

Dorner, D. (1989/1996, English translation). *The Logic of Failure: Recognizing and Avoiding Error in Complex Situations.* New York: Basic Books.

Dossick, C. S., and Neff, G. (2010). "Organizational divisions in BIM-enabled commercial construction." *Construction Engineering Management*, 136(4), 459–67.

Duffy, M. K., and Shaw, J. D. (2000). "The Salieri syndrome: consequences of envy in groups." *Small Group Research*, 31(1), 3–23.

Durkheim, E. (1966/1938). *The Rules of Sociological Method.* New York: Free Press.

Dutton, W. H. (1996). "Network rules of order: regulating speech in public electronic fora." *Media, Culture and Society*, 18, 269–90.

Dutton, W. H., and Kraemer, K. L. (1980). "Automating bias." *Society*, 17(2), 36–41.

Eco, U. (1994). "How to replace a driver's license." In *How to Travel with a Salmon and Other Essays* (pp. 9–18). New York: Harcourt Brace.

Edmondson, A. C. (1996). "Learning from mistakes is easier said than done: group and organizational influences on the detection and correction of human error." *The Journal of Applied Behavioral Science*, 40(1), 66–90.

(1999). "Psychological safety and learning behavior in work teams." *Administrative Science Quarterly*, 44(4), 350–83.

(2004). "Learning from failure in health care: frequent opportunities, pervasive barriers." *Quality and Safety in Health Care, 31*(Suppl. 2), ii3–ii9.

Edmondson, A. C., Ferlins, E., Feldman, L., and Bohmer, R. (2005). "The recovery window: organizational learning following ambiguous threats." In M. Farjoun and W. Starbuck (eds.), *Organization at the Limit: Lessons from the Columbia Disaster* (pp. 220–45). Boston: Blackwell.

Edney, J. (1980). "The commons problems: alternative perspectives." *American Psychologist, 35*, 131–50.

Ehrlich, S. (1987). "Strategies for encouraging successful adoption of office communication systems." *ACM Transactions on Office Information Systems, 5*(4), 340–57.

Einhorn, H. J., and Hogarth, R. M. (1978). "Confidence in judgment: persistence in the illusion of validity." *Psychological Review, 85*, 395–416.

Eisenberg, E. M. (1984). "Ambiguity as strategy in organizational communication." *Communication Monographs, 51*, 227–42.

Eisenberg, E. M., and Goodall, H. L. (1997). *Organizational Communication: Balancing Creativity and Constraint* (2nd edn). New York: St. Martin's Press.

Eisenhardt, K. M. (1989). "Agency theory: assessment and review." *Academy of Management Review, 14*(1), 57–74.

Eisenhardt, K. M., and Westcott, B. (1988). "Paradoxical demands and the creation of excellence: the case of just-in-time manufacturing." In R. Quinn and K. Cameron (eds.), *Paradox and Transformation: Toward a Theory of Change in Organization and Management* (pp. 169–93). Cambridge, MA: Ballinger Publishing.

Ellis, R., Gudergan, S., and Johnson, L. (2001). "Through the looking glass: an agency theoretic foundation for the satisfaction mirror." *Journal of Consumer Satisfaction, Dissatisfaction and Complaining Behavior, 14*, 120–4.

Elster, J. (1983). *Sour Grapes: Studies in the Subversion of Rationality.* Cambridge: Cambridge University Press.

Evans, R. S., Pestotnik, S. L., Classen, D. C., Bass, S. B., Menlove, R. L., Gardner, R. M., and Burke, J. P. (1992). "Development of a computerized adverse drug event monitor." In *Proceedings of the Annual Symposium on Computerized Applications for Medical Care,* pp. 23–7.

Eveland, J. D., and Bikson, T. K. (1989). "Work group structures and computer support: a field experiment." *ACM Transactions on Office Information Systems, 6*(4), 354–79.

Fairhurst, G., Cooren, F., and Cahill, D. (2002). "Discursiveness, contradiction, and unintended consequences in successive downsizings." *Management Communication Quarterly, 15*(4), 501–40.

Farson, R. (1996). *Management of the Absurd: Paradoxes in Leadership.* New York: Simon & Schuster.

Fedor, D., Rensvold, R., and Adams, S. (1992). "An investigation of factors expected to affect feedback seeking: a longitudinal field study." *Personnel Psychology, 45*(4), 779–806.

Feeley, M. (1992). *The Process is the Punishment: Handling Cases in a Lower Criminal Court.* Reprint edition. New York: Russell Sage Foundation Publications.

Feldman, M. S. (2000). "Organizational routines as a source of continuous change." *Organizational Science, 11*(6), 611–29.

Feldman, M. S., and March, J. (1981). "Information in organizations as signal and symbol." *Administrative Science Quarterly, 26*(2), 171–86.

Feldman, M. S., and Pentland, B. T. (2003). "Reconceptualizing organizational routines as a source of flexibility and change." *Administrative Science Quarterly, 48*, +–118.

Felin, T., and Foss, N. J. (2009). "Organizational routines and capabilities: historical drift and a course-correction toward microfoundations." *Scandinavian Journal of Management, 25*(2), 157–67.

Fine, M. (1983). "The social context and a sense of injustice: the option to challenge." *Representative Research in Social Psychology, 13*(1), 15–33.

Fiol, C. M., and Lyles, M. A. (1985). "Organizational learning." *Academy of Management, 10*(4), 803–13.

Fischoff, B. (1975). "Hindsight is not foresight: the effect of outcome knowledge on judgment under uncertainty." *Journal of Experimental Psychology: Human Perception and Performance, 1*(3), 288–99.

Fiske, S., and Taylor, S. (1984). *Social Cognition.* Reading, MA: Addison-Wesley.

Flanagin, A. J., Pearce, K., and Bondad-Brown, B. A. (2009). "The destructive potential of electronic communication technologies in organizations." In P. Lutgen-Sandvik and B. D. Sypher (eds.), *Destructive Organizational Communication: Processes, Consequences and Constructive Ways of Organizing* (pp. 229–51). London: Routledge.

Ford, J. and Backoff, R. (1988). "Organizational changes in and out of dualities and paradox." In R. Quinn and K. Cameron (1988). *Paradox and Transformation: Toward a Theory of Change in Organization and Management* (pp. 81–121). Cambridge, MA: Ballinger Publishing.

Ford, W., and Etienne, C. (1994). "Can I help you? A framework for the interdisciplinary research on customer service encounters." *Management Communication Quarterly*, 7(4), 413–41.

Fornell, C., and Westbrook, R. (1984). "The vicious circle of consumer complaints." *Journal of Marketing*, 48(3), 68–78.

Forrester, J. W. (1980). "System dynamics – future opportunities." In A. Legasto, Jr., J. W. Forrester, and J. Lyneis (eds.), *System Dynamics* (pp. 7–21). Amsterdam: North-Holland.

Frey, B. (1994). "How intrinsic motivation is crowded in and out." *Rationality and Society*, 6, 334–52.

Garvin, D. (1993). "Building a learning organization." *Harvard Business Review*, 71(4), 78–91.

Gaskins, R. (1992). *Burdens of Proof in Modern Discourse*. New Haven: Yale University Press, pp i–xix and 1–11.

Gasser, L. (1986). "The integration of computing and routine work." *ACM Transactions on Office Information Systems*, 4(3), 205–25.

Gattiker, U. (1990). *Technology Management in Organizations*. Newbury Park: Sage.

Gell-Mann, M. (1994). *The Quark and the Jaguar: Adventures in the Simple and the Complex*. New York: W. H. Freeman.

Ghosh, X. M., and Sobek, D. K. II. (2007). "Effective metaroutines for organizational problem solving." Unpublished report. Mechanical and Industrial Engineering Department, Montana State University, Bozeman, MT. Online, available at: www.coe.montana.edu/ie/faculty/sobek/IOC_Grant/Metaroutines_workingpaper.pdf.

Giddens, A. (1984). *The Constitution of Society*. Berkeley: University of California.

(1990). *The Consequences of Modernity*. Stanford: Stanford University Press.

Gilovich, T., Griffin, D., and Kahneman, D. (eds.) (2002). *Heuristics and Biases: The Psychology of Intuitive Judgment*. Cambridge: Cambridge University Press.

Gilsdorf, J. (1998). "Organizational rules on communicating: how employees are – and are not – learning the ropes." *Journal of Business Communication*, 35(2), 173–201.

Goffman, E. (1967). *Interaction Ritual: Essays on Face-to-Face Behavior*. Chicago: Aldine.

(1974). *Frame Analysis*. New York: Harper and Row.

Goleman, D. (1985). *Vital Lies Simple Truths: The Psychology of Self-deception*. New York: Simon & Schuster.

Goodman, P. S. (2000). *Missing Organizational Linkages: Tools for Cross-level Research*. Thousand Oaks: Sage.

(2001). "Understanding time lags." *Academy of Management Review*, 26(4), 651–5.

Goodman, P. S., and Rousseau, D. M. (2004). "Organizational change that produces results: the linkage approach." *Academy of Management Executive*, 18(3), 7–19.

Griffith, T. (1993). "Teaching big brother to be a team player: computer monitoring and quality." *Academy of Management Executive*, 7(1), 73–80.

Grisaffe, D. (2000). "Putting customer satisfaction in its place: broader organizational research perspectives versus measurement myopia." *Journal of Consumer Satisfaction, Dissatisfaction and Complaining Behavior*, 13, 1–16.

Guennif, S., and Mangolte, P. A. (2002). "The analysis of organizational routines: proposal for an analytic framework based on Nelson and Winter and Leibenstein." Paper presented at conference on *Empirical Research on Routines in Business and Economics: Towards a Research Program*, Odense, France, November.

Gunaratne, S. A. (2008). "Understanding systems theory: transition from equilibrium to entropy." *Asian Journal of Communication*, 18(3), 175–92.

Habermas, J. (1984). *The Theory of Communicative Action*, vol. 1. *Reason and the Rationalization of Society*. Boston: Beacon Press.

Hackman, J. R. (1987). "The design of work teams." In J. W. Lorsch (ed.), *Handbook of Organizational Behavior*. Englewood Cliffs: Prentice Hall.

Hackman, J. R., and Morris, C. G. (1975). "Group tasks, group interaction process, and group performance effectiveness: a review and proposed integration." In L. Berkowitz (ed.), *Advances in Experimental Social Psychology*, vol. 8, pp. 45–99. New York: Academic Press.

Hafner, K. (2004, December 30). "Customer service: the hunt for a human." *New York Times*. Online, available at: www.nytimes.com/2004/12/30/technology/circuits/30serv.html?ex=1105472199an dei=1anden=1e2635c40999f3a5.

Halbesleben, J. R. B., and Rathert, C. (2008). "The role of continuous quality improvement and psychological safety in predicting work-arounds." *Health Care Management Review*, 33(2), 134–44.

Halbesleben, J. R. B., Wakefield, D. S., and Wakefield, B. J. (2008). "Work-arounds in health care settings: literature review and research agenda." *Health Care Management Review*, 33(10), 2–12.

Halstead, D. (2002). "Negative word of mouth: substitute for or supplement to consumer complaints?" *Journal of Consumer Satisfaction, Dissatisfaction and Complaining Behavior*, 15, 1–12.

Haney, C., Banks, W. C., and Zimbardo, P. G. (1973) "A study of prisoners and guards in a simulated prison." *Naval Research Review*, 30, 4–17.

Hardin, G. (1968). "The tragey of the commons." *Science*, 162(3859), 1243–8.

Harlos, K., and Pinder, C. (1999). "Patterns of organizational injustice: a taxonomy of what employees regard as unjust." In J. Wagner (ed.), *Advances in Qualitative Organizational Research*, vol. 2 (pp. 97–125). Stamford: JAI.

Harry, M., and Schroeder, R. (2000). *Six Sigma*. New York: Random House, Inc.

Heath, C., Larrick, R. P., and Klayman, J. (1998). "Cognitive repairs: how organizational practices can compensate for individual shortcomings." *Research in Organizational Behavior*, 20, 1–37.

Heaton, L., and Taylor, J. (2002). "Knowledge management and professional work: a communication perspective on the knowledge-based organization." *Management Communication Quarterly*, 16(2), 210–36.

Heinz, M., and Rice, R. E. (2009). "An integrated model of knowledge sharing in contemporary communication environments." In C. Beck (ed.), *Communication Yearbook*, vol. 33 (pp. 172–95). London: Routledge.

Heskett, J., Sasser, Jr., W. E., and Schlesinger, L. (1997). *The Service Profit Chain*. New York: Free Press.

Hirschheim, R. (1985). *Office Automation: A Social and Organizational Perspective*. Chichester: John Wiley.

Hirschorn, L. and Gilmore, R. (1980). "The application of family therapy concepts to influencing organizational behavior." *Administrative Science Quarterly*, 25(1), 18–37.

Hochschild, A. R. (1983, 2003). *The Managed Heart: Commercializaiton of Human Feeling*. Berkeley: University of California Press.

Hodgson, G. M. (2008). "The concept of a routine." In M. Becker (ed.), *Handbook of Organizational Routines* (pp. 15–28). New York: Edward Elgar.

Hodgson, G. M., and Knudsen, T. (2004). "The complex evolution of a simple traffic convention: the functions and implications of habit." *Journal of Economic Behavior and Organization*, 54, 19–47.

Huber, G. P. (1982). "Organizational information systems: determinants of their performance and behavior." *Management Science*, 28(2), 138–55.

  (1990). "A theory of the effects of advanced information technologies on organizational design, intelligence, and decision making." In J. Fulk and C. Steinfield (eds.), *Organizations and Communication Technology* (pp. 237–74). Newbury Park: Sage.

(1991). "Organizational learning: the contributing processes and the literatures." *Organization Science*, 2(1), 88–115.

Huefner, J. C., and Hunt, H. K. (2000). "Consumer retaliation as a response to dissatisfaction." *Journal of Consumer Satisfaction, Dissatisfaction and Complaining Behavior*, 13, 61–82.

Hughes, E. C. (1951). "Mistakes at work." *Canadian Journal of Economics and Political Science*, 17, 320–7.

Hughes, T. (1998). *Rescuing Prometheus*. New York: Pantheon.

Huspek, M. (1994). "Critical and nonfoundational analyses: are they contradictory or complementary?" In B. Kovacic (ed.), *New Approaches to Organizational Communication* (pp. 191–210). Albany: State University of New York.

Jamieson, K. H. (1995). *Beyond the Double Bind: Women and Leadership*. New York: Oxford University Press.

Johnson, B. McD. (1977). *Communication: The Process of Organizing*. Boston: Allyn and Bacon.

Johnson, B. McD., and Rice, R. E. (1987). *Managing Organizational Innovation: The Evolution from Word Processing to Office Information Systems*. New York: Columbia University Press.

Jones, T., and Sasser, W. E., Jr. (1998). "Why satisfied customers defect." *IEEE Engineering Management Review*, 26(3), 16–26.

Kahneman, D., Slovic, P., and Tversky, A. (1982). *Judgment under Uncertainty: Heuristics and Biases*. Cambridge: Cambridge University Press.

Kasouf, C. J., Celuch, K. G., and Strieter, J. C. (1995). "Consumer complaints as market intelligence: orienting context and conceptual framework." *Journal of Consumer Satisfaction, Dissatisfaction and Complaining Behavior*, 8, 59–68.

Katz, D., and Kahn, R. L. (1966). *The Social Psychology of Organizations*. New York: Wiley.

Katz, J. E., and Rice, R. E. (2002). *Social Consequences of Internet use: Access, Involvement and Interaction*. Cambridge, MA: The MIT Press.

Kaufman, O. (1999). *Effective Consumer Complaining: Win – don't Whine*. Philadelphia: Xlibris Corporation.

Keashly, L. (2001). "Interpersonal and systemic aspects of emotional abuse at work: the target's perspective." *Violence & Victims*, 16(3), 233–68.

Keen, P. G. W. (1991). *Shaping the Future: Business Design through Information Technology*. Boston: Harvard Business School Press.

Kendall, K., and Kendall, J. (1999). *Systems Analysis and Design* (4th edn). New York: Prentice Hall.

Kerr, S. (1995). "On the folly of rewarding A while hoping for B." *Academy of Management Executive*, 9(1), 7–14.

Kesting, P. (2004). "Stability and changeability of routines: mechanisms, opportunities, and obstacles." Online, available at: www.gredeg.cnrs. fr/routines/PDF/Kesting1.pdf.

Kiesler, S., and Sproull, L. (1987). "The social process of technological change in organizations." In S. Kiesler and L. Sproull (eds.), *Computing and Change on Campus* (pp. 28–40). Cambridge: Cambridge University Press.

King, R. C., and Xia, W. (1997). "Media appropriateness: effects of experience on communication media choice." *Decision Sciences*, 28(4), 877–910.

Kobayashi, M., Fussell, S. R., Xiao, Y., and Seagull, J. (2005). "Work coordination, work flow, and workarounds in a medical context." *CHI Late Breaking Results* (pp. 1561–4). New York: ACM Press.

Koenig, A. (1995). "Patterns and antipatterns." *Journal of Object-oriented Programming*, 8(1), 46–8.

Kollock, P. (1998). "Social dilemmas: the anatomy of cooperation." *American Review of Sociology*, 24(1), 183–214.

Korac-Boisvert, N., and Kouzmin, A. (1994). "The dark side of info-age social networks in public organizations and creeping crises." *Administrative Theory, and Praxis*, 16(1), 57–82.

Krathwohl, D. R. (1993). *Methods of Educational and Social Science Research*. New York: Longman.

LaFrance, M. (1996). "Why we trust computers too much." *Technology Studies*, 3(2), 163–78.

Lamberton, D. M. (ed.) (1996). *The Economics of Communication and Information*. Cheltenham, UK and Brookfield, US: Edward Elgar.

LaPlante, P. A., and Neill, C. J. (2006). *Antipatterns: Identification, Refactoring, and Management*. New York: Auerbach Publications.

Laszlo, E. (1972). *The Systems View of the World: The Natural Philosophy of the New Developments in the Sciences*. New York: Braziller.

Latour, B. (2005). *Reassembling the Social: An Introduction to Actor-Network-Theory*. Oxford: Oxford University Press.

Lazaric, N., and Becker, M. C. (2007). "On the concept of organizational routines." Online, available at: www.gredeg.cnrs.fr/routines/library.html.

Lehr, J. K., and Rice, R. E. (2002). "Organizational measures as a form of knowledge management: a multitheoretic, communication-based exploration." *Journal of the American Society for Information Science and Technology*, 53(12), 1060–73.

(2005). "How are organizational measures really used?" *Quality Management Journal*, 12(3), 39–60.

Leibenstein, H. (1966). "Allocative efficiency and X-efficiency." *American Economic Review*, 56, 392–415.

(1987). *Inside the Firm: The Inefficiencies of Hierarchy*. Cambridge, MA: Harvard University Press.

Lengnick-Hall, C. (1996). "Customer contributions to quality: a different view of the customer-oriented firm." *Academy of Management Review*, 21(3), 791–824.

Leonard, D. (1995). *Wellsprings of Knowledge*. Boston: Harvard Business School Press.

Levitt, B. S., and March, J. G. (1995). "Organizational learning." In M. D. Cohen and L. S. Sproull (eds.), *Organizational Learning* (pp. 517–40). Thousand Oaks: Sage.

Lewin K. (1943). "Defining the 'Field at a Given Time.'" *Psychological Review*, 50, 292–310.

Lewis, M. W. (2000). "Exploring paradox: toward a more comprehensive guide." *Academy of Management Review*, 25(4), 760–76.

Liebrand, W., Messick, D., and Wilke, H. (eds.) (1992). *Social Dilemmas*. Oxford: Pergamon Press.

Lievrouw, L. (2008). "Oppositional new media, ownership, and access: from consumption to reconfiguration and remediation." In R. E. Rice (ed.), *Media Ownership: Research and Regulation* (pp. 391–416). Cresskill: Hampton Press.

Littlejohn, S. W. (1983). *Theories of Human Communication* (2nd edn). Belmont: Wadsworth.

Litzky, B. E., Eddleston, K. A., and Kidder, D. L. (2006). "The good, the bad, and the misguided: how managers inadvertently encourage deviant behaviors." *Academy of Management Perspective*, 20(1), 91–103.

Lucas, H. C., Jr. (1981). *Implementation: The Key to Successful Information Systems*. New York: Columbia University Press.

Lukasiewicz, J. (1994). *The Ignorance Explosion: Understanding Industrial Civilization*. Ottawa: Carlton University Press.

Luscher, L. S., and Lewis, M. W. (2008). "Organizational change and managerial sensemaking: working through paradox." *Academy of Management Journal*, 51(2), 221–40.

Lutgen-Sandvik, P. (2003). "The communicative cycle of employee emotional abuse: generation and regeneration of workplace mistreatment." *Management Communication Quarterly*, 16(4), 471–501.

Majchrzak, A., Rice, R. E., Malhotra, A., King, N., and Ba, S. (2000). "Technology adaptation: the case of a computer-supported inter-organizational virtual team." *MIS Quarterly*, 24(4), 569–600.

Malone, P. C. (2002). *Organizational Conflict: Coworker "Backstabbing"*. Unpublished Master's thesis, The University of Southern Mississippi.

(2004). "Malicious envy in the workplace." Austin: Dept of Communication Studies, University of Texas. Paper presented to ICA conference, May, New Orleans.

March, J. G. (1991). "Exploration and exploitation in organizational learning." *Organization Science*, 2, 71–87.

March, J., and Olsen, J. (1976). *Ambiguity and Choice in Organization.* Oslo: Universitetsforlaget.

March, J. G., and Simon, H. A. (1958). *Organizations.* New York: Wiley.

Markham, A. (1996). "Designing discourse: a critical analysis of strategic ambiguity and workplace control." *Management Communication Quarterly*, 9(4), 389–421.

Markus, M. L. (1984). "System design features." In *Systems in Organisations: Bugs and Features* (pp. 13–35). Boston: Pitman.

(1987). "Toward a 'critical mass' theory of interactive media, universal access, interdependence and diffusion." *Communication Research*, 14(5), 491–511.

(1990). "Toward a critical mass theory of interactive media." In J. Fulk and C. Steinfield (eds.), *Organizations and Communication Technology* (pp. 194–218). Newbury Park: Sage.

(2001). "Toward a theory of knowledge reuse: types of knowledge reuse situations and factors in reuse success." *Journal of Management Information Systems*, 18(1), 57–93.

Marschak, J. (1968). "Economies of inquiring, communicating, deciding." *American Economic Review*, 58(2), 1–18.

Maruyama, M. (1963). "Deviation-amplifying mutual causal processes." *American Scientist*, 51(2), 164–79.

Marvin, C. (1988). *When Old Technologies were New.* New York: Oxford University Press

Masuch, M. (1985). "Vicious circles in organizations." *Administrative Science Quarterly*, 30(1), 14–33.

McGregor, J. (2008, February 21). "Consumer vigilantes – memo to corporate America: hell now hath no fury like a customer scorned." *Business Week, Special Report*. Online, available at: www. businessweek.com/magazine/content/08_09/b4073038437662. htm?chan=top+news_top+news+index_best+of+bw.

McKinley, W., and Scherer, A. (2000). "Some unanticipated consequences of organizational restructuring." *Academy of Management Review*, 25(4), 735–52.

Meares, M., Oetzel, J., Torres, A., Derkacs, D., and Ginossar, T. (2004). "Employee mistreatment and muted voices in the culturally diverse workplace." *Journal of Applied Communication Research*, 32(1), 4–27.

Mees, A. (1986). "Chaos in feedback systems." In A. V. Holden (ed.), *Chaos* (pp. 99–110). Manchester: Manchester University Press.

Merton, R. K. (1936). "The unanticipated consequences of purposive social action." *American Sociological Review, 1*, 894–904.

(1940). "Bureaucratic structure and personality." *Social Forces, 17*(4), 560–8.

Messick, D. M., and Brewer, M. B. (1983). "Solving social dilemmas: a review." In L. Wheeler and P. Shaver (eds.), *Review of Personality and Social Psychology* (pp. 11–44). Beverly Hills: Sage Publications.

Michael, D. N. (1976). *On Learning to Plan and Planning to Learn.* San Francisco: Jossey-Bass.

Mieczkowski, B. (1991). *Dysfunctional Bureaucracy: A Comparative and Historical Perspective.* Lanham: University Press of America.

Miles, M. B., and Huberman, A. M. (1994). *Qualitative Data Analysis.* Thousand Oaks: Sage.

Milgram, S. (1974). *Obedience to Authority: An Experimental View.* New York: Harper & Row.

Miner, A., Amburgey, T., and Stearns, T. (1990). "Interorganizational linkages and population dynamics: buffering and transformational shields." *Administrative Science Quarterly, 36*, 689–713.

Miner, F. C., Jr. (1990). "Jealousy on the job." *Personnel Journal, 69*(April), 89–95.

Mintz, M., and Cohen, G. (1976). *Power Incorporated.* New York: Viking Press.

Moberg, D. (2006). "Best intentions, worst results: grounding ethics students in the realities of organizational context." *Academy of Management Learning & Education, 5*(3), 307–16.

Molinski, A. (1997). "Sanding down the edges: paradoxical impediments to organizational change." *The Journal of Applied Behavioral Science, 35*(1), 8–24.

Moon, Y., and Nass, C. (1996). "How 'real' are computer personalities? Psychological responses to personality types in human-computer interaction." *Communication Research, 23*(6), 651–74.

Morath, J., and Turnbull, J. E. (2005). *To Do No Harm: Ensuring Patient Safety in Health Care Organizations.* San Francisco: Jossey-Bass.

Morgan, G. (1986). *Images of Organizations.* Newbury Park: Sage.

Moscovici, S., and Zavalloni, M. (1969). "The group as a polarizer of attitudes." *Journal of Personality and Social Psychology, 12*, 125–35.

Nash, J. (1990). "Working at and working: computer fritters." *Journal of Contemporary Ethnography, 19*(2), 207–25.

Natale, E. J., Papa, M. J., and Graham, E. (1994). "Feminist philosophy and the transformation of organizational communication." In

B. Kovacic (ed.), *New Approaches to Organizational Communication* (pp. 245–70). Albany: State University of New York.

Needleman, M. L., and Needleman, C. (1979). "Organizational crime." *Sociological Quarterly, 20,* 517–28.

Nelson, R., and Winter, S. (1982). *Organizational Capabilities and Behavior: An Evolutionary Theory of Economic Change.* Cambridge, MA: Harvard University Press.

Nithamyong, P., and Skibniewski, M. J. (2006). "Success/failure factors and performance measures of web-based construction project management systems: professionals' viewpoint." *Journal of Construction Engineering and Management, 132*(1), 80–7.

Nonaka, I. (1988). "Creating organizational order out of chaos: self-renewal in Japanese firms." *California Management Review, 30*(3), 57–73.

Norman, D. A. (1981). "Categorization of action slips." *Psychological Review, 88,* 1–15.

Nunamaker, J. F., Dennis, A. R., Valacich, J. S., Vogel, D. R., and George, J. F. (1991). "Electronic meeting systems to support group work." *Communications of the ACM, 34*(7), 40–61.

O'Dell, C., and Grayson, C. J. (1998). *If Only We Knew What We Know: The Transfer of Internal Knowledge and Best Practice.* New York: The Free Press.

Olson-Buchanan, J. B., and Boswell, W. (2008). "An integrative model of experiencing and responding to mistreatment at work." *Academy of Management Review, 33*(1), 76–96.

Orasanu, J., and Connolly, T. (1993). "The reinvention of decision making." In G. Klein, J. Orasanu, R. Calderood, and C. Zsambok (eds.), *Decision Making in Action: Models and Methods* (pp. 3–20). Norwood: Ablex.

Orlikowski, W. J. (1991). "Integrated information environment or matrix of control? The contradictory implications of information technology." *Accounting, Management and Information Technologies, 1*(1), 9–42.

(1996). "Improvising organizational transformation over time: a situated change perspective." *Information Systems Research, 7,* 63–92.

Osgood, C. E. (1962). *An Alternative to War or Surrender.* Urbana: University of Illinois Press.

Pace, R. W., and Faules, D. F. (1994). *Organizational Communication.* Englewood Cliffs: Prentice Hall.

Palazzoli, M., Boscolo, L., Cecchin, G., and Prata, G. (1978). *Paradox and Counterparadox: A New Model in the Therapy of the Family in Schizophrenic Transaction.* New York: Jason Aronson.

Pasmore, W. (1988). *Designing Effective Organizations: The Sociotechnical Systems Perspective*. New York: Wiley.

Paton, R. (2003). *Managing and Measuring Social Enterprises*. Thousand Oaks: Sage.

Pava, C. (1983). *Managing New Office Technology*. New York: Free Press.

Pentland, B. T. (2003). "Conceptualizing and measuring variety in organizational work processes." *Management Science*, 49(7), 857–70.

Pentland, B. T., and Feldman, M. S. (2005). "Organizational routines as a unit of analysis." *Industrial and Corporate Change*, 14(5), 793–815.

(2008). "Designing routines: on the folly of designing artifacts, while hoping for patterns of action." *Information and Organization*, 18, 235–50.

Perrow, C. (1984). *Normal Accidents: Living with High-risk Technologies*. New York: Basic Books.

Peterson, I. (1993). *Newton's Clock: Chaos in the Solar System*. New York: Freeman, and Co.

Pettigrew, A. (1972). "Information control as a power resource." *Sociology*, 6(2), 187–204.

Pfeffer, J., and Sutton, R. (2000). *The Knowing-Doing Gap: How Smart Companies Turn Knowledge into Action*. Boston: Harvard Business School Press.

Pidgeon, N., Kasperson, R. E., and P. Slovic (eds.) (2003). *The Social Amplification of Risk*. Cambridge: Cambridge University Press.

Pinch, T. J., and Bijker, W. E. (1984). "The social construction of facts and artefacts." *Social Studies of Science*, 14(3), 399–441.

Platt, J. (1973). "Social traps." *American Psychologist*, 28(8), 641–51.

Pogue, D. (2003). "Checking your bill for a new charge called 'oops'." *New York Times*, December 4, Circuit Section G1, pp. 1 and 9.

Polanyi, M. (1966). *The Tacit Dimension*. London: Routledge and Kegan Paul.

Poole, M. S., Seibold, D. R., and McPhee, R. D. (1985). "Group decision-making as a structurational process." *Quarterly Journal of Speech*, 71(1), 74–102.

Posner, R. (2004). *Catastrophe: Risk and Response*. Oxford: Oxford University Press.

Putnam, L. (1986). "Contradictions and paradoxes in organizations." In L. L. Thayer (ed.), *Organizational Communication: Emerging Perspectives* (pp. 151–67). Norwood: Ablex.

Quevedo, R. (1991). "Quality, waste, and value in white-collar environments." *Quality Progress*, January, 33–7.

Quinn, R., and Cameron, K. (1988). "Paradox and transformation: a framework for viewing organization and management." In R. Quinn and K. Cameron (eds.), *Paradox and Transformation: Toward a Theory of Change in Organization and Management* (pp. 289–308). Cambridge, MA: Ballinger Publishing.

Reason, J. T. (1984). "Lapses of attention in everyday life." In R. Parasuraman and D. R. Davies (eds.), *Varieties of Attention* (pp. 515–49). Orlando: Academic Press.

(1990). *Human Error.* New York: Cambridge University Press.

(1997). *Managing the Risks of Organizational Accidents.* Aldershot: Ashgate.

Rice, R. E. (1987). "Computer-mediated communication and organizational innovation." *Journal of Communication, 37*(4), 65–94.

(1990). "Computer-mediated communication system network data: theoretical concerns and empirical examples." *International Journal of Man-Machine Studies, 32*(6), 627–47.

(1993). "Media appropriateness: using social presence theory to compare traditional and new organizational media." *Human Communication Research, 19*(4), 451–84.

(2004). "Social aspects of implementing a medical information system: cure or symptom?" In P. Whitten and D. Cook (eds.), *Understanding Health Communications Technologies: A Case Study Approach* (pp. 19–29). San Francisco: Jossey-Bass.

(2009a). "Sociological and technological interdependencies of new media." *Journal of Computer-Mediated Communication, 14*(3), 714–19.

(2009b). "Diffusion of innovations: theoretical extensions." In R. Nabi and M. B. Oliver (eds.), *Handbook of Media Effects* (pp. 489–503). Thousand Oaks: Sage.

Rice, R. E., and Bair, J. (1984). "New organizational media and productivity." In R. E. Rice (ed.), *The New Media: Communication, Research and Technology* (pp. 185–215). Beverly Hills: Sage.

Rice, R. E., and Danowski, J. (1993). "Is it really just like a fancy answering machine? Comparing semantic networks of different types of voice mail users." *Journal of Business Communication, 30*(4), 369–97.

Rice, R. E., and Gattiker, U. (2001). "New media and organizational structuring." In F. Jablin, and L. Putnam (eds.), *New Handbook of Organizational Communication* (pp. 544–81). Newbury Park: Sage.

Rice, R. E., and Schneider, S. (2006). "Information technology: analyzing paper and electronic desktop artifacts." In C. Lin and D. Atkin (eds.), *Communication Technology and Social Change: Theory,*

Effects, and Applications (pp. 101–21). Mahwah: Lawrence Erlbaum Associates.

Rice, R. E., and Shook, D. (1988). "Access to, usage of, and outcomes from an electronic message system." *ACM Transactions on Office Information Systems*, 6(3), 255–76.

(1990). "Voice messaging, coordination and communication." In J. Galegher, R. Kraut, and C. Egido (eds.), *Intellectual Teamwork: Social and Technological Bases of Cooperative Work* (pp. 327–50). New Jersey: Erlbaum.

Rice, R. E., and Steinfield, C. (1994). "New forms of organizational communication via electronic mail and voice messaging." In J. Erik Andriessen and R. Roe (eds.), *Telematics and Work* (pp. 109–37). East Sussex: Lawrence Erlbaum.

Rice, R. E., and Tyler, J. (1995). "Individual and organizational influences on voice mail use and evaluation." *Behaviour and Information Technology*, 14(6), 329–41.

Rice, R. E., McCreadie, M., and Chang, S.-J. (2001). *Accessing and Browsing Information and Communication*. Cambridge, MA: The MIT Press.

Ritzer, G. (1993). "The irrationality of rationality: traffic jams on those 'Happy Trails'." In *The McDonaldization of Society: An Investigation into the Changing Character of Contemporary Social Life* (pp. 121–46). Thousand Oaks: Pine Forge Press.

Roberto, M. A., Bohmer, R. M. J., and Edmondson, A. C. (2006). "Facing ambiguous threats." *Harvard Business Review*, 84, 106–13.

Roberts, K., and Bea, R. (2001). "Must accidents happen? Lessons from high-reliability organizations." *Academy of Management Executive*, 15(3), 70–8.

Robinson, S. L., and Greenberg, J. (1998). "Employees behaving badly: dimensions, determinants and dilemmas in the study of workplace deviance." In C. L. Cooper and D. M. Rousseau (eds.), *Trends in Organizational Behavior*, vol. 5 (pp. 1–30). New York: Wiley.

Rochlin, G. (1998). *Trapped in the Net: The Unanticipated Consequences of Computerization*. Princeton: Princeton University Press.

Rodgers, R. (1992). "Antidotes for the idiot's paradox." In U. Gattiker (ed.), *Technological Innovation and Human Resources*, vol. 3 (pp. 227–71). Berlin: Walter de Gruyter.

Rogers, E. M. (2003). *Diffusion of Innovations* (5th edn). New York: Free Press.

Rogers, E. M., and Kincaid, D. L. (1981). *Communication Networks: Toward a New Paradigm for Research*. New York: Free Press.

Romm, C. T. (1998). *Virtual Politicking: Playing Politics in Electronically Linked Organizations*. Cresskill: Hampton Press.

Rosa, P. (1995). *Idiot Letters: One Man's Relentless Assault on Corporate America*. New York: Doubleday Publishing.

Ruane, J., Cerulo, K., and Gerson, J. (1994). "Professional deceit: normal lying in an occupational setting." *Sociological Focus*, 27(2), 91–109.

Rumelhart, D. E. (1980). "Schemata: the building blocks of cognition." In R. J. Spiro, B. C. Bruce, and W. F. Brewer (eds.), *Theoretical Issues in Reading Comprehension: Perspectives from Cognitive Psychology, Linguistics, Artificial Intelligence and Education* (pp. 33–58). Hillsdale: Lawrence Erlbaum.

Russo, J. E., and Schoemaker, P. J. H. (1989). *Decision Traps: Ten Barriers to Brilliant Decision-making and How to Overcome Them*. New York: Doubleday.

Rutte, C. (1990). "Solving organizational social dilemmas." *Social Behavior*, 5, 285–94.

Sandler, T. (2001). "Knowledge is power: asymmetric information." In *Economic Concepts for the Social Sciences* (pp. 110–29). Cambridge: Cambridge University Press.

Schein, E. (1994). "Innovative cultures and organizations." In T. Allen and M. Scott-Morton (eds.), *Information Technology and the Corporation of the 1990s: Research Studies* (pp. 125–46). New York: Oxford University Press.

Schelling, T. C. (1978). *Micromotives and Macrobehavior*. New York: Norton.

Schneider, B., and Bowen, D. (1993). "The service organization: human resources management is crucial." *Organizational Dynamics*, 21(4), 39–52.

Schulman, P. R. (1989). "The 'logic' of organizational irrationality." *Administration & Society*, 21, 31–3.

Schultze, U. and Orlikowski, W. (2004). "A practice perspective on technology-mediated network relations: the use of internet-based self-serve technologies." *Information Systems Research*, 15(1), 87–106.

Scott Morton, M. S. (ed.) (1991). *The Corporation of the 1990s: Information Technology and Organizational Transformation*. New York: Oxford University Press.

Seiders, K., and Berry, L. (1998). "Service Fairness: What it is and Why it Matters." *Academy of Management Executive*, 12(3), 8–20.

Seymour, J. (1990). "Column: little horror stories." *PC Magazine*, April 24, 79–80.

Shapiro, C., and Varian, H. R. (1999). *Information Rules: A Strategic Guide to the Network Economy*. Boston: Harvard Business School Press.

Shirky, C. (2008). *Here Comes Everybody: The Power of Organizing without Organizations*. New York: Penguin Press.

Siggelkow, N., and Rivkin, J. (2006). "When exploration backfires: unintended consequences of multilevel organizational search." *Academy of Management Journal*, 49(4), 779–95.

Simard, C., and Rice, R. E. (2006). "Managerial information behavior: relationships among total quality management orientation, information use environments, and managerial roles." *Total Quality Management and Business Excellence*, 17(1), 79–95.

(2007). "The practice gap: barriers to the diffusion of best practices." In C. R. McInerney and R. E. Day (eds.), *Re-thinking Knowledge Management: From Knowledge Objects to Knowledge Processes* (pp. 87–124). Dordrecht: Springer-Verlag.

Simon, H. A. (1991). "Bounded rationality and organizational learning." *Organization Science*, 2(1), 125–34.

Singer, B. (1973). *Feedback and Society: A Study of the Uses of Mass Channels for Coping*. Lexington: Lexington Books.

(1977). "Incommunicado social machines." *Social Policy*, 8(6), 88–93.

(1978). "Assessing social errors." *Social Policy*, 9(5), 27–34.

(1980). "Crazy systems and Kafka circuits." *Social Policy*, 11(2), 46–54.

Singer, S. J., and Edmondson, A. C. (2008). "When learning and performance are at odds: confronting the tension." In P. Kumar and P. Ramsey (eds.), *Learning and Performance Matter* (Chapter 3). Hackensack and Singapore: World Scientific Books.

Siporin, M., and Gummer, B. (1988). "Lessons from family therapy: the potential of paradoxical interventions in organizations." In R. Quinn and K. Cameron (eds.), *Paradox and Transformation: Toward a Theory of Change in Organization and Management* (pp. 205–27). Cambridge, MA: Ballinger Publishing.

Sitkin, S., Sutcliffe, K., and Barrios-Choplin, J. (1992). "A dual-capacity model of communication media choice in organizations." *Human Communication Research*, 18(4), 563–98.

Sless, D. (1988). "Forms of control." *Australian Journal of Communication*, 14, 57–69.

Smith, P. (1993). "Outcome-related performance indicators and organizational control in the public sector." *British Journal of Management*, 4, 135–51.

Snook, S. A. (2000). Friendly Fire: The Accidental Shootdown of US Black Hawks over Northern Iraq. Princeton: Princeton University Press.

Solomon, M. (2002). *Working with Difficult People* (2nd edn). Upper Saddle River: Prentice Hall.

Spender, J.-C. (1998). "Pluralist epistemology and the knowledge-based theory of the firm." *Organization*, 5(2), 233–56.

Spitzberg, B. (1993). "The dialectics of (in)competence." *Journal of Social and Personal Relationships*, 10(1), 137–58.

Sproull, L., and Kiesler, S. (1991). *Connections: New Ways of Working in the Networked Organization*. Cambridge, MA: The MIT Press.

Starbuck, W. H. (1988). "Surmounting our human limitations." In R. Quinn, and K. Cameron (eds.), *Paradox and Transformation: Toward a Theory of Change in Organization and Management* (pp. 65–80). Cambridge, MA: Ballinger Publishing.

Starbuck, W. H., and Milliken, F. J. (1988). "Challenger: fine-tuning the odds until something breaks." *Journal of Management Studies*, 25(4), 319–40.

Stauss, B., and Seidel, W. (2005). *Complaint Management: The Heart of CRM*. Mason: Thomson South-Western.

Staw, B. M., Sandelands, L. E., and Dutton, J. E. (1981). "Threat-rigidity effects in organizational behavior: a multilevel analysis." *Administrative Science Quarterly*, 26, 501–24.

Steiner, I. D. (1972). *Group Process and Productivity*. New York: Academic Press.

Stewart, D. M., and Chase, R. B. (1999). "The impact of human error on delivering service quality." *Production and Operations Management*, 8(3), 240–63.

Stohl, C., and Cheney, G. (2001). "Participatory process/paradoxical practices: communication and the dilemmas of organizational democracy." *Management Communication Quarterly*, 41(3), 349–407.

Stohl, C., and Schell, S. (1991). "A communication-based model of a small-group dysfunction." *Management Communication Quarterly*, 5(1), 90–110.

Strassman, P. (1983). *The Information Payoff: The Transformation of Work in the Electronic Age*. New York: Macmillan.

Sundaramurthy, C., and Lewis, M. (2003). "Control and collaboration: paradoxes of governance." *Academy of Management Review*, 28(3), 397–415.

Sunstein, C. R. (2005). *Laws of Fear: Beyond the Precautionary Principle*. Cambridge: Cambridge University Press.

(2007). *Worst Case Scenarios*. Cambridge, MA: Harvard University Press.

Susskind, A. (2000). "Efficacy and outcome expectations related to customer complaints about service experiences." *Communication Research*, 27(3), 353–78.

(2001). "I told you so! Restaurant customers' word-of-mouth communication patterns." *Cornell Hotel and Restaurant Administration Quarterly*, 43(2), 75–85.

Susskind, A., Kacmar, K. M., and Borchgrevink, C. (2003). "Customer service providers' attitudes relating to customer service and customer satisfaction in the customer-server exchange." *Journal of Applied Psychology*, 88(1), 179–87.

Taleb, N. N. (2007). *The Black Swan: The Impact of the Highly Improbable*. New York: Random House.

Tarnas, R. (1991). *The Passion of the Western Mind: Understanding the Ideas that have Shaped Our World View*. New York: Ballantine.

Tavris, C., and Aronson, E. (2007). *Mistakes Were Made (But Not by Me): Why We Justify Foolish Beliefs, Bad Decisions, and Hurtful Acts*. New York: Harcourt.

Tax, S., and Brown, S. (1998). "Recovering and learning from service failure." *Sloan Management Review*, 40(1), 75–88.

Taylor, J. R., Flanagin, A. J., Cheney, G., and Seibold, D. R. (2000). "Organizational communication research: key moments, central concerns, and future challenges." In W. B. Gudykunst (ed.), *Communication Yearbook 24* (pp. 99–137). Thousand Oaks: Sage Publications.

Tenner, E. (1997). *Why Things Bite Back: Technology and the Revenge of Unintended Consequences*. New York: Vintage.

Thayer, L. (1988). "How does information 'inform'." In B. D. Ruben (ed.), *Information and Behavior*, vol. 2 (pp. 13–26). New Brunswick: Transaction Books.

Thompson, K. (1998). "Confronting the paradoxes in a Total Quality environment." *Organizational Dynamics*, 26(3), 62–74.

Thompson, M. (1988). "Being, thought and action." In R. Quinn and K. Cameron (eds.), *Paradox and Transformation: Toward a Theory of Change in Organization and Management* (pp. 123–35). Cambridge, MA: Ballinger Publishing.

Tilly, C. (2008). *Credit and Blame*. Princeton: Princeton University Press.

Titmuss, R. M. (1970). *The Gift Relationship: From Human Blood to Social Policy*. London: Allen and Unwin.

Tompkins, P. K., and Cheney, G. (1983). "Account analysis of organizational decision making and identification." In L. Putnam and M. Pacanowsky (eds.), *Communication and Organization: An Interpretive Approach* (pp. 123–46). Beverly Hills: Sage.

Tovstiadi, K., and Beebe, S. (2006). "Cliches in the intercultural communication context." In I. N. Rozina (ed.), *Communication Theory and Practice*, *4*, 76–92. Rostov-on-Don, Russia: Institute of Management, Business and Law.

Tsoukas, H., and Chia, R. (2002). "On organizational becoming: rethinking organizational change." *Organization Science*, *13*(5), 567–82.

Tucker, A. L. (2004). "The impact of operational failures on hospital nurses and their patients." *Journal of Operations Management*, *22*(2), 151–69.

Tucker, A. L., and Edmondson, A. C. (2003). "Why hospitals don't learn from failures: organizational and psychological dynamics that inhibit system change." *California Management Review*, *45*(2), 34–54.

Tucker, A. L., and Spear, S. J. (2006). "Operational failures and interruptions in hospital nursing." *Health Services Research*, *41*(3 Pt. 1), 643–62.

Tucker, A. L., Singer, S. J., Hayes, J. E., and Falwell, A. (2008). "Front-line staff perspectives on opportunities for improving the safety and efficiency of hospital work systems." *Health Services Research*, *43*(5 Pt. 2), 1807–29.

Turner, B. A. (1976). "The organizational and interorganizational development of disasters." *Administrative Science Quarterly*, *21*, 378–97.

(1990). "Failed artifacts." In P. Gagliardi (ed.), *Symbols and Artifacts: Views of the Corporate Landscape* (pp. 365–84). New York: de Gruyter.

Turner, S. F. (2005). "Solid waste collection: examining the impact of organizational routines on organizational performance." Second conference on organizational routines (Nice, 2005). Online, available at: www.gredeg.cnrs.fr/routines/workshop/papers/Turner.pdf.

Umiker, W. (1994). *Coping with Difficult People in the Health Care Setting*. Chicago: American Society of Clinical Pathologists.

Van de Ven, A. H. (1986). "Central problems in the management of innovation." *Management Science*, *32*(5), 590–607.

Van de Ven, A. H., and Poole, M. S. (1988). "Paradoxical requirements for a theory of organizational change." In R. Quinn and K. Cameron (eds.), *Paradox and Transformation: Toward a Theory of Change in Organization and Management* (pp. 19–63). Cambridge, MA: Ballinger Publishing.

Van Lancker-Sidtis, D., and Rallon, G. (2004). "Tracking the incidence of formulaic expressions in everyday speech: methods for classification and verification." *Language and Communication*, *24*, 207–40.

Van Lange, P., Liebrand, W., Messick, D., and Wilke, H. (1992). "Introduction and literature review." In W. Liebrand, D. Messick, and

H. Wilke (eds.), *Social Dilemmas: Theoretical Issues and Research Findings* (pp. 3–28). Oxford: Pergamon Press.

Vardi, Y., and Weitz, E. (2003). *Misbehavior in Organizations: Theory, Research, and Management*. Mahwah: Lawrence Erlbaum Associates.

Vaughan, D. (1996). *The Challenger Launch Decision: Risky Technology, Culture, and Deviance at NASA*. Chicago: University of Chicago Press.

(1999). "The dark side of organizations: mistake, misconduct, and disaster." *Annual Review of Sociology*, 25, 271–305.

Vecchio, R. P. (2000). "Negative emotion in the workplace: employee jealousy and envy." *International Journal of Stress Management*, 7, 161–79.

Vogelsmeier, A. A., Halbesleben, J. R. B., and Scott-Cawiezell, J. R. (2008). "Technology implementation and workarounds in the nursing home." *Journal of the American Medical Informatics Association*, 15(1), 114–19.

von Hippel, E., and Tyre, M. (1994). "How learning by doing is done: problem identification in novel process equipment." *Research Policy*, 24(1), 1–12.

Walsh, J. P., and Ungson, G. R. (1991). "Organizational memory." *Academy of Management Review*, 16(1), 57–91.

Walton, R. (1969). *Interpersonal Peacemaking: Confrontations and Third-party Consultation*. Reading, MA: Addison-Wesley.

Watzlawick, P., Beavin, J., and Jackson, D. (1967). *Pragmatics of Human Communication*. New York: W. W. Norton.

Weick, K. E. (1979). *The Social Psychology of Organizing* (2nd edn). Reading, MA: Addison-Wesley.

(1993). "The collapse of sensemaking in organizations." *Administrative Science Quarterly*, 38, 628–52.

(1995). *Sensemaking in Organizations*. Thousand Oaks: Sage.

Weick, K. E., and Sutcliffe, K. M. (2001). *Managing the Unexpected: Assuring High Performance in an Age of Complexity*. San Francisco: John Wiley, and Sons, Inc.

Wender, P. (1968). "Vicious and virtuous circles: the role of deviation-amplifying feedback in the origin and perpetuation of behavior." *Psychiatry*, 31(4), 309–24.

Wendt, R. F. (1998). "The sound of one hand clapping: counterintuitive lessons extracted from paradoxes and double binds in participative organizations." *Management Communication Quarterly*, 11(3), 323–71.

Wenger, E., McDermott, R., and Snyder, W. M. (2002). *Cultivating Communities of Practice: A Guide to Managing Knowledge.* Boston: Harvard Business School Press.

Westenholz, A. (1993). "Paradoxical thinking and change in the frames of reference." *Organization Studies, 14*(1), 37–58.

Weston, A. (2009). *A Rulebook for Arguments* (4th edn). Indianapolis: Hackett Publishing.

Wexler, P. S., Adams, W. A., and Bohn, E. (1993). *The Quest for Service Quality: Rxs for Achieving Excellence.* Sandy: MaxComm Associates.

Widen-Wulff, G., and Davenport, E. (2005). "Information sharing and timing: findings from two Finnish organizations." In F. Crestani and I. Ruthven (eds.), *CoLIS 2005* (LNCS 3507) (pp. 32–46). Berlin: Spring-Verlag.

Wiener, N. (1948). *Cybernetics, or Control and Communication in the Animal and Machine.* Paris: Hermann, and Cie.; Cambridge, MA: The Technology Press; New York: John Wiley, and Sons, Inc.

(1950/1967). *The Human Use of Human Beings. Cybernetics and Society.* New York: Houghton-Mifflin/Avon.

Wilder, C. (1979). "The Palo Alto group: difficulties and directions of the interactional view for human communication." *Human Communication Research, 5*(2), 171–86.

Williams, L. C. (1994). *Organizational Violence: Creating a Prescription for Change.* Westport: Quorum Books.

Winograd, T., and Flores, F. (1986). *Understanding Computers and Cognition: A New Foundation for Design.* Norwood: Ablex.

Winter, S. (2000). "The satisficing principle in capability learning." *Strategic Management Journal, 21,* 981–96.

Woods, D., Sarter, N., and Billings, C. (1997). "Automation surprises." In G. Salvendy (ed.), *Handbook of Human Factors and Ergonomics* (2nd edn) (pp. 1926–43). New York: Wiley.

Zeithaml, V., Berry, L., and Parasuraman, A. (1988). "Communication and control processes in the delivery of service quality." *Journal of Marketing, 52*(April), 35–48.

Zhao, B., and Olivera, F. (2006). "Error reporting in organizations." *Academy of Management Review, 31*(4), 1012–30.

Zimbardo, P. G. (1971). "The power and pathology of imprisonment." *Congressional Record* (Serial No. 15, 1971-10-25). Hearings before Subcommittee No. 3, of the Committee on the Judiciary, House of Representatives, Ninety-Second Congress, *First Session on Corrections, Part II, Prisons, Prison Reform and Prisoner's*

Rights: California. Washington, DC: US Government Printing Office.

Zmud, R. W. (1990). "Opportunities for strategic information manipulation through new information technology." In J. Fulk and C. Steinfield (eds.), *Organizations and Communication Technology* (pp. 95–116). Newbury Park: Sage.

Zuboff, S. (1984). *In the Age of the Smart Machine: The Future of Work and Power.* New York: Basic.

Zucker, L. G. (1991). "The role of institutionalization in cultural persistence." In W. Powell and P. DiMaggio (eds.), *The New Institutionalism in Organizational Analysis* (pp. 83–107). Chicago: University of Chicago Press.

Index

access costs, 15
accountability, 312
  in service provision, 71
acts, sensemaking theory, 112
ad ignorantiam, 259
Adams, Douglas, *The Hitchhiker's Guide to the Galaxy*, 10
Adams, Scott, 252
administrative time, PeopleData time reporting system, 55–58
affect heuristic, 264
agency paradoxes, 278
agency theory, 77–78
air time fragmentation, 193
ambiguity, sensemaking theory, 111
Anderson, P., 329
antipatterns, 115–17, 146
argument-from-ignorance, 259
Argyris, C., 243–44, 278–79
articulation work, 148
artifact failures, 292
artifacts, 124–25
Ashforth, B., 287
asymmetric information, 77–78
attribution bias, 255, 264
  self-serving, 76
attrition through time, 9
authoritative organizational statements, 13
automated systems, and system error, 293–98
automation surprises, 297
availability bias, 261
availability heuristic, 264
avatars, use while misrepresenting oneself, 11

Bacdayan, P., 241
Bainbridge, L., 295–96
Bair, J., 15

Balanced Scorecard, 138
Baldrige Award process, 138
Bardach, E., 148
barriers to perception, 60
  and crazy systems, 11–13
  Home Sale Automation system, 37
  labor cost system, 28–29
Bateson, G., 221
Bazerman, M.H., 261
Becker, M.C., 126, 327–28
belonging paradoxes, 315
Berry, L., 72
BFQuery system. *see* database query system
Bitner, M., 76–77
Black Swan Events, 12
blame subroutines, 144
  educational institution ICT case study, 163
    camouflaging negligence, 173–74
  Falcon help request system, 46–47
  PeopleData time reporting system, 59–60
blaming the victim, 9, 285
blogs, 73, *see also* consumer vigilantes
Boettger, R.D., 8, 321
Bostrom, R.P., 21, 325
bounded rationality, 253
Brazil (movie, Gilliam), 10
Brenders, D., 222
Brett, J., 321–22
Brown, W.J., 116
Brunsson, N., 273
buffering, 240
Building Information Modeling (BIM) systems, 29–30
burden of proof, 260

carpet shampooer rental, 1–3

case studies. *see* educational
   institution ICT case
   study; information and
   communication technologies
   (ICTs), case studies
Castle, The (Kafka), 10, 14
catatonic non-responsiveness, 240
categorizing, 255
centralization, 282
Cerulo, K., 261–62
Challenger space shuttle, NASA
   briefings, 11–12
Charell, R., 68
charmed loops, 224
Cheney, G., 276, 278
circuits, 14, *see also* subroutines
clichés, 220–21
cognitive dissonance, 253–57, 264
   reducing blaming/defensive
      approaches to, 312–14
cognitive paradoxical processes,
   113–14
Cohen, M.D., 241
collective action, 281
collective reflection, 315
collective traps, 268
common sense, as barrier to
   perception of crazy systems, 13
complicity, 281
computer fritters, 289–90
computer slip, 155–56
computer-mediated feedback, 218–19
confirmation bias, 255
confirmatory responses, 263, 320
conflict spirals, 243
conflicting goals, 61
   and crazy systems, 5–8
   Falcon help request system, 41–42
   Home Sale Automation system,
      32–34
   labor cost system, 23–25, 29–30
   resolving, 321–22
conformance pressure, 185
connotative symbols, 10
constitutive rules, 222
consumer vigilantes, 79–80
content level communication, 221
contingent behavior, 268–69
contradictory expectations, 115
contradictory messages, 276–77

control, conflict with learning, 6–7
cooling out techniques, 9
Coordinated Management of
   Meaning theory, 221–22
counter-bureaucratic coping, 9
counterproductive activities, ICT, 11
cover-ups, 9, 281
co-worker backstabbing, 286–87
crazy systems, 5
   causes
      barriers to perception, 11–13
      conflicting goals, 5–8
      poor feedback, 8–9
      symbolic uses and manipulation,
         9–11
   symptoms, 16
creeping crisis, 282
critically damped feedback loops, 110
Cronen, V., 225
crowding motivation theory, 243
Culnan, M., 73, 218–19
customer complaints
   and complexity of underlying prob-
      lem, 73–74
   and satisfaction, 69–71
   feedback mediation, 72–75
      and technological illiteracy,
         75–76
      by blocking and non-responding,
         79–80
      computer-mediated, 218–19
      perceptions and attributions of
         service quality, 76–77
      through roles and positions,
         77–79
   mishandling, 68–69
   seeking out, 69
customer satisfaction, 81
   and customer complaints, 69–71
customer service interface, 67
   encouraging customer service feed-
      back, 306–10
   literature, 68–69
   service behaviors, 68, *see also* ser-
      vice provision
customers
   as always right, 76–77, 306–07
   problematic, 80–81
cutting corners, 281
cybernetic systems theory, 109–10

cycles of failure, 230

database query system
  delay subroutines, 52–53
  denial, 51
  error subroutines, 53
  manipulation, 50–51
  non-responsiveness, 48–49
  overview, 47–48
  rigidity, 51–52
  secrecy, 49–50
  work subroutines, 52
dead routines, 125
deceptive and equivocal activities
  back-office, 75–76
  ICT, 11
decision-making, 252–53
  educational institution ICT case
    study, 191–94, *see also* natur-
    alistic decision-making
  and leadership, 195–98
decompensation incidents, 298
defensive responses, to customer
  complaints, 69
defensive routines, 243–45,
    see also mixed messages
Dekker, S.W.A., 324–25
delay circuits, 14, *see also* subroutines
delay costs, 15
delay subroutines
  database query system, 52–53
  educational institution ICT case
    study, 174, 178
Deming, W. Edwards, 120
denial, 62
  database query system, 51
  PeopleData time reporting system,
    55–58
denotative signals, 10
deviation-amplifying feedback loops,
    241
diffusion of innovation theory, 117–21
Dilbert (comic strip), 252
direct feedback, 218–19
discrimination, in service provision,
    71
distributed routines, 121
distributive justice, 72
Dorner, D., 7, 252
double binds, 114–15

from mixed messages, 245–49,
    see also Proposition Five
double interacts, sensemaking theory,
    112
double standards, 115
double-loop learning, 13, 341
  cybernetic systems theory, 110
  educational institution ICT case
    study, 167
  PeopleData time reporting system,
    55
driver's license replacement, 3–4

Eco, Umberto, 3–4
  The Name of the Rose, 10
ecological change, sensemaking
    theory, 111
Edmondson, A.C., 135–36, 229,
    231–32, 263, 317–18
educational institution ICT case study
  analytical method, 159
  blame subroutines, 163
    camouflaging negligence, 173–74
  contradictions, 190–91
  data collection, 156–57
  delay subroutines, 174, 178
  double-loop learning, 167
  error subroutines, 175–77
  ICT system implementation,
    204–05
    impact on loosely coupled struc-
      ture, 171–72
  ideology and change resistance,
    187–89
  implications
    for other theories of organiza-
      tional communication, 209–12
    practical, 212–14
  inclusion, 178–81
    respecting all stakeholders,
      182–83
  inclusive decision-making, 191–94
    and leadership, 195–98
  loosely coupled structure
    and change resistance, 170–71
    difficulty managing, 167–69
    impact of system implementation,
      171–72
  new system
    and value chains, 165–67

educational institution (*cont.*)
  as catalyst for policy change,
    164–65
  first-level effects, 160
  forcing social interactions,
    160–62
  second-level effects, 160–67
  upward information flows, 166
  overview, 155, 199, 215–16,
    335–36
  power relations in open meetings,
    184–87
  Proposition One, 160–67, 200–01
  Proposition Two, 167–72, 201
  Proposition Three, 173–77, 201–02
  Proposition Four, 177–91, 202–03
  Proposition Five, 191–98, 203
  representation and process losses,
    181–82
  research site, 155–56
  sampling, 158–59
  student-centeredness, 183–84,
    190–91
  subunit coupling, 162, 171–72
  UR beyond the ICT, 205–06
    validity challenges, 206
  UR dynamics model revision,
    207–08
effort conventions, 127–28
effort discretion, 124
Eisenberg, E.M., 6
eliciting feedback, 218–19
Ellis, R., 78
Elster, J., 257–58
emancipating structures, 319–20
emotional abuse, of employees,
    285–86
emotional labor, 77
employee mistreatment, 283–87
employee relocation. *see* Home Sale
    Automation system
enactment, sensemaking theory,
    111–13
enigmatic episodes, 225
equivocality, sensemaking theory, 111
error circuits, 14, *see also* subroutines
error costs, 15
error subroutines
  database query system, 53
  educational institution ICT case
    study, 175–77

in ICT system implementation, 204
  PeopleData time reporting system,
    58–59
error-amplifying decision traps, 270
errors
  barriers to identifying and report-
    ing, 230–34
  nature of, 228–30
Excellence Model, 138–39
excuses, as form of non-response, 9
expectancy theory, 150–51
exploitation, in service provision, 71
exploratory responses, 263–64, 320
explosive clusters, 242

face-saving, 77
face-to-face communication,
    feedback, 218
failures of foresight, 264
Fairhurst, G., 6
fairness, in service provision, 71–72,
    309–10
Falcon help request system, 47–48
  conflicting goals, 41–42
  manipulation, 45–46
  overview, 40–41
  poor feedback, 42–43
  rigidity, 46–47
  secrecy, 44–45
  symbolic uses and manipulation, 43
farragoes, 225–26
feedback, 61, 217–18, 249
  and crazy systems, 8–9
  challenges for organizations
    defensive routines, 243–49
    learning from feedback, 236–39
    reporting errors through feed-
      back, 228–36
  contextualizing meaning by layers,
    221–22
  contradictions of competence,
    226–27
  discourse and language, 218–21
  elicitation, 218–19
  encouraging customer service feed-
    back, 306–10
  Falcon help request system, 42–43
  fostering learning through, 317–18
  Home Sale Automation system,
    34–35
  labor cost system, 25–26

timing of, 234–35
voicemail system. 38–39,
   see also service provision, feedback mediation
feedback loops
   cybernetic systems theory, 110
   undesired repetitive patterns,
      223–26, *see also* vicious circles
Feeley, M., 16
Feldman, M.S., 9–10, 26–27, 119,
   124–25, 328
Felin, T., 123
filtering information, 44–45, 46
Flanagin, A.J., 11
formalization, 282
forms (documents), 74–75
Foss, N.J., 123
framing, 111
free-riding, 267
Frey, B., 243

garbage can model of organizational
   decision-making, 253
Garvin, D., 217
Gaskins, R., 259–60
general systems theory, 107–08
Giddens, A., 6
Gilliam, Terry, *Brazil* (movie), 10
Goodman, P.S., 298–99, 325–27
government crowding-out theory, 243
Graduated and Reciprocated
   Initiatives in Tension
   Reduction, 321–22
Greer, C.R., 8, 321
Griffith, T., 323
groupthink, 261, 282
Guennif, S., 128–29, 131

Habermas, J., 109
hacktivism, 79–80
Heinen, J.S., 21, 325
help request system. *see* Falcon help
   request system
hiding out, 9
high-reliability organizations,
   strategies for avoiding
   accidents, 323–25
hindsight bias, 260–61, 265
Hitchhiker's Guide to the Galaxy
   (Adams), 10
Home Sale Automation system

barriers to perception, 37
conflicting goals, 32–34
overview, 30–32
poor feedback, 34–35
symbolic uses and manipulation,
   35–37
hospitals
   errors, 230, 231–34, 317–18
   workarounds, 135–37
hybrid traps, 268

identity deception, 11
identity paradoxes, 278
idiot's paradox, 294–95
implementation games, 148
implementation research, 118
implosions of vicious circles, 242–43
impression management, 77
inappropriate activities, ICT, 11
inclusion
   educational institution ICT case
      study, 178–81
   respecting all stakeholders,
      182–83
inconsistent approach, 114
indirect feedback, 218–19
information and communication
      technologies (ICTs)
   and opaqueness of communications,
      8–9
   and strategic information
      behaviors, 10–11
   case studies, 22, 40
   invisibility, embeddedness, and
      routinization of URs, 63–64,
      147
   non-diagnosis of URs, 21–22
   organizational deviance, 282
   system error and automation,
      293–98
   system manipulation, 290–92
   unintended consequences of URs,
      64–66, *see also* database query
      system; Falcon help request
      system; Home Sale Automation
      system; labor cost system;
      PeopleData time reporting
      system; voicemail system
interactional justice, 72
interacts, sensemaking theory, 112
interference finding, 235–36

intrusive activities, ICT, 11
invisible chains, 268
invisible fist condition, 268
invisible hand condition, 268
irrelevant response, 9

Jamieson, K.H., 115
Jeltz, Prostetnic Vogon, 10
Jones, T., 81, 306
just-in-time manufacturing, 6

Kafka circuits, 5, 14–16, 333–34,
      see also subroutines
Kafka, Franz, 126
   The Castle, 10, 14
   The Trial, 14
Kaufman, O., 68
Kerr, S., 6
knowledge intensive routines, 122
knowledge-based mistakes, 228
Koenig, A., 116
Kollock, P., 267

labor cost system
   barriers to perception, 28–29
   conflicting goals, 23–25, 29–30
   overview, 22–23
   poor feedback, 25–26
   symbolic uses and manipulation,
      26–28
labor rates, 24
LaPlante, P.A., 115–17, 313–14
leadership ethics, 281
leadership, and inclusive decision-
      making, 195–98
learning by doing, 235–36
learning, conflict with control, 6–7
Leibenstein, H., 124
Letter-Writing Cowboy, 80–81
Lewin, K., 340
Lewis, M.W., 315–16
linkage analysis, 325–27
Litzky, B.E., 280–81, 283
live routines, 125
local routines, 121
locked-in collective behaviors, 268
logic errors, 257–60
log-rolling, 151
loosely coupled subsystems,
      sensemaking theory, 113

loss aversion, 265
Luscher, L.S., 315–16

malicious envy, 286–87
Malone, P.C., 286–87
managerial rationality, 273
Mangolte, P.A., 128–29, 131
manipulation, 63
   database query system, 50–51
   Falcon help request system, 45–46,
      see also semantic manipulation
March, J., 9–10, 26–27
March, James, 5–6
Markham, A., 219
Markus, M.L., 21
Marschak, J., 14–15
Masuch, M., 241
McGregor, J., 79–80
media transformations, 15–16
meetings, shadow costs, 15
message pads, media transformations,
      15–16
metaphors, 256
meta-problems, 116
meta-routines, 137–39
   unusual, 144–45
Milgram, S., 253–54
Miner, F.C., Jr, 286
mixed messages, 245–49
Moberg, D., 281
mode errors, 297
modification, of customer feedback,
      73
Molinski, A., 278
monitored clusters, 242
monitoring, 218–19
moral dilemmas, 281
moral hazard, 77–78
moral panics, 302
Name of the Rose, The (Eco), 10

NASA, briefings on Challenger,
      11–12
Nash, J., 290
naturalistic decision-making, 325
negative word of mouth (WOM),
      70–71
Neill, C.J., 115–17, 313–14
Nelson, R., 123
no-choice choices, 115

nonproductive activities, ICT, 11
non-responsiveness, 63
    database query system, 48–49
    excuses as form of, 9, *see also* irrelevant response
normal accidents, 292–93, 303
normal lies, 283
normalization of deviance, 230
NOT-time, PeopleData time reporting system, 55–58
no-win situations, 115
Nunamaker, J.F., 185

occasions for structuration, 207
Olivera, F., 231
omission bias, 265
open systems perspective, 109
open systems theory, 108–09
operating routines, 137
operating system fritter, 290
operator error, 21
optimism, about a benign nature, 265
ordinary troubles, 113
organizational bypass, 244
organizational complexity, 269–72
    and rationality, 272–74
    causing organizational deviance, 281–82
organizational cover-up, 244
organizational deviance, 280–83, 303
organizational memory, 236–37
organizational paradoxes
    examples, 278–80, 304
    types, 276–78
organizational routines
    and behaviors, 122
    benefits, 126–27
    change in, 131–33
    conceptualizations, 122–26
    definitions, 121–22
    dimensions, 121–22
    reducing cognitive load, 123–24
    variability in discretion, effort, and performance, 127–31
    workarounds, 64, 133–37, 233, 298–301, 318, *see also* meta-routines; unusual routines (UR)
organizational sensemaking theory, 111–17

organizational truces, 123, 127–28
organizing paradoxes, 315
Orlikowski, W., 119
Osgood, C.E., 321–22
ostensive aspects, 124, 125–26
overdamped feedback loops, 110

paradox cycles, 277
paradoxes, 223, 224, 274–75
    managing, 314–17
    positive and negative aspects, 275–76, *see also* cognitive paradoxical processes; idiot's paradox; organizational paradoxes
passion, 256
pathological communication systems, 241
pathological conflict, 242
pathological growth, 241–42
pathological status systems, 241
Paton, R., 279, 308
Pentland, B.T., 119, 124–25, 328
PeopleData time reporting system
    blame subroutines, 59–60
    denial, 55–58
    error subroutines, 58–59
    overview, 54
performance paradoxes, 315
performative aspects, 124, 125–26
performative routine, 131–32
perfunctory rituals, 225
Perrow, C., 229
personal heuristics, 252–53
petty tyranny, 287
plate spinning antipattern, 116
pluralistic approach, 114
Pogue, D., 291–92
Popper, Karl, 259
positive illusions, 265
Posner, R., 262
power paradoxes, 278–79
precautionary principle, 262–63, 265
predictable surprises, 261
    raising awareness of, 319–20
predispositions, 265
preparation intensive routines, 122
probability neglect, 265
procedural injustice, 16
procedural justice, 72

process gains, 120
process losses, 120
professional deceit, 283
property life cycle, 31
Proposition One, 149–50
  case study, 160–67, 200–01
Proposition Two, 150
  case study, 167–72, 201
Proposition Three, 150–51
  case study, 173–77, 201–02
Proposition Four, 151
  case study, 177–91, 202–03
Proposition Five, 202–03
  case study, 191–98, 203
psychic struggles, 281
Putnam, L., 276

QMF query system. *see* database
    query system
quasi-institutionalization of error, 12

recovery process, after customer
    complaints, 69, 307, 309
recovery window, 263
red tape committee, 311
reflexive loops, 223–24
regulative rules, 222
relational level communication, 221
repertoires, 131
resonances, 108
retention bins, 237
retention, sensemaking theory, 112,
    115–16
revenge effects, 288
Rice, R.E., 15
rigged system design, 40
rigidity, 63
  database query system, 51–52
  Falcon help request system, 46–47
risk
  normalization of, 303
  social amplification of, 304
risk aversion, 265
Ritzer, G., 272–73
Rivkin, J., 271
Rochlin, G., 294–98
Rosa, P., 68
Rousseau, D.M., 327
routine actions, 131
routine decisions, 131

routine nonconformity, 280
routines analysis, 327–29
routines theory, 334
routing information, 46
routing, of customer feedback, 73
rule-based mistakes, 228

safety envelopes, 300–01
Sasser, W.E., Jr, 81, 306
satire, 258–59
satisficing, 253
Saturday Night Live (television
    program), 80–81
Schell, S., 225
schizophrenic systems, 239–41
Schulman, P.R., 270
Schultze, U., 119
scripts
  and URs, 145–46
  diffusion of innovation theory, 117
  in educational institution ICT case
    study, 157
secrecy, 63
  database query system, 49–50
  Falcon help request system, 44–45
Seiders, K., 72
selection, sensemaking theory, 112
self-fulfilling prophecies, 115, 269
self-justification, 254–57
  strategies for escaping, 312–13
self-referential logical approach, 114
self-serving attribution bias, 76
semantic manipulation, 9
sensemaking
  as barrier to perception of crazy
    systems, 13
  case study implications, 209–11
  managing, 314–17
sensemaking theory.
    see organizational sensemaking
    theory
service provision
  examples of URs, 81–82, 106
    next time we just wreck your car,
      94–97
    please call back at your conveni-
      ence, 92–94
    reproducing problems, 97–100
    risky investment, figuring out
      how to fill out forms, 87–89

running out of gas, 89–92
your checks are safe with us,
82–87
fairness, 71–72, 309–10
feedback mediation, 72–75,
see also customer service
interface
and technological illiteracy,
75–76
by blocking and non-responding,
79–80
computer-mediated, 218–19
perceptions and attributions of
service quality, 76–77
through roles and positions,
77–79
Seymour, J., 289
shadow costs, 15
Siggelkow, N., 271
Simon, Paul, xi
Singer, Benjamin, 5, 8–9, 12, 333–34
single-loop learning, cybernetic
systems theory, 110
situated routines, 121–22
Six Sigma, 138
skilled incompetence, 226–27
slips, 228
social action, and reflexive feedback
loops, 223–24
social dilemmas, 266–69, 304
understanding and resolving,
320–21
social fences, 267
social habits, 127–28
social media, 73, *see also* consumer
vigilantes
social systems, 109
social traps, 266–69, 304
understanding and resolving,
320–21
socio-technical systems theory,
117–21
Spear, S.J., 230
Spitzberg, B, 225–26
stealth inflation, 291–92
stereotypes, 220–21
Stohl, C., 225, 278
strange loops, 224–25
strategic information behaviors, 10
strategic manipulation, 240

structuration theory, case study
implications, 211
structure paradoxes, 278
subroutines, 14, 143–44,
see also blame subroutines;
delay subroutines; error
subroutines; work subroutines
subunit coupling
educational institution ICT case
study, 162, 171–72
unusual routines (UR), 148–49,
see also Proposition Two
summarizing, of customer feedback,
73
Sunstein, C.R., 262
Sutcliffe, K.M., 324
symbolic uses and manipulation, 62
and crazy systems, 9–11
Falcon help request system, 43
Home Sale Automation system,
35–37
labor cost system, 26–28
voicemail system, 39–40,
see also manipulation
system contradictions, 277–78
system drift, 300–01, 304
system error or workflow errors, 232
system errors, from automated
systems, 293–98
system neglect, 266
systemic contradictions, 315
systems analysis, 118
systems theory, 107,
see also cybernetic systems
theory; general systems theory;
open systems theory

tacit routines, 121
Taleb, N.N., 12
technology
generating normal accidents,
292–93
inherent complexity, 287–90
mitigating complexity problems,
322–25, *see also* information and communication
technologies (ICTs)
technology of structuration, 207–08
thick rationality, 258
thin rationality, 257–58

third-party effect, 265
Thompson, K., 316–17
time recording, 24
time-delay traps, 267–68
tinkering, 290
Tompkins, P.K., 276
Total Quality Management, 6–7,
    138–39
  mixed messages, 249
tragedy of the commons, 261, 267
transformational shields, 240
Trial, The (Kafka), 14
Tucker, A.L., 230, 232, 329
Twitter, 73, *see also* consumer
    vigilantes

uncompensated interdependencies,
    267
underdamped feedback loops, 110
unintended consequences, of URs in
    ICT systems, 64–66
university continuing education
    programs merger, 119
unrealizable expectations, 115
unusual routines (UR)
  allure of, 331–33
  and meta-routines, 144–45
  and scripts, 145–46
  and subroutines, 143–44
  complexity, 139–43
  consequences, 146–47
  definitions, xi–1, 17–19, 331–32
  future research directions, 214–15
  models
    analytical, 153–54
    preliminary, 333–36
    proposed integrative model, 336
    revision from case study, 207–08
  organization values, 147–48
  organizational processes, 305
  organizational substrate, 147, 154
  overview, 342–43
  resolution and mitigation, 329–30
    complex technology, 322–25
    conflicting goals, 321–22
    encouraging customer service
      feedback, 306–10
    fostering learning through
      feedback, 317–18
    involving stakeholders, 310–12

linkage analysis, 325–27
managing paradoxes and
  sensemaking, 314–17
raising awareness of predictable
  surprises, 319–20
reducing blaming/defensive
  approaches to cognitive
  dissonance, 312–14
routines analysis, 327–29
social traps, 320–21
vicious cycles, 321–22
workplace deviance, 321–22
subunit coupling, 148–49,
    see also Proposition Two
symptoms, 146, *see also* educa-
    tional institution ICT case
    study
unwanted repetitive patterns (URP),
    225
unwritten rules, 7

value expressive rituals, 225
varying approach, 114
Vaughan, D., 230, 280
vicious circles, 241–43
  resolving, 321–22
vividness effect, 261
vividness heuristic, 266
Vogelsmeier, A.A., 136
voicemail system
  overview, 37–38
  poor feedback, 38–39
  symbolic uses and manipulation,
    39–40

walkarounds, 311–12
Watkins, M.D., 261
Weick, K.E., 324
Weick, Karl E., 5–6, 109, 111, 129,
    149
Westenholz, A., 113–14, 316
Wexler, P.S., 68, 306–07
willing awareness of the unwilled,
    258–59
Winter, S., 123, 317
Woods, D., 324
word of mouth. *see* negative word of
    mouth (WOM)
work circuits, 9, 14,
    see also subroutines

work subroutines
  database query system, 52
workarounds, 64, 133–37,
    298–300
  contributing to system drift,
    300–01
  learning from, 318
  preventing correction of
    errors, 233
workflow blocks, 134
workplace deviance triggers, 283

workplace deviance, resolving,
    321–22
workplace mistreatment,
    284–85
worst-case scenarios, 262
  avoiding overreacting to, 319–20

Zhao, B., 231
Zirpoli, F., 126
Zmud, R.W., 10–11, 291
zone of ambiguity, 276